The First Geeks

The First Geeks

*Ray Bradbury, Forrest J Ackerman,
Ray Harryhausen and the Founding
of Science Fiction Fandom*

ORTY ORTWEIN

McFarland & Company, Inc., Publishers
Jefferson, North Carolina

LIBRARY OF CONGRESS CATALOGUING-IN-PUBLICATION DATA

Names: Ortwein, Orty, 1975– author.
Title: The first geeks : Ray Bradbury, Forrest J. Ackerman, Ray Harryhausen and the founding of science fiction fandom / Orty Ortwein.
Description: Jefferson, North Carolina : McFarland & Company, Inc., Publishers, 2024. | Includes bibliographical references and index.
Identifiers: LCCN 2024014984 | ISBN 9781476686301 (paperback : acid free paper) ∞ ISBN 9781476651729 (ebook)
Subjects: LCSH: Bradbury, Ray, 1920-2012. | Ackerman, Forrest J. | Harryhausen, Ray. | Science fiction, American—History and criticism. | Authors, American—20th century—Biography. | Science fiction fans—United States—20th century. | BISAC: LITERARY CRITICISM / Science Fiction & Fantasy | LCGFT: Literary criticism. | Biographies.
Classification: LCC PS374.S35 O78 2024 | DDC 813/.0876209 [B]—dc23/eng/20240408
LC record available at https://lccn.loc.gov/2024014984

BRITISH LIBRARY CATALOGUING DATA ARE AVAILABLE

ISBN (print) 978-1-4766-8630-1
ISBN (ebook) 978-1-4766-5172-9

© 2024 Orty Ortwein. All rights reserved

No part of this book may be reproduced or transmitted in any form or by any means, electronic or mechanical, including photocopying or recording, or by any information storage and retrieval system, without permission in writing from the publisher.

Front cover: (left to right) Forrest J Ackerman, Ray Harryhausen and Ray Bradbury at Archon 20 in Collinsville, Illinois, in 1996 (John L. Coker III); television illustration by Black Digital Cat/Shutterstock

Printed in the United States of America

McFarland & Company, Inc., Publishers
Box 611, Jefferson, North Carolina 28640
www.mcfarlandpub.com

To my father,
Robert K. Ortwein

Table of Contents

Acknowledgments   ix
Prologue: Comic-Con, 2010   1

1. The Bradburys Come to Hollywood   5
2. Shep's Shop   12
3. Hugo Gernsback and the Science Fiction League   14
4. Bradbury Joins the League   25
5. Forry Ackerman   28
6. Bradbury's First Meeting   38
7. *Imagination!* and the Start of Bradbury's Career   40
8. *Imagination!*, the Second Issue   48
9. *Imagination!*, Issues 3 and 4   50
10. Ray Harryhausen Joins the League   55
11. The Two Rays Meet   64
12. Rocket Boys   68
13. The Summer of 1938   71
14. *Futuria Fantasia*   77
15. Ackerman and Harryhausen, 1939   81
16. *Futuria Fantasia*, the Second Issue   83
17. The First Worldcon, 1939   84
18. Bradbury and Ackerman Arrive at Worldcon   86
19. "I have seen the future!" The 1939 World's Fair   89
20. Worldcon, Day One, July 2, 1939   92
21. Worldcon, Monday, July 3, and Tuesday, July 4   99
22. Worldcon, the Aftermath   100
23. Back to LA   103
24. Robert A. Heinlein Joins the League   106

25.	The Los Angeles Science Fantasy Society	111
26.	The End of *Futuria Fantasia*	114
27.	The Second World Science Fiction Convention	116
28.	The Milwaukee Fictioneers	117
29.	Chicon	121
30.	The First Organized Cosplay	126
31.	Ray Bradbury Is Done Selling Papers	128
32.	The First Clubroom	130
33.	The War Comes Home	134
34.	Denvention	136
35.	The Fans Go to War	139
36.	The Second Clubroom	146
37.	The War on Bixelstrasse	150
38.	Goodbye, Morojo; Hello, Tigrina	153
39.	Victory	157
40.	Significant Others	161
41.	*Dark Carnival*	163
42.	*The Beast from 20,000 Fathoms*	166
43.	Forry Ackerman's Agency	172
44.	The Ackermansion	180
45.	Harryhausen Moves to London	186
46.	The First Comic-Con	187
47.	Passing the Torch	190
48.	Growing Old, Never Growing Up	196
49.	The End of the Ackermansion and *Famous Monsters*	199
50.	Afterlife	202
Chapter Notes		205
Bibliography		221
Index		223

Acknowledgments

Without the names listed below, this book wouldn't have been possible. These are the people I would like to thank (and perhaps you will want to blame).

My sister Jeni Tate and her husband Joe, for letting me house-sit their Wisconsin home, giving me the greatest gift any writer can ask for: time.

Molly Ortwein and David Cozzens, whose financial backing made this possible.

Stacia Franus, Schuyler Cozzens, and Mikayla Khramov, who drove me around the lives of Ackerman, Bradbury, and Harryhausen.

Joe Siclari, whose Fanac.org site, with its incredible selection of scans of original zines, made it possible for me to access a trove of primary documents.

The Ritter father-and-son team, whose due diligence, published in their book *The Earliest Bradbury* (some of which can be seen at www.firstfandomexperience.com), saved me hours in tracking down Bradbury's earliest works.

The good people of the Los Angeles Science Fantasy Society. I promise to pay my dues.

John L. Coker III, whose expertise was more valuable than any book or site I could ever find.

The devoted staff at the Center for Ray Bradbury Studies in Indianapolis.

The Waukegan Public Library, for briefly giving me the dream job of cataloging Bradbury's book collection.

And, of course, Ray Bradbury, Forrest J Ackerman, and Ray Harryhausen, who taught me to not be worried when people call you crazy.

"Thank God I met Ray Harryhausen.
Thank God for Forrest Ackerman."
—Ray Bradbury[1]

Prologue
Comic-Con, 2010

By 2010, Comic-Con San Diego had ballooned from its humble origins in 1970 to the carnival it is today, with hundreds of thousands of guests crowding into the San Diego Convention Center. Masses of proud nerds nudged past one another to get their hands on comics, video games, toys, and other geek ephemera displayed among endless rows of tables and booths. In this bazaar one could find quaint cast-offs from yesterday, flotsam and jetsam now commanding hundreds or thousands of dollars. Pulpy comic books originally sold for a dime at the local drug store or flimsy plastic toys that came free in cereal boxes were now going for three, four, sometimes five digits. Plenty of new items were being rolled out as well. Brand name companies hawked products available for the first time anywhere in the world, branding them as exclusive items found only here, only now (assuming, of course, that none of the customers would later sell these "exclusives" online with a markup). One unique item on offer in 2010 was the Lt. Sulu "Oh My!" aftershave.

And then there was Hall H.

Hall H is the largest conference room in the San Diego Convention Center and is logically the site where the best-known names make their appearances. That evening, 6,500 fans crammed into H to see Samuel L. Jackson announce the cast of the upcoming *Avengers* movie, a lineup that included Robert Downey, Jr., and Scarlett Johansson. Later Harrison Ford, Daniel Craig, and Jon Favreau were part of a panel in the vaunted hall to promote their film *Cowboys vs. Aliens*. The mythic hall even turned into a crime scene of sorts when a pair of young men got into a shoving match that ended with one stabbing the other in the eye with a pen. Thankfully the victim suffered only a superficial cut on the eyelid. (The next day dozens of cosplayers dressed up as Guy Who Got Stabbed in the Eye, costumes complete with fake pencils glued above eye sockets.)

San Diego knows what it has in Comic-Con and is determined to hold on to it; it's the equivalent of hosting the Super Bowl every year. In 2019, San Diego Convention Center Corporation signed an agreement with Comic-Con International to keep the convention in their city at least through 2024. Before Covid, more than 140,000 fans flocked annually to the four-day bacchanal celebrating pop culture, and people willing to pay thousands were nevertheless unable to secure a ticket.[1] Comic-Con gets the convention center at a steep discount, but organizers of the convention have nonetheless considered moving their event elsewhere, claiming that the

Bradbury at Comic-Con San Diego, 2008. Note the lipstick from a kiss planted on his cheek (courtesy John Sasser).

The crowd that turned out for Ray Bradbury, Comic-Con, 2008 (courtesy John Sasser).

800,000-square-foot facility cannot accommodate the hordes who flock there every July. Worried the convention may move to Los Angeles or some other greener and roomier pasture, then-mayor Kevin Faulconer lobbied hard for a tax initiative, known as Measure C, that would expand the convention center by 30 percent. It would lead to a hotel room tax hike to pay for expanding the center another 400,000 square feet (the measure would also raise money for street repairs and expanding services to the homeless). San Diego voters turned down the measure in April 2020, but the fight isn't over. Sixty-five percent of voters approved the ballot measure, but it needed a two-thirds majority. Backers of Measure C are now appealing to the courts to allow the initiative to pass anyway since it earned a majority, if not the supermajority it was initially supposed to have. As of this writing, Measure C is still being debated in the California justice system.[2] "It will be interesting to see what happens with the ballot initiative. After that, there will be a true indicator of what we can do and how we plan for the future," said David Glanzer, spokesman for Comic-Con International, words that San Diego hoteliers, restaurant owners, and other business people no doubt hear as a threat.[3]

In all the madness of Comic-Con 2010, in the herds of nerds and geeks, countless Wonder Women, Batmen, and Stormtroopers hushed suddenly as the most famous person in the convention center was passing through. He was neither a director nor a hot young actor. He was 90 years old and needed to be pushed in a wheelchair. More than 1,000 people would pack a conference room to see him and listen as he spoke softly.

"Ray Bradbury coming through!" his runner announced, a volunteer spearheading the effort to move the elderly writer across the convention floor. It was a slow-moving entourage, as the group stopped every couple of minutes while Bradbury autographed items, posed for photos, even accepted the occasional kiss, leaving the lipstick on his cheek as a badge of honor.

Ray Bradbury smiled gently as he parted the seas. Things were a little different more than 70 years ago when it all began.

"This is a story of long, long ago—
when the world was just beginning."
—First line of narration from the
Ray Harryhausen film *One Million Years B.C.*

1

The Bradburys Come to Hollywood

> Good God, I had such a good time. Did I really do all that?"[1]
> —Ray Bradbury to Don Congdon, upon hearing
> Congdon read back Bradbury's own teen diary

> "Let me go back to 1934. Hand me my roller skates. With them I skated through life in Los Angeles when I was 14."
> —Ray Bradbury, undated essay, "L.A., How Do I Love Thee?"

It was a scene right out of Steinbeck, an author Ray Bradbury would one day admire and even briefly meet.[2] The Buick rolled into California in the spring of 1934 bringing a Midwestern family hoping to start again. Bradbury described the family car in his semi-autobiographical novel *A Graveyard for Lunatics*: "It stood, rusting quietly, its headlights dented, its radiator cap flaked, its radiator honey-comb-papered over with trapped moths and blue and yellow butterfly wings."[3] The trek had been arduous, from Waukegan, Illinois, to Los Angeles, a journey that even in the twenty-first century takes four days by auto. The Bradburys were but one of millions of Depression-era families to pack everything they could fit into their car and head west. They were taking part in the largest internal migration in U.S. history save the Great Migration of African Americans from South to North. Unlike many striking out for California, Ray's father, Leonard Bradbury, had family waiting. His brother-in-law, Inar Moberg, a beloved relative Ray would later give wings and immortalize in his short story *Uncle Einar*, was already there. As Bradbury recalled decades later, "My Uncle Inar had moved his family to Los Angeles and sent us pictures of Orange Groves. That did it."[4] Inar had done well in California, inspiring his brother-in-law to try his luck there. Leonard, who typically went by "Leo," hoped this would be the last move for him, his Swedish wife, Esther, and two boys, Ray and Skip. (The Bradburys had two additional children, a girl named Elizabeth Jane and a boy named Sam, but both died as toddlers.) This was the third time Leo had uprooted his family and moved more than a thousand miles away to what he hoped was a better future. Twice he'd relocated them to Tucson, Arizona, first when Bradbury was five and again when he was 12 (it's nothing more than a coincidence, but the first time the Bradburys moved to New Mexico, they briefly, for two weeks, lived in Roswell). Leo hoped this move to the Golden State would prove fruitful. It was a gamble. Ray Bradbury would later find out that the family had all of 50

RAY DOUGLAS BRADBURY
L ikes to write stories
A dmired as a Thespian
H eaded for literary distinction.

LARRY BRADLEY
L ikes life on the sea
A dmired as Boys' Division president
H eaded for Stanford and the sea.

Ray Bradbury's high school graduation photograph. Every student at Los Angeles High School had to come up with an acrostic that worked with the letters LAH. Bradbury ended his with "Headed for literary distinction," having no idea how right this prediction would be (Los Angeles High School yearbook, 1938, *The Blue and White*).

dollars when they reached Los Angeles, an amount that would support the family for maybe a month.

At first, it didn't seem to pay off. Leo Bradbury would leave their apartment in the Mid City neighborhood of LA and spend all day walking in search of work, too poor to afford gas for the family car, only to return home empty-handed. His son later wrote about the shame of seeing his father cry at the kitchen table as he struggled to figure out the family finances, unaware his younger boy was watching. The Bradburys were packed and ready to move back to Illinois when, at the last minute, Leo got a job as a lineman. They were staying in California.

The Bradburys were hardly the only out-of-towners to gamble everything on a better life in California. The Los Angeles of the 1930s was both a young and an old city at the same time. Its roots date back to the time of the American Revolution, but in the decade before World War II, most of the city's inhabitants were born someplace else. According to the immensely fascinating Works Progress Administration guide *Los Angeles in the 1930s*, LA's population doubled, tripled, or quadrupled almost every decade between the Civil War and World War II,[5] and Hollywood's population had exploded from 500 to 50,000 between 1900 and 1920.[6] In 1920, the population of LA was 576,000. By 1940 it had swelled to 1.5 million.[7]

This population of one and half million was more diverse than most cities, with almost 100,000 Mexicans, 21,000 Japanese (there were even Japanese language directories), 3,000 Chinese, and "almost 45,000 Negros."[8] So many people in 1930s LA were transplants that there were "Home-State Picnics" organized for the many Hoosiers, Cheeseheads, Okies, etc., who had moved there. When two strangers met in 1930s LA, the first question was likely "How long have *you* been here?"

The New Yorkers and Texans and Buckeyes flocked to a city that had done better than most during the Great Depression and seemed to be the only corner of America left where an honest man could get a decent job. Tough times fed Hollywood. The Great Depression spawned more desperate souls than ever seeking escape from their dismal world and sent the Dream Factory humming. Film wasn't the only industry booming in southern California in the 1930s. There were still endless acres of orange groves and other crops made famous by John Steinbeck, plus automobile factories, canneries, and oil wells. The castle mansions of stars and producers overlooking the city from the foothills were the exceptions. Most Angelenos lived in modest bungalows or stucco homes. Many humble businesses were located inside of "domed and turreted filling stations, wayside hot dog stands designed to resemble unhappy pups, mammoth ice cream cones, Egyptian temples, baskets of fruit, and piebald pigs."[9] LA was also one of the first places in the world to have regular radio and then television broadcasts, the latter of which began in 1938. This was the world into which Leo Bradbury brought his wife and two boys.

Moving can be traumatic for teenagers who may find it hard to leave everything behind and create a new niche after spending their brief lives carving out a place for themselves. The decision to move is the sort of decision that can turn teens against their parents.

Ray Bradbury couldn't wait.

He loved Waukegan, where his humble home was within walking distance of the Carnegie Library, the cool blue beauty of Lake Michigan, the terrifically terrifying ravine he and his brother Skip walked through on their way downtown to see a picture show at one of the grand movie palaces. He would one day make these favorite spots famous in short stories and novels such as *Something Wicked This Way Comes* and *Dandelion Wine*, always in the fictional locale of Green Town, Illinois. But if there was one place in the world for which he would trade all of this it was Los Angeles, which to this Midwestern boy meant only one thing—Hollywood.

Ray Bradbury loved movies, as did his mother, Esther, who gave her son—Raymond Douglas Bradbury—a middle name in homage to her beloved Douglas Fairbanks. As he once explained to biographer Sam Weller, "When I was ten years old, I would lie in bed night after night and stare at the ceiling. In my mind, I would project movies from my eyes, up onto the bare ceiling. I would watch entire films, from beginning to end, over and over again in my head."[10]

Dimes were scarce for the cash-strapped Bradbury family, and Ray could only afford to see each film once, at least legally—he and his brother Skip were not above staying in the theater for a second showing, or just plain sneaking in altogether (his good buddy Forry Ackerman later claimed that there wasn't a theater in LA Bradbury couldn't break into). Ray reckoned that his mother, Esther Bradbury, took in at least a film a week. Esther's husband—Ray's father—didn't share her enthusiasm for movies, so she often bundled up her toddler son and took him the short distance to the Elite or Academy Theatre or the Genesee in downtown Waukegan. The first movie he saw was Lon Chaney's *The Hunchback of Notre Dame*, and it was love at first sight; he would be a devoted Chaney fan for life. In 1930, 10-year-old Bradbury was first in line outside the Academy Theatre for a re-showing of *The Phantom of the Opera*. The boy stayed all day, watching one screening after another, in spite of a mysterious pain in his abdomen, possibly caused by appendicitis. "I sat there thinking, 'Next week, I won't be alive, but I'll be damned if I leave the theatre. I've got to see The Phantom one more time.'"[11] His father finally had to fetch him from the theater. Another Chaney favorite of his was *He Who Gets Slapped*, the original evil clown film in which men get trapped in a room with a lion, a scene that Bradbury would recreate in one of his best-known short stories.

It was in Waukegan where he saw the first version of *The Cat and the Canary*, the original *Ben-Hur*, and the first *King of Kings*. In 1925 he saw O'Brien's *The Lost World*—a movie that sparked his love of dinosaurs—twice, the first time downtown and the second at Waukegan's Central School. At age eight Bradbury became so enamored with Disney's short film *The Skeleton Dance* that he spent an entire

Saturday sitting through the same boring feature over and over just so he could again watch those magical five minutes of black and white animation in the preview. Leo Bradbury had to drag his son out of this one, too.

During the family's second stay in Tucson, Arizona, the 12-year-old Bradbury got a job working at the KGAR radio station just a couple of blocks from his home. Radio was another love of his, and as an adult writer he proudly adapted dozens of his stories for classic shows such as *Lights Out* and *X Minus One*. After he had taken out trash and fetched food for the adults running the station for a couple of weeks, they asked him if he wanted to read the Sunday Funnies on the radio. The boy jumped at the chance.

Bradbury loved newspaper comic strips and obsessively collected his favorites, eventually filling dozens of scrapbooks with the daily adventures of Buck Rogers, Flash Gordon, Tarzan, and Prince Valiant. He would keep this collection his entire life, becoming a comic collector before comic books existed. Decades later, Bradbury recalled: "The most beautiful sound in my life, dearly recollected, fully remembered, was the sound of a folded newspaper kiting through the summer air and landing on my front porch."[12]

Bradbury went all in on the chance to read the funnies live on the air, narrating the cartoon characters along with other children by use of funny voices and sound effects. KGAR paid him with movie tickets, meaning that, for the first time, this Depression-era lad could see almost as many films as he wanted (legally!). It amazed the boy that adults were paying him to do what he loved, read comics, with another love of his, free tickets to movies. The pre-teen must have wondered what the catch was.

So it was while in Tucson that the boy saw *King Kong, The Mummy, Dracula,* and *The Mystery of the Wax Museum,* films that would have a lasting impact on his imagination and writing. He learned about *King Kong* from the only section of the paper he read, the comics; a special comic strip version of *King Kong* was released in the week leading up to the film's release. After seeing the film, the young writer was so enamored with the great ape that he ran home and, as best he could, typed the screenplay on his toy dial-a-letter typewriter, a machine that only allowed its user to punch one letter at a time. It was on this toy that Bradbury painstakingly typed his earliest efforts, including fan fiction involving John Carter, Buck Rogers, and King Kong.[13] He sat through *The Mummy* in spite of someone, likely a disgruntled union employee, literally dropping a stink bomb in an attempt to clear out the theater. (Oddly, stink bombs and other types of bombs were a common occurrence in movie theaters during the 1930s, the result of disputes between unions and owners. In *Twilight at the World of Tomorrow*, about a terrorist attack at the 1940 New York World's Fair, James Mauro writes: "The most popular targets for bombs in the 1930s were movie theaters. Throughout the city [New York], an assortment of smoke bombs, tear gas bombs and bottle bombs ... were set to go off at a specific hour.") He was so enamored with *The Invisible Man* that as a teenager he used his newspaper money to go to a studio and record himself reading passages of *The Invisible Man* as Claude Rains.[14] He later got to work with Rains directly, when the actor played the lead in Hitchcock's adaptation of Bradbury's story *And So Died Riabouchinska*.

The derring-do of Douglas Fairbanks, the terror of Lon Chaney Sr., the dinosaurs of *The Lost World* and *The Mysterious Island,* all of this planted a seed in the young boy's heart, influences that stayed with him forever. Bradbury later claimed he saw every movie ever released through his childhood and teen years.

And now, he was here, in the City of Angels, where Quasimodo's Notre Dame still stood and Marlene Dietrich made men swoon. The one place any dream could be made a reality. His very first morning in LA, the day after the Bradburys moved into their new apartment on Hobart Boulevard, 13-year-old Ray strapped on his roller skates and asked a complete stranger where he could find MGM Studios.

* * *

In an era when people spend hours lining up to meet B-list celebrities and household names are prisoners of their own fame, it is hard to picture just how accessible movie stars were in the Golden Age of Hollywood. George Burns, Al Jolson, W.C. Fields, and Marlene Dietrich are but a few of the VIPs the teenaged Bradbury met before the world knew his name.

The stranger Bradbury encountered just outside his new home explained that MGM was at least five miles from where they stood, so Bradbury settled for the closer Paramount Studios. Within a week he had W.C. Fields's signature. The actor called the 13-year-old a "little son-of-a-bitch" but gave him an autograph all the same. Obsessed, the teenager soon made a habit of strapping on skates, autograph book in hand, and garnering signatures simply by asking, making friends with other autograph hounds along the way. (Decades later these same hounds would ask *him* for an autograph after he became a screenplay writer.) On one occasion he was seated at an Al Jolson radio broadcast when, to his amazement, Al leapt off the stage, snatched Bradbury's skates, and started to put them on. Bradbury snatched them back and yelled to the audience, "My transportation!" Later that year he approached George Burns and Gracie Allen outside of the Figueroa Street Playhouse, where they weekly broadcast their radio show to a nationwide audience, a show they would later transfer to television. Bradbury asked that he and his friend Donald Harkins be allowed to sit in on the recording. Burns's show wasn't before a live audience; the two boys were the only spectators in the studio. Bradbury later sent Burns some radio scripts he had written. Burns bought and used one of Bradbury's jokes on his show. Bradbury ran into Burns 40 years later at a banquet honoring Steven Spielberg and they embraced for the first time in decades. Burns knew who Bradbury was because Bradbury was a well-established author by then. Bradbury introduced himself as the boy who used to sit in on Burns and Allen's recordings. Burns was stunned to learn that that pre-teen boy grew up to become the world-famous science fiction writer. Until then, he had not made the connection.

The Bradbury apartment on Hobart was on the second floor of a two-story building, with a balcony that allowed young Ray to see the roof of the Uptown Theatre. A red light on top glowed whenever Paramount premiered a new movie. This was a beacon for the film-obsessed boy, who grabbed his autograph book and roller skates every time he saw that red glow, like a fireman springing to the alarm. He shadowed every premiere he could and got the autographs of Jean Harlow, Clark Gable, Laurel and Hardy, and many others. He had a lifelong love of Laurel and Hardy and worked the duo into a few of his short stories, such as *The Laurel and Hardy Love Affair*.

Once, he and his pal Donald Hawkins cut through Hollywood Cemetery, already the resting place of Hollywood's earliest tragic stars, like Rudy Valentino and Barbara

La Marr. The graveyard abutted the back lot of Paramount, making it easy for the boys to jump onto a woodpile and climb over the wall. Bradbury's first visit onto a Hollywood lot was short-lived, as he was confronted by a security guard who escorted him out. But Ray Bradbury would return to Hollywood.

Through a neighbor he met the three Gumm Sisters, the youngest of whom would be known to the world as Judy Garland. Once he sat next to Gary Cooper during the radio broadcast of *The Lives of a Bengal Lancer*. He watched as Shirley Temple impressed her little feet into wet cement outside Grauman's Chinese Theatre. He literally bumped into Greta Garbo as she secretly exited a theater. According to his own diary, as an undiscovered 20-year-old he once bought a $2 seat (admittedly not a small sum in 1940) at the El Capitan, where he saw a Noël Coward play. After the show, he recorded in his diary that he chatted with "Jo Ann Sayers and beau, Burns and Allen, Jack Benny [who was also a Waukegan native] and Mary and saw Joan Fontaine, Henry Fonda, Burgess Meredith and Harold Lloyd."[15]

Against his better judgment Leo Bradbury sometimes let his energetic son borrow the family's expensive Brownie box camera, which is how the 14-year-old snapped a photo of himself with George Burns and, later, Marlene Dietrich, whom he followed into her favorite hair salon for an autograph. After getting her signature he was kicked out, only for him to see her outside of Paramount, where he asked if she would pose with him. Leo allowed Ray to borrow the camera, understanding that the hyperactive boy would keep the camera strapped to his body with a string. This string can be seen in the photo with Burns, snapped just outside the Brown Derby. The teen often lingered outside the Brown Derby and the Vendome, hoping for autographs. Sometimes he got multiple signatures from the same VIP three or four times. His estate is said to include more than 20 snapshots of the teen Bradbury posing with Hollywood royalty of the time. He would gather more than 1,000 signatures of actors, executives, music composers, and radio personalities.

California worked out for the rest of the family, too. Not only did his father land a job with the General Cable Company, but also his brother, Skip, eventually worked for the Civilian Conservation Corps. The good fortunes of the Bradbury family allowed them to move into a more upscale apartment on South Saint Andrews Place.

Bradbury was an okay student at Los Angeles High School, not great. He submitted 20 stories for publication in his school's anthology of creative verse, all of which were rejected. He only had a couple of good friends, and the only girls he kissed in his teen years were his first cousin Vivian and a prostitute he and a buddy visited to lose their virginity.[16] As he recounted in *Green Shadows, White Whale*, he tried to woo uninterested girls—"one or two unlucky girls who, when I brought my stories over to the house, ran off whining with boredom after the first hour"—with his stories and poetry. A self-described wimp, he was often the target of bullies. At age 11 he wrote his first story on a roll of butcher paper,[17] then continued to write every day, musings often modeled on his first loves: radio shows, horror and science fiction movies, the comics he still scrapbooked daily, and the worlds of Poe, Baum, and H.G. Wells that he checked out from libraries. He continued to painstakingly peck away at his toy dial-a-letter typewriter, his first efforts being a fan fiction sequel to one of the Martian stories of Edgar Rice Burroughs.[18]

The Bradburys happened to rent an apartment adjacent to one that had a girl about Bradbury's age, who said he could use her typewriter whenever he wanted.

But for the most part, there were few who got him and his writing. His young Aunt Neva understood and inspired him, giving him books of fairy tales and imagination. He wrote during his high school lunch breaks on a school typewriter, after begging the typing teacher to let him spend his break in her classroom rather than the cafeteria, pounding away furiously for 45 minutes before saving a few last minutes to eat. He took a short story course and doubled the output of anyone else in the class.[19] He got praise and encouragement from a pair of teachers, Snow Longley Housh, who published one of his poems in the 1937 edition of LA High School's *Anthology of Student Verse*, and Jennet Johnson, who once wrote at the bottom of short science fiction story he'd written, "I don't know what it is you're doing, but don't stop."[20] Bradbury never forgot her early encouragement. Throughout his career, he gifted Johnson signed copies of his books, and dedicated *Something Wicked This Way Comes* to her. His gifted books to her were appraised on *Antiques Roadshow* and judged to be worth thousands.

As a teenager he was already writing about the ravine that cut through his native Waukegan in a story that would eventually become one of his first radio adaptations and then the short story "The Whole Town's Sleeping"; the landform would later to be a key element of his novel *Dandelion Wine*. He wrote periodically for the school paper, *The Blue and White Daily*; joined the glee, art, and poetry clubs; and participated in theater. A lover of the stage who considered becoming an actor, his first taste of acceptance came when he wrote a play that would be staged in the school auditorium. Another boost came just a few days before his 16th birthday, when the boy was elated after his native *Waukegan News-Sun* published a poem of his, an ode to the late Will Rogers, marking the first time his name appeared in a professional publication. All told, though, few in the bookish boy's orbit understood his love of dinosaurs, space travel, and concepts that were out of this world.

This changed on the fateful day when, while walking out of the bookstore Shep's Shop at the corner of Hollywood and Western, Bradbury saw a flyer advertising an upcoming meeting of the Science Fiction League (SFL). On Thursday, October 7, 1937, Bradbury went to his first meeting of the SFL at Clifton's Cafeteria downtown.[21] Neither his life nor the world of science fiction would ever be the same.

2

Shep's Shop

Shep's Shop was a unique bookstore in a Los Angeles that suffered no lack of unique bookstores.

The late 1930s saw LA become a magnet for authors from all over the country. The relatively young motion picture business attracted these men and some women because Hollywood, flush with cash—at this time, 80 percent of the world's movies were made in LA—paid writers considerably more than any other industry. The booming motion picture business drew plenty of beautiful and pretty dreamers hoping to be the next Valentino or Mary Pickford, but it was also a siren call for anyone with a portable typewriter.

The money made authors drool. A writer could expect somewhere between $500 to $1,000 for a script, at a time when pulp magazines paid a penny per word. This is why many of the better-known writers of the decade (and more than a few forgettable ones) at least tried their typing talent at screenwriting. Raymond Chandler, F. Scott Fitzgerald, Dashiell Hammett, John Steinbeck, Aldous Huxley, Tennessee Williams, and William Faulkner are but a few of the notables who lived in or around Los Angeles and handed in screenplays. "Junior writers"—unknowns working for a studio exclusively—could still expect $50 a week, not a bad wage for the time. The major studios employed teams of readers whose only job was to pore through books, plays, and magazines for plots that would make good motion pictures.[1] Sometimes, a studio would register a catchy title and then put an anonymous scribe to work coming up with a script to match the name.

Pre-war Los Angeles was full of directors, starlets, and writers, and where there are writers, there are inevitably bookstores, more than 100 in 1937, according to the LA City Directory. Sixth Street and Hollywood Boulevard were both loaded with them. Many of them catered to unique tastes and sold more than just books. Some had art galleries, and others were known for selling booze under the table during Prohibition to the inevitably alcoholic writers who came by. Many became hangouts for like-minded authors. Across the street from the Screen Writers Guild, the Stanley Rose Book Shop was frequented by the likes of John Steinbeck, Dashiell Hammett, and F. Scott Fitzgerald, where the boys often played poker. It is said to be the inspiration for the bookshop in *The Big Sleep*.[2] A couple of nearby shops specialized in books on the occult and mysticism.

Competing with the dozens of bookshops was the Los Angeles Public Library. Built in 1926 on Fifth Street between Flower Street and Grand Avenue, the low stucco building was the nexus of a system that had 48 branches and 69 book stations, including three "parasol libraries"—outdoor libraries where the check-in station was under a large patio umbrella. A photo of one of these shows a sign that says, "Borrow a book. Read in the park."[3]

Most of these spots would have had little, if any, science fiction, however. Shep's Shop filled this gap, selling materials not so easy to find. "Bookstore" may not be the most accurate description of the business. Lucie B. Shepherd—despite what one might infer from the name, this shop was owned by a woman—stocked her store at the corner of Hollywood and Western (The Mayer Building) with secondhand magazines, a used magazine shop being a common business back then. She sold both pulps (like *Amazing Stories* and *Weird Tales*) and slicks (*Life*, *Time*, etc.). She advertised her store in the pages of the amateur fan publication *Imagination!* as a "second hand mag shop" that claimed to have the "LARGEST stock backdate Mags in H'Wood!"[4] That it was a cantina bar for local science fiction fans is confirmed in another ad that ran in that same amateur fan magazine, which declared Shep's a "regular rendezvous of FJA, Morojo, RJH, Yerke, Paul Freehafer, Bob Cumnock, & bunch othr localities"[5]— all names that would have been familiar to active science fiction fans of the era. T.B. "Tubby" Yerke was an active fan at that time who introduced Bradbury to the rest of the bunch. His memoir likely has the most complete description of the shop.

> SHEP'S SHOP was a favourite hangout for SFL members in them thar times. Lucille B. Sheppard [*sic*] did have a fabulous collection of scientifiction magazines up on Hollywood Blvd.... I considered the place to be quite a paradise. I often dropped in after school to enjoy this rapture, this virtual wallowing in vast piles of WONDER STORIES, SCIENCE WONDER STORIES, AMAZING STORIES QUARTERLY, and endless piles of later Astoundings and Wonder.[6]

Knowing that her customers often couldn't spare a dime, Shepherd ran her shop as something of a library, letting customers check out pulps or books for a penny a day. She also stocked her shop with movie stills and materials about Esperanto, an artificial language that was supposed to unite the world and a passion of Forry Ackerman's, the most devoted fan in the world (much more on him later). This was the heyday of the pulps, with some 200 publications cranking out about 10 million copies per month.[7]

Back issues of pulps like *Weird Tales* and *Amazing Stories* weren't easy to find, so this corner bookshop was a honeytrap for anyone in 1930s LA addicted to Wells or Jules Verne. Sooner or later Ray Bradbury would find his way to Shep's, and it was a flyer at the back of the bookshop that gave his life meaning. It was there that he saw a poster advertising an upcoming meeting of the Science Fiction League.

3

Hugo Gernsback and the Science Fiction League

When Bradbury saw that poster, he had no way of knowing the organization he was joining was the brainchild of the man many consider to be the founder of modern science fiction, Hugo Gernsback.

Science fiction, like all literary genres, has no one single Edison-like inventor, but a strong case can be made for Hugo Gernsback as the father of at least modern science fiction as we know it. Decades later, Forry Ackerman would point to his vast collection and say Gernsback "is responsible for everything you see in this room."[1] Before Gernsback there was H.G. Wells, preceded by Jules Verne, who came after Edgar Allan Poe, and before him Mary Wollstonecraft Shelley. If Gernsback wasn't the inventor of science fiction, it could be argued that he did for that genre what Ford did for cars: streamlined it and made it something more accessible to the masses. He is even credited with dreaming up the name "science fiction" in the first place.

Born Hugo Gernsbacher to Jewish parents in 1884 Luxembourg, young Hugo began tinkering with electronics at age six when a handyman hired by Hugo's wine merchant father installed a series of bells attached to a battery. Little Hugo soon became fascinated by all things electronic. The boy earned a reputation as the kid to call whenever phones or electric bells needed to be installed. He claimed that he was granted permission by Pope Leo XIII himself—boy though Hugo was—to enter an all-female convent and install a series of electric-powered call bells.[2]

While clearly curious, he did poorly in school outside of his favorite topics. He developed a fascination with American culture, particularly the music of John Philip Sousa, Westerns, and the writing of Mark Twain. He eventually wrote a few pieces under the pseudonym "Huck Gernsback."[3]

His parents did not approve of his tastes or his tinkering, but when his father died at the age of 57, Hugo, only 19, immigrated to America. It was 1904 and he floated into the United States with 200 dollars in his pocket.

He embarked on a series of battery-related inventions and businesses before launching the Electro Importing Company. One of the first mail order radio retailers in America, it specialized in importing from Europe radio and electrical parts otherwise unavailable in the US. His Telimco radio receiver was a wireless telegraph "guaranteed to work up to one mile." The device was so far ahead of its time that the police actually came to his shop to make sure he wasn't selling some sort of scam. Hugo published the *Electro Importing Company Catalog* as a means of selling his

3. Hugo Gernsback and the Science Fiction League 15

wares. The catalog evolved to include articles, editorials, and letters and turned into the magazine *Modern Electrics*. This publication later morphed into *The Electrical Experimenter*, which would become *Science and Invention* in 1920. He also published a companion magazine, *Radio News*. In a further sign of how prescient he was, he launched a magazine called *Television News* in 1931, over a decade before TVs would become household items. His company also published a series of books and manuals on electronics, mostly regarding amateur radio, with titles like *Wireless Telephone* and *The Wireless Course*.

The purpose of these publications was initially to keep readers abreast of the latest technological breakthroughs in the same vein as *Popular Science* and *Popular Mechanics*. The articles he wrote and/or published were amazingly prescient, predicting inventions some of which have only recently come to fruition. His writings include "Television and the Telephot," in which he predicts an interactive two-way TV, which he published in 1909 at a time when radio was still a novelty.[4] In 1924 he wrote a piece called "A Radio-Controlled Television Plane," which foresaw drones. ("They can be used in pursuit of the enemy, for taking aerial photographs, and for any other military or peace-time operation, just the same as a present-day plane piloted by an aviator."[5]) He published an article on the world's first "portable" telephone, which he called a "Stovepipe Radio" because the massive tubes resembled a chimney. Whether it was really portable is debatable—according to the accompanying photo, the phone needed a two-man team to operate it. Nevertheless, Hugo reported, "Mrs. Macfarlane ... was talking thru the wireless telephone to her husband seated comfortably in a moving automobile 500 yards away."[6] An article on a helicopter appeared in 1919, one on solar panels and another on moon rockets in 1920. He would later set up one of the first regular television broadcasts in America.[7]

The world's first cell phone, the Stovepipe Radio of 1919 (*Electrical Experiment* 7, no. 74 [June 1919]: 115).

Not all of what he foresaw would come to pass.

The cliché that science fiction becomes science fact is true, but less understood is that science fact from yesterday reads like so much steampunk now. Many of Gernsback's proposals are reminiscent of pulpy sci-fi, with color-loaded magazine covers that would have looked perfectly at home on the cover of *Amazing Stories*. During the Great War (a.k.a. World War I, 1914–18) many of his publications theorized on the machinery of planes, submarines, and electric hot-air balloons. It is just as well that not all of Gernsback's ideas saw the light of day. Brilliant as Hugo was, he could be wickedly cruel when conjuring up new weapons.

The Germans occupied Gernsback's native Luxembourg during the First World War (and again during World War II). This may explain why he was more eager than the Americans of his adopted homeland to beat back the Hun. In the pages of *Electrical Experimenter* he devised weapons that looked like they sprouted from the mind of a sadistic 12-year-old. In the February 1918 issue he earnestly proposed the "Gyro-Electric Destroyer"—think of a Ferris wheel mechanized to roll over enemy trenches and at least a few unlucky Germans. Gernsback assured his readers that the Destroyer would somersault at "40–60 miles per hour, instead of creeping along as do the 'Tanks'" (quotes in the original).[8] He also published designs for "The Automatic Wireless Soldier," an army of robotic turrets controlled by soldiers via radio-remote in faraway bunkers. These spinning cylinders of doom were to be equipped with machine guns, poison gas, and flamethrowers—imagine R2-D2 armed to the teeth. ("These automatons cannot only be used to pump bullets into the oncoming enemy, but ... to belch forth liquid fire or to let loose a gas attack."[9]) Hugo believed wholly in his machines. An automaton "never surrenders and never turns traitor," and "there is not a soldier living who would stand up under the withering fire of such automatons who know no fear."[10]

More mundane inventions he speculated on were an electric water purifier, electrically operated step-escalators, a cow milking machine, a stoplight (an "electrical traffic regulator"), a device that sorted coffee beans, and a vending machine that dispensed hot pies for a nickel.

He also routinely devoted column space to critiques of the earliest science fiction films ever made, what were then called "scientific movies." *A Daughter of Uncle Sam* was apparently about a radio-controlled torpedo and a "theoscope" that allowed people to see through walls and across vast distances. Another film, *The Mystery Ship*, is lost to history but centered on a vehicle that could travel on land, sea, or air and was rendered "semi-invisible" by use of a special paint.

Gernsback also published "scientifiction" stories, tales to help the reader grasp what a new world with these inventions would look like. Many of these stories were written by his own readers with his full backing and encouragement, but he also published some of the better-known scientific fiction writers of the era, like George Allan England and Ray Cummings. While some of his readers felt these fictional stories a waste of space, Gernsback defended them with a line that just may be the best defense of science fiction anywhere: "There can be no progress without prediction."[11] Perhaps his most prescient foretelling was the gradual acceptance of science fiction as a respected genre: "In time to come, there is no question that science fiction will be looked upon with considerable respect by every thinking person."[12] In order for scientifiction stories to be published in his pages they had to be at least somewhat plausible. That science fact was crucial to science fiction was enshrined in the emblem of scientifiction that Gernsback commissioned, depicting a machine of three cogs. One large cog is flanked by two smaller ones, one labeled "fact" and the other "theory." Both cogs were connected to a pen in the process of writing "scientifiction."

In the pages of these magazines readers found stories about a fictional duel

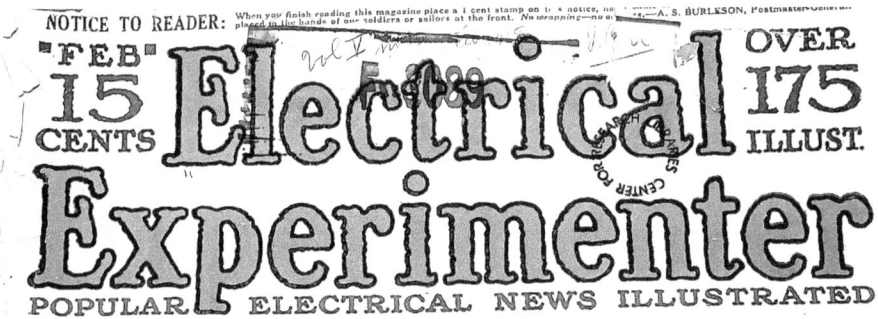

How does it stop? Hugo Gernsback's Gyro-Electric Destroyer ploughs through German trenches (cover of *Electrical Experimenter* 5, no. 58 [February 1918], painting by George Wall).

between two men fought with electric swords,[13] an entire army losing its electrical capabilities at the hands of an enemy strike,[14] a murder mystery that involves a primitive drone strike.[15] It was in the pages of *Modern Electrics* (between April of 1911 and March 1912) that he serialized what many consider to be the first modern science

Gernsback's "Wireless Soldiers" (*Electrical Experimenter* 6, no. 66 [October 1918]).

fiction novel, *Ralph 124c 41+; A Romance of the Year 2660*. The story is the sort of damsel-in-distress melodrama common at the time, but it is Gernsback's prescience that makes the novel stand out. Much of what he envisioned in that book has come to pass in some form or another, including an interactive TV that allows users to speak with people all over the world; "Tele-Theaters" that let the audience dial up whatever performance they wish to see; houses with lights that turn on using voice commands; inkless newspapers that are updated every half hour, the type of news based on the reader's habits; ocean crossings in "trans-continental air liners"; and climate-controlled buildings that don't use wood or coal. Other predictions have not come to pass but would become tropes of science fiction, such as routine visits to a Mars inhabited by intelligent Martians, one government ruling all of Earth, individuals flitting about in personal "aeroflyers," and weather that is totally under human control.

Other predictions have yet to come true and hopefully never will, most notably the godawful food tubes in restaurants: "A flexible tube hung down to which one fastened a silver mouthpiece.... The silver mouthpiece was then placed in the mouth and one pressed upon a red button. The liquid food which one selected would then begin to flow into the mouth." Not surprisingly, Ralph explains to his love interest, Alice—most of the novel is Ralph explaining things to Alice—"it took people a long time to accept the scientific restaurants." While the novel portrayed a mostly sunny outlook on the future, Gernsback admitted that, "with all the labor-saving devices they have," the lives of the novel's characters "are speeded up to the breaking point."

Everything Gernsback predicted was to his mind at least theoretically possible,

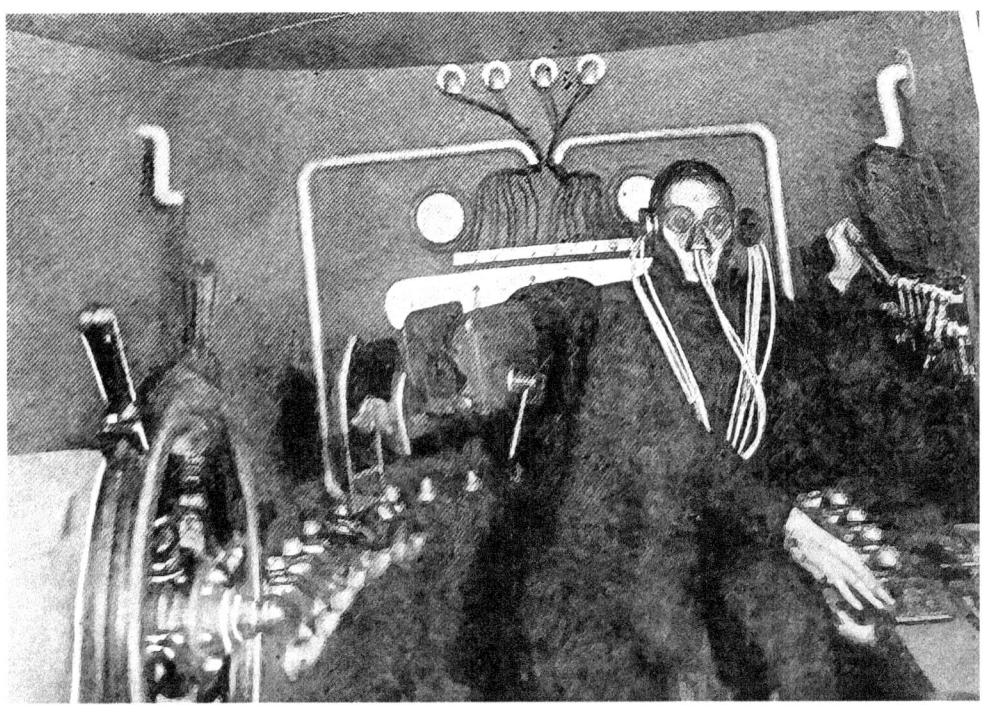

A still image from *The Mystery Ship* (1917).

including contact with aliens. He would always be a firm believer that all science fiction should be grounded in fact, even if these facts led to wildly imaginative journeys. In a 1950 reprint of *Ralph*, Gernsback wrote in the introduction: "While quite a number of the scientific predictions made in Ralph have come to pass, many more are still unrealized. I have, however, little concern that all—or most of them—will come about in the not too distant future."

Building on past publications, Gernsback launched the first ever science fiction magazine in 1926, *Amazing Stories* (*"Extravagant Fiction Today—Cold Fact Tomorrow"*). For the first time, a magazine would publish nothing but "scientifiction" stories, a genre Gernsback described as "charming romance intermingled with scientific fact and prophetic vision."[16] On the very first page of the first issue he introduced *Amazing Stories*: "There is the usual fiction magazine, the love story and the sex-appeal type of magazine, the adventure type, and so on, but a magazine of 'Scientifiction' is a pioneer in its field in America." And it certainly was. Within 15 years dozens of imitators glowed on the news racks, many of the titles short-lived (the average life span for a pulp magazine was five years), with interchangeable names employing seemingly every superlative in the English language, often combined with something scientific-sounding: *Astonishing Stories, Startling Stories, Marvel Science Stories, Dynamic Science Stories, Stirring Science Stories, Super Science Stories, Fantastic Adventures, Fantastic Stories, Planet Stories*, and *Galaxy Science Fiction*, to name but a few. While other magazines had printed futuristic fiction here and there, and others, like *Weird Tales*, published stories of fantasy and/or the supernatural, *Amazing Stories* is thought of as the first to publish science fiction exclusively. *Amazing* initially reran stories from some of the best-known names in science fiction, such as H.G. Wells, Edgar Allan Poe, and Jules Verne, and later ran with original work from the likes of E.E. "Doc" Smith, Ray Cummings, and Edmond Hamilton. Gernsback and his editors even haunted used book shops in search of material they could reprint.[17] The 1920s and '30s was a time when fiction magazines began specializing in genres, with an increasing number of pulps devoted just to detective stories or Westerns, romance or sports. Some got ludicrously specific, such as *Zeppelin Tales* and *Submarine Stories*, both of which quickly folded. *Amazing* would be the first to publish nothing but science fiction.

Indeed, it was in the pages of *Amazing Stories* that the genre first began to be called "science fiction." In the January 1927 edition of *Amazing Stories* Gernsback wrote: "Jules Verne was a sort of Shakespeare in science fiction."[18] The new genre had a name. Gernsback had published an issue of *Science and Invention* in 1923 titled *Scientific Fiction Number*, thought by many to be a trial balloon for *Amazing Stories*. Throughout the '20s Gernsback referred to the genre as scientific fiction or "scientifiction" (a word MS Word doesn't recognize). When he first ran *Amazing Stories* it was subtitled "The Magazine of Scientifiction," and the term "scientifiction" (which Forry Ackerman and other early fans called simply "stf," pronounced "stef") would be used throughout the '20s and early '30s. The works of earlier authors, like H.G. Wells and Jules Verne, were often published under the label of "fantastic voyages" or "scientific romances," and Wells's later works were called "scientific fantasies." Other early terms for science fiction were "scientific," "impossible," "futuristic," "imaginative," "pseudo-scientific" (a word Gernsback hated—there was nothing "pseudo" about the science in his fiction), or just plain "different" fiction, with science fiction films often called "scientifilms" or "science films," phrases that still turn up in the various pulps and mimeographed publications of the '30s. Gernsback himself continued to stick with the phrase "scientifiction" throughout his run at *Amazing Stories*. He began using the term "science fiction" more frequently when he launched *Science Wonder Stories* in 1929, as a way of distinguishing his new publication from the one that had been taken from him. He lost *Amazing Stories* as part of a bankruptcy hearing. Brilliant though he was, Gernsback was not a businessman (but there is some speculation as to whether Gernsback had really "lost" *Amazing Stories* or whether he deliberately folded). He even tried, without success, to patent the phrase "science fiction"—the patent office ruled the term too similar to "scientifiction."

The Science Fiction League

Besides *Amazing Stories* and the subsequent invention of the term "science fiction," the other great contribution Gernsback made to early fandom was the creation of the Science Fiction League.

Being a science fiction fan in the 1930s could be lonely at a time when there was relatively little scientifiction to be enjoyed and the public mostly looked down on consumers of pulps, comics, and silly space movies. If you were a science fiction fan (what from this point forward will be called simply a "fan") anywhere besides in a large city, you were likely the only one. When Roy Test, all of 14 years old, hosted the first meeting of the LA chapter of the Science Fiction League in his garage in 1934, fewer than a dozen people showed up, the most fans he'd ever seen in one place. The era where small towns and suburbs could support subgroups of fans and host comic book conventions was 70 years off. In the 1930s, a fan was lucky to have one friend who also enjoyed Edmond Hamilton or Edgar Rice Burroughs, or even knew who those writers were.

Desperate to communicate with like-minded souls, fans reached out to each other the only way they could in the late 1920s and '30s, via mail. Whereas other genre magazines and pulps published letters simply to fill space and received sparse correspondence, science fiction fans were passionate, and their pulps received more letters than editors could print. By one estimate, in its roughly first decade of existence, *Amazing Stories* published more than 2,100 letters from more than 1,500 fans, a not small minority of which came from overseas.[19] Some fans wrote hundreds of letters and were known in the business as "letterhacks," their names as well known to fans as those of published authors. The fans, mostly boys in their teens or early twenties, thought nothing of signing off with their names, addresses, and sometimes phone numbers. The mostly young, white males saw each other's addresses and struck up pen-pal friendships. Some of the magazines had a special correspondence section in the very back where fans could publicize their contact information and whom they wanted to communicate with.[20] *Thrilling Wonder Stories* also offered a "swap column," where readers advertised items they were willing to trade: "Will swap perfect voice singing course for good camera." Another: "A young female Persian cat and also black male racoon to swap for what have you."[21] The more active fans of the '30s had dozens of pen pals.

It was in these brown, grainy back pages of the pulps that science fiction fandom spawned. Writing to other fans was fun, but soon many of these boys (and a few girls) felt the urge to meet one another in person. Fans who noticed addresses that weren't too far away reached out to each other and began meeting. In bigger cities, these individual friendships became cliques, which became clubs, eventually forming nationwide organizations.

In the early 1930s, a teen named Julius Schwartz saw that another boy, Mort Weisinger, also lived in the Bronx. Schwartz mailed Weisinger a postcard, and they eventually met in Weisinger's basement. The boys would be friends for life, and both had stellar careers in science fiction, including founding the first science fiction literary agency and editing DC Comics. T. Bruce Yerke wrote in his self-published *Memoirs of a Superfluous Fan, Vol. 1* (it does not appear that any further volumes were written) that after his family moved from the suburbs into LA proper, he realized he lived two blocks away from Forry Ackerman's house, an address he'd seen printed many times in the pulps. He excitedly wrote Ackerman, who invited him to join the local chapter of the Science Fiction League. Chicago fan Erle M. Korshak found like-minded souls when he bought used magazines and sometimes saw the name and address of a fan written on the back. In the summer of 1930, Walter H. Gillings saw a letter published by another Londoner, Leonard A. Kippin, in *Wonder Stories*. The two struck up a friendship and formed the first British fan club, The Ilford Science Literary Circle.[22] In September of 1938 Isaac Asimov got a letter from someone named Frederik Pohl inviting him to join a group called The Futurians.

In the fall 1929 edition of *Science Wonder Quarterly*, Gernsback reported: "There are also in existence several clubs whose prime purpose is to discuss science fiction."[23] In 1928 a boy named Aubrey MacDermott contacted other fans in the Oakland area and formed the Eastbay Science Correspondence Club, one of the earliest known fan clubs. (Among their other activities, they visited a fellow fan whose name and San Francisco address they'd seen in the letters column of *Science Wonder Quarterly*, Forry Ackerman.) *Amazing Stories* soon began to devote column space to keeping up with various scientifiction clubs around the country. In the November 1929 issue, one Leonard May mailed in a letter about the recent establishment of the Science Correspondence Club, whose 50 or so members included the afore-mentioned MacDermott and a Milwaukee fan named Ray Palmer. It would later become the International Scientific Association. The Science Correspondence Club, as its name suggested, was more devoted to the interests of science that science fiction (Leonard May finished his letter with a formula explaining the relationship of a cube to a sphere), but it did include many young men who would later be active in the fantastic fields (e.g., Ray Palmer would eventually edit *Amazing Stories*). A later letter to *Wonder Stories*[24] claimed the club had been founded in 1927. In December of 1929 a handful of New York fans—fewer than a dozen initially—who had been corresponding formed the Scienceers.[25]

By one estimate, by the late 1940s there were about 30 to 50 science fiction groups across the country and in other English-speaking lands, some with multiple chapters.[26] As more and more of these groups formed, it was inevitable that someone would suggest they coalesce into one national front. It made sense for that someone to be the man who began the whole craze, Hugo Gernsback.

Gernsback and his very young editor, Charles D. Hornig (he was not even out of high school when he first began editing *Wonder Stories*), announced the formation of the Science Fiction League in the April 1934 issue of *Wonder Stories*, the magazine Gernsback founded after giving up *Amazing Stories*. The goal was to combine the myriad groups and fans under one umbrella, to unite fandom and turn it into a force for good. As Gernsback put it, the league was "for the betterment and promotion of scientific literature in all languages."[27]

Gernsback had become devout in his faith in science fiction, not just as a respected genre but also as a force for good in the world. Not long after launching the league he wrote in the May 1934 issue of *Wonder Stories* that "the purpose of the Science Fiction League, naturally, is to disseminate and spread the cult and art of Science Fiction in the most energetic manner." The world needed to turn away from "meaningless detective and love trash to the elevating and imaginary literature of science fiction."[28]

He often referred to science fiction simply as "the Cause." He believed fully that Westerns and romances where all well and good for simple entertainment, but science fiction alone had the potential to make the world a better place. It could get people interested in science and knowledge, and the more people subscribed to science, the more progress there would be. In another issue of *Thrilling Wonder Stories*, he proclaimed: "The founders of the Science Fiction League and the editors of *Thrilling Wonder Stories* sincerely believe that they have a great mission to fulfill. They believe in the seriousness of science fiction. They believe that there is nothing greater than human imagination, and the diverting of such imagination into constructive channels. They believe that science fiction is more than a form of entertainment. They believe that it can become world-force of unparalleled magnitude."[29]

Skeptics have argued that while he may have believed in all of the good science fiction could do, the league's purpose was really to sell magazines. While he insisted that the league was not for any financial gain, he no doubt hoped some of this good force would help *Wonder Stories* compete with his usurpers, *Astounding Science Fiction* and *Amazing Stories*, Gernsback's old publication. Whatever his motives, he needed a church and flock to promote the wonders of science fiction, and a nationwide club with local chapters was just the way to do it.

After the announcement of the formation of the Science Fiction League, the response from the fans was immediate, with hundreds clamoring to join. Frederick Pohl recalled sending off a letter to be a member as soon as he read the April announcement, but he was still member #490.[30] Science Fiction League fans got an official lapel pin, a certificate of membership, an official member number, and league stationery embossed with the emblem of a red, yellow, and blue logo depicting a rocket shooting through a field of stars, leaving Earth behind. Gernsback claimed that flashing the official league lapel pin at bookstores and magazine shops would get one a discount on scientific literature, but it's not known if that really worked. (Ray Bradbury did claim that the SFL button could be used to literally get a free ride—on the bus: "I find that they clog up the mechanism very easily & by the time the busman gets the darned thing out you'll be at the street where you want to get off."[31])

If there were enough league members in a certain area, a chapter could be organized. In order to form a chapter a fan needed to write to *Wonder Stories*, ending his letter with his mailing address. The eager fan then hoped that others in the area contacted him. If at least three fans in a certain locale showed interest, Gernsback recognized the chapter.

The SFL was not the first organization devoted to science fiction, but it would be the most prominent, with chapters spread out across the US and even the world. Well-known author Edmond Hamilton and a young fan named Forry Ackerman were among the executive directors. The league went international, with chapters springing up in Europe, Australia, Canada, Mexico, and India. The goal of these chapters was to give fans a place to meet, be informed of the latest developments in the world of science fiction, and often hear talks from prominent scientists, writers, and other people of interest in the field.[32] *Wonder Stories* ceased publication in 1936, and officially the league was disbanded, but the various chapters continued to meet.

The league and its 36 chapters made a huge difference in the lives of its members. As authors Mike Ashley and Robert A.W. Lowndes pointed out in their Gernsback biography, *The Gernsback Days*, "The Fan magazines had only united them in spirit. Gernsback united them in body."[33] In an era before Facebook or Meetup, the league found a way to bring together young people who were often targeted or bullied elsewhere, many of whom would have admirable careers in science fiction. LA chapter member T.B. Yerke wrote about meetings of the league: "The World of the future seemed awfully close, though. Here were people who thought about it, much as I did. Schoolmates laughed at such things, but when I could tell them that I knew adults who spent their time in such a manner, I felt that my own interest was justified."[34]

Most of the chapters consisted of only a handful of members and met sporadically, with those of New York, Chicago, Philadelphia, and Los Angeles being the ones to have the most impact. The Leeds, England, chapter was also highly active, even going as far as to organize what was arguably the first science fiction convention (more on that in Chapter 15).

Los Angeles had the honor of hosting the fourth chapter, started by a 14-year-old named Roy Test in his family garage. The first meeting was recorded as being on October 27, 1934, attended by eight chapter members, two guests, and Roy's mom, Wanda. Officially she was there to keep meeting minutes, what would eventually be known as "Thrilling Wanda Stories." Unofficially, she was just making sure her teen boy was in good company. She soon threw her full support behind the club, even once baking a cake for the boys with "long live SFL!" written in icing. The first chapter director was a man named E.C. Reynolds (in the August 1935 issue of *Wonder Stories* it was reported that he resigned from the league due to his night employment). Roy Test would continue to work to promote the league throughout 1936. Test was so keen on science that in the back pages of *Fantasy Magazine* he advertised that he was selling a printed list of the known 92 elements with their symbols and atomic weights.[35]

Initially the LA chapter of the league met in Pacific Electric Building and at members' houses. For the next two years *Wonder Stories* published regular reports of meetings of various chapters, then continued to do so after it morphed into the magazine *Thrilling Wonder Stories*. This pulp printed the meeting minutes of different chapters, giving us an idea of what typical meetings were like. By the time of Ray Bradbury's first meeting in October of 1937, they had been meeting twice a month at a downtown establishment called Clifton's Cafeteria.

4

Bradbury Joins the League

> "So I came down to the Brown Room and met all the weird people. We were all weird, because we were all ahead of our time."
> —Ray Bradbury, 2004[1]

Ray Bradbury attended his first Chapter 4 meeting on October 7, 1937, at age 17.[2] Now called the Los Angeles Science Fantasy Society (LASFS), this group still meets every Thursday, making it the oldest continuously running science fiction club.[3]

There are different versions of how exactly Bradbury came into the Little Brown Room at Clifton's Cafeteria that night. He would always say he left his name and address with the owner of Shep's Shop and was eventually contacted by T.B. Yerke. Yerke, in his own memoirs, said a fan named Robert L. Cumnock wrote to the league saying that a kid named Bradbury asked about them. In any case, it was Theodore Bruce Yerke (pronounced "yerk-ee") who sent a mimeographed letter to Bradbury on official league stationery personally inviting the high school senior to a meeting. Bradbury's first words when he burst into the Little Brown Room were, "Is Mr. Yerke here?" (Yerke was affectionately known as "Tubby," both because of his initials "T.B." and because, at five feet, eight inches, he weighed 185 pounds. For his 19th birthday, LASFS gave him a cake inscribed "Chubby from Clubby." In the second issue of *Imagination!*, it was reported that he ate seven donuts in one sitting.)

Clifton's Cafeteria

Clifton's Cafeteria was not, as one might speculate from its name, a simple affair serving tater tots. It was a multi-storied theme restaurant before people knew to call it that. A forest of faux redwood trees (made with real redwood bark wrapped around support beams) stood up the interior, along with walls covered in forest murals. A waterfall spilling over plaster cliffsides and fake caves completed the illusion of eating outdoors.

The downtown location was built by Clifford E. Clinton in 1935 as Clifton's Brookdale at the corner of Broadway and 7th Street, considered the terminus of Route 66. Clifford was a devout Christian and ran his restaurants (a total of eight) with the golden rule that no one during this Depression era had to pay if they couldn't afford it (the Clifford's on Olive Street was called "Clifford's of the Golden Rule"). A bulletin board outside of both of the LA locations had postings not just for jobs, barter, and sightseeing, but also "appeals for congenial friendship"[4] and a guest exchange that promised to find "friends for lonely diners."[5] According to his biography—called *Clifton's and Clifford Clinton: A Cafeteria and a Crusader*—at the bottom of the check was written, "This is our estimate of the value of your meal. Please pay what you wish."[6] A separate dining room in the basement served a meal for either a nickel or whatever the customer could afford. Customers could get the food free with a meal ticket supplied by a local charity. At one point, about 10,000 to 15,000 meals were eaten every day.[7] The main dining hall for paying customers was upstairs. Ever the Christian, Clinton eventually installed a chapel that depicted a life-size Jesus praying in the garden of Gethsemane, complete with rubber olive trees. It's not typical for a soup kitchen to be located in a privately owned restaurant. But then there was no place else in the world quite like Clifton's.

The multi-level vast interior, more than reasonable prices, and separate rooms made it an attractive place for a wide variety of groups to gather, including Christian associations, political debaters, different immigrant organizations, and people with shared hobbies—everyone from the Southern California Timing Association (devoted to early hot-rodders) to the Conchological Club of Southern California. Clifton's establishment is recalled in dozens of books and memoirs about pre-war Los Angeles, the most honorable mention being in the *Green Book*, a Jim Crow–era guide telling African Americans where they could safely stay and eat. Clifford Clinton welcomed everyone. After changing ownership many times and several renovations, Clifton's is still operating as a multi-leveled bar and restaurant. Among the drinks served are The Two Rays, Something Wicked, and The Forest J.

For all of the dazzling interior of Clifton's, the Little Brown Room on the third floor, where Chapter 4 met, was an aptly named, simple affair, nothing more than stout wooden chairs and tables. Basic though it was, dozens of science fiction's top artists, writers, and editors would meet in this chamber.

A typical meeting of Chapter 4 of the Science Fiction League began with a reading of the prior meeting's minutes. According to chapter director Russ Hodgkins, reporting in the first issue of *Imagination!*, "Meetings are held with as little ceremony as possible. After the business has been conducted the meeting is open to informal discussions of mags, storys, authors, artists."[8] T.B. Yerke wrote in his *Memoirs of a Superfluous Fan*:

> The meeting itself was operated along a modified parliamentary procedure which called for reports from the Treasurer, Librarian, and the Secretary and his minutes. After this there was the matter of business, which in 1937 constituted little more than answering letters, collecting dues, and a few items of club transactions, mostly the library....[9]

After the official business and formal talks were finished, members kept one another up to date on the latest stories to be published in *Amazing* and other pulps. They would often read magazines brought by other members right there at Clifton's because, in the words of Ray Bradbury, "a lot of us couldn't afford the magazines."[10] When the meeting was over the boys and girls took advantage of the giant 10-cent malts, the free sherbet, and the "endless Limeade waterfall."[11] Sometimes after meetings they would gather at a hamburger stand at Third and Vermont and get hamburgers for a nickel. Bradbury always bought three ("they tasted better when you bought three of them"[12]). He was no one's idea of a healthy eater and it's a miracle he lived to be 91. In the August 1942 issue of the hand-cranked zine *Shangri-L'Affaires* it was reported that he made something called Ghoul's Broth, a combination of lemonade, stale coffee, and strawberry sherbet. No one else took better advantage of all Clifton's had to offer.

When Bradbury went to his first meeting, he was in heaven. For the first time he was in a room full of people who also scrapbooked comics, read scientifiction stories, and took in as many science fiction and horror films as they could. The teen writer made it clear to everyone within shouting distance that he was happy to be there. This was not the white-haired Ray Bradbury the world would come to know, a sort of elder statesman of science fiction and fantasy. Seventeen-year-old blond Bradbury was brash, bold, and bouncing off the walls. The teenager's enthusiasm was on full display; he was laughing, cracking jokes, flat out hyper. Yerke described him as a "wild-haired, enthusiastic individual" who infuriated fellow members with "endless pranks and disturbances"; victims often retaliated with "trays and hammers."[13] He would also recall that Bradbury had "mad, insane, hackneyed humor." Early fan Walter Sullivan described a visit to the Little Brown Room in 1940 that had Bradbury "dashing in."[14] By his own admission decades later, Bradbury was an obnoxious brat.

Another member remembered: "He was loud, boisterous, always hamming it up with impersonations of W.C. Fields or Hitler ... lucky that we didn't strangle him and rob the world of one of the greatest literary talents and socially stimulating individuals of the 20th Century."[15] That comment came from a lanky, gangly 21-year-old named Forrest J Ackerman. He eventually stopped putting a period after the *J*, one of his many quirks. Most people just called him Forry.

5

Forry Ackerman

"Anything, as long as it's fantastic."
—Forry Ackerman

"Without Forry, an important part of my life would not have been started."
—Ray Bradbury[1]

Looking at how similar their tastes and loves were, it was inevitable Forry and Ray would meet once they were in the same city. Both loved horror, science fiction, and all things magical. Both loved movies and hounded actors for autographs. Both scrapbooked *Buck Rogers*. Both would stuff their homes with sci-fi memorabilia (if the opening credits of the cable series *The Ray Bradbury Theater* are to be believed, Bradbury's office looked like a room from Forrest Ackerman's house of memorabilia, the Ackermansion). While Bradbury was inspired by his love of the fantastic, Ackerman made loving science fiction his career. Long before fanatics earned a living critiquing movies and books via the internet and podcasts, Forry was doing as much in the '30s with typewriters and mimeograph machines. He was that rare person who invented the career that defined him. He was the world's first professional fan.

Forrest James Ackerman[2] was born on November 24, 1916, in LA to William Ackerman, a statistician for the Pacific Western Oil Corporation (later Getty Oil), and Carroll Cridland Wyman, a homemaker. Carroll and William provided Forry with everything he needed, but it was Forry's maternal grandparents, George and Belle Wyman, who truly indulged the boy who would one day edit *Famous Monsters of Filmland* and garner the largest horror and science fiction collection. Forry would always joke that he picked the right pair of maternal grandparents, who he often referred to as "the last of the big-time angels."[3] Grandpa Wyman routinely sketched aliens and other monsters, art that Forry kept well into his adult years. His grandmother Belle read him *Ghost Stories Magazine* until she was hoarse.

Science fiction seemingly flowed in Ackerman's ancestry. As a young man, his grandfather George Wyman was contracted to build the Bradbury Building (no relation to Ray), LA's first million-dollar skyscraper. Legend has it that his inspiration for the design came from the nineteenth-century novel by Edward Bellamy called *Looking Backward*, about a man who falls asleep in 1885 and wakes up in the year 2000. Young George wasn't sure he was up to the enormous task, so he and Belle consulted the spirit world via a planchette, a precursor to the Ouija board. The wooden heart with a pen through the center scrawled on paper that if George built the Bradbury Building he would be successful, a message from his deceased brother. Forry Ackerman inherited this piece of paper and held onto this message from beyond the grave his entire life. An atheist who had no belief in the afterlife (nor in ghosts, vampires, or anything else supernatural), Forry nevertheless was enamored by an actual message from the dead. With its open cage elevators and iron railings, the Bradbury Building has been featured in numerous films and is a designated landmark. As an odd coincidence, it is seen in the opening credits of late '80s/early '90s show *The Ray Bradbury Theater*.

The Wymans introduced little Forry to the world of film, taking him to plenty of movies. This was in the peak years of the Los Angeles movie palaces, when there were 22 theaters just on Broadway. In the documentary *The Ackermonster Chronicles*, Forry claimed he went with his grandparents to 356 films in one year: "We'd start off at 11 in the morning, see 2 pictures & 5 acts of vaudeville, have lunch, see 2 pictures, have dinner, see 2 pictures and 7 acts of vaudeville at the old Orpheum Theater."[4] They saw as many as seven films per day, and would have seen even more if not for the vaudeville acts.

Seeing films in the '20s and '30s was a spectacle, showing at a time when adult audiences were used to live performances. Often these films were billed as double features with vaudeville acts, which is how Forry Ackerman saw Al Jolson (Ackerman's father had worked with Jolson as a teenager and collected all of his records) perform on stage. Later Ackerman got his autograph, after Jolson put his arm around him and called him "sonny boy." Another actor Forry saw live was Bela Lugosi, in a stage version of *Dracula*, and got his autograph as well. Ackerman would later say it was the only time Lugosi signed as "Count Dracula." When he was 15 Forry personally met Marlene Dietrich, along with a young, unknown actor named Cary Grant.

From an early age little Forry gravitated towards what he often called "imagi-movies," "scientifilms," or "fantastic movies." He would later say that the 13 years of 1923–1936 were the "greatest consecutive years of imaginative movies." Many of these are tragically lost to history and exist only in the recollections of fans, vanished treasures such as *One Glorious Day*, Forry's first film at age five, in which Ezra Botts (Will Rogers) is possessed by a not-yet-born soul; *The Young Diana*, seemingly an early Benjamin Button, a film about a woman who reverse ages; *Aelita, Queen of Mars*, partly set in the USSR and partly on Mars; and *A Blind Bargain*, about a mad scientist turning an ape into a "bestial man." Then there are the classics thankfully still with us, such as *Dante's Inferno*, *The Thief of Bagdad*, *The Mysterious Island*, and *The Lost World*, the last of which Forry saw at Grauman's Egyptian Theatre. Some of the stop-motion dinosaurs from *The Lost World* were on display as little Forry passed through the Egyptian's ornate foyer. The collector needed all of his willpower to avoid grabbing one and bringing it home. Like his future pal Ray Bradbury, he loved anything and everything Lon Chaney Sr. did. As far as he was concerned, Mary Philbin ripping off the mask of the eponymous character in *Phantom of the Opera* was the most significant moment in the history of cinema.[5] His top six favorite horror films were *Phantom of the Opera*, *Frankenstein*, *Dracula*, *Dead of Night*, *King Kong*, and *The Mummy*. The young fan spent one New Year's Day seeing *Frankenstein* not once but twice. A fully staffed ambulance was parked outside in case anyone in the audience found the film so frightening as to need medical attention. During Forry's first viewing the teen was shocked when a woman ran screaming from the audience. When the same woman screamed out of the theater during the next showing, the boy learned an early lesson about the business of Hollywood. (Having medical staff on hand during extra scary shows was nothing new. When the stage version of *Dracula* debuted in 1927, with Bela Lugosi as the title character, a nurse was on hand in case anyone fainted. It's not known if anyone actually did.)

His grandparents planted another seed in the young collector's mind when they gifted him a series of stills from the 1930 film *Just Imagine*, a musical comedy—generally credited as the first sci-fi "talkie"—depicting life in the faraway year of 1980. Forry had seen plenty of lobby cards in his career as a film buff, but it had never occurred to him that he could own them. Soon the boy was off and running to the local National Screen Service, a company that controlled distribution of most movie posters, where he asked for stills.[6] "Nobody but me was interested in collecting movie stills," he explained in the pages of *Collecting Monsters of Film and TV*. "They cost 10 cents a piece, and I would always buy a dollar's worth." He also made the rounds at dozens of local cinemas. The staff thought the boy odd but often gave him stills and press kits for free, and sometimes the posters (oddly, he wouldn't collect lobby cards and posters until later in life). This ephemera soon piled up in his parents' basement. No one could have imagined a time when these mementos would sell for hundreds or thousands of dollars. Forry would eventually accumulate more than 100,000 stills, a gallery he would one day use to launch the magazine *Famous Monsters of Filmland*.

His greatest collecting passion was the written word, the books and magazines that described the possible impossible. It was one pulp in particular that sparked his imagination.

Decades later, time and again, Forry would tell the same story of his first encounter with the legendary magazine *Amazing Stories*. The script always went something like this: "You're too young to remember, but back then, magazines spoke! And this one cried, 'Take me home, little boy, you will love me!'" Exactly how Forry first came across his first issue of *Amazing Stories* is up for debate. In one version of his telling, his mother sent him to a corner drug store at the intersection of Santa Monica Boulevard and Western Avenue to buy milk of magnesia, as he wasn't feeling well. In other accounts his mother bought this copy for him, as a way to bribe him into drinking the milk of magnesia. However he first came across that issue of *Amazing Stories* with its amazing Frank R. Paul cover, it was love at first sight. The cover's depiction of a large centipede-like creature towering over an earthling survivor of a space wreck (a scene from the A. Hyatt Verrill story "Beyond the Pole") gripped young Forry and sparked a lifelong obsession. No one would have guessed at the time that this simple magazine would be the acorn that would sprout the largest science fiction collection ever in private hands. He soon began hoarding pulps like *Amazing Stories*, *Ghost Stories*, and *Scientific Detective Monthly*, along with any magazine, like *Argosy* or *Blue Book*, that happened to have a fantastic story in it. As he later explained, "I was fearful that all of a sudden there wouldn't be any more science fiction, so I figured I better collect as much as I possibly could."[7] His fears were not totally unfounded. Science fiction pulps began on shaky ground when they first appeared in the late 1920s and early 1930s. Even the best-known science fiction magazines of the era, *Amazing Stories* and *Astounding Stories*, both faced bankruptcy and stopped printing for a time. It wasn't uncommon for a science fiction magazine to run for a few issues, sometimes even only one, only to then vanish or reappear under a different title. Science fiction books and anthologies were rare. If a reader should stumble across a story he especially liked, there was no certainty he would be able to find it anyplace else. Some fans, including Forry, went as far as excising their favorite stories from magazines and having them bound between a couple of marble boards, library-style.

The boy felt the urge to gather as many fantasy rosebuds as he could and kept this trove in the family garage. If he knew a magazine was going to come out on the 25th, he would start haunting the newsstand on the 23rd. If one of his few friends called and said they'd seen a new scientifiction magazine at a drug store across town, Forry would run all the way there. He soon began collecting entire print runs of various pulps, including obscure ones like the German-language *Der Orchideengarten*, which only ran from 1919 to 1921. He would always say that if he could keep but one item from his mansion of collectible treasures—a collection that would one day include Bela Lugosi's ring and original dinosaur models from *King Kong*—it would be his first issue of *Amazing Stories*.

He scrapbooked every article and ad about his favorite films and collected countless magazines about movies. His mother confronted her boy about the growing collection, pointing out that he had, at last count, 40 magazines and might, by the time he was an adult, have well over 100, an estimate that would end up being short by more than 100,000. (Forry claimed in an interview with a New Mexico oral history project that he had the complete run of more than 49 magazine titles. In different interviews over the decades, he estimated the number of titles he had the complete run of to be anywhere from 20 to 200.) She pressured him to sell these copies. He relented, sold them to another boy, and soon regretted it. His mom saw how much the loss burdened him, called the boy, and got him to sell them back. When the Ackerman family moved to San Francisco in 1927, the pre-teen Forry kept this pile in the family's garage, what he proudly named the Leaning Tower of Pisa of Pulps. Each issue either had his address on it using personal stickers or he had stamped his name on them, as he somehow managed to get a personalized rubber stamp.

Even his doting grandparents wouldn't buy him every issue of every pulp magazine he wanted unless, the boy figured, he could somehow get his name on those brown pages. Surely if he managed to get something published, the adults in his life would buy the magazine for him?

Ackerman saw his first letter printed in the 1929 Gernsback publication *Science Wonder Quarterly*. His was the first letter in the first issue. It read:

> Although I am only 12 years old, I have taken a delight in reading the magazines you have published for almost the last four years.... Take every word that means excellent out of the largest dictionary in the world, multiply those words by the number of seconds in two thousand centuries, and add to that amount the number of stars in the heavens and the sum will give you a very slight idea of what I think of your magazine.

Even as a boy, Forry was always Forry.

He signed off: "HIP, HIP, HURAYYY!"[8]

While his parents seemed bemused by their son's obsessions, they were proud to see his name in print. Eventually, Forry's father had his secretaries type up short stories the boy had written in longhand. Decades later, Forry's mom would work for her own son's magazine.

After seeing his name printed, Forry began to dash off as many letters as he could to the pulps. He soon became one of the most prolific pulp magazine letter writers of the time, if not of all time, getting his name in hundreds of issues of *Amazing Stories*, *Thrilling Wonder Stories*, and *Air Wonder Stories*, among others. He wrote so often that, as Gernsback explained in the back pages of *Wonder Stories*,[9] "Whenever an issue of *Wonder Stories* appears without one of his letters, readers wonder what has happened to him." Ackerman wrote more than *Wonder* could print. According to one estimate, Ackerman had more than 200 letters published before World War II.[10]

Writing, young Ackerman quickly learned, could get you things. Once he fired off a letter of praise to the artist who painted the cover work for a pulp called *Miracle Science and Fantasy Stories*. The grateful artist shipped Forry the autographed cover painting for free. By the time he was in his early twenties Ackerman would have a collection of original pulp art from such masters as Frank R. Paul and Virgil Finlay, works that would later be worth thousands of dollars. In 1931 he wrote to Fritz Lang, director of his favorite film of all time, *Metropolis*. In response the director sent him stills of that film. Forry replied to an ad in *Photoplay* magazine, where Universal president Carl Laemmle asked for reader criticism on films, both released and proposed. Forry wrote more than 60 letters. Besides offering his opinions of films, Forry asked if they had any film props they no longer wanted. Laemmle replied by writing the following memo to his secretary: "Give this boy anything he wants." Ackerman would get the sound discs from *Murders in the Rue Morgue* and Whale's *Frankenstein*[11] and an invitation to visit the set of *Bride of Frankenstein*.

Besides the discs, Laemmle would also send him stills, pressbooks, lobby cards, and posters of *Frankenstein*. By the time he was 21, roughly the time he met Bradbury, Ackerman already had one of the most, if not the most, impressive science fiction collections in the world, and he loved to tell the world about it. Below is a description of his collection that he typed up for the zine *The Fantasy Fan* in 1933:

MY SCIENCE FICTION COLLECTION by Forrest J Ackerman Part Two

My stf books and magazines lie behind sliding panels. These panels are decorated with various original stf illustrations. Two are by an artist friend showing the rocketship STF over a foreign world, and the other a city of the future. One is by Morey. There is a Tarzan jig-saw puzzle, and one of the mighty 56 foot prehistoric ape, King Kong, engaging in a battle with a flesh-eating allosaur. From "The Swordsman of Mars" comes another drawing. Two striking Paul illustrations are prominent, one being what I consider one of his very best: the inside drawing for "The City of Singing Flame," picturing the towering black and ivory edifices of that weird world. Buck Rogers in his interesting costume with rocket pistol smiles down. And Elliott Dold, Jr. has autographed his original frontispiece for Miracle Stories' first issue, "The Midnite Mail takes off for Mars." Paul's original Wonder Stories' cover for "The Dust of Destruction" hangs on a side wall.[12]

As a 14-year-old then living in San Francisco, he wrote a letter to the writer Charles R. Tanner, asking him not only for an autograph, but also his desk and typewriter. The latter two requests were jokes, but Ackerman would have been thrilled if the scribe had sent them.[13] He also fired off a letter to Edgar Rice Burroughs, complaining that his teacher wouldn't let him do a book report on any of that writer's *Tarzan* and *John Carter of Mars* books. Not content to simply gather their autographs, Ackerman made it a point to meet writers in person. He somehow learned that Aladra Septama was a pen name for Judson W. Reeves. The 11-year-old looked up Reeves in the San Francisco phone book and simply showed up on his doorstep. Amused, the author invited the pre-teen inside, where his wife served him milk and cookies. When the Ackermans were still in LA, 10-year-old Forry managed to visit author Bob Olsen.

Like most fans, Ackerman was inspired to at least try his hand at writing science fiction. As a 13-year-old he won a short story contest sponsored by the *San Francisco Chronicle*, his opus titled "A Trip to Mars."[14] Later in life, as a young man, he teamed up with Indianapolis-based writer Catherine L. Moore to publish "Nymph of Darkness," first in *Fantasy Magazine*, then in *Weird Tales* in 1939. He got a few stories placed after teaming up with Francis Flagg. The first, "Earth's Lucky Day," was placed in the last issue of *Wonder Stories*. Perhaps Ackerman's best-known fiction is "Cosmic Report Card: Earth." It's only one letter long (no spoilers as to which letter that is). It has been anthologized (and translated) many times, and Ackerman often bragged about how many hundreds of dollars he got paid for typing just one letter. He also wrote the second-shortest story in the history of the genre, called "World War Three," which had only two words: "The end."

For the most part though, he preferred writing *about* science fiction.

Like most fans, when Ackerman sent a letter to *Amazing* or *Wonder Stories*, he thought nothing of publishing his name and address (and sometimes phone number) for the world to see. One day while he was sick in bed, a letter arrived from a Missouri boy named Linus Hogenmiller, who explained that he had seen Ackerman's address in the letters column and wanted to strike up a pen-pal friendship. Little Forry suddenly felt better. He bounded out of bed, composed a letter, and had it mailed. Later he thought of more he wanted to say and wrote another letter, and then another. He composed six letters in a few days, and a new obsession was born.

He soon became one of the most prolific "letterhacks," a fan term for anyone who often got letters printed in prozines (professional magazines) or "fanzines" (amateur publications normally hectographed or mimeographed), where he typically included not just his name but his address, which led to him soon getting mail from other fans. At the time, the world of science fiction fandom was small enough that a fan could get renown simply for writing a lot of letters. For whatever reason, fans of science fiction tended to send in more fan mail than fans of other genres. According to Moskowitz, in his book *Explorers of the Infinite*: "Since the earliest days, a characteristic of the reader of this literature has been his enthusiasm for writing letters.... New publishers of science fiction magazines, accustomed to getting one or two letters a month for their other magazines, have been astonished to find their science fiction venture getting from 50 to 200 every issue."

Letter writing was his window to the world. As a boy at San Francisco's Balboa High School, Ackerman was skinny, unathletic, and terrified of girls. About the only school activity he liked was editing the school paper, *The Buccaneer*, and the yearbook, *The Galleon*. He said he only had three face-to-face friends. "Schooling was unreal to me," he once explained to an interviewer. "The real world was getting home to the typewriter and the 117 boys and girls I found around the world who shared my interests."[15]

He later claimed he was routinely corresponding with 116 fans across the US, in Canada, Britain, and even one in the USSR. This was done at a time when the postal service ran trains around the clock and letters often arrived overnight, frequently even on the same day. In 1929 13-year-old Forry contacted two of these friends to begin the Boys Scientifiction Club (female fans of science fiction were as rare as "unicorn horns," Forry often said). The purpose of the club was to "promote scientific interests among boys between the ages of 10 and 15, to encourage the reading of Science Fiction and scientific works, and to create a bond of friendship between them."[16] Forry was president and librarian of the club. In order to join, a member had to pay dues of a dime, which granted him access to science fiction magazines and books. Decades later Ackerman explained how his little lending library worked:

> You sent in a little snapshot of yourself. You also sent in either three issues, consecutive, of one of the magazines that had a serial in it, or a hardcover book, of which there weren't too many at the time. In return, you got to keep either three magazines or a book for a month. Pretty soon, it got to where I was staggering five or six blocks to the mailbox, just to send off the books or magazines to the members.[17]

He shipped these all over the country, some to Canada, some even to England and the Philippines.[18]

Besides the lending library, he also published a zine for the club. Fellow club member Jim Nicholson—one of Ackerman's few face-to-face friends—introduced him to the cheap printing technology of hectography. Soon the pair were producing their own zine, *The Meteor*. (Jim Nicholson later had a career in film as a co-founder of the production company American International Pictures. Forry often promoted Nicholson's films in the pages of *Famous Monsters of Filmland*.) *The Meteor* would be the start of a new career for Forry. He would soon contribute to other zines with other fans across the country, many of whom would have legendary careers in science fiction.

In 1932 he wrote for a zine called *The Time Traveller* ("Science-Fiction's Only Fan Magazine"). He was the "scientifilm editor," and his primary contribution was keeping readers up to date on the latest science fiction/fantasy/horror films—or "imagi-movies" as he was then calling them—coming out. Ackerman would later say that the arrival of this mag in his mailbox was one of the most important events in his life. The team that produced this paper—Julius Schwartz, Mort Weisinger, and Conrad Ruppert (the staff also included an early fan named Allen Glasser, although he would later drop out amidst charges of plagiarism)—would later quit the project and launch the highly respected *Science Fiction Digest*, which would become *Fantasy Magazine* in 1934.

The adolescent fans he was publishing with would go on to be founders in the new industry of science fiction. Julius Schwartz and Mort Weisinger, the Bronx duo, later founded The Solar Sales Service, the first agency to focus on science fiction.[19] Schwartz was the first agent to represent Ray Bradbury, among other writers. (Schwartz later advertised his company saying he represented "Bradbury, Bester, Binder, and Bloch, and that was just the Bs."[20]) Both Weisinger and Schwartz became editors at DC Comics. Another contributor to *Science Fiction Digest* was Ray Palmer, future editor of *Amazing Stories*, a magazine he saved from certain death (he was a member of the Milwaukee Fictioneers, more on them in Chapter 28). Forry Ackerman was all of 17 at this point, with Ray Palmer being the senior man at age 23.

The Time Traveller ran ads for another zine called simply *Science Fiction*, produced by a pair of Cleveland teens named Jerry Siegel and Joe Shuster. Forry

Ackerman and Ray Palmer both contributed to *Science Fiction* (subtitle: *The Advance Guard of Civilization*), and this zine, first printed in 1933, is credited as being the first publication to use "science fiction" in the title. But *Science Fiction*'s biggest claim to fame is the birth of Superman.

"The Reign of the Superman" appeared in issue #3 of *Science Fiction*. The story, read by no more than a handful of people at the time (which is just as well, because it is terribly written: "Suddenly, as he lay there on the ground, a veritable holocaust of confusion burst upon his mind"), is remembered as the first appearance of Superman, sort of. In this early piece "the Superman" is a bald villain, an ordinary hobo transformed by a mad scientist's experiment. The lunatic with superpowers is investigated by a reporter Siegel named after his buddy Forry Ackerman. ("Was it true that Forrest saw the look of hate swept from the Superman's face and terror replace it, or was it mere fancy?"[21]) Schwartz explained in the pages of *Science Fiction Digest* why Siegel had decided to quit the zine: "he is working on a scientifiction cartoon strip which a number of syndicates are interested in handling ... the artist is supposed to be a top notcher in his field."[22] It would be another five years before Superman first appeared on the cover of *Action Comics*, now with a full head of thick, dark locks and in tights and a cape. Forry Ackerman kept all five issues of the Siegel/Shuster fanzine. *Science Fiction* was unremarkable at the time, as it was the work of a couple of kids using their high school's mimeograph machine, but since these issues contain original work by Ackerman, along with sci-fi writers Raymond Palmer and David H. Keller, plus the debut of Superman, the collection is appraised at $35,000 to $88,000.[23] Actor and comics fanatic Nicolas Cage has managed to separately collect issues 1 through 4. Jerry Siegel also hectographed a fanzine called *Cosmic Stories*, consisting of his own tales rejected by the pulps and contributions from others. Some say this is the first amateur zine devoted totally to science fiction, not also science or what is happening in the world of fandom. This can't be verified, since no copies have been found, making *Cosmic Stories* something of a Lost Ark for collectors.[24]

Ackerman was seemingly anywhere and everywhere in science fiction, in touch with both the famous and anonymous. Ackerman started to correspond regularly with various writers, including Edgar Rice Burroughs and H.P. Lovecraft (although his relationship with Lovecraft was mixed—see Chapter 7). Writers and film insiders began sending him information about upcoming projects that Ackerman then shared with the world. Insiders soon learned the value in letting Forry know about upcoming movies and books, information he would share with other fans. He was an influencer before anyone knew to call it that.

While not exactly a happy student, Ackerman decided to stay in school another year; senior year was optional in those days, but he liked editing the school paper. Ackerman didn't want to go to college; he wanted to see if, somehow, he could make a career out of science fiction. His parents balked, understandably. Their son had tried, without much success, to run a business selling science fiction books and related materials. In the pages of *Science Fiction Digest* and other zines, teenaged Ackerman often advertised his own science fiction wares ("Tons of Science Fiction—For Twenty Five Cents!"[25]) without profit. After he finished high school in 1933 (in his senior yearbook, he predicted a "scientific future" for himself and picked "inventor" as his future career), Forry worked out a deal with his parents, who said he should try Berkeley for a year. If he didn't like it, he could quit. He tried it for an academic year,

1933–34, didn't like it, and quit (unsurprisingly, he studied journalism and paleontology). He soon thereafter moved back to LA to live rent-free at a home owned by his grandparents, 236½ N. New Hampshire. Los Angeles was the center of the film industry that he wanted to work in somehow, plus it was the home of Chapter 4 of the Science Fiction League.

Ackerman would always claim that he was at the very first meeting of Chapter 4 when it was founded on October 27, 1934, in the garage of 14-year-old Roy Test. The chapter's October founding was announced in the February 1935 issue of *Wonder Stories*; the list of the young men present at the launch does not include Forry. Initially Roy Test did seem to be running the show: "Roy Test, one of the most active members, has started a one-man campaign to make the Los Angeles Chapter one of the finest in the world. He is contacting the fans in the local area who are not yet members."[26] Gradually, though, Ackerman took over operations, making Chapter 4 arguably the premier chapter of the Science Fiction League. LA's chapter was relatively quiet in 1934 and '35, especially when compared to those in New York and Chicago. But by mid–1936 the league began meeting regularly (at least every other Thursday) in Clifton's Cafeteria, and the gatherings were better attended and more lively. Ackerman religiously went to each and every meeting, and would even manage to keep attending meetings when he was stationed in San Pedro after being drafted into the army during the World War II.

As much as Forry loved any tales of the imagination, he did not personally believe in God or anything supernatural. He turned to atheism as a boy and never looked back, in spite of the shocked prodding of his parents, who took him to more than a dozen churches, Sunday schools, and even a synagogue, hoping he would at least believe in something. (There was no shortage of religions to choose from in 1930s LA. As the WPA guide put it, "Frequently a 'Messiah' of one of the dozens of bizarre local religious cults, garbed in biblical robes made of flour sacks, pads barefoot along a crowded sidewalk.") Forry didn't buy into any of it. He often asked others how they would feel in a world where everyone took Santa Claus and the Easter Bunny seriously. He would always say that science fiction was his only religion, and he was a devotee.

If Gernsback was an evangelical preacher of the genre, then Ackerman was a devout follower. Ackerman led charges to get local theaters to show more "imaginative movies" and made sure members of the chapter knew which houses were showing them. He stuffed flyers in the pages of pulps at newsstands and put up posters in stores, advertising upcoming meetings of the Science Fiction League. According to the minutes of the LA chapter of the Science Fiction League, published in *Thrilling Wonder Stories*, Forry and other members printed between 500 and 1,000 announcements to be distributed to members and then slipped them into the "imaginative mags of the great LA newsstands."[27] The handbill Bradbury saw in Shep's Shop was almost certainly Ackerman's handiwork.

Onward Esperanto

Another rabbit hole Forry fell into was Esperanto, a language invented by Polish-born Dr. Ludwik Zamenhof as an attempt to create peace and understanding by use of a universal dialect ("Esperanto" is Esperanto for "he who hopes"). Living as a Jew in Russian-occupied Poland in the late 1880s, Dr. Zamenhof (he was an eye doctor) had seen plenty of strife in his time and thought that a universal language would lead to better understanding between people of different backgrounds. Forry read about Esperanto in the writings of Francis Flagg and thought it was a fictional language, until his grandfather spotted an ad for classes being taught downtown. Soon Forry was attending night classes at Los Angeles City College in 1934, and he would later claim he learned it faster than anybody.[28] Esperanto was trendy for a time and gave Ackerman the ability to write fans in Germany, Czechoslovakia, Argentina, "Jugoslavia," and elsewhere, communicating with fans in this synthetic language.[29] It was also through Esperanto that he met Myrtle Douglas, a young woman who would play a key role in his life and in fandom.

In subsequent issues of his own self-published magazine, *Imagination!*, Ackerman wrote a column called "Onward Esperanto" (under the pseudonym Erdstelulov). Here he spoke about the goings on in the Esperanto community, wrote occasional words or phrases in Esperanto, and sometimes offered synopses of translations of science fiction works originally written in Esperanto by Europeans. He would use the language to communicate with fans overseas, proving its practical utility.

He was not the only member of the league to buy into the universal world language. Several members of Chapter 4 and fandom in general at least dabbled in the language. His girlfriend Myrtle Douglas was a convert, as well as Lucie B. Shepherd, proprietor of Shep's Shop. In issue #8 of *Imagination!* (May 1938, edited by Russell J. Hodgkins), Ackerman writes about piling into a car with Myrtle Douglas and a few league members and driving to a mountain residence to hear the first broadcast in Esperanto in America.

Esperanto was the closest he came to any kind of organized religion, though he dabbled with other ideas. Later in life he was intrigued by cryogenics. The idea of going to sleep and waking up 20 years later interested the lifelong fan, and he even considered doing this to himself when his time came (he didn't).

Like Bradbury, he hounded celebrities for autographs and photos. He hoarded the signatures of hundreds of authors and Hollywood royals, among them Karloff, Lugosi, and director Fritz Lang. He went to many a premiere and was at least in the same building with various celebrities, including James Cagney and Douglas Fairbanks. Unlike Bradbury, he was not averse to selling these signatures to pen pals, especially if he had extra autographs. He was a budding businessman. In 1934, he offered a fan with whom he corresponded regularly a photo of himself for 10 cents.[30] He routinely sold pieces of his collection in classified ads in *Wonder Stories* and other magazines and fanzines.

It was no surprise that Ackerman was there that Thursday evening when Bradbury first visited the Little Brown Room at Clifton's. He would be at all of the rest of the meetings Bradbury attended, too.

6

Bradbury's First Meeting

Bradbury's first meeting of Chapter 4 of the Science Fiction League featured a display of original drawings from E.E. "Doc" Smith's *Galactic Patrol*, a story being serialized in *Astounding Stories* that would later be published as a novel.[1] This interesting type of display was typical for meetings of Chapter 4 and explains why turnout was high. A meeting of a dozen attendees was considered low; a typical attendance ran between 20 to 30 fans at these biweekly gatherings in the Little Brown Room. Some of the happenings at different meetings included proofs of a new pulp magazine, *Startling Stories*, being passed around, courtesy of the publisher; a Mr. Marshall showing off a strip of three-dimensional cinema celluloid[2]; artist Jim Mooney, who would eventually work for DC Comics and Marvel, displaying some of his inked and colored illustrations, along with a Frankenstein mask he'd made[3]; visits from Charles D. Hornig or Mort Weisinger, the teenaged editor of *Wonder Stories*[4] and the young editor of *Thrilling Wonder Stories*, respectively; Jack Parsons and his partner Ed Forman speaking about the new technology of rockets, passing a few photos around, and leading the gang to the parking lot to look at metal models; and a hypnotist doing a live demonstration of his powers (he convinced several members their eyes were glued shut). Being in Los Angeles put Chapter 4 in close proximity to a lot of writers, more than a few of whom visited them at Clifton's. When writer Arthur J. Burks visited the chapter, he was amazed at their intelligence and enthusiasm:

> These youngsters, ranging in ages from twelve to sixty, are keen as hell. What they don't know about science, today and tomorrow, hasn't been written yet.... They get together twice a month, and they're rabid fans.... Forrest J Ackerman, a fashion-plate of twenty or so, asked me over and sprung me as a surprise on 'em. Reeled off the titles of stories I had done during the past ten years.... Someone asked me about one I'd published about ten or eleven years ago.[5]

Meetings began with a reading of the last meeting's minutes, plus reports from the treasurer and the librarian. "Meetings are held with as little ceremony as possible," explained chapter director Russell J. Hodgkins. "After the business has been conducted the meeting is open to informal discussions of mags, stories, authors, artists."[6]

It wasn't uncommon for league attendees themselves to give a talk. Many of the members were or would become professional authors, like Bob Olsen, Henry Kuttner, Arthur K. Barnes, and of course, eventually, Ray Bradbury. One of the key advantages of joining a chapter was meeting professionally published authors, some already quite well known. The lines between amateur and publisher, fan and published author were blurry and almost nonexistent. Joining the league meant Bradbury would eventually meet some of the top names in the field even if he himself was a no-name. One of the most common members to entertain the crowd was Forry Ackerman himself, who often brought some of his movie stills to show off to the group, along with photos of celebrities he'd managed to take. A typical example of this show-and-tell was reported in the meeting minutes in *Wonder Stories*: "Scenes from the scientific-serial 'Flash Gordon' have been exhibited by Ackerman, in addition to stills from several Soviet fantasy films; and pictures from his kodak collection passed around of various science fiction celebrities."

If there was no guest speaker, attendees frequently talked about the topics of the day, usually recent science fiction publications or actual scientific breakthroughs. Sometimes, they would simply do a reading of a recent science fiction story and then critique it. Often members exchanged copies of pulps with each other, issues of magazines not so easy to find in the pre-internet era. T.B. Yerke was amazed at how Ackerman and other fans traded pulps: "I presume an archeologist being allowed to view undestroyed Mayan relics drools and slobbers no less than when I was wallowing in piles of quarterliesand the like back in 1937."[7] If members weren't able to buy or barter, they often read the magazines on the spot. This was the case with Bradbury, then so broke that he often showed up on roller skates, not always able to spend a quarter on the red car trolley downtown. When the gang went out to eat, he frequently mixed ketchup with hot water to make a free tomato soup.

A topic discussed at Bradbury's first meeting was the disastrous debut of Chapter 4's latest project, their own fanzine, *Imagination!*.

7

Imagination! and the Start of Bradbury's Career

There were two basic types of science fiction magazines before the Second World War. The "prozines," or professional magazines, such as *Amazing Stories* or *Thrilling Wonder Stories*, and the "fanzines," or amateur publications typically run off a mimeograph machine by devoted fans. The differences were not always solid. Most of the fanzines looked like the amateur publications they were, but some, like Hornig's *The Fantasy Fan* or Schwartz and Weisinger's *Science Fiction Digest*, were done by young men who worked elsewhere in professional publishing and put out a quite impressive zine. (Both *The Fantasy Fan* and *Science Fiction Digest* were printed by fan Conrad Ruppert, who set the type by hand. Earlier, he printed issues of *The Time Traveller*. He owned a small hand press, and his experience gave the zines he worked on a much more professional look.) The fanzines didn't typically pay their authors, while the prozines paid an average of a penny per word. It was a common complaint among science fiction authors of the Golden Age, however, that the prozines didn't always pay on time or what they were supposed to, and sometimes not at all.[1]

A fanzine then was really what its name implied, a magazine published by fans. A unique attribute of the first generation of science fiction fans compared to fans of other genres, like Westerns or mysteries, was the urge to write and publish, neither of which was easy to do in the pre–World War II era. The technology involved the same cheap printing methods used to create church bulletins and high school newspapers. Part of the reason so many early fans published is because they tended to be the same kids who wrote and edited their schools' newspapers and yearbooks. Loneliness also played a role. "Buying science fiction magazines from a small town's two drug stores and one pool hall, I never once met another who read the stuff," one early fan recalled.[2] Many of these boys had few if any friends who shared their tastes or didn't laugh at their obsessions with Mars or Flash Gordon, and the fanzines gave them a way to connect with the handful of like-minded dreamers. In the 1930s, the only way for this loose collection of fans to communicate across the country was via pages sent through the US Mail, written on typewriters and duplicated with mimeographs or hectographs.

As soon as fans began clustering in the late 1920s and early 1930s, they began publishing, and they would prove more prolific publishers than fans of any other genre. Forry Ackerman would always claim that *The Time Traveller*, a zine he contributed to under the leadership of Julius Schwartz, Mort Weisinger, and Allen

Glasser, was the first science fiction fanmag, but that claim is debatable. The Science Correspondence Club (founded in 1929) had been putting out a fanmag called *The Comet* since 1930. Purists have pointed out that the first issue of *The Comet* had no science fiction, and wouldn't until the second issue.[3] The first issue consisted of 10 one-sided mimeographed sheets. That same year, the Queens-based Scienceers started up a fanmag called *The Planet*. The purpose of *The Planet* was to keep readers up to date about the goings on of the Scienceers, talk about developments in science fiction, and "prove that science is not a dry-as-dust study, but a vital, interesting, and entertaining subject."[4] There were reports regarding the biweekly meetings, reviews about the latest scientific fiction, and lots of smart remarks, as this fanzine was edited by boys in their early twenties: "It was recently announced that the radius of the Universe is approximately 9,500,000,000,000,000,000,000 miles. We intend to check up on this."[5] Some have theorized that *The Planet* may have inspired the "S" symbol of Superman. At the bottom of the pages of *The Planet* is the logo of an "S" in a diamond-shaped field.

Others bestow the honor of first science fiction fanmag onto Superman co-creator Jerry Siegel's *Cosmic Stories*, published in 1929. He filled the pages of his own zine with stories rejected by the pulps, so some say it was at least technically the first fanzine devoted purely to science fiction. But since no copies have been found, this can't be verified.

Whoever was first, the trend caught on. By the end of the '30s, these cheap newspapers sprouted from any group of fans as predictably as a houseful of unneutered cats produces kittens. Any science fiction club with access to their high school's or employer's mimeograph machine, or who were willing to shell out for a hectograph kit, or sometimes, simply crammed carbon copy paper into their mom's typewriter, could publish a zine, and they did. These titles were pure labors of love that didn't pay for themselves, at least at first; many if not most of the amateur publishers of the Golden Age would go on to become professionals, as editors and/or writers. Many of these boys became men who turned their hobbies into their jobs.

Fans sometimes ran surveys in their own publications to get a sense of who their fellow fans actually were. These surveys revealed a group of mostly unmarried men, under 30 and white, a clique of about 200 boys and a few girls who knew one another, or at least of one another. In his book *All Our Yesterdays*, Harry Warner, Jr., published a survey in the late '30s showing that there were 216 active fans,[6] an active fan defined as somebody who participates in fandom, such as by contributing to a fanzine or by joining a science fiction club. By one estimate, 150 fans became professionals in some way, either as writers, editors, or artists.[7]

By 1937 there were enough science fiction fanmags that fans, writers, and eventually editors Donald A. Wollheim and John Michel proposed a system of distribution.[8] The result was the formation of the Fantasy Amateur Press Association, or FAPA.

Fans got copies of these homemade zines either through subscription, by trade (I'll send you a copy of mine if you send me one of yours), or for free if they themselves contributed writing and/or artwork. While some customers did pay subscription fees, most got copies via trade or contributing. These fanzines were mostly money-losing endeavors, done out of a combination of love and egotism. First fan and future writer Damon Knight described the fan mag process thusly:

The editor cut the stencils himself, ran them off, collated the sheets, stapled the magazines, mailed them to an exchange list of other fan editors and to a few paid subscribers, and waited for the letters of comment which, far more than cash, are the rewards of amateur publishing.[9]

To get an idea of just how many of these amateur newspapers there were, at least 47 different fanmags produced more than one publication in 1940.[10] In his excellent essay "A History of Fanzines," Harry Warner, Jr., estimated that, throughout the '60s, approximately 11,000 zine pages were printed *every year*. (Warner's essay was written in 1994 and ends: "Popularity is growing for the distribution of electronic fanzines by computer links via telephone lines to fans who possess the necessary equipment.... Several fanzines have taken the forms of videotapes."[11])

Initially, most fanzines had print runs of 100 copies or fewer, with some reaching 200, and most folding after a few years. Eventually, though, they grew in sophistication, with some running for decades and printing off thousands of copies, becoming near prozines. *Fanews* had a run of 500 copies and *Fantasy Advertiser* around 1,000.[12]

The primary purpose of the fanzines was to keep other fans in the loop of what was happening in the world of science fiction and fantasy. As author Arthur Louis Joquel II put it, a zine was a "'sound off' sheet for our pet peeves and manias."[13] Forry Ackerman routinely contributed to different zines by publishing news about upcoming "imagi-movies," sometimes typing up a complete list of all known science fiction films in an era when so few were made that it was possible to do so.

The zines also kept tabs on the lives of the fans: where they went, when and how they partied, what movies they saw, who recently had a birthday—all manner of data were fed into typewriters and mimeographs, which is how we now have a good idea of what the LA fans were doing in their spare time. Fans also preached strong opinions of trends in science fiction and fantasy and wrote not always flattering opinions of one another. Among other people, Forry Ackerman got into a notorious dispute with none other than H.P. Lovecraft.

In the zine *The Fantasy Fan*, Ackerman described Clark Ashton Smith's story "Light from Beyond" as a "sorry piece of science fiction." He also felt that another story of Smith's, "Dweller in the Martian Depths" (better known as "The Dweller in the Gulf"), was fantasy instead of science fiction, and should have appeared in *Weird Tales* instead of *Wonder*. Smith, along with his friend and fellow writer H.P. Lovecraft, soon pounced. Ackerman and Lovecraft would have something of a rivalry for a time, both taking shots at each other in *The Fantasy Fan* column The Boiling Point. "He evidently enjoys verbal pyrotechnics for their own sake," Lovecraft wrote, not inaccurately, about Ackerman.[14] Elsewhere he called Ackerman an "ebullient youth with no imagination."[15] Other fans followed the dispute, some chiming in with comments of their own. The two men made up, but for years the Ackerman-Lovecraft feud would follow Ackerman. In 1936 Ackerman wrote, "Even today, when I make a weird fan's acquaintance, same seems apt inevitably to mention 'my pal' Lovecraft and wink knowingly."[16] The Boiling Point was discontinued after six issues because of the "ill-feelings aroused."[17] Other feuds and disputes were common, with fans forming intense rivalries. The titles of the memoirs of early pre-war fandom reflect the tension, such as *The Immortal Storm, Ah! Sweet Idiocy,* and *Memoirs of a Superfluous Fan.*[18]

7. Imagination! and the Start of Bradbury's Career

While gossip and science fiction news were a key part of these zines, these publications were also a medium for the not-yet-discovered to place original fiction, art, and/or poetry. Besides the trio of friends—Ray Bradbury, Ray Harryhausen and Forry Ackerman—who are the focus of this book, other notables who published in pre–World War II zines include Robert A. Heinlein, Robert E. Howard (best remembered for Conan the Barbarian), Arthur C. Clarke, and H.P. Lovecraft. Established writers who normally got paid well for their writing sometimes contributed to the fanzines for free. Heinlein published pieces in the zines of different LA fans, including Bradbury's. (Bradbury's good friend "Tubby" Yerke was to publish a satirical piece on Heinlein in the zine *The Damn Thing*, but Robert A. Heinlein, a.k.a. "Bobsy," evidently found nothing funny about it and demanded its retraction. Yerke complied.[19]) Even the best-known authors had some pieces rejected by the prozines, and it was better to publish somewhere than have these pages sit in a desk drawer. Publishing in the fanzines also advertised an author's name and helped win over fans.

Given its prominence and given that Chapter 4 had several members with experience in amateur publishing, it was inevitable that this group would join the ranks of fans to publish. Chapter 4 voted to spend $7.50 on *Imagination!* on September 2, 1937, for the cost of the needed hectograph equipment.

Hectograph was an early, cheap alternative to the more common mimeograph machine. It involved typing a master copy on special paper designed specifically for the hectograph. The editor then placed this master face up into a tray full of gelatin. One had to let this master copy sit for about five minutes for the impressions of the typed letters to sink into the gel. The gelatin itself was made from a special formula, often sold in the pages of the Sears Roebuck catalog. After it was mixed with water, the formula could take as long as 24 hours to settle into a gel. (Sometimes, though, the regular edible dessert was used. According to Warner's book *All Our Yesterdays* [page 238], a Milwaukee-based zine called *Frontier* was reportedly made using standard orange Jell-O.) The creator then slowly peeled the master away and was left with a reverse impression in the gelatin mold. Next, he or she placed a special type of hectograph paper onto the tray. The page needed to set anywhere from five seconds to a couple of minutes in order for the image to impress, depending on the gel. The paper was then delicately peeled away with a fresh imprint on one side of the page. The image faded with each successive print, until finally the underpaid or volunteer editor had to once again make a fresh gel and start again. "Hecto" is a prefix meaning 100, supposedly the number of copies one could get from a single gel; teachers, secretaries, and church bulletin editors claimed 50 copies was a more realistic count. A disclaimer published in the first issue of *Imagination!* read: "If the good readable copies are exhausted, we will refund Ur dime."[20] In another zine, *Sun(t)rails*, the editor lamented he needed to hectograph due to rising printing costs, so he could distribute "only as widely as the medium permits."[21] The hectograph and the more advanced mimeograph were to early science fiction zines what Gutenberg's press were to the early Protestant faith, a way of cheaply spreading the word.

The beauty of the hectograph was that, unlike the mimeograph, no machine was needed. "All one needed was a cakepan, a pound of hectograph gelatin, a special typewriter ribbon, and some ink," said early fan and fan historian Bob Madle.[22] If a fan had a yearning to publish but couldn't get to a mimeograph machine, the hectograph was within reach.

Myrtle Douglas

The initial team behind the first issue of *Imagination!* was Ackerman, Yerke, and Ackerman's girlfriend, Myrtle Rebecca Douglas. Douglas would play a crucial role not just in the production of the league's first zine, but in several publications thereafter. She would also become the founding mother of cosplay, which will be discussed in Chapter 18.

Yerke recalled Myrtle Douglas first coming to Clifton's in April of 1937. According to the brief biography of her, published in the pages of *Imagination!*, Myrtle R. Douglas was pretty and quite small, a "feminine fenomenon" just shy of five feet. Her slight stature and youthful appearance may explain why no one seemed to notice she was older than most of the other league members, turning 33 in 1937. Not only did she have about 10 to 15 years on typical fans, she had also been married twice and had a son, Virgil, 13 years old by the time of *Imagination!*'s first printing. Her parents both died before she was 34. Myrtle grew up fast.

She was bright, eventually teaching classes on Esperanto. The 1940 census listed her occupation as an accountant. Her office skills of typing and mimeographing would prove crucial to the success of *Imagination!* and other zines the group produced. Myrtle Douglas was almost always referred to in prozines as "Morojo" (pronounced *moe-row-yo*), a moniker derived from Esperanto. As Ackerman (Esperanto name, "Fojak") explained decades later, "She was such a superfan of Fojak (that's me) in those days that she in effect thot of herself as a female counterpart of FJA and hence called herself the Esperanto equivalent of ERJ. As if, in English, she had called herself Emerjay."[23] In any case, Morojo would be her handle in the pages of *Imagination!* and dozens of other fanzines. (It was also common for fans of the era to go by their three initials. Donald Wollheim was DAW and later started a company called DAW Books, Ackerman was known as FJA, Ray Palmer called himself RAP, David Kyle was DAK, etc.)

Myrtle was not the only fan to use an Esperanto name. Her cousin, an attractive young heartbreaker named Patti Gray (full name Mary Corinne Gray, later Wood after she got married), went by "Pogo."[24] Morojo's son, Virgil, was often referred to as "Vodoso."

Morojo was "one of the most kindhearted persons in Los Angeles," Francis T. Laney wrote in his memoir *Sweet Idiocy!*, "the first person most of the older members think of when they are in trouble, and in this selfish civilization people like that are rare."[25] Laney did not think so highly of everyone and especially loathed Forry Ackerman, so his was high praise indeed.

While she has often been described as Ackerman's sidekick, Morojo was very much a fan in her own right. Born in San Diego but raised in Arizona, she grew up admiring Edgar Rice Burroughs and Jules Verne. Her favorite film was the adaptation of H.G. Wells's *Things to Come*, which would play a key role later when she attended the first science fiction convention. She kept some of Ackerman's collection of "fantasymags" in her apartment on Bixel Street, a Mid City pad that became a frequent hangout for other fans.[26] She was that rare "unicorn horn" Ackerman spoke of, a female fan, although women in early fandom may not have been quite as rare as Ackerman believed. According to at least one source, women composed 11 percent of fans by 1948.[27] Most of the photos of the early days of Chapter 4 show at least a few women, making it one of the more female-friendly chapters in the country (it was typical for a chapter to have no women at all).

Morojo, Ackerman, and Yerke slapped together the first issue of *Imagination!* in September of 1937, with 13-year-old Vodoso (Virgil Douglas, Morojo's son) contributing artwork. It was a cheap but complicated process, as Yerke outlines in his memoir. After school Yerke would type up the material for publication, then take a streetcar to Ackerman's flat. There the young editor Ackerman would make corrections— Yerke acknowledged that both his spelling and grammar were pretty bad. Ackerman then hopped a streetcar to Morojo's apartment so he could type the corrected copy onto the carbon paper needed for the hectograph, as Myrtle's standard typewriter was better suited for the unique sheets of carbon. Then her son Virgil took it back to Yerke's apartment, where the hecto-pads were kept. Yerke had the fun chore of making the actual copies.

Yerke described the process of printing the first issue in the second issue of *Imagination!*:

> The hecktograph was purchased Sept. 3d. First affair attempted.... But initial try pulled a lot of jelly off the hekto. (50 pgs wasted,) Tried again—50 more mutilated. Started over, & succeeded to produce 8 pgs (400 sheets)... Because of scandalous spelling (YE ED responsible), the entire output was condemned to destruction: First slashed to ribbons & then incinerated—with the exception of several examples of each article, which were retained as reminders of the too-true proverb, "Haste Makes Waste." After this marvelous muddling, it evolved that Ackerman & Morojo must do the typing, if we were to appear at all.... Every afternoon, after school, YE ED hurried home to prepare proof; which was rushed to Forry's to make haste with to Morojo's to be typed on her 'writer when she returned from work, as Forry's was different from mine—larger. Thus, whatever was set up on mine had to be re-arranged to fit his. After the Masters were typed, Vodoso (Virgil, Myrtle's son) would slop on some illustration &, while it was still wet, hop the streetcar for my "office." Immediately I'd grab the m.c. (master copy-ed.), & slap it on the goo— which was still blotchy from use the previous nite. This crazy merry-go-round continued 10 mad nites, at the end of which we all were sights. "Hektographer's Hand" (fingers stained with indelible inks) was prevalent, & tempers taut from combustion of the cylinder of solidified fat at opposite extremities. But on the 11th nite we stapled the "stuff," mailed the mag out to those who luckily had ordered in advance, 6 days, & we were sold out.[28]

The result was an illegible mess of a zine. (When this author contacted a university about getting scans of the originals of *Imagination!*, I was not charged for the first issue, because it was completely unreadable.) The purple ink was smudged and uneven, and 13-year-old Virgil's drawings looked like they were drawn by a 13-year-old. The league wound up not being pleased with the result. Every subsequent issue of *Imagination!*, or "Madge" as some insiders called it, would be done via mimeograph.

Imagination! was advertised gratis in the pages *Thrilling Wonder Stories* in the February 1938 issue. The editors gave it this sunny review: "The first Issue, which we have seen, carries interesting personality sketches of prominent science fiction writers, science fiction news, scientifilm and scientibook reviews, poetry, humorous articles, and many other features of Interest to the science fiction follower."

Imagination! was rife with Ackerman's shortened, pun-style spellings and invented slang (e.g., "egoboo" = "ego boost"). Ackerman also didn't see the point in indenting and frequently saved time by just skipping a line to start the next paragraph. He called these space-saving shortenings "telescoping," and they were seemingly derived from Esperanto, a language totally phonetic with no silent letters, no inconsistent spellings, no irregular verbs, none of the exceptions that make learning a language so difficult. Ackerman insisted his simplified spellings were better for everyone and the world as a whole. "Why waste time & typ on 'thought' & 'through' & 'vaudeville' too?" he wrote in the second issue of *Imagination!*, "when unnecessaryly lengthy or clumsy complicated words may be reduced to simplr terms? such as 'thot, thru, vodvil.'"[29]

This dialect of his would eventually be known as "Ackermanese." While Ackermanese took some getting used to, one could usually make sense of it, but at times his weird spelling could reach the point of near incomprehensibility: "If U'v a Q that's got U best& which at th same time'll be of interest to othr fans, just send it in & we'll be glad to use it in th col." In any case, this author has chosen to both not correct the countless misspellings when quoting Ackerman and his followers, a.k.a. Ackolytes. To correct Ackermanese would be as sinful as somehow adding dialect to old Charlie Chaplin shorts, not to mention very time-consuming.

Ackerman published an entire essay in the first issue of *Imagination!* devoted to the wonders of Esperanto: "To create, out of chaos of baroque babel 3,400 tongues on La Tero today Universal understanding. Utopian aim!"[30] Chapter 4 director Russell J. Hodgkins acknowledged the created language may not be of interest to all readers: "If you don't like our Esperanto column remember, this mag is published in Los Angeles, and so most of its circulation is in Los Angeles, and since most of the readers are interested in Esperanto."[31]

Others in the league insisted on correct spelling, arguing that the phonetic spellings of words made the entire affair less professional looking. Some common examples of "Ackermanese" were "dawter" instead of "daughter" and "Autograft" instead of "autographed." As Hodgkins stated in *Imagination!*, "What stopt the battle was the offer of the staff to withdraw entirely & let whoever wisht to, carry on with Madge in their own orthodox way."[32] In other (often misspelled) words, some members would stick to proper English, while others, like Ackerman and Bradbury, would go on with their simplified spellings. If Ackerman and others wanted to dabble in their own little dialect, fine, but they had no right to change the writing of anyone else, and that would be the compromise.

Good idea or not, Ackerman's language had its detractors, especially his readers in England. In the British zine *Novae Terrae*, he replied to his English critics who were horrified by his butchering of their cherished language, defending his techniques as time-saving: "And so it is that when fingers fly, I employ all logical time-saving cuts I can. Meaning omission of many unnecessary indefinite articles, use of obvious abbreviations, simplified spelling to expedient extent, etc."[33]

The first issue of *Imagination!* also contained book reviews, news of upcoming science films, a report from President Hodgkins, and a summary of what happened at the meeting of the league. There was also information from Mort Weisinger about the future of *Thrilling Wonder Stories*. The issue ended with advertisements promoting other zines of other fan clubs, along with classified ads from fans both willing to sell and buy pulp magazines.

Whatever its shortcomings, *Imagination!* intrigued the league's latest member,

Ray Bradbury. While most biographies of Bradbury record that he first learned of Chapter 4 at Shep's Shop, one source, *Seekers of Tomorrow* by Sam Moskowitz, claims that Bradbury was at an "unnamed member's" house on September 5, 1937, when he saw a copy of *Imagination!* that sent his mind spinning and convinced the teen to splurge a quarter on the red car ride downtown.[34]

The idea that he could get published somewhere, after years of anonymous typing, intrigued young Ray. No matter that he wouldn't be paid, and that these initial efforts would be read by only a handful of fellow fans. *Imagination!* had the potential to give him the recognition he so craved, the stepping stone to his dream of becoming a real writer.

8

Imagination!, the Second Issue

> "Forrest Ackerman immediately put me to work on his magazine, *Imagination!*, writing terrible articles—supposedly humorous articles—and illustrating the cover on occasion. Really dreadful illustrations."
>
> —Ray Bradbury[1]

Not long after his first meeting at Clifton's, Bradbury joined the inner circle of league members who put out the zine. Bradbury may not have been as talented as some of the other members, and he was certainly not as mature as some of the boys already editing national magazines, like 17-year-old Charles Hornig, editor of *Wonder Stories*. But he was devoted. Ackerman knew he could count on the boy to help with the sticky, messy process of editing a mimeographed zine. (Yerke described the process of creating *Imagination!* in his memoir, *Memoirs of a Superfluous Fan*: "To Ackerman ... fell the job of stenciling, dummying, corresponding, and a good bit of the editing. The rest of us turned the crank, learned the Speed-O-Scope, assembled and stapled or else sat on the side-lines.") If all Bradbury wanted in return was to publish little bits and pieces, it was a deal Ackerman was willing to make.

Bradbury's debut in *Imagination!* was in the second issue, November 1937, run off the mimeograph of Morojo's employer. He wrote a brief column called "FOOLOSOFY by Kno Knuth Ing, Combined with SCIENTIFRAX." This column had appeared in the first issue and almost certainly—judging from the endless bad puns ("Use Television in a sentence. 'Can U Television When U See One?'"[2])—originated with Forry Ackerman. Bradbury took over this section in the second issue and continued Ackerman's witty, pun-filled humor. Example: "Feedng fuel to th fires of life only makes it burn fastr. Don't be a—fuel." Another: "Anny: I bought a dress th other day to put on around my house. Monjo: Goodness! How big's Ur house?"[3] While uncredited, Bradbury is also believed to have contributed the masthead of the Francis Flagg/Weaver Wright (Forry Ackerman) story "The Hazy Hord."[4] In issue #9 of *Imagination!* a biography of him—Yerke is often attributed as the author—described Bradbury as "the funny man of the Los Angeles League." Bradbury's works in mimeographed publications would be full of bad jokes, puns, and harmless cracks at others in fandom. In another issue he admitted that his jokes were so bad that people were likely to burn the page but, he advised, "be careful not to burn the other side." He also sometimes tried his hand at illustrating. Towards the end of his life Bradbury would recall that he contributed "terrible covers" and "awful articles."[5] But it was a start.

The second issue of *Imagination!* also ran an apology for the low quality of the first issue: "Honestly, readers, I'm sorry the fifth page didn't turn out well, but there's nothing I can do about it, &, anyway, it was only one-twentieth of the whole issue."[6] Issue #2 also had interviews with established authors Catherine L. Moore and Arthur K. Barnes, another column of "Onward Esperanto," and updates on what was going on in the league.

There were likely fewer than 100 issues printed of each edition of *Imagination!*, but those who were reading it were among the most prominent members of the nascent science fiction fandom community, a much smaller world at the time. The handful of fans who read or at least knew of *Imagination!* included professional editors and writers like L. Ron Hubbard, Hugo Gernsback, and Charles D. Hornig. Readers of *Imagination!* lived across the county and as far away as Britain.

The members of Chapter 4 continued to meet on Thursdays. On Sundays the 15 or so members directly involved in the printing of *Imagination!*, among them Ackerman, Walter J. Daugherty, Morojo, Bradbury, and Henry Kuttner, met at the Hodgkins home and helped get the newsletter published.

Russell J. Hodgkins was the director of Chapter 4 and clearly had the qualifications to be an elder statesman. Not only was he 28 years old, making him a near senior citizen in a club dominated by high school and college-age kids, but he also was a veteran employee of the Bank of America, giving him practical real-world experience the younger people lacked. According to Yerke, he had an impressive library of science fiction, organized by his "incessant filing, cross-filing, and counter-filing of all the items on his shelves. One could find any given story by either magazine, author, or title, and there was still a fourth file where stories were listed by type."[7]

The printing sessions led to informal meetings, and soon topics were being broached at the Hodgkins pressroom rather than at Clifton's. Yerke recalled that while official motions and discussions about money took place at the Thursday meetings, Sundays led to spontaneous discussions. "The scene of the real activities began to move out to 84th place," which was Hodgkins's address.[8]

9

Imagination!, Issues 3 and 4

The third issue of *Imagination!* kicked off with a reluctant essay by director Hodgkins that included a dig at Ackerman and Ackermanese: "My messages, I understand, will be run <u>exactly as I write them</u>" (underline in the original). The second installment of the story "The Hazy Hord" appeared, courtesy of Francis Flagg and Weaver Wright (a pseudonym of Ackerman's). Then there was the usual report on upcoming science fiction and fantasy publications and films, where it was reported that Bradbury had just written a piece called "Among the Metal Gods," a story that he optimistically sent off to *Astounding*. As a teen, the hopeful writer was already sending off his stories to national magazines, not easily discouraged by the endless rejections. Bradbury was also back with more bad jokes. ("Bees dispose of their honey by celling it. This is considered good bee-havior.") Chapter 4 printed interviews with writers Clark Ashton Smith and E. Hoffmann Price and letters from fans all over the county.

The fourth issue of *Imagination!* demonstrates just how many future science fiction stars were involved with the league at the time. The table of contents lists mostly authors and artists who would have stellar careers in the genre. Jim Mooney, who had already sold some work to *Weird Tales*, illustrated the cover. He would eventually find work with both DC and Marvel, contributing to Batman, Supergirl, and Spiderman comics, among others. Henry Kuttner published extensively with his wife, C.L. Moore, and is considered one of the most important science fiction writers of that era. The league reprinted a letter of H.P. Lovecraft, who was not well known at the time but is now one of the best-known horror fantasy writers of the era. And then there's Ray Bradbury and Forry Ackerman. In issue #4 Henry Kuttner wrote: "I believe that in 5 or 10 years many of the names we now see in the commentors columns will be well known authors of imaginative fiction."[1] Even he likely didn't realize just how prescient he would be.

Imagination! #4 is also notable for its inclusion of the debut fiction work by Bradbury, though it wasn't the very first time the world saw his writing. That honor belongs to the *Waukegan News-Sun*, which ran Bradbury's ode to Will Rogers on the near one-year anniversary of the radio personality's death on August 18, 1920, four days before Bradbury turned 16. Bradbury's high school included exactly one poem of his in its annual *Anthology of Student Verse for 1937*, a work called "Death's Voice."[2] At the end of his senior year, another poem of his, "Truck Driver after Midnight," was published in *Morning Song*, a city-wide anthology of student verse.[3] He wrote a few nonfiction pieces in the Los Angeles High School paper, *The Blue and White Daily*, mostly movie reviews and a short bit about his hometown hero, Waukegan native Jack Benny.[4]

He had plenty of stories on hand. Throughout high school he wrote fiction profusely, including a piece called "The Night" that takes place in Waukegan's ravine, a location he would revisit in works like "The Whole Town's Sleeping" and *Dandelion Wine*. He submitted 20 short stories to his high school's annual fiction anthology, all of which were rejected.[5]

So the fourth issue of *Imagination!* had the honor of being the first to publish a fiction work of Ray Bradbury's, in a fanzine mailed to subscribers all over the country and even overseas. No longer was he being read by teachers, Aunt Neva, or buddies in the Science Fiction League. The story, "Hollerbochen's Dilemma," would be read by strangers.

His opus was not well received.

Bradbury's Dilemma

The "dilemma" of the title involves a man named Hollerbochen who has two unique abilities, to foresee the future and to "stand still" in time for a few minutes. He can both see events in the near future and also stay rooted in a place in time while people and a vision of himself move on. Put simply, Hollerbochen can see what will happen in the next few minutes. While staying at a hotel he learns that if he takes the stairs he'll be murdered, whereas if he tries the elevator, it will crash to his doom, taking the other passengers with him. Most confusing, whether he uses stairs or elevator, the vision always ends with "himself being blown to bits by a tremendous explosion."[6] So what to do?

The writing in "Hollerbochen's Dilemma" is simplistic and evokes none of the imagery prevalent in Bradbury's later works. This was not the writing that earned him the moniker "Poet of the Pulps." (From the first paragraph of Hollerbochen: "He could see when he would die—& it was very distressing, as you may well imagine.") Still, we do see in Hollerbochen themes that would pop up in some of his best-known writing: facing mortality and the dangers of time travel.

Jack Speer, a noted "letter-hack," wrote in to say that "Hollerbochen's Dilemma" was "the biggest mistake of the issue."[7]

According to Bradbury's own diary, "One guy in Kansas said it was 'unscientific, uninteresting, poorly written, and……?'"(ellipses Bradbury's).[8] Ackerman would later say that the work was weak, but that he needed the material.

Bradbury responded to his initial flop with his usual humor, and the name "Hollerbochen" became something of an inside joke among early fans. In another zine he contributed to, *Mikros* (edited by his friend T. Bruce Yerke), Bradbury wrote a sequel called "Hollerbochen Comes Back." Here, Hollerbochen breaks the fourth wall and comes to avenge Bradbury's humiliation:"He had received thotwaves from Earth sent by Bradbury, pleading with him & clear the good name of the family. Hollerbochen realized his author was suffering great torment under the haranguing of his friends & readers, so he decided to come back!"[9] Bradbury would sometimes publish under the pseudonym Hollerbochen, winkingly knowing that others in the fandom community would get who was behind the name. (Decades later, Forry Ackerman gifted Bradbury a book he'd written. Ackerman signed his own book, "For Hollerbochen's Dilemma...'Till the end of the line, forever.")

Inwardly, Bradbury despaired. He took pride in his work and was devastated at the poor reception of his opus, as his teen diary proves: "Felt pretty low because noone enjoyed my story 'Hollerbochen's Dilemma'... I think it was terrible myself. Must clear my name."[10]

He would redeem himself soon enough.

Imagination! #5—*Ackerman the Nudist*

Madge #5 featured a bare-breasted young woman strutting across the cover, courtesy of member and artist Hannes Bok. Ackerman later claimed this was the first nude cover of a fanzine. Ackerman, known to be obsessed with female nudes himself—later in life he joined a nudist colony (as did Morojo, though not at the same time, and years after she'd parted ways with Forry)—was certainly an authority on the topic (Bok himself was understood to be homosexual). Ackerman often printed nudes not only in his zines, but also in personal correspondence.[11] He once wrote that he dreamt of the day when the current counterparts of Marilyn Monroe would be able "to uninhibitedly exhibit their unclothed simulacrums on the screen in total nudicolor."[12] Later in life, a nude of Trina Robbins loomed over his bed at the Ackermansion.[13] In issue #13 of *Fantast*, Forry wrote: "I will defend to the death (beyond the grave I cannot go, being an atheist) that nice nudes are NOT dirty pix."[14] In another fanzine Ackerman edited, a disgruntled fan asked, "Just what is science-fictional about a nude?" Forry's candid response was, "Nothin'."[15] Another wrote: "Say, the cover for this issue was rather pornographic. Hans Bok ought to watch his step or Uncle Sam will stop in and make things uncomfortable."[16] The writer of this letter had a point—in those days an artist could be jailed for obscenity.

Imagination!, #6 & #7: *A Visit to Tarzan's Home*

In the spring 1938 issue of *Imagination!*, Ackerman, as usual, reported what was happening in the world of fantasy and science fiction. This included a letter he had received from Edgar Rice Burroughs, announcing an upcoming work, *The Lad and the Lion*. The letter, printed on Burroughs's own official stationery, began "To The Imagi-Nation!," addressing the league directly.[17] Ackerman had been corresponding regularly with Burroughs since he was a child. Bradbury also contacted the creator of Tarzan and the John Carter of Mars series, asking Burroughs to visit the league at Clifton's (an invitation the author politely declined).

In *Imagination!* #7, Ackerman floored everyone in the fan community by reporting what for many of the readers would have been a dream come true: a personal visit to the office of Edgar Rice Burroughs himself. Ackerman and Morojo, along with league members Fred Shroyer and Russell J. Hodgkins, drove out to his office. While the great author wasn't there, his secretary nonetheless let the fans inside. Hodgkins described Burroughs's office in the pages of *Imagination!* #7: "Imagine ... a great open fireplace in the corner, spread before it an enormous polar bear robe, head, claws & all. On the walls are the original illustrations of many the memorable scenes from the Tarzan & Martian storys."

Whatever anybody thinks of his writing, Burroughs was one of the most popular authors of the twentieth century. Given that he didn't publish anything until he was 37, and then only as a means to an end, it's amazing how much influence he would have on the twentieth century. He had been an unremarkable pencil sharpener salesman until he turned to writing solely as a source of income (one of his more famous quotes: "I write to escape—to escape poverty"). He published *Tarzan of the Apes* in the October issue of *All-Story Magazine* in 1912 (this issue was also the first time Tarzan was depicted visually, seen on the cover wrestling a lion). The Chicago-based publisher A.C. McClurg printed the hardback book edition two years later, and in 1918, the movie *Tarzan of the Apes* came out under the direction of Scott Sidney. With Elmo Lincoln as Tarzan, it became one of the first films to gross over a million dollars.[18]

Burroughs is best remembered for his Tarzan books, but he also contributed greatly to science fiction. His first novel, *Under the Moon of Mars*, was the start of his John Carter of Mars series. Other sci-fi sagas are David Innes adventures, about a man who ends up in a land in the center of the Earth called Pellucidar, and Carson Napier, who lands on Venus. Not one to miss a marketing opportunity, he combined characters and settings, so that Tarzan somehow ended up in the center of the Earth (*Tarzan at the Earth's Core*) and John Carter crossed paths with Carson Napier. Burroughs's writing sold so well that he bought a huge estate that he later sold in parcels, and to this day that neighborhood in San Fernando Valley is known as Tarzana. At the time of his death his estate was valued at about 10 million, or almost 100 million dollars today.[19] As late as 1962 his books were responsible for approximately 1/30 of all paperback sales.[20] Ackerman would later get to interview Burroughs for one of his zines,[21] at the writer's house. The young fan reported visiting a humble but exquisite home, where Burroughs showed his own adapted films to friends and family. Bradbury would later say that Burroughs was the most important author of the twentieth century. Whatever one's opinion of Burroughs or his writing, there's no doubting his influence on a generation. One of Bradbury's earliest efforts was attempting his update of the John Carter of Mars series, pecking out the whole thing on his toy dial-a-letter typewriter as a 12-year-old.

Michelism

Issue #7 also included an essay by T. Bruce Yerke, "A Reply To Michelism." It was his critique of a movement that had been dominating the pages of zines, a Socialist/Communist ideal that its subscribers sincerely believed would save the world.

The idea that science fiction could actually make Earth a better place had been part of the genre since its earliest days. Gernsback theorized that science fiction could get people more interested in science, leading to more learning, and more learning meant that the world would improve. The aim, as Ackerman often put it, was "saving humanity through science and sanity." It is not surprising that some fans took this idea a step farther and argued that science fiction should be an actual political movement. None made this argument louder than a clique of New York City fans known as the Futurians. Led by a pair of teenaged boys, Donald Wollheim and John B. Michel, the movement was also known as Michelism.

Who were the Futurians, and what did these Michelists want? Michelism was steeped in Communism. This is not a slur but a fact; Michel was a member of the Young Communist League (YCL) along with Frederik Pohl, who edited some issues of the YCL's zine. In a letter to Forry Ackerman, Wollheim explained that he was really a Socialist but described himself as a Communist because he felt "socialism" was a term most people didn't understand. "When I speak of communism, I mean socialism." He said in that same letter: "Fascism is capitalism in fighting trim."[22]

In his notorious speech at the Third Eastern Science Fiction Convention on October 30, 1937, Michel outlined his beliefs (witnesses say that Wollheim actually gave the speech, as Michel had a slight difficulty in speaking). Science fiction could no longer be content to simply indulge in fantasies that went nowhere. The transcription of his speech is littered with phrases like "dumb" and "baloney bending" and is a call to arms towards "working for a more unified world, a more Utopian existence, the application of science to human happiness, and a saner outlook on life." The fans, with their heightened intellect and scientific curiosity, needed to use their gifts to create a better world, a world that was coming apart.

The debate about Michelism soon ignited the fanzines, and *Imagination!* was no exception. Members of Chapter 4 got into a protracted debate with Wollheim, both sides using language that would likely get them banned from social media today. In issue #9 of *Imagination!* Wollheim took a shot at league member Erick Freyor, who had written critical essays regarding the Michelist movement. Wollheim's response ended with: "Mr. Freyor apparently has no faith in man's ability & does not recognize any such thing as progress or change ... if you have no faith in a finer future & have no regard for an ugly present, why not carry your beliefs to the only logical conclusion? You canescape PERMANENTLY for a dime's worth of liquid in any drugstore!"[23] Freyor's reply was printed in that same issue, ending with, "Personally, I prefer that $2.49 (plus tax) escape that you also buy at drugstores."[24]

While some fans supported or were at least open to Michelism, most were ambivalent at best. The general consensus was that science fiction should be more about intellectual curiosity and fun, and less about politics. According to issue #10 of *Imagination!*, copies of two speeches by Wollheim and Michel were read out loud at Chapter 4's June 16, 1938, meeting. Next, "it was disclosed that Michelism has supporters in the Chapter, who heretofore have refrained from bringing 'politics' into the meetings. DUE to the wishes of the majority, the Michelism debate which has been carried on in the pages of Madge, has been dropped." Because of the controversy caused by the Michelism issue, Chapter 4 appointed a council to oversee the publication of similar controversial topics in the future.

The three wise young men chosen to be on the council were Yerke, another member named Frank Brady, and Chapter 4's newest member, an 18-year-old by the name of Ray Harryhausen.

10

Ray Harryhausen Joins the League

The world premiere of *King Kong* at Grauman's Chinese Theatre took place on March 24, 1933, an event as outsized as the great ape. (Actually *Kong* premiered in two theaters almost three weeks earlier in New York, at Radio City Music Hall and the RKO Roxy. Grauman explained that New York's was the national premiere, but his was the "world" premiere.) Kong's big head—the 50-foot bust used in the film for close-ups, such as when Kong chews on a poor native—sat in the outdoor forecourt of Grauman's Chinese. This court was a "miniature World's Fair" with live flamingos wandering among palms and ferns as part of an overall Skull Island jungle motif, along with a display of live monkeys, penguins, and someone called the "Mystery Man: Ape or Human?"[1] And that was just the forecourt.

The movie's premiere was preceded by a 17-act live show that included a troupe of Black performers putting on a piece called "The Dance of the Sacred Ape," along with other politically incorrect routines such as "Studies in Ebony" and "Voo-Doo Dancers."[2] LAPD sent extra manpower, along with members of the California National Guard, to handle the throngs of tourists and sightseers hoping to catch a celebrity glimpse. Fay Wray, Bruce Cabot, Robert Armstrong, and other cast members attended, along with an impressive galaxy of stars including Jean Harlow, Harold Lloyd, and Al Jolson.

Sitting in the audience was an anonymous 13-year-old named Ray Harryhausen.

It is hard to say whether his life, or the world of filmmaking, would have been the same if not for the twist of fate that Ray Harryhausen's aunt happened to be taking care of Sid Grauman's elderly mother. The box-office showman gratefully gifted her tickets to the premiere of *King Kong*, having no way of knowing he was creating a film legend. Ray Harryhausen remembered every detail of that day the way others remember Kennedy's assassination or their first kiss. Decades later he could still recall the jungle dancers, the flamingoes, the giant bust of King Kong. He would one day reflect, "I walked into Grauman's Chinese Theatre and when I came out I haven't been the same since."[3]

As awed as Harryhausen was by the prologue before the film, it was just another day for Sid Grauman, who once hired a couple of pilots to stage a mock dogfight in the skies above Hollywood for the premiere of the war epic *Hell's Angels*. Extravagant live theater was par for the course in the movie palaces of the '20s and '30s, but Grauman hit on the original idea of making his "prologues" tie into the picture.

HARRISON, JANET
Secretarial Club 4
Euodia 2
Commercial Club 2

HARRYHAUSEN, RAY
Publicity Club 4
Masquers' Club 3, 4
Movie Club 1, 2
Cartoon Club 2, 3, 4

Ray Harryhausen's 1939 high school yearbook photograph. His interest in making movies was already well established.

For the opening of Charlie Chaplin's *The Circus* the prologue was—what else?—a circus, complete with a Chaplin look-alike. He constructed a special Munchkinland in the forecourt of the Chinese Theatre for the premiere of *The Wizard of Oz*. After a showing of George Fitzmaurice's *Mata Hari*, 75 girls dressed in outfits from the era of King Louis the XVI jumped into a pool to perform an underwater ballet, emerging with headdresses that sprayed water.[4] Grauman spent anywhere from $5,000 to $50,000 on these stage shows, not adjusting for inflation. *King Kong* would actually be one of the last premieres to have a prologue and was relatively toned down with a mere 17 acts. The Depression caused Grauman to cut back on expenses.

Thirteen-year-old Ray Harryhausen was transfixed and transformed. He had seen dinosaurs before, in *The Lost World*, and had seen impressive fantasy and science fiction before, as in *Metropolis*. He teethed on *Dracula* and *Frankenstein*. But *King Kong* changed him forever. He left Grauman's Chinese obsessed, trying to fathom how what he had seen was possible. For years he had made his own clay dinosaurs based on the monsters from the La Brea Tar Pits, never thinking he could make them move. He knew he hadn't watched a stuntman in an ape costume, but just what had he seen? How was any of this even possible? The boy was bitten. He desperately sought any and all information on the techniques of stop-motion animation.

Stop-motion animation is as old as film itself and the first special effect. The technique was discovered by Georges Méliès, the French filmmaker who also pioneered double exposures, hand coloring film, time-lapse photography, and countless other techniques. Even those who have never heard his name have likely seen his classic image of the man in the moon annoyed at an Earth-rocket plunging into an eye socket, the iconic scene from his 1902 film *A Trip to the Moon* (*Le Voyage dans la Lune*). Years earlier, in 1896—about a year after he sat in on the Lumière brothers' Cinématographe exhibition, making him a member of the first film audience ever—Georges had set up filming adjacent to the Paris Opera House when his camera jammed, an annoyingly common issue with first-generation movie cameras.

It took him about a minute to clear up the jam and resume shooting. He hadn't reckoned for what happens when you stop filming, the world moves on, and then you start shooting again. When he had the film developed he was pleasantly surprised to see a bus turn into a hearse and Parisians vanish into thin air while others appeared magically. At roughly the same time, Thomas Edison's men in America (Edison claimed some of the earliest patents in America regarding filmmaking) also noticed the effect of actors or inanimate objects moving as if by magic, the accidental result of stopping the shooting briefly and picking up again. Soon Méliès and others realized the potential of interrupting shooting, moving a few objects, and filming again, resulting in actresses vanishing and skeletons suddenly popping onto the screen. It was the first time that filmmakers understood the potential of this new technology. Movie cameras could depict more than simple reality—they could create magical worlds.

The upshot was a series of European and American short films that we would now call science fiction or fantasy, silent dreams depicting cars taking to the stars and devils haunting old castles. The very titles give one an idea of what to expect, like *A Trip to the Moon* (Méliès, 1898), *Summoning the Spirits* (Méliès, 1899), *Santa Claus* (George Albert Smith, 1898), and *The Enchanted Toymaker* (Melbourne Cooper, 1904).

These were not animated films per se, as they more often relied on substitution techniques. The first example of a true, full stop-motion animation film, meaning models moving without strings, the result of the filmmaker painstakingly shifting characters $\frac{1}{24}$ of a second, is thought to be *The Humpty Dumpty Circus*, released in 1898. British-born director James Stuart Blackton manipulated his daughter's toy acrobats and animals to animate the circus. Sadly this film has been lost. The earliest three-dimensional animated film we can still see is likely *Matches: An Appeal*. Made by the British director Arthur Melbourne Cooper, it depicts a series of matches coming to life and writing on a chalkboard. The "appeal" was for British citizens to spend one guinea to send matches to soldiers in the Boer War.

While other directors and filmmakers dabbled in stop-motion, California-born Willis O'Brien elevated this technique to blockbuster status. The former jockey, boxer, artist, cartoonist, and sculptor shot his first film on top of the Bank of Italy building in San Francisco, depicting a dinosaur and a caveman that he created using clay over a flexible wooden frame. The film impressed a nickelodeon owner enough to pay O'Brien $5,000 to shoot a short film, *The Dinosaur and the Missing Link*. It was five minutes long and took two months to make.[5] He was next hired by Thomas Edison (whose company was appropriately called Conquest Films) to make a series of shorts set in prehistoric/dinosaur times. Edison's company took a hit when the US government ruled his outfit an illegal monopoly, but O'Brien found work soon enough, eventually contracted for the most ambitious stop-motion film yet, a feature-length version of Sir Arthur Conan Doyle's *The Lost World*. It took a total of 14 months and 50 models (the models created by Mexican-born genius Marcel Delgado), with O'Brien frequently working 18 hours a day to shoot 30 seconds of footage. His hard work paid off; *The Lost World* was the smash hit of 1925.

O'Brien's career stalled. He invested in and was hired for several projects that went nowhere. However amazing his effects were, they were expensive (*The Lost World* had cost an incredible $1 million to make) and time-consuming in an era when producers were used to films being shot in less than a month. He spent years working on what was supposed to be another epic, *Creation*, only find that RKO wanted to cancel the project. O'Brien would use the footage of *Creation* to convince RKO to fund something else entirely, a film about a giant ape.

King Kong was released in 1933 to much well-earned fanfare. It is considered the first true Hollywood blockbuster, in that essentially everyone in America saw it. It earned $89,000 in its first four days alone, astounding when considering that it only opened in two New York theaters selling most tickets for 15 cents. Many were awed and inspired; plenty were curious to know exactly how O'Brien had done what he did. In the case of 13-year-old Ray Harryhausen, *King Kong* changed his life.

"No one ever got religion quicker, had it last longer. I went home running a fever," Harryhausen later reflected.[6]

Raymond Frederick Harryhausen was born on June 29, 1920, in LA to a machinist father, Frederick, and mother, Martha, parents who encouraged his every interest and passion. The boy seemed to inherit his father's knack for working with his hands. As a grammar school student he was assigned the homework of constructing miniatures of historic California missions. He threw himself into the work, making model churches and other buildings. He soon spent his free time making dioramas of prehistoric scenes, "occupied with clay saurians with toothpick teeth."[7]

His artistic mother taught him to make papier-mâché heads. At Audubon Junior High he learned the basics of model making and occasionally did skits before the class with puppets, little bits he brought to life with dragons, robots, and, one December, his own puppet Santa Claus. After *King Kong* he made an increasing number of dinosaurs from cloth and old rags, using papier-mâché for the prehistoric animals' faces, and built a marionette of Kong himself. The future special effects wizard re-enacted favorite scenes from *King Kong* in front of the school using his homemade Kong, along with his brontosaurus and T.rex. In a sign of what would make him famous, he also made skeletons for a Halloween puppet show that he put on both at school and for friends at parties in 1939. Inspired by Disney's *Skeleton Dance*, the paper bones were designed to come apart. Martha Harryhausen did the costuming, but he did the rest, learning lessons on making small sets that he would put to good use in making his fairy tales after the Second World War.

Like boys everywhere, young Ray was fascinated by dinosaurs, and he was in a unique position to see them. LA was home of the active peat field in Baldwin Hills, where he would watch the mist rise and imagine a prehistoric landscape. Martha and Frederick took him to the LA County Museum, complete with skeletons of mammoths, saber-toothed tigers, and dinosaur bones. All of these creatures had been pulled out of the nearby La Brea Tar Pits, full of bubbling ooze that had trapped those doomed creatures eons ago. It was at this same museum that young Ray Harryhausen first saw the dinosaurs of Charles Knight, who painted a mural depicting the pits as they would have looked eons ago, complete with saber-toothed tigers and looming vultures. When Harryhausen was stationed in New York during the war, he managed to look up Knight and call him personally.

Like the future friends he would make, little Harryhausen was a bookworm, consuming the works of H.G. Wells and Sir Arthur Conan Doyle. He inhaled the Wonder Books, a set of children's encyclopedias full of illustrations of dinosaurs and mythical creatures. The budding young artist enjoyed and was influenced by the animal and dinosaur drawings of Gustave Doré and Charles Knight. Other artists he came to admire were the apocalyptic works of John Martin and the architectural portraits of Joseph Michael Gandy.

And then there were the films.

His parents took him to see movies all of the time, including *The Lost World* in 1925 and the sci-fi adventures of Fritz Lang. But it was one film that changed his life.

"I had seen movies with men in gorilla suits, but when Kong appeared from behind those trees I knew he was something special, a real 'Eighth Wonder of the World,'"[8] Harryhausen recalled, decades after that fateful afternoon at Grauman's Chinese. It was *Kong* that created the Ray Harryhausen the world came to know and love, and all of his wonderful creations after.

After that day at Grauman's Chinese Theatre, the 13-year-old became obsessed. He begged his father to drive him to the Pathé Lot in Culver City to see Kong's Wall, the gargantuan structure that kept the giant beast from devouring the village on Skull Island. He and friends—including eventually, Ackerman and Bradbury—would stare through the wire gate at the piece of cinema history, Harryhausen reciting the chieftain's words from the film that he had memorized after so many viewings, "Tabe, Bala kum nono hi, Bala! Bala!" (Dozens of movies and TV shows were filmed at the sets on this back lot in Culver City, including *The Adventures of Superman*, *The King of Kings*, and *All Quiet on the Western Front*. Kong's Wall was built from pieces of the sets for *The King of Kings*. The wall was then torched for the Atlanta burning sequence in *Gone With the Wind*. Hollywood was never a sentimental place.)

In his diary, the teen recorded seeing *Kong* 39 times by 1939, no easy feat in an era when the only way to see a film was in the movie theater. Once, when he was an established filmmaker, he traveled all the way to Nias Island, just off the coast of Sumatra, simply because it is mentioned briefly in the film as the possible original home of the Skull Island natives. Once ashore this island, Harryhausen recited a few lines of native dialect from *King Kong*, only to have the natives reply in English, "Just what are you talking about?"

He read anything and everything he could find on stop-motion animation, often doing experiments at home. As luck would have it, his machinist father had done some freelance work for RKO and knew a few people who had worked on *Kong*, men who filled the boy in on details about the stop-motion animation process. Among other projects, his dad was responsible for destroying the cars in the Laurel and Hardy shorts *Busy Bodies* and *Hog Wild*. Another stroke of luck came by way of the Museum of Arts and Sciences at Exposition Park in LA. For years this museum displayed mattes, dinosaurs from *The Lost World*, test footage of the never-made film *Creation*, and the wooden stand-in figure of Kong, all gifted by O'Brien himself. Harryhausen spent hours at the museum, learning all he could. (Decades later, Harryhausen was invited to revisit the museum. Harryhausen was then a well-known special effects artist, and the museum wanted him to inspect some of the *Lost World* models that had been uncovered. It turned out some of the miniature dinosaurs had been accidently sealed up in the walls during a remodeling decades earlier. It's just possible that a couple of O'Brien's dinosaurs might still be trapped in the building somewhere.[9])

Having learned the basics, he then got his long hands on the most accurate information he could in the pre-internet era regarding stop-motion animation. A crucial article in *Look* magazine outlined the basics, including scaled-down props, painted scenery on glass, and ball-and-socket joints that were moved in front of a special camera that gave its user the ability to advance the film one frame at a time.

Armed with this knowledge, the teenaged Harryhausen began making films in the grand tradition of greatness in the garage. Already accustomed to model-making and dioramas, he evolved to the next step of making moveable creatures.

His first moving model was a cave bear. Its skeleton—known in the business as an "armature"—had limbs made of wood glued to decorative beads for sockets. The hair came from an old fur coat of his mother's that he sliced up (he would later insist that she gave him her blessing). The bear had a moving tongue and glass eyes. His next experiment was a six-foot-long brontosaurus with a wooden frame and papier-mâché torso. Only the neck and tail—made from the necks of flexible table lamps—moved. He next created a stegosaurus, then a woolly mammoth. He carved the mammoth's tusks from wood; the hair was Siberian goat hair from a taxidermist; the trunk was one of his mom's old stockings. The flexible joints were again salvaged from old angle-poise lamps. The skin consisted of sponges stuffed into his mother's stockings that he painted over. With his father's help he created a sloth and a pterodactyl. The LA Museum hosted a model-making contest. Harryhausen submitted a 20-inch stegosaurus on a prehistoric miniature set and came in first (elsewhere he has said he came in second, but *The Harryhausen Scrapbook* said he came in first and had been previously mistaken about coming in second). This time the ball-and-socket joints were made by using the hinges of rearview mirrors from old cars, courtesy of his machinist father.

He borrowed a movie camera from a friend, a 16 mm Victor. Meant for amateurs, it didn't give Harryhausen the ability to shoot one frame at a time. He filmed his dinosaurs in his own little prehistoric world, the Harryhausens' backyard garden. The boy had no choice but to quickly push the release button on and off in quick succession, hoping to only advance one frame, but often advancing two or three. Hence, in the teen's first effort, a few minutes of the cave bear moving through the Harryhausens' backyard plants, the beast lopes along jerkily.

Still, the future filmmaker learned some things, most notably that shooting outdoors was problematic, with the changing position of the sun making shadows move quickly and distractingly, as in a time-lapse film.

The parents of the first generation of fans often frowned upon the useless obsessions of their children. Bradbury's athletic brother and outdoors-loving father were bemused by the boy's love of the fantastic. Forry Ackerman's father once told his son that he would never amount to anything. When John W. Campbell, Jr., got his first piece published in *Amazing Stories*, his father hissed, "It isn't the *Saturday Evening Post*."[10]

Harryhausen's parents, on the other hand, completely backed their eccentric son. Mr. Frederick Harryhausen helped set up a studio in the corner of the family garage and built a bench where Ray could work on his miniatures; eventually he would build a shack for his son to create prehistoric worlds in. His mother helped sew the backcloth of Ray's sets and made the tiny palm trees and ferns for his little jungles. Years later, both mom and dad helped Harryhausen with the fairy tale shorts that were his first professional ventures, his mom sewing costumes and his dad building miniature castles and gingerbread homes. Mr. Harryhausen helped his son throughout his career, among other things developing the aerial brace used to show models flying, like UFOs or pterodactyls. Frederick Harryhausen also built the title saucers in *Earth vs. the Flying Saucers*, making them toys that could rotate so Ray could create the illusion of them spinning as they whirred through the sky. Frederick Harryhausen's last contributions to his son's career were the armatures for the models of Selenites, or creatures who live on the Moon. Meant to be used in the film *First Men on the Moon*, it was decided it was more cost effective to use children in moon-man suits for away shots (shots from far away, meant to show a panorama of an entire set; children in costumes created the illusion of depth, making it seem like the characters were further away than they really were, and thus making the set seem a lot bigger), so Mr. Harryhausen's models were never used.

Eventually, Harryhausen bought his own camera, a 16 mm Kodak Cine II with the much-needed one-frame shaft. The future special effects genius read more, practiced more. He began to draw intricate black and gray sketches of the sequences he wanted to film, hundreds of sketches. Ray conducted early experiments with a static matte, a technique in which part of the camera's lens is covered, exposing only half of the film as the director shoots a live action sequence with human actors. The film is then rewound and the matte is moved to the other half of the lens—think of transferring a seeing person's eyepatch from one eye to the other—and shot again, this time slowly exposing the un-filmed half as it captures the model being moved, one frame at a time. The result is combining live action with models. Harryhausen was able to film himself ducking a swipe from his cave bear, a short project that also included King Kong and his pet German shepherd (his dog was named—what else?—"Kong").

He spent weeks not just on building models but also on creating sets, intricate jungles painted onto plate glass that he then set between camera and diorama, creating the illusion of depth. He soon had a semi-professional studio, with lights towering over miniature prehistoric worlds of extinct creatures. He embarked on a project called *Evolution of the World* (begun in 1938), that was to depict exactly what the title called for, the creation of the planet Earth, or, in his words, "from the swirling gases in space, through the age of dinosaurs, to the appearance of mammals."[11] For this ambitious project he created a brontosaurus, a T.rex, and a triceratops, all of which would be uncovered in his storage garage in California almost 80 years later.

As in all work of genius, it's the little details that matter. In his early footage, what stands out already are the spices not totally necessary that added hours to the project, such as the swirling tails of the dinosaurs, or the T.rex's final snarl to the camera. He abandoned *Evolution* after he saw Disney's *Fantasia* and felt he could never top their dinosaur sequence. Still, it was his little reel of *Evolution* that he showed to producers to find work in his early days.

Among other lessons, he also learned to control his emotions. It was while working on his almost-opus that he lost his temper, threw a hammer, and accidently smashed a glass matte that had taken him hours to paint.

King Kong led him to his hero, the father of Kong himself, Willis O'Brien. Harryhausen noticed a girl in his social studies class reading a bound script of *King Kong*, with illustrations. He introduced himself to her and explained that he'd been obsessed with Kong since he was a kid, and told her all about his own experiments. The girl's father, as fate had it, had worked with O'Brien, or "O'bie" as he was known. She asked Harryhausen why he didn't simply call O'bie, a bold idea that had never occurred to the shy teen.

Harryhausen dialed the number and to his shock heard the voice of Willis O'Brien himself on the other end. The teen somehow managed to stutter who he was and why he was calling. O'Brien asked that he swing by the studio sometime. Stunned, Harryhausen gathered up his dinosaurs, stuffed them in a suitcase, and headed for MGM studios.

At the time, O'Brien was working on a film called *War Eagles* (the project was never finished). Ray's jaw dropped as he walked into Obie's office and saw the walls bedecked with paintings and drawings of giant, Kong-sized eagles leashed by Roman soldiers. After talking at length about his interest in animation, he finally showed his models to O'Brien and held his breath. He was a writer showing his latest sonnet to Shakespeare, a hockey player demonstrating his slapshot to Gretzky. The master was kind but firm in his appraisal of the boy's models. The stegosaurus's legs looked like "wrinkled sausages." The boy needed to pay attention to dinosaur anatomy, learn which muscles did what, illustrate where muscle connected to bone. Harryhausen wasn't offended; he was flattered to be taken seriously by the adult who had inspired him.

Six months later the boy's parents took him to see O'Brien and his wife Darlyne at the O'Brien home. This time, Harryhausen showed him his early film experiments, once again getting constructive criticism from O'Brien. Darlyne flattered the boy's work. She reported years later that after the Harryhausens left, her husband looked at her and said, "You realize you're encouraging the competition."

Harryhausen followed his mentor's advice, taking night classes at Los Angeles City College in art and anatomy while still a high school student. During the day, he took art instruction at his Manual Arts High School, learning how to draw nudes. (Yes, nudes, at a high school. 1937 was a different time.) He also joined the Manual Arts masquers, film, and cartoon clubs (the masquers were devoted to Hollywood makeup techniques). After high school he studied cinematography at the University of Southern California, which had one of the nation's first film schools, and took classes in art direction, editing, and photography. Throughout his career he routinely visited zoos to see how primates, tigers, and octopuses moved. He also tried his hand at acting as part of a troupe that presented a play on the local radio station every Saturday night. He soon learned that acting was not his true calling, but he kept the lessons that he learned, making it a point to instill emotions and empathy in his creations. His models were also actors.The Ymir and Mighty Joe Young often emoted better than their human counterparts.

By the time he was 21, he was featured in *Popular Mechanics* in an article titled "Cashing in on a Fantasy." (Quote: "Filming weird monsters has been converted from a hobby into a profitable venture by Ray Harryhausen of Los Angeles, California."[12])

And he saw *King Kong*, a lot. Every chance he got. The eighth Wonder of the World was released in 1933 and re-released in 1938, and young Harryhausen scanned the papers and took the red car to whatever theater was showing it. (At the time, there were two basic ways to get around LA without a car, the yellow cars of the Los Angeles Railway that served the city and the Pacific Electric red cars that sprawled all over LA County. But this system was already under attack. According to the WPA guide published in 1940, "The Los Angeles of the future is likely to evolve along highways ... in some instances the city has left outlying districts devoid of any method of travel except by automobile or on foot." Los Angeles also already had

10. Ray Harryhausen Joins the League

more cars per capita than any other city.) By the time he walked into the Hawthorne Theater (a "fleapit," he later recalled) on that day in May 1938 and paid a dime for admittance, he would have seen the great ape dozens of times before. But this time, the lobby was bedecked with beautiful 11 × 14 stills depicting scenes from the film.[13] He asked the manager if he could borrow the stills to photograph and sketch. Luckily, the person behind the ticket counter was Roy Test, the young man who first began the LA chapter of the Science Fiction League and was a personal friend of Forry Ackerman. He gave Harryhausen Forry's phone number. Harryhausen would always say that the big gorilla was responsible for introducing him to Fay Wray, Willis O'Brien, and Forrest Ackerman.

The young man eagerly dialed Forry, and the pair had an instant rapport. Harryhausen explained he was an artist obsessed with King Kong and that he'd seen the movie about the great ape more than 30 times. Just how many times Harryhausen saw *King Kong* in his life is incalculable. In a 1977 article written by Ray Bradbury, Harryhausen is quoted as having seen it "some 87 times," this in the time before VCRs, though Bradbury seemed to think his good friend saw it even more than that.[14]

Harryhausen wanted to borrow the images of the great ape, promising to return them after taking some pictures of his own and making some sketches. If there was one fan who understood being obsessed with a movie, it was Forry, who later in life would fly across the world just to view different editions of *Metropolis*. (During the First World Science Fiction Convention, Forry distributed an entire fanmag that he'd printed devoted to *Metropolis*. There he compiled opinions of other fans of the movie. Bradbury thought the film "well worth [his] money any day" but did have some criticism: "The plot was moth-eaten. The directing, well, could have been better.") Ackerman said he could indeed borrow the stills—Forry later said he just plain gave the *Kong* photos to Harryhausen. Always eager to show off his collection, Ackerman then invited the eager young fan to his flat on New Hampshire, where he showed the artist his infinite stash of stills, original art, and magazines. Ackerman also explained that there was a club that met every other Thursday downtown and told Harryhausen that he would fit right in. The Science Fiction League minutes of the June 2, 1938, meeting recorded that there was a new member, "Ray Harryhauser."[15]

Harryhausen would join the league, though he wasn't quite as gung-ho about the future as his friends. As his later filmmaking would show, he cared more for the ancient past of gods and goddesses, monsters and swords, a time he described as "so much more romantic."[16]

11

The Two Rays Meet

"It was the dinosaur that was responsible for our first meeting at the Los Angeles Science Fiction League, and the long friendship that followed."

—Ray Harryhausen[1]

Ray Bradbury and Ray Harryhausen told different stories about when exactly they first met. Sometimes, Bradbury would claim that Ackerman invited him to meet Harryhausen at his home on New Hampshire Street: "When I was eighteen years old, Forrest Ackerman called me and invited me over to his house because there was a young man there who he wanted me to meet. That man's name was Ray Harryhausen."[2] Elsewhere, he said he was at Ackerman's place editing an issue of *Imagination!* when Harryhausen dropped by to look at the stills of Kong. Then there's what Bradbury wrote in the introduction to Harryhausen's book, *The Film Fantasy Scrapbook*: "I have known and loved Ray Harryhausen and his work since the night in 1937 when he walked into the Little Brown Room at Clifton's Cafeteria in Los Angeles ... and showed me his drawings and told me his dreams." During an interview with both Bradbury and Ackerman published over a half century later in an issue of *Famous Monsters of Filmland* magazine, Bradbury summed up his first encounter with Harryhausen thusly: "He [Harryhausen] called you [Ackerman], you told him to come to the club, and I met him there." To which Forry replied, "And the Three Monsterteers were born!" Elsewhere, Ackerman referred to the trio of Ackerman, Bradbury, and Harryhausen as "The Bat Pack."

For his part, Harryhausen remembered first seeing the dishwater blond boy rolling into Clifton's on his roller skates after an afternoon of selling newspapers on the corner of Olympic and Norton.[3] Bradbury was a newsie then. Out of high school and needing a job, he received a loan from his dad and brother to buy a corner from another newspaper boy.

However or wherever it was the two Rays met, it was love at first sight. The boys shared a first name, had been born only about a month apart, and, most importantly, both loved dinosaurs. A few years earlier, 13-year-old Bradbury, still living in Illinois, attended the Chicago World's Fair with his family and was taken in by the animatronic dinosaurs of the Sinclair exhibit. The beasts so hypnotized Bradbury that he walked backwards on the moving, Jetson-style sidewalks that shepherded everyone through the fair so he could spend more time with the prehistoric beasts. He would eventually have to be escorted out of the exhibit. Bradbury later revealed in an interview that he built his own little World's Fair in his Waukegan backyard, using Christmas lights and coming up with architectural drawings.[4] When Ray Bradbury went to New York for the World Science Fiction Convention in 1939, his first stop was the American Museum of Natural History to look at the dinosaurs.[5]

Harryhausen, meanwhile, was so infatuated with the beasts of the Jurassic and Triassic eras that he built his own stegosauruses and T. rexes and brought them to life in his backyard garden. Bradbury was amazed to learn the boy had a garage full of dinosaurs and that he could make them move. "Make them move?" Bradbury asked.

Harryhausen explained that he animated dinosaur films in his garage in Leimert Park. This was something Bradbury had to see, and soon the teen was in the garage of a master, looming over Harryhausen's prehistoric world. Decades later, this is how Bradbury would describe visiting Harryhausen's studio for the first time: "There on the garage floor I saw these miniature dinosaurs that he animated with 8mm film, and I realized we were similar people. He loved dinosaurs as much as I did. We had a friendship that began when we were both eighteen. We hoped that one day I would write a screenplay about dinosaurs and he would animate it."[6]

Bradbury was enamored with the tiny animals living in a jungle of paper ferns. He not only got to see the beautiful miniature world Harryhausen created, his new friend also showed him his own home-made films.

Soon the boys went to movies together, lots of movies. With *Kong* playing in theaters, the first time it had been re-released since

Ray Bradbury selling newspapers on the corner of Olympic and Norton in Los Angeles, circa 1938 (from the collection of John L. Coker III).

Ray Harryhausen in his Los Angeles studio circa 1941 (from the collection of John L. Coker III).

its initial run in 1933, Ray and Ray simply had to see the great ape as many times as they could. Harryhausen scanned LA papers for announcements of *Kong* playing in LA, Pasadena, anyplace within driving distance. Harryhausen would call Ray and tell him that *King Kong* was playing somewhere for 15 cents, pick up his buddy—and sometimes Forry—and off they'd rush together to go see it. The boys either hopped on a red trolley or borrowed Aunt Neva's car to see the great ape one more time. Bradbury never learned to drive, so Harryhausen would have been at the wheel. They also saw other hits, like *She* and *The Last Days of Pompeii*. At a theater in Pasadena screening of *King Kong*, the boys had been there so many times that they knew the projectionist. When it was time to start the movie, the manager would command, "Okay Bill!" and the film began. Sometimes, an impatient Bradbury yelled, "Okay, Bill!" and the film started ahead of time.[7]

Bradbury would eventually pay what, in his world, was the ultimate compliment: he made Harryhausen a character in a work of fiction. He cast his good buddy in the short story "Tyrannosaurs Rex." In this story, an arrogant producer gets his comeuppance from a mistreated 3-D animator. In the story Bradbury revealed just how familiar he was with Harryhausen's monster-making process: "All liquid latex, rubber sponge, ball-socketed steel articulature; all night-dreamed, clay-molded, warped and welded, riveted and slapped to life by hand. No bigger than my fist, half of them; the rest no larger than this head they sprang from.... Glue plastic sponge over lubricated skeleton, slip snake pebble-skin over sponge, meld seams with fire..."

Bradbury based this story on a real encounter Harryhausen had with a producer who wasn't willing to pay him what he was worth. In Bradbury's words:

> So together we went over to Raleigh Studios ... [Robert] Lippert was there, but he didn't get up. He didn't even say hello. He said, "Give your film to the projectionist." So Ray and I sat in the front row while Lippert screened this incredible footage of Ray's wonderful dinosaurs. When it was over, the projectionist handed Ray his films, and Lippert didn't say a word. He didn't say thank you. He didn't even say goodbye....[8]

Two years after this encounter the film would be released, and curiosity led Ray and Maggie Bradbury to attend the sneak preview of the film at the Pickwick Theatre in Los Angeles. It turned out to be a low-budget B-movie (*The Lost Continent*, 1951). "The dinosaurs were nothing but men in suits and gila monsters with fins—it was terrible!" Bradbury explained.

> When it was over, my wife and I went out in the lobby, and over in the corner was Robert Lippert, surrounded by all of his yes men.... I plunged through a sea of yes men and said ... "Mr. Lippert? My name is Ray Bradbury. And the film we just saw? It won't make a dime!" I walked away very happy, because I had given that terrible man his comeuppance. And I was right—the movie never made a dime![9]

Bradbury also made himself and Ray Harryhausen into fictional characters in his mystery *A Graveyard for Lunatics*, in which "Roy Holdstrum" uses his special effects powers to help solve a crime. Ray Bradbury sent Ray Harryhausen a copy—he mailed Harryhausen a first edition of most of his books. For the edition of *Lunatics* Bradbury signed it: "For Diana and Ray, with love over 52 years—and hope you enjoy yourself as Roy Holdstrum* in this book!

*Don't Sue!"[10]

Bradbury had met a soul mate, someone so crazy about dinosaurs that he actually recreated them. Ray eventually explained to his biographer Sam Weller: "We had a mutual interest in dinosaurs, and we both loved King Kong—and so did Forry—and the three of us would many times jump on the red car and go to Eagle Rock or Pasadena to find a replay of *King Kong* or *The Most Dangerous Game* and all the Merian Cooper pictures."[11]

The two Rays would spend hours on the phone, spending a nickel for an unlimited call. Other teen boys talked about sports, girls, or cars. Harryhausen and Bradbury chatted endlessly about dinosaurs, space elevators, trips to Mars, and how they—Harryhausen with his clay, Bradbury with his typewriter—could bring these ideas to life. They also told each other about the latest theater to be showing *She* or *King Kong* and hopped on whatever red car would take them there. The boys promised to make a great dinosaur picture together. They made a pact then and there: grow old, but never grow up. Time would march on and they would grow into adults, but never would they stop loving the creatures that brought them joy. Both would make a tidy living from these monsters—and change culture at the same time.

12

Rocket Boys

In issue #9 of *Imagination!*, it was reported that Chapter 4 had a visit from Caltech's engineers John Parsons and Ed Forman, to talk about rockets. Parsons spoke at length about nascent rocket technology, then brought members of the league out into Clifton's parking lot to look at some models he'd brought.[1] John, better known as "Jack" Parsons, would later help found the Jet Propulsion Laboratory. The fans were enthused, as many of them had become infatuated with the new technology of rocketry.

What has always set apart science fiction fans from those of other genres was the belief that what they are reading can and will exist someday, if not quite as originally imagined. Most romance readers don't really believe they'll be swept off their feet by a hunky cowboy who is also somehow a billionaire, nor do readers of Westerns expect to have a showdown on a dusty street at high noon. Science fiction fans, on the other hand, believed and believe that much of what they are reading is fantastic today but could be a reality someday, and more than a few tried to personally bring about this reality. Case in point, rocketry.

The fanzines and prozines of the later '20s and early '30s routinely published reports from the rocket societies of America, Britain, and Germany. More than a few fans felt inspired to try their hands at this new art (the first known successful launch of a liquid fuel rocket was by Robert Goddard in 1926), often with disastrous results.

Like the greater world of fandom, the rocket boys initially worked as individuals before meeting like-minded types and forming nationwide organizations, often finding each other via the letter columns of the pulps. *Amazing Stories* and other early publications journaled the progress of these amateurs. Rocket science being new, these boys, some as young as 14, had no choice but to make everything up, creating their own fuel and rockets from scratch. The rockets were metal and fueled by the boys' own homemade brews.

A prominent fan who tinkered, quite dangerously, with rockets was William S. Sykora. He was a member of different early fandom groups in the Queens, New York, area, eventually becoming head of the International Scientific Association, or ISA (originally, the Science Correspondence Club). Though Sykora was not universally well liked, no one could deny his love of science. He had a lab in his basement, where he hand-made rockets with his father. Sykora filmed his experiments and showed these movies to members of the Queens Science Fiction League and other fans.[2] Sometimes he demonstrated his rockets live in front of friends and fans, much to their eventual regret. In the fall of 1935 he loaded a pair of rockets full of letters labeled "via first American rocket-flight, Sept. 22, 1935," hoping to demonstrate the feasibility of mail by rocket. Both rockets exploded, shredding and scattering the letters. One rocket was made of steel, and the other aluminum, so one can imagine how dangerous it was for them to blow up. According to Donald A. Wollheim, a fellow ISA member (the association was actually sponsoring the experiments) who was with Sykora when attempting to make history, a piece of one of the rockets tore into a small boy's arm. Sykora was arrested and fined.[3] In his book *All Our Yesterdays*, Warner writes that one boy in Memphis was temporarily blinded while trying to stir up some fuel in his basement lab.[4] Warner adds, "History is silent on the question of whether the lab recovered as fully as his eyes."

In an issue of *Thrilling Wonder Stories*, the Leeds, England, director of the Science Fiction League, Harold Gottliffe, reported on the goings-on of the Manchester Interplanetary Society, an optimistic name for a group that could barely get their rockets in the air: "Bill Heeley made one of his first rockets with an aluminum casing; its premature explosion was rather a surprise, though. Mr. Osbourne a cinema operator, was not so lucky."[5]

Gottliffe does not say what happened to Mr. Osbourne.

The Manchester Interplanetary Society and the Leeds Rocket Society were early local rocketry groups. America had smaller organizations as well, such as the Cleveland Rocket Society and the Peoria Rocket Association, but the premier rocket club in America was the American Rocket Society. It began life as the American Interplanetary Society, which was devoted to interstellar travel, a.k.a. rockets. This organization was founded by 11 men and one woman in New York in the spring of 1930. Nine of the founders were editors or writers for Gernsback's *Wonder Stories*,[6] which explains why so much information about the society was printed in that magazine. The purpose of the society was to gather books, newspaper clippings, and any other information available on the new science of rocketry, and make this information available to anyone who was interested. Fans from all over the country and the world wrote in that they would like to join the AIS and help in any way possible to break the confines of Earth. The society published *The Bulletin of the American Interplanetary Society*, later to become a respected magazine called *Astronautics*.

In January of 1932, the American Interplanetary Society put its theories into practice by building a 7-foot, 15-pound aluminum rocket, its engine fired remotely by members using a control pad attached by wires while sitting in a self-made dugout. It failed to launch after it was accidently dropped while being loaded into the wooden proving stand. A year later they built a second rocket and launched it. It split apart after an altitude of 250 feet.[7]

In 1939, one of the society's rockets was on display at the World's Fair, where it eventually vanished. The American Rocket Society conducted other experiments that resulted in neighbors complaining about shattered windows and blasts that could be heard miles away. Once, a young woman bystander stepped from behind a tree to snap a photograph of one of their motors in action just when it happened to explode, a mistake that required her to be rushed to a hospital. She would need a year to recover.[8]

The pulps also printed reports of a rocket powered "comet car" by the German Dr. Paul Heylandt; a rocket ice-sled in Syracuse, New York; other cases of failed mail-by-rocket attempts in Australia and Germany.[9]

Not to be outdone, the British oversaw in 1933 the first meeting of the British Interplanetary Society,[10] an organization run for a time by a young Arthur C. Clarke. Clarke later claimed that a journalist who came by his flat asking about rockets turned out to be a German spy.[11]

The premier rocket society in Germany, dating back to the 1920s, was the Verein für Raumschiffahrt (Society for Spaceship Travel), whose 800 members included men from France, Russia, and Austria.[12] It was in Germany that rocketry claimed its first martyr. On May 17, 1930, a German named Max Valier was killed while experimenting with a rocket car.[13] *Wonder Stories* also reported on German experiments with "rocket airplanes."

Initially, German, American, and British rocketeers openly shared information in a spirit of camaraderie and mutual interest, but the adults running the world had other ideas. After taking over Germany, the Nazis forbade the German boys from leaking data about rocket science. Officially, Germans were forbidden from conducting private rocket experiments or publishing any information about them. The only legal rocket testing was to be done for the Reich. One prominent German rocket scientist, Willy Ley, would end up defecting to America before Pearl Harbor. He continued his research in the States, where he helped develop a mail rocket/glider at NYU.[14] Rockets were especially attractive to Hitler because they were not covered by the treaty that ended the First World War, which specifically forbade Germany from investing in new military technology. Hitler was paranoid enough to ban Fritz Lang's movie *Frau im Mond* (*Woman on the Moon*) from screening in America, afraid the enemy might learn a thing or two about rockets.

13

The Summer of 1938

> "I stood on that street corner and friends, coming to visit, would ask me what I was doing there and I said, 'Becoming a writer.' Selling newspapers gave me a chance every day to write in the morning until three in the afternoon. I went to the corner and I sold my newspapers until six and made my money and went home and wrote some more."
>
> —Ray Bradbury[1]

Right out of high school Bradbury started selling the *Herald-Express*, the late afternoon version of the *LA Herald Examiner*, making about ten dollars a week. He worked the corner of Norton and Olympic, walking or roller-skating home at the end of each day. It was the only time he made money doing anything besides writing, and he loved it. It was the perfect gig for a gregarious boy like himself, plus it allowed Ackerman and other friends to drop by. John Barrymore and Buster Keaton were regular customers of his. Not only did this job give him the chance to socialize outside Acton's Drugstore, but he only worked about three hours day, from roughly 3 to 6 p.m., leaving plenty of time to write.[2] Plus, he sometimes traded in unsold newspapers for movie tickets. He would always say that he never worked a day in his life, and that included his days as a newsie. Every other Thursday he skated the grueling five miles from his corner to Clifton's.

He didn't just focus on writing. In a pattern that he would keep up throughout his adult life, he always had his hands on different projects and interests. His first year after high school Ray Bradbury was active in local theater, including a playhouse run by Laraine Day, who would one day star opposite John Wayne, Cary Grant, and Ronald Reagan, and almost got Donna Reed's role in *It's a Wonderful Life*. She was one of many people Bradbury knew before they became Hollywood royalty, including Ray Harryhausen, Jo Ann Sayers, and Sam Peckinpah, who as a student wanted to film one of Bradbury's stories. Ray volunteered to be an usher at an outdoor venue, the Hollywood Bowl, exposing him to classical music, opera, and ballet. He continued to write plays and radio dramas. According to his own diary, he once agreed to adapt a story of L. Ron Hubbard's for radio. He still haunted the Brown Derby for autographs but saved money by eating at Hugo's Hot Dog Stand across the street. He would later estimate he spent something like three million words before he got anything published professionally. Starting in high school he wrote a story a week, because, as he once said, there can be no quality without quantity. The hopeful teen submitted these works to high-end "slicks" like *The New Yorker*, *The Saturday Evening*

Post, and *Harper's Magazine*, as well as the plethora of short-lived pulps. There were no takers.

When it came to publishing unprofessionally, his work still appeared in every issue of *Imagination!* after his debut in #2. He illustrated the cover of issue #9, a line drawing of a muscular, Egyptian-styled man striking a gong. Most likely he based this illustration on the "Rank Gongman" that introduced every film by a British company called the Rank Organization, much like MGM's lion. This issue also had a poem by "Hollerbochen" called "IF" ("If U can be a fan & sing a song & make a noise just like King Kong").

The league soon put their newest member, Ray Harryhausen, to work. His art graced the cover of the September 1938 issue (#12) of *Imagination!* along with appearing in other zines coming out of Chapter 4.

The boys and girls of Chapter 4 socialized outside of Clifton's, throwing a beach party in August. They also saw lots and lots of movies.

At the meeting on August 4, 1938, Chapter 4 reported that eight members went to a triple feature showing of *Frankenstein*, *Dracula*, and *Son of Kong*.[3] Ackerman had the inside scoop about upcoming movies and often invited his friends to go with him to premieres of any fantastic film that was coming out. They saw *The Invisible Man Returns* with Vincent Price (Bradbury hated it—Vincent Price was no Claude Rains). The gang also took in the latest version of *Hunchback of Notre Dame* at the Fine Arts Theatre in Beverly Hills, where they ran into Lon Chaney, Jr., and Peter Lorre in the lobby. Ackerman gushed, told Chaney Jr. how much he admired his late father, congratulated him on his recent roles in *The Wolf Man* and *Of Mice and Men*, and then told Lorre how much he loved him in *M* and *The Maltese Falcon*.[4] At a tribute to Ackerman after he had died, Bradbury mentioned going with Forry in 1939 to the Regina Theatre on Wilshire Boulevard and watching *Frankenstein* and *Dracula*, which was playing there, he claimed, 365 days a year, all night and all day.

In the October 1938 issue of *Imagination!*, Chapter 4 reported on the bulk of horror and science fiction screening that month.

> Marquees in movieland have more than featured fantascience films during the month, including (often 2 at a time) "Deluge, Frankenstein, Bride of F., Kong, Son of K., Werewolf of London, Things to Come, Trans Atlantic Tunnel, Walking Dead, Invisible Man, Mummy, Ghoul, Raven, Gabriel Over the White House, She, The Scoundrel, Man who Lived Again, Clairvoyant, Invisible Ray, FPL, Crime of Dr Crospi—At many revivals of Dracula, Bela Lugosi has appeared in person." Topping their own records, Harryhausen has now seen King Kong 25 times!, Forry THINGS TO COME for the dozenth (also "Lost World" for the 10th time), & Morojo is up there with 8 to date on Wells.

The Movie Palaces

The boys and girls of Chapter 4 happened to be living in the best place anywhere ever to see movies. There never was before or after a better place to see a film than 1930s Los Angeles. According to the 1938 Los Angeles City Directory, there were 247 movie theaters in LA, along with 60 stage theaters, for a combined total of 450,000 seats. This in a city whose population was 1.3 million people. Thirty percent of the city could fit into LA's theaters at any time.

By the late '30s cinemas had graduated from posting "No Spitting" signs to hanging the art of Italian masters, from places without bathrooms to boasting waiting rooms and smoking lounges, from a single piano-man or woman playing the accompaniment to full-blown orchestras of more than 60 pieces. (Female piano players were not uncommon in the days of early silent films. Often they were local church organists or piano teachers looking to make extra cash.) In the late 1890s and early 1900s, "movie-men" toted reels and projectors to flicker films inside of tents and saloons. By the 1930s movies were playing in buildings bigger than most cathedrals. By 1920 100 million people went to the cinema every week, almost the entire US population.[5]

Both Forry Ackerman and Ray Bradbury claimed to have visited a local movie house four or five times weekly. This may sound obsessive, but in the age before television the only way to see a movie, newsreel, cartoon, or anything else moving at 24 frames per second was at the movies. Millions of Americans went daily the same way that plenty now watch TV for two or three hours a day. Seeing one, two, even three films in a day was nothing unusual and is why we in America talk about going to the *movies*, plural, even if now we rarely see more than one. Bradbury typed in his teen diary about celebrating New Year's Eve 1939 rolling over into 1940 by seeing five films, leaving The Forum at 3 a.m. He saw two more the next day and thought about seeing *Gone With the Wind* but decided not to as he had already seen it twice. Bradbury saw so many films that, decades later, as an established writer and celebrity, he frequently appeared as a guest commentator in documentaries about silent horror films. He claimed to have seen every movie that was released when he was a boy. While this isn't the literal truth, in the decades leading up to World War II it was possible for a film buff to see every feature film screened nationwide, as there wasn't nearly as much content in the pre–Netflix era.

By 1920 the question was not how to get Americans to the movies, but how to convince them to go to *your* theater. Soon the men of the industry began constructing greater, more opulent theaters, often one-upping each other to the point where one wondered if they were actually turning a profit. The Big Five film studios—Warner Brothers, RKO, Fox, MGM, and Paramount—often either financed the movie theaters or bought them up. By 1930 70 percent of movie ticket sales passed through a theater owned by one of these studios,[6] so there was plenty of money to be spent on the construction of cinemas. No expense was spared. It was as if movie theaters were financed by Jay Gatsby.

Entire books have been written about the exquisite movie palaces of the 1920s and '30s, but here are a few anecdotes to give an idea of just how ostentatious they were.

The Roxy in New York City had a marquee that gleamed "The Cathedral of the Motion Picture" with no fewer than 6,214 seats when it opened in March of 1927. It owned not one but three golden organ consoles, each costing thousands of dollars. On the Roxy's opening night the NYPD devoted 150 men to holding back the crowds of people, most of whom had no chance of actually getting in but were just hoping to catch a glimpse of the paradise inside. This interior included crystal chandeliers, five columns of Verde marble, and the world's largest oval rug, weighing 2.5 tons. That was just the foyer, which could hold about 2,500 people and whose walls were bedecked with paintings any museum would be proud of, including works by Benjamin West and Luca Giordano. For the performers, there were five floors of dressing rooms served by two elevators. Animal acts were so routine that the Roxy had a special backstage ramp installed.[7]

The Uptown in Chicago had an "acre of seats" according to its own advertising. A perfuming system percolated pretty scents beneath the 4,381 seats that faced a pair of golden gates guarding the screen, which opened before each show. The conductor of the orchestra could control the speed of the film, lest the movie not run in tandem with the music.[8] Customers entered through a six-story grand lobby decorated with reproductions of European master paintings and sculptures before walking up a double-sweeping staircase into the main hall. The architects modeled Uptown after Versailles. It was then the largest example of a theater with an "atmospheric setting," meaning the ceiling was decorated with twinkling lights to mimic sitting under a starry sky.

Fans did not need to travel to Chicago or New York or LA to enjoy a motion picture in style. Most mid-sized cities were home to at least one movie palace. In 1928 the city of Racine, Wisconsin, then with a population of 67,000, listed five movie houses that could seat upwards of 1,000.[9] A couple of hours northwest of Racine lies the small town of Baraboo, where in 1915 the oldest of the native Ringling Brothers gifted an 800-seat movie house. The population at the time was less than 1,000, meaning the entire town could fit inside the Al Ringling Theatre. Originally home to a $9,000 Wurlitzer organ and a ceiling with no fewer than 17 hand-painted murals, it is considered by some to be the first movie palace. Purists deny the Ringling this distinction because it has fewer than 1,000 seats. Either way it is still operating today, making it one of the oldest running cinemas in the world.

Besides the film itself the palaces offered an entire night of live entertainment, with complete orchestras led by a conductor and a tuxedoed organist who was a minor celebrity in his own right.[10] A 1921 program guide printed in the trade publication *Motion Picture News* laid out the entertainment at some of the country's biggest movie theaters of the time, listing lineups of musical acts longer than the actual movie. Before showing the film *Lessons in Love* starring Constance Talmadge, The Mark Strand Theatre of Brooklyn showcased a dozen live classical music pieces. The entertainment continued after the film, with the showing of a short flick called *A Day with Jack Dempsey* followed by an organ solo.[11] Forry commented in more than one interview that he and his grandparents saw as many as seven films per day and would have seen even more if not for the vaudeville acts. Initially vaudevillians looked askance at the movie industry, worried that this new technology would replace them. This prediction proved to be tragically prescient, but for the decades between the wars vaudevillians routinely performed in tandem with movies, before or after the screening (the "K" in RKO stood for the B.F. Keith-Albee Vaudeville Exchange, a talent agency that represented vaudevillian performers. Among the performers little Forry saw before different films were Eddie Cantor and the great Black baritone Paul Robeson, who would be best known for his solo "Old Man River" in the musical *Showboat*. Other acts Ackerman attended included Blackstone the Magician; a Chinese singer named Sing-along Foo, who sauntered across the stage touching things that sprouted water, until there were 25 fountains firing at the same time; and Vern Coriell, who would hop up a set of stairs while drinking a glass of water.[12]

While extravagant movie theaters were not hard to find, Los Angeles had, if not the largest or most expensive, then certainly the most unique cinemas of its

13. The Summer of 1938

time. There were 22 movies houses on Broadway alone, all between Third and Ninth Streets, making LA's Broadway the most movie theater–saturated stretch of road anywhere ever, blocks of gleaming neon that would have rivaled the Vegas Strip. The Big Five studios owned many if not most of these, and sometimes named the theaters after themselves; there were five theaters in the LA area whose names began with Fox, three Warner Bros, and two Paramounts. That the movie studios themselves owned theaters is part of the reason there were so many movie houses. Fox's theaters only showed movies made by Fox, Paramount only showed Paramount pictures, and so on, meaning there were more cinemas than the free market demanded.

The United Artists at 933 South Broadway, with its vaulted ceilings, 2,200 seats, and extravagant murals, was so holy that it was used as a church for a time. The Warner Theatre (on Hollywood Boulevard and Wilcox) boasted walnut paneling, a smoking room, a music room, a nursery for toddlers, and the biggest theater in Hollywood up to that point. The Mayan (1044 South Hill) was brightly colored with a façade guarded by seven heads of "warrior-priests." Then there was The Shrine Auditorium (665 W. Jefferson Boulevard), at the time of its construction the biggest theater anywhere, holding more than 6,000 seats and meant to resemble a Moorish palace. It is from the Shrine that King Kong escaped in 1933 after being dragged to America. The simply named Los Angeles Theatre (615 S. Broadway) was built in 1931 and billed itself as "the most beautiful theatre in the world." Its interior was as opulent as any other movie palace of the time, with a grand sweeping staircase topped by a crystal fountain, everything illuminated by a crystal chandelier. The men's room had a pink Carrara marble shoeshine stand.

Sid Grauman's Million Dollar Theatre was not much of an exaggeration; he is estimated to have spent about $800,000. Grauman had each of the 2,300 seats wired so that when a customer sat down, a light glowed inside the box office, making it easy for ushers to see which seats were open. He had an identical grid installed in his own office. Grauman also built The Egyptian, which gave off the impression of being built by a pharaoh, with an ornate interior of stone walls bedecked with hieroglyphics, the screen flanked by sphinxes and hidden behind a curtain decorated by the two-dimensional drawings of Egyptians styled after those found on pyramid walls. The forecourt was meant to look like an ancient bazaar, with potted palm trees as decorations and actual shops inside the stone stores. The final touch was a bearded actor dressed as a Bedouin in striped robes and carrying a spear (cultural appropriation be damned) who patrolled the parapet overlooking the forecourt before each show.

Most exotic of all was and is Grauman's Chinese Theatre, still standing as a tourist trap for anyone who wants to see how their feet measure against those of John Wayne or Shirley Temple. It would take 18 months and 2 million dollars to build what is still the most famous movie theater in history. At the time of its opening, the Chinese had the largest stage of any cinema anywhere: 150 feet wide, 71 feet high, and 46 feet deep, all behind a golden silk curtain decorated with silver trees and fronted by an orchestra pit that housed as many as 65 musicians in addition to a Wurlitzer pipe organ estimated to have cost $26,000. Entire 20-foot sections of the stage could be raised or lowered to configure sets. A pair of "heaven dogs"—antique sculptures thousands of years old imported from China—guarded the entrance. The Chinese had its own power supply, making it completely independent of the grid.

Most exotic of all was the air conditioning hidden in a series of octagonal pillars seven feet in diameter that bordered both sides of the auditorium.

Almost anyone could enter the Chinese or other movie paradises, since admission to most shows was less than a dollar. A premiere with a concert may have cost a whopping two or even 10 dollars, but matinees and weekday screenings typically went for less than 50 cents.

Predictably, the Great Depression brought a halt to the era of the movie palace. When the Los Angeles Theatre opened in 1931 crowds lined up for a premiere whose guests included Gloria Swanson and Albert Einstein, while across the street desperate souls stood in a bread line. The Los Angeles would close less than 10 months after it opened. Even if they could afford the price of admission, fans no longer wanted to be reminded of the 1920s lavishness that many blamed for the crash of '29. The decade following the '20s saw theaters done with a style that would eventually be called art deco. The simple geometric patterns of basic colors were sleek, modern, and, most importantly, a lot more cost-effective than palaces of infinite ceilings and art.

This was the world of Ray Bradbury, Forry Ackerman, and Ray Harryhausen. It was a moviegoers paradise, Shangri-La for obsessive fans.

14

Futuria Fantasia

> "If nobody wants you, believe in yourself and create your own career."
> —Ray Bradbury, in the intro to the
> bound collection of *Futuria Fantasia*

The issue that Ray Harryhausen illustrated was almost the last edition of *Imagination!*. In 1938 Ackerman began working for his father's Associated Oil Company, after a stint as a civil service senior typist. Working for his father's employer was not a good fit. The straight-laced business world didn't work for the future editor of *Famous Monsters of Filmland*: "My job was to add columns of numbers and then at the end of the month, subtract the same column. And Heaven help you if you didn't come up with zero at the end of the month. I hate numbers and love words."[1] Having a real job competed with his duties at *Imagination!*, and the fanzine would lose. The one-year anniversary issue of *Imagination!*, October of 1938, announced the end of the publication: "U may've read rumors to the effect that Madge is moribund. The rumors were rite. ...4e was working from 4 pm til midnite.... Eventually it was decided 'twould be best to bring the business to a stop while Madge was on top, rather than sadly to watch her decline."[2]

Publishing *Imagination!* had been a labor of love, but it was labor intensive, with Forry and Morojo doing the bulk of the work. As Yerke wrote in his memoir: "Since he [Ackerman] was the mainstay on the editing and stenciling end of IMAGINATION!, a fact which until then had been begrudgingly admitted only as necessary, it became suddenly obvious that the magazine would have to do some rapid telescoping."

The death of *Imagination!* seemed to portend the death of Chapter 4. Lower turnout at meetings soon became the norm, although Chapter 4 still had more members than most, a low turnout defined as "only" 15 members. December 2 was the nadir so far, with just eight.[3] Things took a slight turn for the better when the league held its annual Christmas party, with dozens attending during a rare deluge in December.[4] Members exchanged gifts from a grab bag. Yerke recalled getting a Buck Rogers water pistol. Otherwise members exchanged mostly books or magazines. They played a record of the film *Things to Come*, courtesy of Forry Ackerman. At the first January meeting, the showman Bradbury performed a skit with a couple of other members "being a discussion between Life, Death and Fate, in regards to mankind."[5]

The Christmas party evidently breathed new life into the club. In January of 1939 Forry and Morojo were once again running a zine, a sequel of sorts to *Imagination!* called *Voice of the Imagination*, or *VoM* (always a lowercase "o"), consisting mostly of letters from fans. Ackerman and the league also backed a fanzine printed by Ray Bradbury, a brainchild he called *Futuria Fantasia*.

Bradbury had been wanting to do his own fanzine for quite some time and had offered to take over *Imagination!*, an offer Forry declined. Bradbury had typed millions of words he was eager to show the world, Hollerbochen be damned. It wouldn't be the first time Chapter 4 had helped along his writing career; it was through Chapter 4 that Bradbury, still in high school, bought his first typewriter for $12, from member Perry Lewis. The 17-year-old didn't have the money, so he paid Lewis a dollar a week, skipping lunch to come up with the cash.[6] In 1942 he wrote an ode to this machine:

> "A paradise of keys where stories dwell
> The characters who work within your womb
> That I push out, give birth, and kill, entomb
> Line after black-light line, page after page."[7]

With his own machine now, Bradbury was eager to show his work to the world. His was not the only zine Chapter 4 supported. The boys and girls of the league got behind several publications spun off of Chapter 4's mimeograph machines. Members not only submitted writing and artwork to one another's zines, they also helped with the labor of actual printing. One zine hinted at just how much other members supported one another with free labor: "Upon entering the Little Brown Room, it appeared to be a continuation of the work left last Sunday … the tables were piled high with copies of Futuria Fantasia & Polaris in process of being bound & addressed."[8]

Subscribers to *Imagination!* would have seen ads for "Fufa," as Bradbury's zine was nicknamed, in the last few issues, and Ackerman also granted him free ad space in the pages of *VoM*. Since this latest zine of Ackerman's consisted solely of correspondence, Bradbury once sent a letter that was really an ad for his own zine: "Futuria Fantasia is only ten cents, see, and it ain't gonna hurt you to kick through with the money either, cause it's the best damned rag in the business."[9] He threatened to send Slith, a snake-like creature he doodled himself, after anyone who didn't subscribe (this ad was also accompanied by a pretty bad drawing of himself). Bradbury advertised in other LA-based zines, hoping to build a following.

Bradbury was both writer and editor, meaning he could finally publish his own material, which he did, prolifically. Besides using his birth name, he published under pseudonyms like Ron Reynolds, Guy Amory, Doug Rogers, E. Cunningham, Brian Eldred, Cecil Claybourne Cunningham, and sometimes his old Hollerbochen. He used these not just for *Futuria Fantasia* but also for other zines that he contributed to. For the most part Bradbury (and his partners, like Ackerman and Bok) received praise, though one fan, an editor named J. Chapman Miske, found Bradbury's poetry lacking: "Melodramatic, obvious, a bit wandering, it still shows you might be able to do some pretty good stuff."[10]

Technocracy

The first issue of *Futuria Fantasia* largely dealt with Technocracy, a movement popular with many LA fans at the time, a set of ideas similar to the Michelism of the Futurians. In fact, in an issue of the fanzine *VoM*, it was stated that Michel and the more devout Futurians were literal card-carrying members of Technocracy, Inc.[11] Technocracy was so identified with the West Coast that Illinois fan Bob Tucker, something of a Mark Twain of early fandom, joked that a technocrat was someone who lived in LA. To an outsider, the differences between Michelism and Technocracy aren't readily apparent, but those in the Technocracy saw it differently, as Bradbury's friend T.B. Yerke explained.

> You Michelists are predominantly Communistic, and Communism is a reversion to hand-tool methods. They may work in Europe and on any other Continent, but Technocracy is the only thing which will work on this Continent, where an economy of abundance instead of scarcity is the only solution. Technocracy has the biggest array of scientists, engineers, technicians, and plain ordinary thinkers behind it, of any movement in history![12]

Technocracy has mostly been forgotten, but for a time in the late '30s it was in vogue, especially among early fans. It argued for a world governed by men of science, rather than the silly, narrow-minded politicians. People's wealth and importance would be tied to their intelligence and contributions rather than to how much money they had. Scientists, not politicians, would make all the decisions. Economists would decide economic policy, agricultural experts would make any choices regarding planting, engineers would be in charge of transportation, and so on. No meddling from elected leaders.

The leader of the Technocracy movement was a man named Howard Scott, who also personally taught classes on it. Scott genuinely believed that by 1945 America's system would collapse totally (he had predicted earlier collapses that never happened). The only hope was for scientists to control the country with absolute authority.

How would it work? T.B. Yerke laid Technocracy out in the first issue of Bradbury's zine. Each industry would have its own national, and then regional, leaders, the leaders chosen by the workers themselves. The regional leader of welders would be elected by other welders, for example, and these leaders would then pick a national leader. Instead of cash, people would spend energy certificates that would have the person's name, address, job, "worker's number," etc. stamped on them. An individual could only spend his/her energy certificates like personal checks. When a person went to buy, say, a pair of shoes, where the shoes were bought, by whom, what materials, and what size, would be teletyped to the Minister of Shoes, or whatever the national leader of shoemakers was to be called. Funneling this information promised no more shoes were made than needed, thus cutting back on inefficiency. The system would be so efficient that Americans would work only 24 hours a week and earn $20,000 per year (about $430,000 in today's money). In this utopia, everyone would have more than enough, negating the need to steal.

In that same issue, Bradbury published a piece called "Don't Get Technatal" by "Ron Reynolds." It depicts a Technocracy-run world so perfect that a frustrated crime writer no longer has anything to write about. ("Something like a tear rolled down Sam's check. 'No more gangsters, no more bank robberies, no more holdups, no more good, old-fashioned burglaries, no more vice gangs!'"[13]) Bradbury thought so highly of the movement that in his first issue of *Futuria Fantasia*, he stamped the yin-yang looking logo of Technocracy on the mailing flap, with the motto, "America Must Decide."

Technocracy's insistence that the US government, with its capitalist price system, would soon collapse, was an easy enough sell to people who saw bread lines and their fathers put out of work. As Bradbury once wrote in a letter, "When they put men on relief they cannot tax them. Therefore what will the government run on?"[14] Technocracy also seemed to be the only movement that could create the world he'd dreamed of. A country run by engineers looked poised to bring about the magical cities of wonder otherwise found only in pulp art. As Bradbury wrote in a letter, "We can have the magnificent civilization of science fiction dreams in twenty-five years once the technate comes in."[15]

Technocracy soon lost steam. Outsiders were turned off by the fascist leanings of its leaders, who typically wore military-style matching gray suits as uniforms and drove gray cars with the emblem of the Technocracy on their doors, looking like a police shield. When Bradbury went to see the leader of the movement, Howard Scott, speak in person, he was dismayed by the way his followers saluted him.[16]

Fans were particularly worried about the movement's Communist leanings, this being a time when being an out Communist was almost as bad as being an out homosexual. Then there was the problem that Technocracy was, by definition, undemocratic. No "meddling" from politicians in reality meant voters not having a voice, with decisions made by a handful of insiders. The death blow came in 1942, when Technocracy, Inc. placed ads in 100 newspapers, calling for an end to aid to countries fighting the Nazis.[17] The technocrats later changed course and got behind the war effort, but the damage was done. By the time of Pearl Harbor, the LA crowd had mostly turned away from Technocracy, such as in this joke in the February 1942 issue of *Shangri-L'Affaires*: "Tell me, Mr. Johnson, is it true that the Univ. of So. Cal. is going to offer a course in Technocracy under the heading Fascism I-A?"

Besides T.B. Yerke and Bradbury, the only other author whose work appeared in the first issue of Bradbury's zine was Forry Ackerman, who submitted a story called "The Record." Written when he was 16, it reflects his love of music; in this tale, one of the few remaining phonograph players saves the world. The last paragraphs were written by Bradbury.[18] Bradbury signed off with a poem called simply "Space," then encouraged readers to send opinions to the Bradbury home, now located at 1841 Manhattan Place. The Bradburys had moved again.

The cover art was done by young man named Hannes Bok. Like so many of the boys in Bradbury's pre-war world, Bok was unknown at the time but would have one of the more memorable, albeit tragic, careers in science fiction, painting cover art for 150 pulps and belonging to the first round of Hugo Award winners in 1953 (only six total were handed out that first year). He won his Hugo, an award for people in the world of science fiction, for Best Cover Illustrator.

15

Ackerman and Harryhausen, 1939

Harryhausen contributed art to some of the other fanzines, but his focus in 1939 was trying to break into filmmaking. Briefly he kept a diary in the spring of 1939. The entries reflect a hard-working boy who labored over his dinosaurs every day. He and his father made the rounds at different studios trying to find film work for Ray, leaving photos of his concepts behind (March 22, 1939: "Went to Paramount and RKO and Colombia [*sic*]"). Harryhausen routinely called on Willis O'Brien, the legendary director who was now starting to take serious interest in his protégé. Harryhausen wrote about his night school classes, and his models—always the models. ("Dressed the two 'stop motion men' in blue. They look nice. Also made belly for Stegosaurus."—March 15, 1939.) He worked on his paintings and his dinosaurs, and did puppet shows at his alma mater, Manual Arts.

And Ray Harryhausen saw lots of movies, including *Stagecoach*, *She*, and the one that started it all, *King Kong*, for the 31st time on May 21, at the Ritz. He once saw four movies in two days (*Dr. Jekyll & Mr. Hyde*, *Son of Frankenstein*, *All Quiet on the Western Front*, and *Things to Come*). His pal Bradbury frequently accompanied him, and he often dropped in on Bradbury at home.

Ackerman 1939

In 1939 Forry Ackerman had moved on from his father's hellish corporation to working in the movie business. It was not yet the Hollywood career he'd dreamed of. Initially he found work as a film projectionist, but later he got a job at the Academy of Motion Picture Arts and Sciences, after meeting an employee who was also a fan. It was not glamorous exactly: he was the "Chief Varitypist."

The VariTyper Composing Machine was a special typewriter that allowed its user hundreds of different fonts (including italics) and dozens of different languages by means of changing the carriage. It produced neat copy that could be sent directly to the printer. The VariTyper looked like a souped-up typewriter, with multiple discs, wheels, and brackets. According to an ad, it had more than 600 changeable types and "composes directly on stencils, spirit or gelatin masters. Work produced on Vari-typer looks like printing."[1]

It was routine office work, but not without its moments. One of his duties was to be backstage during the Academy Awards ceremony at the Coconut Grove, guarding the Oscars for *Gone With the Wind*.

The most significant event for young Forry in 1939 was the death of his beloved maternal grandfather, the man who sketched aliens for him as a boy and took him to so many grand movies. George Herbert Wyman died on August 1, 1939.

16

Futuria Fantasia, the Second Issue

Bradbury published the second issue of *Futuria Fantasia* in the fall of 1939. As with the first issue, he wrote most of the material under different names (Antony Corvais, Doug Rogers, Guy Amory). Contributing authors who weren't Bradbury were Henry Hasse with a poem as well as a column about the recent divisions in fandom, and Erick Freyor, who published an atheist piece called "God Busters." Bok contributed both the cover art and the interior, which included more nudes, such as the same bare-breasted girl that caused a stir on the cover of *Imagination!*. He also contributed a piece called "The Galapurred Forsendyk—A tale of the Indies."

Bradbury's "Fall" issue of *Futuria Fantasia* didn't come out until after Halloween, due to the typical production delays of running a mimeographed zine. ("One month ago Bradbury stenciled and printed the editorial to this second issue of FuFa, only to be delayed by various troubles, mostly typewriter and stencil scourges, until now."[1]) Most significantly, in issue #2 Bradbury published a story called "The Pendulum," which would later (after rewrites with Henry Hasse) be the first story he would be paid for.

Besides his own fictional pieces under fictional names, Bradbury also continued talking about what the fans were doing. In *FuFa* #2 he gave brief descriptions of some of the better-known names in fandom:

> Charlie Hornig: The dark horse who says neigh to every manuscript I write for him. Dark-haired, dark-eyed, dark-skinned fiend who deals from the bottom of the manuscript pile over at Science-Fiction. He has just learned to speak English during the past week and now he finds it much more fun picking out the manuscripts instead of leaping into a pile of them and bobbing up with one between his teeth…

Hornig was the former editor of *Wonder Stories.* In 1939 he was editing a magazine simply called *Science Fiction*, along with two companion publications, *Future Fiction* and *Science Fiction Quarterly*. As usual, Bradbury had a sense of humor about the fact that so far none of his submissions had been accepted.

"Morojo, short and sweet, commonly referred to as the VOICE OF MIDGE." Here, Bradbury references the fact that Morojo was largely responsible for editing *Voice of the Imagination*, Chapter 4's publishing organ.

"Forrest J Ackerman, dressed in future garb at convention, looking like a fugitive from a costume shop." This was in reference to the history that Ackerman had made at that most historic of events, the great granddaddy of all cons, the World Science Fiction Convention of 1939.

17

The First Worldcon, 1939

Both Forry Ackerman and Ray Bradbury attended what is considered to be the first major science fiction convention, The World Science Fiction Convention of 1939, often called simply Worldcon.

Between 1935 and 1938 there was a string of fan conferences, although some of these "conferences" really stretched the definition of the term. In June of 1935, a clique of Chicago fans met up with some fans in New York. In October of 1936, a contingent of fans from New York met with a group of fans in Philadelphia and decided to declare the event an official convention.[1] Really though, it was just a gathering. The boys toured Philly together and then met at a member's home.[2]

A solid case for the first national convention can be made for the conference in Leeds, England, on January 3, 1937, under the leadership of the Leeds Science Fiction League. Roughly 14 young men from across England attended, including Arthur C. Clarke.[3]

The British fan group called the Science Fiction Association organized conferences in April 1938 and May 1939, both of them in London. Back in America there would be a handful of conferences in Philadelphia and around the New York/New Jersey area between 1937 and 1939, attracting between 25 and 100 fans, organized by key players in fandom at the time, including Donald Wollheim, William Sykora, Charles D. Hornig, and Sam Moskowitz.[4] Each successive con approached something more like a traditional science fiction conference as we would recognize it today. The Second Eastern Science Fiction Convention on February 21, 1937, was attended by some of the top names in science fiction and had about 40 fans. Movies were screened, including a Buck Rogers cartoon and footage of some of Sykora's rocketry experiments.[5]

The First National Convention on May 29, 1938, in Newark, New Jersey, attracted more than 100 people and was the first to have special zines devoted just to the convention. It was also the first to have an auction of collector's memorabilia,[6] many of the items—mostly magazines—contributed by Forry Ackerman. There was a falling out between Ackerman and the organizer of the con, Sam Moskowitz. Ackerman had wanted half of the proceeds plus copies of convention fanzines that he could add to his collection. Because his correspondence was written in his garbled "Ackermanese," Moskowitz misunderstood his meaning and instead simply paid Forry with magazines. Moskowitz's confusion is understandable. Here is a quote from Ackerman regarding the mix-up; "If U disposed of my stuff at $3 and I got $1.50 & U the opportunity to sell me $1.50 worth of Ur stuff for Ur 'trouble' (fun)."[7] The First

Front, from left: Ray Bradbury, Leo P. Margulies. Back, from left: Manly Wade Wellman, Mort Weisinger, Erle Melvin Korshak. First World Science Fiction Convention, New York City, July 2, 1939 (photograph by Conrad H. Ruppert, from the collection of John L. Coker III).

National Convention also showed films, including *Aladdin and the Wonderful Lamp* and *The Lost World* (the latter cut short because most fans had already seen it). There was soon talk of a more ambitious convention, one that would attract fans nationwide. The result was the World Science Fiction Convention of 1939.

While it wasn't the first science fiction convention, Worldcon 1939 (as it is now known) set the basic formula for other cons that would follow. There was an auction of rare science fiction memorabilia (mostly original artwork from the pulps). There were celebrity guests, lectures, and discussions about science fiction. And while no one called it that at the time, this con also sparked the birth of cosplay.

18

Bradbury and Ackerman Arrive at Worldcon

By the time the bus pulled into Elizabeth, New Jersey, where 19-year-old Bradbury disembarked before making his way to New York for the first time in his life, the young man had endured a storm of emotions: giddiness, love, terror, and relief, all layered in his own sweat, as Greyhound had no air conditioning or toilets in 1939 and it was June.

Nevertheless, he was overjoyed to be taking this trip, and not just because he passed the hours speaking to a curvy young swimming instructor. He had read about the World Science Fiction Convention for months in the back pages of *Thrilling Wonder Stories* and other pulps, along with the amateur zines he was always reading and contributing to. He would be going to the largest science fiction convention in the world up to that point, almost 200 fans, writers, and artists in one spot. There would be dozens of top men in the field. Hoping against hope, he'd taken with him a portfolio of his stories and his ever-present typewriter. One never knew when inspiration might hit. While en route he somehow managed to type every day. Here are his thoughts after the first day: "The road stretches endlessly away. I can't help thinking how much sweat must have been worked out of hot hides making these miles of concrete—of the headache and creaking bones and sun-scarred faces that resulted."[1]

His good friend Forry Ackerman lent him the $50 (elsewhere Bradbury said it was $90) needed for a bus ticket plus a $5-a-week room at the local YMCA when he got to New York. Ackerman was still living rent-free and earning 85 cents an hour working for The Academy, so he had some extra income.

During the four-day sojourn the bus stopped every two to three hours and left quickly and without you if you weren't careful. Bradbury was shaving in a restaurant bathroom outside Denver when the bus took off, leaving him behind.[2] Frantic, the teen chased after to no avail. He was devastated. It wasn't so much that he missed his bus—he could catch the next one. It was that his typewriter and anthology of stories were on board, no copies anywhere. Luckily for the sake of science fiction literature, Greyhound recovered his stuff and everything was waiting for him in a locker when he disembarked in New Jersey. There Ray met up with pulp editor Charles D. Hornig. The pair took a ferry to Manhattan.

Ackerman Arrives

Ackerman took a train to New York, incredibly nervous. When it stopped in Chicago, he thought about turning back. He couldn't shake the notion that plenty of people there would know who he was, and that he might be asked to make a speech. One day he would make a living doing talks and making speeches, but 22-year-old Ackerman suffered from stage fright: "I thought, 'Oh my God, what if I'm in an audience and somebody notices me.' They might say, 'Ladies and gentleman, I believe it is Mr. Ackerman. Forrest, won't you stand?'"[3]

When he pulled into New York, about a half dozen fans were there to meet him. It was not the most welcoming of welcome committees. A smoking 15-year-old with a paunch stood among the crowd. He stepped up to Forry and snapped, "So you're the Forrest Ackerman who's been writing all of those ridiculous letters to the science fiction magazines." Then he punched Ackerman in the gut. It was Cyril Kornbluth. (Kornbluth was one of the "Excluded Six" not allowed to enter the convention. More on the "Exclusion Act" later.) Ackerman thought, *I came three thousand miles for this?*[4]

Ackerman's next move was to change into the costume his girlfriend had made. (Ackerman described the change as "like Clark Kent when he steps into the telephone booth."[5]) No one knew it at the time, but he and Myrtle Douglas were about to make history as the first cosplayers.

Ackerman would later say he wore a costume

The first cosplayers. Forrest J Ackerman (4SJ) and Myrtle R. Douglas (Morojo). Visitors from the Future. First World Science Fiction Convention, New York City, July 2, 1939 (photograph by Charles D. Hornig, from the collection of John L. Coker III).

because he had simply assumed everyone would: "It had never occurred to me that at a first World Science Fiction Convention everybody wouldn't come as future men from Frank R. Paul paintings, or as vampires or something."[6] Ackerman's costume of high boots, a long-sleeve yellow button-down with "4SJ" emblazoned on the chest, and a green cape[7] was based on the outfits from the H.G. Wells film *Things to Come*. The "futuricostume," as he would eventually call it, had been designed by Morojo, who herself attended Worldcon in a cape and a short red satin romper repurposed from a ball gown, cleverly designed so the cape could revert back into a gown. They walked the Manhattan streets standing out among a sea of gray suits and fedoras, capes billowing behind them. "Buck Rogers!" kids called out. "Flash Gordon!" Adults looked at the pair quizzically. More than one stopped them in the street and asked them what the hell they were doing. So it was for the first cosplayers.

Ackerman and Morojo eventually made their way across Manhattan to the one place where their space-age costumes wouldn't stand out quite as much, the World's Fair.

19

"I have seen the future!"
The 1939 World's Fair

The New York City World's Fair, in Flushing Meadows in Queens (a special train was set up just to whisk fairgoers), was the perfect backdrop for the first science fiction convention. At first the plan had been to actually have the con at the fair, but the admission fee of 75 cents was not in every fan's reach.[1] The centerpiece architecture of the fair was a 700-foot obelisk called the Trylon and a 200-foot globe known as the Perisphere, which stood next to each other and loomed large enough to literally become the combined symbol of the fair itself. A 65-foot statue of George Washington towered over Constitution Mall.

The era Gernsback and his followers had been predicting for decades was starting to bloom at the fair, and on display were marvels hitherto only suggested in the pulps. There was a virtual rocket ride to London, a 3-D movie showing a car assembled by invisible workers, even a cow-milking machine (the "Rotolactor"). Westinghouse built a giant robot called Elektriko that could walk, talk, and smoke a cigarette. After visiting Futurama, a sprawling diorama in which thousands of visitors coasted above a 36,000-square-foot model town consisting of mini-miles of miniature houses, skyscrapers, mountains, farms, roads, and General Motors cars (GM sponsored the shrunken city), the visitors were given a button that said "I have seen the future." Many felt they had.[2]

Most fascinating of all was television. Millions were awed by their first glimpse at the glowing sets on display. On April 20 RCA broadcast images of the Trylon and Perisphere to the few hundred sets scattered throughout New York.[3] Decades later writer David Kyle would recall visiting the fair with Julius Schwartz, and being awed when his friend's face, that of Mort Weisinger, was broadcast live on a glass screen.[4]

Many of the pleasures were much more earthly and attracted men for reasons unchanged since caveman days. Girls were on display everywhere. Oscar the Obscene Octopus wrestled a near-nude woman in a tank at a display called "Twenty Thousand Legs Under the Sea." Another attraction involved Olympian Eleanor Holm splashing in a pool with several other shapely swimmers in sync with a waltz.[5]

When President Roosevelt opened the fair on April 30, 1939, he declared that it was for all of mankind, but this was proving naively optimistic. Twenty-two countries were represented with pavilions,[6] many of which looked at one another askance, knowing they would be at war soon if they weren't already. The Soviet Union constructed a marble tower topped by a red star and worker with Lenin's creed: "The

Russian Revolution must in its final result lead to the victory of Socialism." Czechoslovakia erected a building that *Life* called a "brave memorial to a vanished nation."[7] By the time the fair wrapped up in 1940, dozens of other nations suffered the same fate as their Czech brother, enslaved under the heels of Nazi boots and/or Stalin's Red Army. When the fair opened for its second season in 1940, 10 nations did not return to their pavilions at the Lagoon of Nations, bordered by the increasingly ironic Court of Peace.[8] The metal and lumber that went into the fair would be carted off and sold for scrap, to be turned into munitions for the war effort.

Even at the fair, where participants were encouraged to wear traditional outfits of their native countries, Ackerman and Morojo stood out. At one stage there was a microphone where people from other nations were asked to record a greeting in their native language. The man of the future stepped up to the microphone and greeted the world in Esperanto, the language of tomorrow. Ackerman had gotten over his shyness. "As long as I was in this futuristic costume I had enough nerve to perform."[9]

After thankfully retrieving his stuff from his locker and riding the ferry with Hornig to Manhattan, Ray Bradbury checked into the Sloane House YMCA.[10] (He would return to this particular YMCA in 1949. Still broke, he stayed there while in town to meet with Walter Bradbury [no relation] of Doubleday about his upcoming *Martian Chronicles* project. Ray typed up an outline for *Martian Chronicles* at the Y.) He toured the World's Fair with Julius Schwartz, Charles D. Hornig, and Conrad Ruppert, the printer who had lent much of his talent to early fanzines.[11] His meeting with Julius Schwartz would prove crucial.

Julius Schwartz was not yet 25 but already a force in the fledgling world of early science fiction. Together, Schwartz and his boyhood pal Mort Weisinger founded the first literary agency representing science fiction, with the very cool name of Solar Sales Service. Schwartz also edited the highly respected zine *Fantasy Magazine*. This was after he helped start one of the earliest science fiction zines, *The Time Traveller*, which he edited along with Weisinger, Allen Glasser, and Milwaukee fictioneer Ray A. Palmer, with contributions from Forry Ackerman. Schwartz would go on to edit All-American Comics, which in time became DC Comics, where he was largely credited with saving Batman, Superman, and Wonder Woman, whose sales had slipped after the war. He also resurrected the Green Lantern, the Flash, and other Golden Age characters who had been canceled. One of the heroes he brought back was called The Atom, whose alter ego he named after his good friend, the pint-sized Ray A. Palmer.

Schwartz was not interested in Bradbury or his work. Ray's early writing lacked promise, so Schwartz politely told the the young man truthfully that he only represented writers who had already published professionally. Bradbury persisted, and Schwartz eventually agreed to at least let the fledgling writer send him stories. He sensed, as did so many others in Bradbury's world, that while he may not have been a gifted writer, Ray was willing to make up for lack of talent with hard work and hone his craft. "In due time this young kid got a hold of me and expressed the desire to become a writer," Schwartz recalled. "I said, 'Yes, yes, my boy, keep writing, send me your stories.' I did it because he was a friend of Forry. So sure enough, I kept getting stories and stories.They weren't too good but they started to improve."[12]

Sometimes, according to Schwartz, Bradbury was so bankrupt he couldn't even afford the postage to send stories.

Throughout his time in Manhattan, Ray Bradbury was his usual obnoxious self. He almost got kicked out of a hamburger joint for making his signature Ghoul's Broth, once again mixing ketchup with water and other ingredients to make a free soup, his way of eating in a restaurant without paying. He sang so loudly while riding a boat in Central Park that "authorities intervened."[13] Bradbury also made it a point to go to New York's natural history museum and look at the dinosaurs.

On the Friday before the convention, he met John W. Campbell, Jr., of *Astounding Science Fiction* fame, although this encounter would not be as fruitful as his meeting with Schwartz. As the editor of *Astounding*, Campbell was something of a kingmaker in the Golden Age of science fiction, the one man responsible for discovering Isaac Asimov, L. Ron Hubbard, and Robert A. Heinlein, among others. Yet Ray Bradbury would succeed more in spite of, rather than because of, Campbell.

Years later, even after Bradbury was somewhat established as a science fiction writer, Campbell passed on stories that would eventually become part of the Bradbury canon, including "Zero Hour," "Mars is Heaven," and "The Million Year Picnic."[14] As someone who had attended MIT and Duke, Campbell preferred writers with more of a science education, like Heinlein, graduate of the Naval Academy who served on one of the first aircraft carriers, and Asimov, who began college at 15 and graduated with a degree in chemistry. Bradbury had no education past public high school. Campbell may have thought what many have since said about Bradbury, that he was more of an emotional, sentimental writer, opinions Bradbury himself wouldn't necessarily argue with. (To quote Bradbury, "My writing is completely emotional and immediate."[15])

Bradbury sold two pieces to the Probability Zero department, a section of *Astounding* that Campbell set up specifically for stories with zero chance of coming true. Scientifically inaccurate flights of fancy, in other words. Both of Bradbury's submissions won first place in the Analytical Laboratory poll, a poll of *Astounding* readers in which the stories were ranked by popular opinion.[16]

Still, Campbell continued to pass on Bradbury, even as the young writer's name began popping up on the covers of other pulps. Campbell believed that science fiction could solve real, practical problems of the world, and used the pages of his magazine to suggest methods to beat back the Axis. Bradbury, on the other hand, was a dreamer, a boy who sent men to Mars, Venus, and beyond our solar system, without giving much thought to how this could be. Whatever the reason, as Ackerman once quipped, "Campbell seems to be allergic to him and he [Bradbury] has not appeared in asf [*Astounding Science Fiction*] in ten years!"[17] In a short piece published in the fanzine *The Alchemist*, Bradbury playfully shot at Campbell's rejecting of him so many times: "Dear Mr. C, I have read your rejection.... I must reject your masterfully written rejection."[18]

Bradbury also met Donald A. Wollheim and Frederik Pohl, but not in the actual hall where the convention was held. These two young men would not be allowed into the convention.

20

Worldcon, Day One, July 2, 1939

The Futurians versus New Fandom

Planning the convention had not been a pretty process. Two rival factions fought for control: the Futurians, led by Donald A. Wollheim and John Michel, and New Fandom, a group led by William Sykora and Samuel Moskowitz. The key difference was politics. The Futurians, as outlined in Chapter 7, believed science fiction should be a movement to create a better, more just world, their beliefs largely rooted in socialism. New Fandom simply wanted science fiction to be science fiction, and to stay out of politics.

Initially, the Futurians were charged with running the convention, but they lost control of the planning to New Fandom. The Futurians were an outspoken group of about 20 boys who had alienated many. (William Sykora had actually been one of them, and had even been kicked out of the Science Fiction League, along with Michel and Wollheim. But then Sykora had a dispute with Wollheim and defected.) Damon Knight, a former Futurian himself, defined the Futurians as "more like an extended family than like an organization ... a strong sense of us-against-them."[1] The Futurian coat of arms was a screw over the Latin inscription "Omnes qui non Futurianes sunt" (all who are not Futurians).

Years earlier, Futurian leader Donald Wollheim had circulated an open letter criticizing *Astounding* editor John W. Campbell for publishing Thomas McClary's story "Three Thousand Years," calling it "fascist" and an "outrage."[2] Wollheim and other Futurians continued to rail against Hugo Gernsback, initially because Gernsback had been slow to pay Wollheim and Michel for stories upon acceptance. Wollheim, Michel, and other authors successfully sued for payment, but the Futurians continued to be outspoken critics of Gernsback,[3] often attacking him and the Science Fiction League (an organization begun solely to sell magazines, they claimed) in the pages of different fanzines.

Wollheim was also no friend of Ackerman's. He wrote this about Ackerman in the zine *Aroturus*: "He doesn't know it, but when his name is mentioned in stf-circles, it causes considerable snickers and suppressedlaughter. This obstreperous author-pester, silly-letter writer, and what-have-you, is now going off half-baked onEsperanto and Universal Languages." Ackerman fired off an angry letter, which Wollheim replied to, and that is where Ackerman decided to leave it. He would eventually work with Wollheim on future projects, evidently forgiving.

The Futurians also sometimes literally attacked other fan groups. In 1936 Charles D. Hornig (someone else they didn't like) was presiding over a League meeting when Wollheim and a few friends stormed in and actually shoved Hornig aside, then railed against Gernsback's *Wonder Stories*. Sam Moskowitz summed up the affair in his book, *The Immortal Storm: A History of Science Fiction Fandom*:

> Suddenly the clumping of many shoes was heard, and in burst Sykora and Wollheim at the head of eight other youths ... recruited from the streets for rough action if necessary. Sykora walked up to Julius Schwartz, a member of the audience, and shook a fist under his nose as a gesture of defiance.... Then with the aid of his comrades he chased Hornig from the platform. Producing a gavel of his own Sykora proceeded to call the meeting to order in the name of the New York branch of the International Scientific Association.... Wollheim then ascended the platform and vividly outlined his grievances with Wonder Stories....[4]

Moskowitz's description needs to be taken in context; he and the Futurians were not friends. But Moskowitz was hardly their only adversary. Donald A. Wollheim and John B. Michel were eventually thrown out of the league for disrupting chapter meetings. "Every time they organized an SFL [Science Fiction League] chapter in New York, we would attend its meetings and subvert them into joining the International Scientific Association [a Futurian group]," Wollheim would later brag. "We ate up three or four Science Fiction League chapters."[5] In 1941, perhaps hoping to bury the hatchet, the Queens Science Fiction League invited the Futurians to a meeting in January. The result was a shoving match and fight that got the league thrown out of the building, the building superintendent commenting that "this thing has happened before. I told them what would happen if it occurred again."[6]

New Fandom, meanwhile, had successfully organized a couple of conferences without incident and would be granted control of the first World Science Fiction Convention. But the Futurians were not done yet.

The Exclusion Act

The World Science Fiction Convention took place on the fourth floor of Caravan Hall on East 59th Street, the walls festooned with original pulp art. When it came time to open the doors on July 2, 1939, Moskowitz and his boys, William Sykora and James Taurasi (another of the event organizers), were ready and waiting. They anticipated the Futurians attempting to enter and wreak havoc, and they wanted to cut them off at the pass. When the Futurians arrived, Taurasi even went as far as to call the police, though the officers took no action. Six Futurians were denied entry by Moskowitz and his New Fandom allies. Moskowitz would always claim that he was willing to allow the Futurians entry as long as they promised to behave, and that Wollheim, Michel, and the rest of the "Excluded Six" (Frederik Pohl, Robert W. Lowndes, Jack Gillespie, and Cyril Kornbluth[7]) had declined to make such a promise. Those excluded claimed no offer was ever made. Futurian Isaac Asimov had supposedly been allowed to enter after promising not to cause any trouble. Asimov would always say he remembered no such thing and that he simply walked in. Isaac Asimov would go on to be the most famous Futurian, though there is some debate about whether he was really one of them. In Nevala-Lee's excellent book about John W. Campbell, Jr., *Astounding*, he argues that the Futurians were simply the group that Asimov fell in with and that he "might have been equally pleased to have stumbled into the ranks of their rivals."

Moskowitz's decision to deny entry was largely influenced by the discovery in the hall of a leaflet called "Warning! Beware the Dictatorship!" that referred to New Fandom as "ruthless scoundrels." Wollheim claimed to know nothing about it. It turned out he was telling the truth; the pamphlet had been printed by David A. Kyle, a Futurian who had been allowed entry after promising to behave. He would go on to enjoy the entire conference, not admitting to his sins until decades later.

The Futurians would set up camp in an automat cafeteria across the street from Caravan Hall, eventually meeting most of the attendees. While they may have been excluded from the conference, they were not barred from the world of science fiction. Former Futurian Damon Knight wrote in his memoir, *The Futurians*: "Out of this little group came ten novelists, a publisher, two literary agents, four anthologies, and five editors (with some overlapping roles)" (parentheses in original, from the foreword). Their exclusion actually won them sympathy in the greater fan community, with many feeling that Moskowitz had gone too far. Wollheim soon after became the editor of both *Cosmic Stories* and *Stirring Science Stories*, where he published works by his fellow Futurians. Pohl would go onto edit *Super Science Stories* and *Astonishing Stories*, at age 19 no less. Donald Wollheim later edited the anthology called *The Pocket Book of Science-Fiction*, considered the first science fiction pocket book.

But on July 2, Moskowitz filled the door like the 200-pound ex-boxer he was, to bar the Futurians entry. Bradbury, Ackerman, and the rest of the attendees had to awkwardly file past. It was time for the convention to begin.

The doors opened at 10 a.m.; the official kickoff was at two in the afternoon. Sam Moskowitz gave the welcome address, followed by speeches by prominent men of science fiction, including John W. Campbell, Jr., and Mort Weisinger. The convention screened the movie *Metropolis*. Fan responses to the classic were mixed. Asimov hated it. Moskowitz found the acting "antiquated" and unintentionally funny at times, but acknowledged the movie was "the most ambitious of pre-talky efforts."[8] The print used was only two hours long, not long enough for Ackerman and other diehard fans (the original was 153 minutes). According to his own special zine devoted to *Metropolis*, Ackerman brought some 150 stills with him to the conference. In the publicity leading up to the convention, Moskowitz was quick to point out that the German movie had been bought from an American firm and "not one pfennig will go to the Vaterland," an important distinction for the many Jews in early fandom.[9]

That evening they held the official Science Fiction Auction, consisting primarily of original manuscripts, hard-to-find books and fanzines, and art from the pulps, many of them painted by the guest of honor himself, Frank Rudolph Paul.

Frank R. Paul

One for Paul, and Paul for one!
—Ackerman letter to *Thrilling Wonder Stories*, October 1936

What made *Amazing Stories* stand out from the hundreds of other pulps on the magazine rack was the artwork. These bright and colorful surreal works, bought for a quarter and displayed with cigarettes and gum, would plant acorns in the minds of many future science fiction greats. These images all came from one man. Pulps were judged by their covers, and there was no better cover artist than the Austrian-Hungarian man born as Franz Rudolphe Paul.

Forry Ackerman, Ray Bradbury, Isaac Asimov, and Arthur C. Clarke all remembered their first covers of *Amazing Stories*. For Clarke living in Somerset, England, it was the very first edition, depicting a scene from the Jules Verne story "Off on a Comet," showing humans ice-skating happily on a distant frozen landscape, the ringed planet Saturn looming on the horizon. Asimov picked up this same first edition in 1926, for sale at his dad's candy store. Mr. Judah Asimov told his son that those magazines were "for bums," but the boy eagerly anticipated *Amazing*'s arrival every month, always sure to handle the merchandise carefully. (Asimov's dad's disregard for *Amazing Stories* is suspect because, as Isaac pointed out, his father read that trashy magazine as well. His Russian father explained he only read it to practice his English.) For Ackerman it was the October 1926 issue, showing a pair of bug-like creatures towering over a human in ragged clothing, the survivor of space shipwreck, from A. Hyatt Verrill's "Beyond the Pole." For Bradbury it was an issue being read by one of his grandmother's boarders in Waukegan, Illinois, the fall 1928 *Amazing Stories Quarterly*, showing a giant ant attacking a black explorer, an illustration for A. Hyatt Verrill's "The World of the Giant Ants."[10] Bradbury spoke for many fans of his generation when he summed up Paul's works: "You want to live inside them. You want to go inside the covers and never come out of those great architectures."[11]

Frank R. Paul was born in Austria-Hungary in 1884 and studied art in Vienna, Paris, and London, focusing on drafting and mechanical drawing, skills he would put to good use as a pulp artist creating not-yet-invented machines and futuristic cities. He moved to America as a young man, first to live with a sister in San Francisco. Then he moved to New York, where he met fellow German-speaking immigrant Hugo Gernsback. The two men soon hit it off. Gernsback hired Paul on a freelance basis to do technical illustrations for his early publications, including *Modern Electrics* and *Electrical Experimenter*. Paul also did cover art for various issues of Gernsback's Education Library, how-to booklets on various aspects of radio and early television. His work depicted men working on radios under such titles as *How to Read Radio Diagrams* and *How to Make the Most Popular All Wave 1 and 2 Tube Receivers*. The most interesting work from this time is his cover illustration for the summer 1927 publication *All About Television*, depicting a family watching a football game on an oval-shaped living room TV set, a prescient drawing over 20 years ahead of its time. He would go on to do the first issue of *Amazing Stories*, and hundreds of following issues of Gernsback publications. He was a machine, cranking out not just the covers but also the black and white interiors. Fan mail poured in praising Paul and begging to buy the original works. The powers that be at *Amazing* literally gave away these beauties or sold them for a fraction of what they would be worth. The handful of Paul originals still in existence now sell for tens of thousands of dollars.

Paul genuinely enjoyed the work. When Gernsback lost *Amazing Stories*, Paul did most of the cover and interior art for the variety of *Wonder* publications Gernsback turned to next. He would also lend his talents to the budding comic book industry just before the war, illustrating *Marvel Comics #1*, which introduced the Human Torch among other heroes and was the first comic book from Timely Comics, later known as Marvel Comics.

Frank R. Paul also found time to raise three girls and a boy, become a skilled mandolin and violin player, design actual buildings, and compose music. He seemingly never stopped.

In the world of Frank R. Paul, buildings stretch into infinity, giant buzzsaws slice planes in half, and Earthlings take to the skies in all sorts of contraptions. He put his technical background to good use and focused on machines more than men. In an era when newsstands hawked hundreds of covers, his brilliant blues and yellows grabbed the customer's attention. (Paul may have bought into the idea that certain colors sold on the magazine rack better than others. According to Fred Cook, in his essay "The Cover Artists and Their Publishers" [published in the book *Pulp Art* by Robert Lesser], Harry Steeger, head of Popular Publications, believed that yellow and red attracted male eyes, while blue and green attracted women. He was known to set up a newsstand in his office so he could see how his own magazines looked on the racks.) When people refer to a "classic science fiction" look, they are (often unknowingly) talking about Frank R. Paul.

The Literal Art of Science Fiction

At the first Worldcon, organizers sold works of Frank R. Paul, Virgil Finlay, and other pulp artists, with Moskowitz as the chief auctioneer. These works would go for a fraction of their worth, but it was one of the first times these pieces were even seen as anything worth keeping.

The process of producing pulp magazine art before the war was straightforward enough. The artist created a color painting, or, if it was an interior illustration, a black and white ink drawing. Then a photographer snapped an image and sent the print off for color separation. Every issue of every pulp birthed easily a dozen original works of art. What to do with them?

Most were thrown out. It's estimated that only about one percent—a few hundred—of the roughly 50,000 cover paintings of the pulp era still exist.[12] Sometimes the artists painted over an original canvas to do a fresh cover for someone else. The artists, many of them classically trained and working to pay the rent, often felt indifferent and mildly ashamed of what they were doing. In 1961, when Condé Nast bought pulp publisher Street & Smith, they found themselves with hundreds of cover paintings on their hands. Unable to sell or even give away the works, not to the employees, not even to the artists themselves, they wound up trashing them.[13]

The history of pulp art is full of such heartbreaking losses. When cover artist John Newton Howitt died, his wife burned his pulp paintings because she wanted him to be remembered as an "artist."[14] Collector and dealer Charles G. Martignette once got a phone call from an elderly woman interested in selling him a few Western paintings created as cover art. Her husband rescued them from a couple of workers in the basement of the building where the Street & Smith office was located. Her husband had an office in the same building and had reason to go into the basement, where he saw two men hurling paintings into the furnace. The men told him he could take whatever he wanted. A reader of the pulps, he went home that day with works by the likes of Tom Lovell, Walter Baumhofer, H.J. Ward, and Harry Parkhurst.[15] Popular Publications kept all of their cover paintings in their attic and periodically asked artists to clean house and take what they wanted. Artists often did not want all, or even any, of their creations. One anecdote goes that artist Norman Saunders came to fetch his own paintings but instead left with several of Walter Baumhofer's, an artist he had always admired. Baumhofer had taken what he wanted of his own repertoire and left the rest behind.

Rumor has it that John Newton Howitt, one of the best in the business, destroyed hundreds of his own paintings in a puritan rage of hatred for how he earned a living. The best proof of this urban legend is that almost none of his originals have been found, although that is shoddy evidence, since hardly any original pulp art is left anyway.

More science fiction and fantasy art survives than from any other pulp genre, thanks to the fact that the fans were the first to see value in these works. The lovers of the fantastic collected art more than readers of crime, romance, or Westerns did.

Any fan before World War II could have gotten his hands on an original Paul or Finlay without too much trouble. They could buy original artwork for less than a couple of bucks, and could frequently get something for free. When a group of Chicago fans went to New York to meet up with editor Charles D. Hornig, Hornig allowed each of the Chicago boys to go home with one original Paul painting.[16]

Giving away original works by artists like Paul, Virgil Finlay, and H.W. Wesso was a common practice during the Gernsback era. In the February 1940 issue of *Thrilling Wonder Stories*, it was announced that a reader would be awarded an original Paul cover illustration by winning the Scientific Treasure Hunt, i.e., by finding the most chemical elements mentioned in that particular issue. Runners-up got black and white illustrations by artists Virgil Finlay and H.W. Wesso. Sometimes, readers of *Thrilling Wonder* could win original Paul pen and ink drawings by writing letters that answered the question "What can I do to promote science fiction?"[17]

Other times, fans like Ackerman simply wrote a letter requesting a certain original painting or drawing. At the World Science Fiction convention in '46, Ackerman fell ill and had to leave early. He was gifted a Paul painting as a consolation.[18] By the time he was in his early twenties, *Thrilling Wonder* reported that Ackerman had a collection of roughly 25 paintings (in their weird words, "1/4 of 100"). He and other members of Chapter 4 frequently raffled art or sold pieces to one another at their parties and meetings to raise funds. In issue #27 of *Shangri-L'Affaires*, Chapter 4 offered a sort of eBay-in-print auction, where they listed original pulp art they were willing to sell and readers could mail in bids. Work from lesser-known artists started at 25 cents. A watercolor by Paul and signed by both Paul and Ray Palmer began at $1.50; the highest opening bids were for original works by Finlay and also Roy Hunt, each at $5. In 1943, a group of LASFS members auctioned paintings to one another, with someone paying a whopping $26 for a Virgil Finlay. Others were raffled off.[19] Another fanzine, *Ad Astra*, summed up a contest Ray Bradbury and Morojo participated in. Members of Chapter 4 had to listen to sound discs of fantastic films (*The Invisible Man*, *Old Dark House*, etc.) and guess their titles. The winners had their pick of "Original illustrations—by Krupa, Binder & Orban as prizes.... Morojo got all ryt & pickt the illustration from 'World Reborn' as her reward, Bradbury was in

2d place & took 'When the Half-Gods Go,' leaving a panel-pic from an early New Amazing for 'Franklyn Brady."[20] Robert Heinlein finished dead last and was awarded the "booby prize," an original drawing done by Bradbury. Members of Chapter 4 often gifted each other original pulp art for Christmas.

When fans Allen Class and Dale Hart decided to visit editor Ray Palmer at the offices of *Amazing Stories* after the '41 Worldcon, Palmer gave them free copies of the magazine and their "choice of a color painting."[21]

Palmer was particularly generous with these artworks. He gave away hundreds of them at the Second Worldcon in Chicago (see Chapter 27). Science fiction publisher Erle M. Korshak was in the office of Ray Palmer when he feasted his eyes on an *Amazing Stories* cover by J. Allen St. John that featured John Carter and the City of the Mummies.

"You like it?" Ray asked.

"I love it!" Erle replied.

"You can have it."

Korshak's son Stephen slept in a bedroom decorated by that painting, later valued at $75,000.[22] The Korshaks garnered one of the largest collections of pulp art, along with Sam Moskowitz, collector and author Robert Lesser, and Forry Ackerman. The Korshak collection still exists. This author was lucky enough to see the display at the Worldcon in Chicago in 2022.

The first auction at the first Worldcon was not exactly a smashing success; there weren't always buyers, so some items wound up being sold in bundles. The Depression-era fans found $10, $5, even $2.50 too much. Bradbury successfully bid on a few items in spite of his meager funds.[23] Arguably he paid too much, since unsold paintings were tossed out into the audience, like so many posters at a concert. The most paid for any one item was $3 for an *Amazing Stories* cover; the least was a nickel for a Buck Rogers comic book.[24] Besides art, another collectible to hit the auction block was a copy of Stanley Weinbaum's memorial book *Dawn of Flame*, which went for $2.50 (these now retail for about $3,500). Ever the businessman, Ackerman convinced the original buyer to sell Weinbaum's anthology to him for $2.75.[25] The auction at the first World Science Fiction Convention netted all of $65.[26]

21

Worldcon, Monday, July 3, and Tuesday, July 4

The second day of Worldcon kicked off with a reading of the minutes from the first day. Moskowitz gave a second lecture, "The Future of the Fan World," followed by a speech by Sykora. Next there was a documentary called *Seeing the Universe*. In his description of the film, Moskowitz referred to it as simply the greatest documentary ever made: "It started with the sun, and then the planets, one by one, from Mercury to Pluto, including asteroids and all important moons."[1] The film was followed by a variety of talks and discussions and the second day of the auction—so many items were still for sale that the auction spilled into the next day. Moskowitz insisted the auction was a success since everything sold, although he admitted that "originals were offered in sets of 6, 8, and 12 in order to assure a complete sell out."[2]

That night they held the fan banquet in honor of pulp artist Frank R. Paul, who gave a speech called "The Spirit of Youth." The evening ended with a speech from Willy Ley, the writer and rocket scientist who defected rather than work for Hitler. Ackerman attended the banquet at the Wyndham restaurant. Ray wasn't able to go as Forry couldn't quite spare the one dollar the dinner cost (most fans couldn't—only about 28 attended). Other reports have Ray simply waiting in the back of the restaurant, attending without paying in typical Bradbury fashion, sitting next to Paul's wife.[3] After the formalities Bradbury personally met Willy Ley and Frank R. Paul, the man whose art first inspired him in Waukegan at his grandma's house.

The following day the highlight of July 4 was a softball game that Bradbury refereed between the Queen's Science Fiction Society (the "Queen's Cometeers") and the Philadelphia S-F Society (the "PSFS Panthers"). None of the fans being particularly good athletes, the score wound up being 23–11 in favor of the Cometeers.[4] They were so inept that only one "player," Art Widner, managed to hit a home run. He didn't knock it out of the park or even the infield, but the fans manning the bases fielded so poorly that he ran all the way home. Will Sykora filmed the entire game. Later, Bradbury piled into a car with other fans and headed to Coney Island. Bradbury ended the night by attending the World's Fair and watching the July 4 fireworks outside the Russian pavilion.[5] He wept as he saw the rockets explode. He had thoroughly enjoyed his day in the World of the Future, but the pyrotechnics reminded him that the planet was at war, and this beautiful world would not be for long.

22

Worldcon, the Aftermath

Bradbury and Ackerman lingered for about a week after the con, relaxing, going to the movies and Coney Island, passing time with friends, and making key connections.[1]

For a couple of days (July 7 and July 8) Bradbury, Ackerman, and Morojo, along with Chicago fans Mark Reinsberg and Erle M. Korshak, toured the city together, seeing the offices of some of the best-known magazines in the business. Ackerman, older than his friends and having been in touch with various editors for years, had been able to arrange these visits. They called on *American Weekly* editor A. Merritt, who introduced them to pulp artist Virgil Finlay. They dropped in on Mort Weisinger at the combined office of *Thrilling Wonder Stories* and *Startling Stories*. Weisinger invited them to his home that weekend, a gathering that included Charles D. Hornig, Robert Madle, Julius Schwartz, and Ross Rocklynne, along with convention organizers James V. Taurasi and Will Sykora. They also paid a visit to the office of *Marvel Science Stories*. One of the editors there offered an original Paul painting to whichever of the visiting fans made the best pitch for it. Ackerman and Bradbury desperately pleaded their case to no avail. The six fans present wound up drawing straws. Both Bradbury and Ackerman offered to buy the painting from the lucky winner, Donald Wollheim, who declined and took the masterpiece home.[2]

Next it was on to *Weird Tales* and its editor, Farnsworth Wright. Bradbury showed Wright the paintings Bok had sent ahead of time to the Sloan House YMCA, where the future writer was staying. Wright's wife Marjorie was in on the meeting, a woman rumored to have key sway over her husband's decisions (Farnsworth was also racked with Parkinson's and would resign a year later). She remembered Bradbury; he'd submitted poetry to *Weird Tales*, which they rejected.[3] They were still not sold on Bradbury's talent but agreed to buy some of Bok's work and told Bradbury his friend had a job in New York.

On the following Monday, Hornig and Rocklynne sat in Central Park with Bradbury, critiqued his writing, and felt nothing was worthy of the pulps. Bradbury wasn't disappointed—he still had made vital connections.

Going Home—July 12

Bradbury left New York and took the scenic route going back to LA. He swung through his hometown of Waukegan to see his old haunts and friends, buying a copy of Steinbeck's *Grapes of Wrath* from a cigar store. He read Steinbeck's classic all the way to Seattle on the bus, where he returned Bok's portfolio. Bok was now in Seattle and working as an artist for the local WPA, but he wouldn't be there for long. Bradbury told Bok the good news, that he had been hired by *Weird Tales*. Ray hadn't had the funds to send a wire or telephone; this was the first Bok heard that he was now a professional pulp artist.

Bradbury was overjoyed for his friend, as if the accomplishment were his own. Never the jealous type, he continued to promote Bok in the pages of the pulps via fan letters. Here is an example, from the January 1941 issue of *Fantastic Novels*:

> But if you asked me who wants Hannes Bok in Fantastic Novels, I would be the one of the first to exclaim all of we readers would like to see Bok doing more work.... In case you haven't discovered what this letter is about by now, I guess I might as well add his name once again. Boy, do I like Hannes Bok's work! Don't lose him! Use him![4]

Bradbury was not averse to self-promotion; he signed off as the editor of *Futuria Fantasia*. Bradbury jumpstarted one of the better-known careers of pulp art, albeit one laced with tragedy.

Bok's name (his birth name was Wayne Woodard) was derived from the composer he admired most, Johann Sebastian Bach (Hannes Bok pronounced his first name "Hahn-es"). Starting in 1934 he began publishing as an amateur, his opus beingthe cover art of the book version of *Cosmos*, a Round Robin series that initially appeared in issues of *Fantasy Magazine* before being separately bound as a book in 1934 (a collection of different writers contributed a chapter each, includingE.E. "Doc" Smith and John W. Campbell, Jr.). He next illustrated Emil Petaja's mimeographed chapbook *Brief Candle*. He would room with Emil when both moved to LA.

Bok's works were surreal, he himself explaining that he set out to depict not what's factual but imagining what could be. Unlike Paul's world of sharp edges and magnificent machines, Bok depicted satanic figures and pixies made up of soft tones. The largest difference between Paul and Bok, however, was that while Paul could easily whip out a cover painting a week, Bok took weeks or even months on a single project.

Bok was a purist, insisting on reading at least one of (sometimes, all of) the stories of whatever magazine he'd been commissioned to paint the cover for so that his work would correspond to one of the plots inside. This may sound like common sense but was not the standard practice of the time. In fact, it wasn't uncommon for the cover painting to have nothing to do with the interior content. Sometimes, pulp editors would even make a contest of writers submitting stories to go with the painting. However talented an artist was, he (sometimes she) only got paid about $5 to $50 per work, just as authors got paid one or two pennies per word. Asimov, Bradbury, and Heinlein may have done some of their greatest work in the pulps but initially made little from these efforts. According to Harry Warner, Jr.'s book *All Our Yesterdays*, which details fandom in the 1940s, the average full-time writer made about $3,000 per year in 1950, less than the average elevator operator. The same rule applied to pulp artists as to writers: it was fine to be talented, but to make money you had to be *prolific*. Damon Knight recalled in his memoir *The Futurians* being paid $5 for a single page drawing and $10 for a spread in such magazines as *Weird Tales*.[5] At these low rates, there simply wasn't time to read everything. Paul was said to have his daughters read a story out loud to him while he was working on a piece for another story, to maximize his time.

Bok had plenty of skill but was not known for great output. In a letter to science fiction editor August Derleth, Bok vented:

> It takes me at least a week to make a simple drawing—often up to 10 or 14 days for a black & white pulp illustration. Currently I'm going nuts doing a cover design for MAGAZINE OF FANTASY AND SCIENCE FICTION—have worked on it (in color) 17 days and the end is still not in sight! By the time it's finished, I'll receive about 70 cents per work hour on it....[6]

In another letter to Derleth, he complained, "I still don't feel like doing pulps at $5 per." The date of this letter is hard to discern. He sent the letter on stationery from something called the Aetna Barber Supply Corp., and on the paper was a line for the year, "193_," where the letter writer was supposed to put in the last digit to complete the date. Bok crossed out the "193" totally and penciled in "1940's." This author could only discern that the letter was written on September 13, sometime in the 1940s. His need to use free, outdated stationery spoke to how destitute he was. "I haven't been so broke, so willowy-thin, since I first hit New York!"[7] Hannes Bok wrote in another letter to Derleth. He was so cash-strapped that he often corresponded via penny postcards, sometimes using three or four mailed separately to combine into one letter.

In a letter written in 1963, Bok complained bitterly about fans dropping by day and night, so much so that neighbors though he was running a "dope den." These fans expected him to gift them a painting for free, which he refused to do, because "since I've never earned enough to save-up a nest egg or emergency fund … I can't afford to risk a long-term investment of a painting." He would die alone at age 50 in 1964, evidently of a heart attack, surrounded by the art that earned him a reputation but not much else. The police estimated he'd been dead for days. It was only because of a friend that his works were not thrown out by the building super.[8]

Decades later, Bradbury wrote the introduction to a coffee table book devoted to Bok, *A Hannes Bok Treasury*, where the writer claimed to own "dozens of his sketches, and a half dozen of his tempera paintings." Bradbury said he "would have wished for Hannes the same fame that came to another close friend, Ray Harryhausen," an allusion to the sad turn that Bok's life took.

23

Back to LA

All told, Worldcon was a success, in spite of the controversy and the fact that it didn't make much money, having only cleared about $50.[1] It set the tone for every con to follow. It also helped promote fandom to the wider world. *Time* magazine wrote an article about the con, where it referred to the gathering as the "jitterbugs of the pulp magazines."[2] It was the most publicity science fiction fans had ever received. Many in fandom found the article condescending and insulting, but it was the beginning of bringing this tight-knit group into the wider world. (To quote *Time* at length: "Scientifiction's fans, mostly boys of 16 to 20, are the jitterbugs of the pulp magazine field. Many keep every issue, and a copy of the magazine's first issue often fetches $25 from collectors. Publishers soon discovered another odd fact about their readers: They are exceptionally articulate.")

Fanzines came out with special Worldcon issues, outlining the events and the fan personalities present. The most extensive coverage came from *New Fandom*, a zine edited by Sam Moskowitz, who also organized the event. Never one for humility, Moskowitz described the first World Science Fiction Convention as "the greatest scientifiction event of the year" and peppered his summary with lots of "great," "extraordinary," and "prominent," with more than one paragraph ending with an exclamation point.He began his summary with this not-so-humble opening: "We will do away with the self-glorification and launch ourselves directly into an account of the greatest convention of all time." He went on to write, "And hardly a one did not come away with the remark that it was the greatest event they had ever witnessed. They were in veritable ecstasy throughout the entire affair."[3] Moskowitz did acknowledge that "there was a little trouble at first when some communists attempted to break in with a stack of communistic and anti-convention booklets. It was finally necessary to call the police."[4]

Frederik Pohl, one of the Excluded Six, decades later made this dry remark: "It was a gala affair, so I am told."[5]

When he was done with the scenic route back home, Bradbury soon began contacting the connections he'd made at Worldcon. Shortly after the debacle of the Exclusion Act, the exiles moved up quickly, and Bradbury hoped to take advantage of his recent acquaintance with them. In August of 1939 he wrote Frederik Pohl, who agreed to represent Bradbury as a literary agent,[6] but the partnership bore no fruit. In 1940 Pohl became the editor of both *Astonishing Stories* and *Super Science Stories*, but he refused Bradbury's submissions on the grounds that they were stories Bradbury had already published in *Futuria Fantasia*. Bradbury pleaded with Pohl—fewer than 100 copies of any individual issue of his zine had been printed, after all—but Pohl refused. Bradbury had no better luck with Wollheim when that Futurian became the editor of *Stirring Science Stories* and *Cosmic Stories*.

Ray Harryhausen, Mask Maker

The boys soon got back to their zines and writing and monster making. And they went to movies, lots of movies. Bradbury, Ackerman, and other members of Chapter 4 celebrated Halloween of 1939 by seeing a screening of Bob Hope's version of *The Cat and the Canary* at the Paramount. Bradbury almost got himself thrown out when he snuck up on a teen girl while donning a gruesome green mask so terrifying that the blonde almost fainted.[7]

The young woman had nothing to be embarrassed about, as she had been petrified by one of the best monster men in the business. The mask Bradbury wore that night had been created by his friend Ray Harryhausen. It's worth noting that the girl was hardly the only one to nearly pass out at Harryhausen's creation. Bradbury snuck up on Ackerman as well. Forry was so stunned by "this terrible toothy one-eyed fiend confronting him" that the atheist momentarily shirked his belief system, letting out a cry of "my God" instead of his usual "Sacred Science!"[8]

Another hobby Harryhausen pursued in the family garage was mask making. As a teen at Manual Arts he had been a member of the masquers' club, the purpose of which was to help young students learn the ins and out of movie makeup. As he did with all of his hobbies, Harryhausen took his hobby to an extreme, achieving professional perfection.

Harryhausen once made a life mask of young Forry Ackerman by covering his friend's face in plaster of Paris, shoving a couple of straws up Ackerman's nose so the young man could breathe. Ackerman had to lie on his back outside with the plaster molding onto his face. Harryhausen's pet German shepherd, Kong, kept licking Ackerman's bare feet, causing him to giggle. When the mold of his face was finished it would be left with a slight Mona Lisa smile. Ackerman kept this Harryhausen artifact his whole life, forever having the 24-year-old version of himself on hand, eventually turning it into a bust wearing a space helmet.

Ray Harryhausen made the life masque because Ackerman wanted to go to 1941's Denvention, the third World Science Fiction Convention in Denver, as the science fiction character Odd John (in the July 1941 issue of *Shangri-L'Affaires*, Ackerman mentions he will wear a "made-to-order mask"). The mask never came out right, so Ackerman went in a different Harryhausen mask, that of Quasimodo, a costume that earned Ackerman third place.[9] For this costume, Harryhausen recalled that Ackerman borrowed his Hyde mask (as in Mr. Hyde, opposite Dr. Jekyll) and refashioned it. Harryhausen had created this mask himself and at age 21 went as Mr. Hyde to a Halloween dance with his then girlfriend.

Other mask creations of his included the title character from *She*, after "she" has aged rapidly in a few seconds, and something called "Homo Superior," a sort of caveman mask, "complete with white realistic wooly hair."[10] Homo Superior would eventually be nicknamed Uncle John and serve as a sort of mascot for the boys and girls of Chapter 4. Decades later, in only the fourth issue of *Famous Monsters of Filmland*,

Walter J. Daugherty in a mask made by Ray Harryhausen, Los Angeles, California, ca. 1941–1942 (from the collection of John L. Coker III).

one of Bradbury's four daughters, Ramona, sent in a picture of her dad in the Harryhausen mask her father wore that Halloween night years earlier (he made a life mask of Bradbury as well). In the snapshot the masked Bradbury is seen dressed as a grim reaper, holding in one hand the life mask of Ackerman, threatening his friend's head with a scythe.

24

Robert A. Heinlein Joins the League

Forry Ackerman immediately recognized the handsome 30-something in Shep's Shop. The older but still young customer was asking if they had the issues of *Amazing Stories* that had serialized Doc Smith's *The Skylark of Space*. They didn't, but as the man was leaving, the gangly young Ackerman approached and explained that he had every issue of *Amazing Stories*—and just about any issue of any magazine you could name. Forry didn't need to be told that the man he was talking to was Robert A. Heinlein, as he recognized him from the campaign posters Heinlein had plastered all over town. Ackerman explained that he could come over to his place on New Hampshire and get copies from his garage, which Heinlein did. By now, Ackerman's "GarageMahal" was devoted to just his collection of extra magazines and books, a trove he'd amassed after years of being in touch with almost every fan in the country. Forry was fond of having fans over to his flat. After showing off his amazing collection of movie stills and other memorabilia, he next took visitors on a tour of his garage stuffed with extra *Amazing*s and *Weird*s, hoping to make a sale.

One day, Heinlein would be one of the most famous writers in science fiction. He is now best known for *The Moon Is a Harsh Mistress, Stranger in a Strange Land*, and, because of the movie series, *Starship Troopers*. But he was all but anonymous in 1939. A few weeks after Heinlein's visit to his flat, Ackerman was stunned when he picked up a copy of *Astounding Science Fiction* and saw Heinlein's name printed under the story "Life-Line." It was Heinlein's first professional publication. Ackerman looked up Heinlein in the phone book and called him.[1]

Heinlein had recently settled in Southern California with his wife, Leslyn, still unsure of the future while living off of his military pension. In his 32 years he had already done a lot; after graduating from the Naval Academy, he served on two ships, including the USS *Lexington*, itself something of science fiction concept as one of America's first aircraft carriers. He was a proud military man and would likely have spent his life in the navy, if not for a diagnosis of tuberculosis having him honorably discharged at age 27. Heinlein came to LA's University of California to study mathematics and physics but dropped out due to further health issues. He would fall in with Upton Sinclair, socialist author of *The Jungle*, who led a movement called End Poverty in California (EPIC), which was the basis of Sinclair's campaign for governor. Heinlein, himself without work, volunteered at EPIC and was given command of seven precincts. Upton Sinclair lost, but Heinlein remained active with the movement, running unsuccessfully for California State Assembly in 1938. He tried real estate and mining, among other ventures, before he saw a call for submissions in *Thrilling Wonder Stories* and decided to give writing a shot.

His first effort was a novel titled *For Us, the Living* that failed to get published but did help him on his way to becoming a better writer.[2] His next effort took him four feverish days of writing in April 1939. "Life-Line" was either a fantasy or science fiction, he wasn't sure which, so he sent it to editors of various magazines.[3] Within two weeks he received an acceptance letter from *Astounding* editor John W. Campbell, Jr., offering to buy his story for $70. A new writer was born. "Life-Line" was published in *Astounding* in August 1939, followed a couple of months later by "Misfit," then "Requiem" in January of 1940.

Campbell's early acceptance of Heinlein cemented Heinlein's career. Campbell was impressed, not just with Heinlein's writing but also the fact that the 30-something was an ex-military man brimming with technological knowledge. Campbell himself liked to tinker with electronics and spent spare time in his hobby shop attempting to develop improved batteries. He did not accept everything Heinlein wrote, but even his rejections included advice on how to make the submissions better. (About his story "Lost Legacy," Campbell wrote to Heinlein, "It's good. It should be great.") Heinlein took the advice, and the rewritten stories were printed.

Heinlein's next short novel, titled *If This Goes On*, about a revolution against a false prophet in a dystopia, was praised by Campbell as "one of the strongest novels I have seen in science fiction."[4] Heinlein soon became a favorite not just with Campbell but science fiction fans in general. Isaac Asimov wrote him directly. He published stories in other pulps, such as *Astonishing* and *Super Science Stories*, under the name Lyle Monroe. He saved his real name for Campbell. His star rocketed up quickly. In 1938, no one had heard of Heinlein. By the year of the third World Science Fiction Convention in 1941, he was the guest of honor. Nineteen months after his first story appeared in 1939, a 1942 poll published in the February issue of *Fantasy Fiction Field* named him as the most popular author.

Heinlein soon put in regular appearances at Clifton's, and he would have a key influence over the young Ray Bradbury.

The Mañana Literary Society

The third issue of Bradbury's *Futuria Fantasia* (winter 1940) had original artwork by Bok, who also contributed a story under the name H.V.B. League members Ross Rocklynne and Henry Hasse contributed as well, and there was poetry by Emil Petaja. *FuFa* #3 ended with Bradbury congratulating his new friend Heinlein on another success:

> I seem to remember being at someone's house not so long ago and glancing thru a thick manuscript under submission to John W. Campbell. I seem to remember that the author was Robert A. Heinlein, member of our LASFL. And the other day that story popped up in Astounding as a Nova, "IF THIS GOES ON—" And it seems to me that here and now Bob should take a bow for a swell story.

Bradbury had indeed seen Heinlein write. In 1940 Heinlein launched a writers group called the Mañana Literary Society, the joke being that forever-procrastinating writers would turn in their manuscript tomorrow (*mañana*).[5] Members included some of the top writers to publish in Campbell's *Astounding*, including Lafayette "L." Ron Hubbard, Anthony Boucher, Jack Williamson, Henry Kuttner, Leigh Brackett, and C.L. Moore (Leigh Brackett and C.L. Moore were both women, a fact they hid from the reading public by use of gender neutral names). They met at the Heinlein home on Lookout Mountain.

Heinlein also allowed 20-year-old Ray Bradbury into the fold, sort of. Bradbury later recalled that he would sip a coke while the adults drank booze, but Heinlein said he never allowed drinking at the gatherings because of the sharp, winding roads en route to his home.[6] "I could have served liquor, and would have eliminated all of my competition overnight," he once joked.[7]

Bradbury was happy just to be in their presence, but he wasn't welcomed by everyone. Leslyn Heinlein in particular found him annoying, obnoxious, and brash (though the two later struck up a long friendship). Julius Schwartz reported in his book *Man of Two Worlds* that Heinlein described Bradbury as a "noisy kid," a "loudmouth" who "asked too many questions" and asked Schwartz to stop bringing him over.[8]

Nevertheless, Heinlein would play a crucial role in Bradbury's career. Besides inviting him into his inner circle of writers, he also personally mentored the young man, once inviting Bradbury to come and watch him write. Bradbury never forgot that moment: "I was lucky to be able to go to Robert Heinlein's house. He let me stare at him while he used his typewriter."[9]

Bradbury later described the work he showed to members of Mañana as "dreadful crap," including one particularly bad piece called "Black Symphony" about a dictatorship that somehow controls people through music.[10] His mentors included men whose writing he admired as a boy growing up in Waukegan, such as Edmond Hamilton and Jack Williamson, both of whom had been publishing in the pages of *Amazing Stories* since the late 1920s. Bradbury used to read their works by swiping issues left behind by the boarders at his grandmother's Waukegan house. Now he was in their presence, and, to his amazement, they were taking him seriously.

None of this is to say that Bradbury was any good. He would later say of Williamson's review of his early works, "He could hardly keep his gorge from rising they were so bad."[11] Nevertheless, the writer took Bradbury in, critiqued his work, and often took him to a movie later. Sometimes, it was Williamson who drove the young man to Heinlein's house. "He treated me as an equal even though I wasn't," Bradbury would say decades later.

Edmond Hamilton introduced Bradbury to writers outside of the world of fantasy and science fiction, such essentials as Alexander Pope, Robert Louis Stevenson, Emily Dickinson, and Shakespeare, among many others. The pair spent hours touring Acres of Books, a bookstore in Long Beach. He sent the blond boy with lists of books to check out at the library.[12]

Another writer who helped Ray was Henry Kuttner. Kuttner was born in LA, and, according to a biography he published in *Thrilling Wonder Stories*, he had worked in a bookshop but spent more time reading than selling the books.[13] He is often considered one of the most important science fiction writers of the Golden Age. Kuttner was a lot more blunt with his protégé, though only four years older. Bradbury often dropped into Kuttner's Beverly Hills apartment. After a particularly substandard bit of prose, Kuttner would tell Bradbury, "If you ever write another story like this, I'll kill you."[14] He flat out told Bradbury that he was writing "purple prose," that he was far too wordy, and that he just needed to shut up and get out of his own way. But he continued to critique the boy's work. Like so many others in Bradbury's life—Williamson, Brackett, Schwartz, and the Heinleins—Kuttner recognized genuine passion beneath the wordy writing. These early mentors of Bradbury's understood that what he lacked in talent he would more than conquer with hard work. It was through Kuttner's mentoring that Bradbury learned to just *write*. Bradbury soon developed a habit of sitting at his typewriter and letting everything out in one quick outburst, getting a first draft down in a few hours.

The writer to have the most influence on him, and whom he would have a lifelong friendship with, was Leigh Brackett. She was five years older than Bradbury and had already broken through into the pages of Campbell's *Astounding Science Fiction*. Some say her success in the boys' club of science fiction may be due to her gender-neutral name; her fans didn't know she was a girl. Upon reading one of her stories, Henry Kuttner decided that "this guy" deserved better representation and asked if "he" would be interested in meeting the literary agent Julius Schwartz. It was not uncommon for other women writers or artists—such as C.L. Moore (the C stood for Catherine)—to hide behind initials or gender-neutral names. The writer Lucile Taylor Hansen submitted her work under the name "L. Taylor" Hansen with a headshot of her brother, a ruse that resulted in her work getting published.[15] The story and ink drawing of her brother were published together in *Wonder Stories* in October 1930. For a while she insisted she wasn't an author but was only placing stories for her brother. Hence this summary of her visiting Chapter 4 at Clifton's: "We had Louise [sic] Taylor Hansen—Authoress of 'The Man From Space, Prince of Liars-. What the Sodium Lines Reveald,' etc in our midst a whole evening & couldn't get her to tell us who she was."[16]

Brackett was something of a tomboy who often signed off her letters to Ray as "muscles." From 1941 through the summer of '44, Bradbury fell into a routine of biking from Venice to Santa Monica, where they would meet and she would critique his writing. They called this partnership "The Santa Monica Muscles, Malts, Manuscripts and Ah Bergman and Bogart Society."[17] She would later go on to have a career as a screenwriter, including *The Big Sleep*, *Rio Bravo*, and the first draft of *The Empire Strikes Back* (she got *The Big Sleep* assignment because its original writer, William Faulkner, had succumbed to drinking). Bradbury and Brackett collaborated on the space opera "Lorelei of the Red Mist," published in the summer 1946 edition of *Planet Stories*. Bradbury would later say he couldn't recall where Brackett ends and Bradbury begins.[18] Bradbury credited Brackett's advice as crucial in helping him break into the pages of *Planet Stories*, where she had been dominating.[19]

Brackett showed romantic interest in Bradbury, but he wanted to keep their relationship platonic. It was through him that Brackett met the science fiction writer Edmond Hamilton. The two were married, with Bradbury as best man, in 1946.

All of these writers sensed that while Bradbury was not the most talented of the group, and though he may have been loud, annoying, and hyper, this all stemmed from passion. Given time, if he kept going at the rate he was going, he would develop into a pro. "The Young Ray was brash and over-the-top," Ackerman once said, "but his raw talent was immense and his enthusiasm was contagious."[20]

Eventually, it was Heinlein who gave Bradbury his first professional break.

Heinlein knew the editor of an LA-based magazine called *Script* and sent in one of Bradbury's stories. In the fall of 1940, Ray got an envelope from *Script* informing him that his story "It's Not the Heat, It's the Hu—" had been accepted. He and his mother, Esther, literally danced on the lawn of their home on 12th Street. No matter that he wasn't paid with anything but three free copies of the magazine. He was a real writer now. He would have a total of five stories published in *Script*.

25

The Los Angeles Science Fantasy Society

In March of 1940, Chapter 4 of the Science Fiction League announced that they were something else. The group's name was now officially the Los Angeles Science Fantasy Society, or LASFS (pronounced *lahs-fahs*). It is still known by that name today, and members still meet every week. There were a couple of reasons for the name change. Gernsback was gone from *Wonder* and the league was no longer his, and so it was quaint to be named after something that didn't exist anymore. Meanwhile, there had been a lingering feud between Charles D. Hornig, who had worked for Gernsback and is generally credited with starting the league, and the Futurian Frederik Pohl, who was leading his own group, the Science Fictioneers. By changing its name, Chapter 4 could claim neutrality and independence from the fighting fans of the East Coast. Forry Ackerman had also announced his resignation as executive director of the Science Fiction League. (As Ackerman explained in the February 1940 issue of the zine *Le Zombie*: "I had come to the conclusion that the SFL was fakey & wisht my name removed from the masthead of an organization which was one in name only.")

The name change announcement was printed in the fanzine *Shangri-LA*, the latest organ of Chapter 4. In this same issue, T.B. Yerke also announced that the league (now LASFS) would be pulling financial support from its other zines, including Bradbury's, and focusing its efforts on *Shangri-LA*. Also, Yerke, explained, Chapter 4 continued with its "SEW" program, or Speaker Every Week. In the past three weeks their guest speakers in the Little Brown Room had been the head of the Hollywood High School history department, an engineer from the North American Aircraft factory, and an expert on rocketry.[1]

It was also announced that Hodgkins had stepped down as director and was replaced by Walt Daugherty. Under Walt's leadership, many new members spoke at the biweekly meetings of Chapter 4, including teachers, professors, and airplane technicians, and recruitment and membership of LASFS both went up. The son of silent movie actors (his parents' names were Lillie May and "Two-Gun" Montana Williams), Daugherty was keen on technology, notably photography and sound recording. Many of the early photos of LA fandom are his. He later used his photography expertise to work for Forry Ackerman on *Famous Monsters of Filmland*, and the two men were lifelong friends. He enjoyed tinkering with technology and had members of LASFS record their voices to phonographs and also recorded Heinlein's speech at the third World Science Fiction Convention in Denver. He was responsible for being the first to record the voices of Bradbury, Heinlein, Ackerman, and other early fans, though these recordings have been lost to history. He was also an expert on King Tut and an award-winning dancer. His professions were as varied as his hobbies, as his obituary outlined: "He was a production control manager for large manufacturing and aircraft companies, a private detective, a motion picture stand-in and stuntman, a photography instructor, a photographer and a museum curator."[2]

Recording Fan History

In *Voice of the Imagination* #10, Ackerman announced that a record with the voices of himself, Bradbury, Yerke, Morojo, and others would soon be circulating throughout the world of fandom. He compiled names of fans and sent exactly one copy of the album to the first person on the list as a Christmas gift, with the understanding that each person in turn was supposed to send it to the next on the list, a plan that bogged down. Eventually, someone in the chain failed to forward the album, and there's no knowing what happened to it (inevitably, Ackerman explains all of this in an article headlined with the pun "Off the Record").[3]

Because no known copies of the record exist, we have only descriptions from those who listened to it. The first to receive this album, Damon Knight, gave his impressions of this unique keepsake in the pages of *Voice of the Imagination* (*VoM*). He had to play it on a high-end system in a furniture store and said the salesman at the shop was taken aback by the screams, howls, and whistles that followed the opening of "Greetings stfans & stfettes! This is 4E Ackerman speaking to you over station VoM!" Knight was disappointed in Ackerman's "silly" voice, was pleased by Morojo's southern drawl, and felt "no surprise whatever at Bradbury's mouthings."[4] Another person to hear the album claimed that Tubby Yerke sounded "chubby" and Morojo completely confident, but that Ackerman had seeming stage fright and Bradbury was the total opposite of masculine.[5] The record passed through a few more hands before it simply vanished.

In the pages of *VoM*, Ackerman also reported that their clubhouse kept records either mailed in by fellow sci-fi lovers or dropped off by fans now in the military who were passing through en route to the Pacific theater of the war. These "fonographs" (to use Ackerman's simplified spelling) stored the personal voices of young men eager to have their messages saved for posterity. Later, with Walt Daugherty, Ackerman recorded an album called the *Shangri-LA Record* that they advertised in *VoM* #15 for 15 cents. Hopefully copies of these are waiting to be found in the basement of a departed fan.

Ackerman kept busy, continuing to work for the academy during the day and editing or helping to edit multiple fanzines at night. Seemingly every member of LASFS had a fanzine of his own. Seven fanzines were being published in the LA area,[6] with names like *Sweetness and Light*, *Polaris*, and *Mikros*, all of them sprung from Chapter 4's equipment. An article published in *Mikros* stated that LASFS put out 12 to 14 issues of different magazines per year.[7]

Ackerman continued to entertain at his home/museum on New Hampshire. Forry loved having friends over to drool at his collection of movie posters, stills, and other Hollywood collectibles, beginning a trend he would continue throughout his life. Already a businessman, he would tour visitors through his garage full of redundant copies of pulps and fanzines, hoping to make a sale. Ackerman often brought his stills to the meetings at Clifton's, passing around images from his collection. Some of his artifacts were quite rare, like stills from a Soviet film called *Around The World* and a Polish version of *Flash Gordon*.[8]

Yerke later recalled in his *Memoirs of a Superfluous Fan*: "There was something remarkably exhilarating going up to the Ackerman den and looking at movie stills from *Metropolis, Deluge, Things to Come, The Golem, The Girl in the Moon*, and countless others. It seemed to make a faith in the future justified."[9]

26

The End of *Futuria Fantasia*

The fourth issue of *Futuria Fantasia* was an all-star lineup of the not-yet-famous. Bradbury was back, of course, so was Bok, and Henry Kuttner. Most notably, Heinlein contributed a piece, "Heil," under his usual pen name of Lyle Monroe. One of Bradbury's fourth issue stories, "The Piper," is memorable as his first story set on Mars, which he published under the name Ron Reynolds. It would also be the first story he would sell to the pulps as a solo artist, unlike earlier efforts that were collaborations with Henry Hasse. Bok's cover painting was printed on a multilith machine Ackerman had access to as an employee of the Academy, increasing the quality to a near professional level.

Issue #4 would also be the last edition. Bradbury was losing money on each copy, as the 10-cent price didn't cover the costs. Like most of the fanzines, *FuFa* was a fun but money-losing endeavor, and Bradbury's only income was still from hawking papers on the corner. LASFS had decided to pull the plug on all zines except its own *Shangri-LA*, though plenty of Chapter 4 members could use the printing equipment for free. Even with the reduced overhead, Ray couldn't afford to run his zine on his own, and he didn't want to keep accepting Ackerman's money, to say nothing of how time-consuming the whole endeavor was. He wouldn't just stop printing his own zine, he also gradually scaled back on contributing to other amateur publications. From his days in high school to the age of 21, Bradbury published about 50 different pieces, a miscellany of drawings, stories, poetry, nonfiction reviews, and satirical pieces, all in a potpourri of amateur publications.[1] Now, he needed to focus on his writing, and to take it more seriously. This not only meant no more fanzine editing, but he would also soon be spending less time in the Little Brown Room and more in front of his typewriter.

Bradbury fell into a routine, outlined in the introduction to the reprint of *Dark Carnival*: "I wrote the first draft of a story on Monday, the second on Tuesday, the third, fourth and fifth on Wednesday, Thursday, and Friday, and mailed the thing off on Saturday morning."

He wrote about life on Mars, Venus, and dozens of planets not yet discovered. Like so many of the writers he admired, Bradbury took it for granted that the galaxy was as teeming with life as his own native planet. In many circles, including those populated by respected men of science, life on other planets was taken not as science fiction, but science fact. Fans hopefully looked at the sky at night believing there were others out there. Nothing we knew at the time could have told us better. *The War of the Worlds* radio hoax worked in part because, for all we knew, intelligent life on Mars was real.

26. The End of Futuria Fantasia

In the introduction to the December 1930 issue of *Amazing Stories*, Gernsback seriously speculated that life on Mars had advanced far past ours but went extinct while Earth was still developing, and that said life evolved into a totally different form. In another issue (January 1933), he theorized that this ancient race built machinery that is still running on Mars today. He also came up with the theory that the Martians may be blind, like so many intelligent termites, and thus unable to visit Earth.

He was not the only scientist to believe in life on Mars. When German-born William Herschel, living in Bath, England, spied polar ice caps on Mars, he also interpreted different dark and light areas on the Martian surface as oceans and land and sincerely believed that the Martians enjoyed a life "in many respects similar to our own."[2] Herschel believed all of the known planets, including the one he discovered in 1781, Uranus, to be awash in life.

These beliefs continued well into the twentieth century. A May 5, 1907, article in the *Los Angeles Times* gave considerable space to the theory that Martians irrigated their planet using water found frozen at the poles. Titled "Irrigating an Arid World; Life Sustained on Mars Through the Medium of its Wonderful Canals," it devoted a full page spread to an artist's rendition of a Martian digging a canal. The article quoted top men of science.

An article in *Life* dated July 31, 1939, showed a murky black and white photograph of the Red Planet that "easily" displayed reddish deserts and green forests. A globe of Mars at the Hayden Planetarium was crisscrossed by straight lines in perfect geometric patterns. Based on photos of Mars, the globe depicted a series of perfect blackened rows thought by some to be Martian-made canals. Canals on Mars was a favorite theory of Percival Lowell, who also speculated on a then unknown body that would eventually be identified as Pluto. Contributors to Gernsback publications theorized about the possibility of life on Mars, and how we might communicate with the intelligent beings there. One author argued for a gargantuan collection of searchlights blinking in sync to send a pulsating signal to the Martians.

It was not until the NASA probe Mariner 4 brought back the first close-up images of Mars that we knew for sure we were more alone than generations of astronomers and writers had imagined. President Lyndon B. Johnson spoke for many when he drawled that life as we know it "is more unique than many have thought."[3]

Bradbury wrote feverishly about the universe out there. Still, he made time to socialize with his old friends. There was an Easter party in the spring of 1940, with league members chasing each other around the Planetarium, going to the zoo, and watching Bradbury eat a half-dozen hot dogs.[4] He went to Clifton's with such irregularity that by the April 1941 issue of *Shangri-L'Affaires* they mentioned Bradbury "rejoining" LASFS. In September of '43, a group of fans including Morojo and 4e were waiting in line to see a revival of *The Lost World* and bumped into Ray Bradbury, who happened to be doing the same thing.[5] It was the first time they'd seen him in a while. He had turned inward.

Among other events, he skipped the second Worldcon in September of 1940, being held in Chicago.

27

The Second World Science Fiction Convention

The second World Science Fiction Convention was organized by a group of Illinois fans called the Illini Fantasy Fictioneers, a clique who came together to plan this con. The leaders were an Illinois trio consisting of Erle M. Korshak, Mark Reinsberg, and Arthur Wilson Tucker, who normally went by "Bob." After the first convention in New York, it was not necessarily a given that the World Science Fiction Convention would be an annual event. It was primarily because of the lobbying of the Illinois fans that there was another con the following year in Chicago. In an interview in 2021, Korshak claimed that it was Mark Reinsberg who first suggested not just having the con in Chicago, but in Denver the year following and LA after that, to give fans across the country a chance at attending.[1] Publicity about Chicon, as it was christened, soon began popping up in fanzines and prozines alike in early 1940. (Forry Ackerman is generally credited with tacking "con" onto the end of each city, "Chicon" for Chicago's convention, "Torcon" for Toronto, etc.) The decision to have the con in Chicago served the double purpose of taking the event away from the bitter politics that dominated New York's Worldcon (although, as seemed to be inevitable with all early fans, the young Illinois fans also feuded, to the point where Bob Tucker complained about "a long, running, dirty fight that just about wrecked the Old Chicon"[2]). It was also hoped that having the event in the Midwest would help make fandom more of a national force, since up until now most of the major conventions had been in the New York area. LA fans in particular were not eager to make another trip all the way out to the East Coast.

It also helped that a small but influential clique of fans lived just north of Chicago, in Milwaukee.

28

The Milwaukee Fictioneers

The Milwaukee Fictioneers were a group of men who would have a tremendous influence on the Golden Age of science fiction. They were more laid back than Chapter 4 and other groups of the era. Whereas LASFS elected officers, had a written constitution, and kept meeting minutes, the Milwaukee Fictioneers were informal, meeting biweekly at members' houses. Their only rules were no booze, no guest speakers, no women (this rule would change after the war), and no manuscripts.[1] This was not a place to read stories out loud. Rather, it was where Milwaukee's most talented got together to discuss their latest works and flesh out ideas. Some of the authors wrote fiction, others nonfiction; some were Marquette professors, others were journalists; some wrote crime, others wrote Westerns, but it would be the science fiction and/or fantasy writers who would become the best known. They ranged in age from teens to early forties. Their more notable members included the following:

Ralph Milne Farley

Ralph Milne Farley was the pen name of Massachusetts state senator Roger Sherman Hoar. When he initially entered politics at age 23, his opponent accused him of being full of wide-eyed dreams, which turned out to be true. Among other things, the mathematician and engineer invented a device for aiming large guns by use of the stars.[2] He was also a published cartoonist. His legal career took him to Milwaukee, where he fell in with the Fictioneers. His writing appeared in several pulps—his obituary lists him as having published 13 volumes of science fiction—and is best known for his Radioman series. According to a biography of him that appeared in the fanzine *Spaceways*, he studied genetics and in his spare time tried to create a "race of dwarf lop-eared white rabbits."

Raymond A. Palmer

Ray Palmer (like many fans of the era, he often went by his initials, "RAP") is easy to spot in any photo with other fans of the 1930s, as he's two heads shorter than everyone else. His stunted growth was the result of a childhood horrific even by the standards of the early twentieth century. His problems began at age seven when, as author Richard Toronto described in his book about Palmer, *War over Lemuria*: "While playing in the street near the truck, Ray Palmer's leg became lodged in the wooden spokes of its rear wheel. As the truck began to move, it took young Ray with it." This was only the beginning; poor Ray also suffered from tuberculosis, fell off a roof, somehow broke several fingers while bowling, and broke still more digits playing baseball. At age 13 he had to spend two years in bed. After this recovery, the teen bought the first issue of *Amazing Stories* and soon started buying further *Amazing* issues and early fanzines, a collection he hid from his disapproving parents under floorboards. Success did not end his troubles; in 1950 a car accident left him temporarily paralyzed. Perhaps to his own relief, he died at age 67.

As a 20-something, he edited or contributed to some of the earliest known zines, including *Science Fiction Digest*, *The Comet*, and Jerry Siegel's *Science Fiction*. *The Comet* (later called *Cosmology*) was the publishing arm of the Science Correspondence Club (later known as the International Scientific Association), an organization he'd co-founded.

Farley had initially been offered the job of editing *Amazing Stories* after it was purchased by Ziff-Davis but turned the position down, instead recommending his fellow Fictioneer, Ray Palmer. In February of 1938 Palmer was put in charge of the pulp. Ziff-Davis explained to the 28-year-old Palmer that *Amazing* was dying, had been for years, and that they didn't really expect the publication to survive. After *Amazing Stories* was taken from Gernsback, its sales plummeted. Ziff-Davis had in fact only bought *Amazing Stories* as part of a larger package.[3] Palmer had one issue to turn things around, but no one was expecting great things. He mostly rejected the slush pile of unwanted manuscripts and instead published some of his own work and turned to his contacts for submissions, including fellow Fictioneers like Robert Bloch. Some criticized Palmer for publishing more juvenile and stereotypical stories, based more on action than substance. "Pulp magazines are not intended to promote great literature," Palmer himself once said, and "when the action begins to slow down, drop a body through the skylight."[4] He also forecasted the explosion of geek culture. "The day isn't far off, when science fiction will shed its cloak and blossom forth in its party gown, to make its play for fame on publicity's great stage," he predicted in the zine *Ad Astra*.[5] Whatever the critics thought of the content he chose for *Amazing Stories*, the numbers spoke for themselves: his first issue sold 45,000 copies, his second 75,000,[6] putting *Amazing* back on top. It is not hyperbole to say that the Milwaukee Fictioneers saved *Amazing Stories*.

Palmer's most famous, or infamous, contribution to science fiction is the Shaver Mystery. Starting in 1945 he began publishing a series of stories from Richard Shaver, about an ancient civilization living in the hollow Earth. What made the stories unique was that they were nonfiction, according to their author, Shaver, who in real life had been in an institution. Shaver insisted that the world of the Teros (an ancient race of humans) and the Deros (evil robots that especially liked to torture Teros females) existed. Some have argued the Shaver stories were the start of a crackpot conspiracy theory, reinforcing the stereotype that science fiction fans were lunatics. Palmer would also publish nonfiction articles about "flying discs" or UFOs, and is arguably more responsible than any other one person for kicking off the genuine belief in aliens visiting Earth.

Robert Bloch

> "I have the heart of a small boy. I keep it in a jar on my desk."
> —Robert Bloch

Robert Bloch got his first story accepted by *Weird Tales* when he was 17, a short story called "The Secret in the Tomb" that appeared in the May 1935 issue. Shortly after this publication, the *Milwaukee Journal* ran a story about him.[7] Bloch received a phone call from the Fictioneers and he agreed to attend the group's next meeting on the city's south side. He arrived and found himself talking to the dwarf-sized Palmer, as if one of the *Weird Tales* had been brought to life. Bloch would go on to write dozens of novels and hundreds of stories.

Bloch corresponded with H.P. Lovecraft regularly (Lovecraft even devoted a story to him), and through this correspondence he was introduced to the Moskowitz/Weisinger duo, who published some of Bloch's earliest work. Bloch's first book was later published by fellow Wisconsinite August Derleth (typically known as Auggie), who would also publish Ray Bradbury's first book, *Dark Carnival*, in 1947. Bradbury himself was a good friend and fan of Bloch, and he approvingly critiqued Bloch's "Unauthorized Autobiography," *Once Around the Bloch*, calling it a "Bloch buster!" Bloch will always be best remembered as the author of *Psycho*, loosely based on Wisconsin murderer Ed Gein.

Stanley G. Weinbaum

When the editing boys on the East Coast first heard about a young writer from Milwaukee named Weinbaum, they assumed it was a pseudonym for Ralph Milne Farley, evidently not thinking there could be another writer from Milwaukee.[8]

Weinbaum published his first and most famous science fiction story, "A Martian Odyssey," in the July 1934 issue of *Wonder Stories*. While he had published before, his 15-month career in science fiction would shoot him to fame and leave a permanent imprint on the genre. In those 15 months he published a total of 12 stories; 11 more were published posthumously.

Ackerman wrote about "A Martian Odyssey" in the next issue of *Wonder Stories*: "Why have you been keeping this talent scientifictional from us? ... I really haven't read such an interesting story of Mars in a long time." This was high praise from the man who had read almost everything science fiction had to offer. Most other fans agreed. Weinbaum's first story introduced new ideas to the saturated genre of creatures from another world. His aliens were often intelligent, empathetic, and looked not even remotely human. He introduced concepts other writers would use for decades to come. In "Valley of Dreams," he suggested that Martians may have been what inspired Egyptian mythology. His influence on Bradbury is apparent, suggesting ideas Ray would incorporate into some of his best work. In Weinbaum's "Parasite Planet," two Earthlings are stranded on Venus, an almost perpetually moist world with vegetation instantly growing and overrunning anything that sits still for more than a moment. In "A Martian Odyssey," creatures can mimic whatever forms others most want to see, as a means of entrapping them.

Unfortunately Weinbaum's chain smoking caught up with him, leading to early lung cancer that worsened with time. Bloch described Weinbaum's voice as husky, and also said he was prone to constant coughing spells and hoarseness. Whereas he previously paced frantically during meetings of the Fictioneers, Stanley later was quite sedentary. Towards the end he was too ill to attend meetings at all, so instead Palmer went to visit him. Palmer described one of his last meetings with Weinbaum, saying his friend was "propped up on a divan, and attended by his wife."[9] After his death, Ray Palmer printed a Weinbaum collection, *The Dawn of Flame and Other Stories*, generally thought of as the first science fiction memorial collection published. Bound in leather with gilded letters on the cover, it looked like a bible. Its cost may have been the problem, as Palmer had a hard time selling copies for $2.50. Original copies now retail for about $2,200.

In an unscientific poll published in the fanzine *Le Zombie*, where fans named their favorite writer, Weinbaum finished between H.G. Wells and Lovecraft.[10] In another poll of 60 active fans published in 1945, 10 years after Weinbaum's death, "A Martian Odyssey" was still ranked as the #1 science fiction story of all time. (This poll was published in a one-off zine called *After Ten Years: A Tribute to Stanley Weinbaum*, published by Moskowitz in 1945.) Decades later, in 1970, Weinbaum's "A Martian Odyssey" was voted second best science fiction story of all time by the Science Fiction Writers of America.

Weinbaum died on December 13, 1935. When Julius Schwartz received the telegram from Ray Palmer, the young editor broke down and cried, having never met the man. Weinbaum is the great might-have-been of American science fiction. Many felt that if his life hadn't been tragically cut short at age 33, Weinbaum would have been one of the gods, alongside Bradbury, Asimov, and Vonnegut. Forty years after he died, Isaac Asimov wrote in his introduction to the collection *The Best of Stanley G. Weinbaum*: "Weinbaum ... would surely be in first place in the list of all-time favorite science fiction writers."[11]

29

Chicon

The second World Science Fiction Convention took place on the second floor of the Hotel Chicagoan on September 1 and 2, 1940. It was a small affair, costing all of $145, less than the $270 spent on the first con. Cover paintings by the likes of Paul and Krupa decorated the walls and would later be auctioned off.

LA fans Paul Freehafer,[1] Ackerman, Morojo, and Pogo came by way of Santa Fe. Most fans took trains or drove; some hitchhiked; none flew. Some of the fans made admirable sacrifices to attend the second Worldcon, Homeric odysseys that make Bradbury's four-day Greyhound sojourn to reach New York seem downright comfortable. A group of Futurians (Donald A. Wollheim; Elsie Balter, Wollheim's future wife; Cyril Kornbluth; Robert W. Lowndes; and John B. Michel) piled into one of their cars and got into an accident. The Futurians showed up covered in mud, the windshield and windows gone after their car ran off the road.[2] Another pair, Olon F. Wiggins and Lew Martin, rode the rails all the way from Denver to Chicago, hanging between two cars the entire trip. One of them fell asleep and almost fell to his death.[3] One couple, a Mr. and Mrs. Rich Frank, attended during their honeymoon. As was typical of the era, some of the thriftier fans stayed at the local YMCA. Morojo booked at the Chicagoan, and her room became something of an unofficial headquarters, with one count having 50 attendees in the room at the same time. Room 689 was the place to change into costume for the masquerade ball on Sunday night.

On the Saturday before the kickoff, Mark Reinsberg, Erle Korshak, and Bob Tucker—the three young men who organized the event—visited the office of Ziff-Davis, publisher of *Amazing Stories*, and walked away with a literal pushcart full of original illustrations (about 200) from the magazine and 300 copies of the magazine itself, to be sold at auction. These gifts were courtesy of Milwaukee Fictioneer Ray Palmer, editor of *Amazing Stories*. The Chicon program booklet included illustrations done by Buck Rogers artist Dick Calkins. Calkins worked for the Chicago-based Dilly Company and lived there in the Windy City. Mark Reinsberg convinced Calkins to do the drawings of his most famous creations, Buck Rogers and other characters in that universe, totally *gratis*, and his work appeared in the guide to Chicon.

Flash Gordon and Buck Rogers

Buck Rogers is a blond World War I fighter pilot who gets trapped in a mine and passes out from a gas that awakens him 500 years later. He finds himself in love with the female soldier Wilma Deering—society has progressed so that war is a not just a man's sport (though women who have families are still mustered out of the military)—and he joins her in the fight against an Asiatic race called the Red Mongols. Wilma's very first line of dialogue is "Half-breed!" It's a world of flying cars, laser guns, and interplanetary travel. Later the young couple team up with an elderly scientist, Old Doctor Huer.

Buck Rogers was the brainchild of John Flint Dille, president of National Newspaper Syndicate of America, who saw the success of *Amazing Stories* and wanted to bring that universe into the strips. He recruited the writer/illustrator team of Philip Nowlan and Dick Calkins.

A few years later, a comic strip called *Flash Gordon* appeared. Flash was forever at war with the Asian Emperor Ming the Merciless and in love with a girl named Dale Arden. He had a middle-aged scientist for a sidekick and sometimes enemy, Dr. Zarkov. There was no disputing that King Features Syndicate, the company launched by William Randolph Hearst and the biggest rival to National, had blatantly stolen Dille's idea, and there wasn't much to be done about it. To be fair, there are differences—Flash, Dale, and Hans Zarkov are from Earth and on a different planet, whereas Buck Rogers is the sole Earthling from the twentieth century. In any case, Flash was one of many Sunday strip imitations spun off in the wake of Buck Rogers's success.

Buck Rogers and Flash Gordon were key influences on not just Bradbury but most of the first fans. Buck Rogers jetted into a 1929 where plenty of Americans went without electricity and had horses delivering ice to their homes. Space or fantasy films were few and far between, not many science fiction books were published, and pulps like *Amazing Stories* were published once a month. Buck Rogers and Flash Gordon appeared in the papers that essentially all Americans subscribed to and are the first example of science fiction enjoyed and adored on a daily basis. Bradbury wrote, in his introduction to *The Collected Worlds of Buck Rogers in the 25*th *Century*: "Buck Rogers burst upon our vision like some grander July Fourth, full of rockets celebrating tomorrow."

M. Brundage

While in Chicago, Ackerman and a few other fans called on an artist whose work he had admired for years. Ackerman wrote about visiting the pulp artist M. Brundage, whose scantily clad—sometimes entirely unclad—women graced the covers of Chicago-based *Weird Tales*.[4] Brundage painted a total of 66 covers for that magazine, including a run of 39 consecutive issues from June 1933 through October '36.[5] Ackerman, famously obsessed with nude women, could not resist the chance the meet an artist whose tastes were seemingly and strikingly similar.

That M. Brundage drew attractive young women leaving next to nothing to the imagination was hardly unusual. The pulps were as close to legal porn as anyone could find in 1930s America. Occasionally the crusaders scored a victory and forced the girls to put their clothes back on, but the moralists never held the high ground for long. At any given newsstand, dozens of magazines fought for dimes by displaying leggy blondes menaced by a beast who'd tied them up and/or already ripped half of their dresses off. What did make M. Brundage so unusual was that she was a woman.

The M stood for Margaret. Like so many other women in the world of science fiction or fantasy, she didn't advertise what she was.

According to his own report, Forry simply called Brundage and asked if he could visit. He and three others (Erle Korshak, Walt Liebscher, and Ross Rocklynne) visited her and were able to see two so far unpublished works, in Forry's words, "the most delicately done and delectable of damozels." Some have speculated on her sexual orientation. Little is known of her private life other than that the she was married, had a son, and later divorced. (One strange rumor about her is that she sometimes used her own daughters as models. She only had the one son.) Brundage had previously worked in the fashion industry, which explains her thinly drawn beauties. She likely simply produced what she knew would sell. One need not be attracted to women to draw them convincingly: Hannes Bok, infamous for his nudes, is now generally believed to have been homosexual.

Brundage was to *Weird Tales* what Frank R. Paul was to *Amazing Stories*, the artist who made the sales for the magazine. She was paid 90 dollars per cover, painted on paper so thin a single finger could tear it, mounted on cardboard. Brundage originals now sell for tens of thousands of dollars.

The Fans on Parade

On the Saturday before the official kickoff of Chicon, Ackerman and other costumed fans were seen parading down Madison Avenue to a local bus depot to greet other guests, some of the greeters carrying signs. One witness remembered: "They linked arms and sang the entire time."[6]

Fans began converging in Morojo's hotel room at the Chicagoan to try on their outfits for the first time, and an impromptu costume party ensued. Forry Ackerman had an idea. Maybe thinking of the national coverage the first Worldcon got in *Time*, he suggested his fellow costumed fans march to a local newspaper. This parade almost finished before it started. As the dozens of early cosplayers marched the Chicago streets, a suspicious policeman confronted attendee Jack Speer, who was dressed in a "golden radio helmet, flying belt vest, helium gun, and shorts."[7] What exactly the officer was suspicious of God only knows, but the cop tossed several of the fan's collectibles, presumably paintings, into the street and threatened to call a paddy wagon. The officer only cooled when Speer showed him his identification proving him to be a federal employee.

The 25 masqueraders continued and marched to the office of the Chicago *Herald-American*, taking the night editor by surprise. In the words of Ackerman:

> With a very straight face—as the editor looked up at these spacemen and vampires, wondering what all of this was about—I explained to him that we were time travelers. I said, "You see, tomorrow we picked up your newspaper, and saw that there was a photograph of us and an interview, so naturally we had to get in our time machines and come back here to be with you tonight."[8]

Ackerman's actions evidently altered the timeline. While the staff on hand did take pictures of the group, the photos didn't appear in the *Herald-American* or any other paper.

Later that night attendees gathered at a bar on Eighth and Wabash, the same intersection as the YMCA where many of the young guests were staying. Other fans imbibed, but Forry refused to drink even a soda, worried that his friends would spike his drink and end his lifelong abstinence from alcohol. As the evening wound down, Reinsberg stood atop a garbage can outside the hotel Chicagoan and howled at passersby, declaring, "This is not an invasion from Mars! ... This is a science fiction convention!"[9]

One hundred twenty-eight attendees would be the official tally.[10] There is sometimes confusion about who attended. The official Chicon Program Guide listed Ray Bradbury as a "Fictioneer," but he was not present. Neither, for that matter, were Hitler and Mussolini, whom the program guide also listed. In 1940 one could still joke about such things.

Chicon began on Sunday, September 1, 1940. Mark Reinsberg was to give the opening address, but as he was about to speak all of the color drained from his face. The young man was evidently exhausted from the planning. Erle Korshak, another of the Illinois Trio, wound up taking over. Forry Ackerman also gave a speech. Using his usual pun-style humor, he said his address would be short, then read off his LA home address.[11]

The guest of honor was E.E. "Doc" Smith, best known for his Skylark and Lensman novels. In his opening remarks, he denied science fiction was escapist, since, after all, wasn't all fiction a form of escapism, and that fantasy and science fiction were not so wholly different. He then addressed the fact that only a handful of people got science fiction, and that that likely would always be the case. "The science-fantasy mind does now and probably always will limit our number to a very small fraction of the total population. In these personal meetings, there is a depth of satisfaction, a height of fellowship which no one who has never experienced it can even partially understand."[12] He received a standing ovation.

Sunday's activities included screening a film called *Monsters of the Moon*, "pasted together from various sources" by southern Illinois fans Bob Tucker and Sully Roberds.[13] Forry Ackerman gave an introduction to the showing. This "film"—it was really just five minutes of footage, more of a preview, originally shot to entice producers into backing a never-realized science fiction project—would pop up at various cons over the years.[14] It displayed an impressive sequence of moon monsters created via stop-motion animation. Tucker and Roberds didn't actually make the film; it was a Frankenstein monster of clips, the science fiction portion shot by a totally different pair of filmmakers about five years earlier. Ackerman, with his Hollywood connections, had gotten ahold of the footage and handed it off to the Illinois duo—both young men worked as projectionists—for splicing. According to Tucker, this mashup monstrosity also showed "cowboys galloping across the plains with shooting irons smoking.... In another scene, Earthmen and Martians are staring at a round television screen mounted on a wall, and this is followed by a girl doing a strip-tease."[15] Decades later, Ackerman would say that he spliced a few minutes of "girly" footage on the end—that may be the "strip-tease" Tucker refers to. But this particular print has not been found. This film was thought totally lost until collector and restorer Eric Grayson managed to buy a print on eBay. He has restored it and released it to Blu-ray, along with other unique treasures (which can be purchased at his site, DrFilm.net).

The Chicon Auction

As at the first Worldcon, Chicon would host an auction. Once again, unique treasures that would one day fetch a fortune in future auction houses went for a song, and sometimes for free.

The auction was overseen by Erle M. Korshak, the same Illinois young man who took over the festivities after Reinsberg fell ill. Korshak would be the auctioneer for the next 14 cons.[16] He was very young, in fact—17 years old in 1940 (so young that he only passed recently, in 2021, at age 97, one of the last surviving first fans). Once again, the works of Virgil Finlay and Frank R. Paul were auctioned off for a fraction of what they would one day be worth. In the July 1941 issue of Bob Tucker's fanzine *Le Zombie*, Tucker printed the official tally of the auction. Paul and Finlay covers sold for somewhere between two and four dollars; original interior illustrations went for as little as a dime. Ackerman spent exactly $11.35 on more than a dozen cover and interior works by the likes of Paul, Finlay, Krupa, and others, along with some original zines. Morojo spent just shy of $3. The entire auction netted $120. Those who spent a few dollars actually overpaid; at the end of the night Korshak tossed unsold paintings into the audience.[17]

A Finlay cover that sold at Chicon for $3.40 went at a 2005 auction for $11,000.[18]

30

The First Organized Cosplay

The first night of Chicon—Sunday, September 1—there was a masquerade ball, the attendees attacking one another using water pistols and toy dart guns. It was the first time there had been organized cosplay at any con, unlike the previous year, when Forry and Morojo surprised everyone as two people from the future. In the months leading up to Chicon, the fanmags discussed who would be wearing what at the planned costume ball.

Competitors took turns walking across the dais. Ackerman and Morojo were back in their futuristic costumes from the '39 convention, and this time did a skit that earned them third prize. The act involved Ackerman menacing Morojo, who was to be rescued by Reinsberg, dressed as Buck Rogers. The routine was ahead of its time in that it cast Morojo as a strong female lead worthy of Princess Leia or Buffy the Vampire Slayer; Buck is so comically inept (riding in on a "rocket horse") that she has to rescue herself.[1]

Other costumes included three Buck Rogerses; an Invisible Man; Pogo as the High Priestess of FooFoo (a totally made-up character); writer E.E. Smith as Northwest Smith, a science fiction hero created by female author C.L. Moore, Smith completing the costume brandishing a ray gun equipped with a couple of silver buttons, one of which fired off a real light beam; Smith's daughter Honey dressed as Nurse MacDougall, the very Lensman character she inspired her father to create; Bob Tucker as "Hoy Ping Pong," a satire of the Asian Buck Rogers villain that was also Tucker's pen name; ErleKorshak as a Roman centurion, the costume rented from a local shop; the intelligent bear Johnny Black, straight from the L. Sprague de Camp story "The Command"; a mad scientist; and Superman co-creator Jerry Siegel in "normal garb, representing his famous character not yet stripped down for action"—in other words, he simply wore a suit and said he was Clark Kent.[2] The winner of the costume contest was Futurian David Kyle (DAK), dressed as Ming the Merciless, the Asian foe of Flash Gordon. (Originally Wollheim was to be Ming, but he was too proper to wear the outfit, so fellow Futurian Kyle donned it instead.) His prize was an original pulp painting. The second prize winner was Robert Lowndes as Bar Senestro of *The Blind Spot*, a popular science fiction novel from the '20s.[3]

The next day saw fewer attendees but important business. Ackerman lobbied for Heinlein to be the guest of honor at the 1941 Worldcon: "I've been living in the future. I've been privileged to read wonderful stories by Heinlein that won't be appearing for six months or a year. I think that a year from now he will be the hottest thing in the science fiction field."[4] Ackerman was right about Heinlein's career, and he would get his wish.

It was also time to decide the site of the next Worldcon. After contingents from different cities made their bids, Denver was chosen, the logic being that a central location would favor neither the New York nor LA fan factions. This despite worries that the Mile High City was too far from either coast to be attended by many (a prediction not so inaccurate). This was almost the only feud. The bickering and physical fighting, the Exclusion Act, all of that had seemingly evaporated. A banquet was held that night with E.E. Smith and family at the head of a U-shaped table, 62 in attendance. It was much more peaceful, and while there would be other issues and rivalries, there would be no shoving, street toughs, or exclusions. "There seemed to be a strange peace reigning in fandom," recalled fan Jack Chapman Miske. "Everyone seemed willing to be fair and aboveboard, desiring only to have a good time, so dozens of petty feuds were forgotten forever."[5]

31

Ray Bradbury Is Done Selling Papers

Julius Schwartz was exhausted. He and his friend, science fiction writer Edmond Hamilton, had been driving across the country. They sojourned first from New York to Denver, where they attended Denvention. They next pushed on to California, where agent Schwartz had clients he needed to visit, one of them being Ray Bradbury. After he and Hamilton found the bungalow they rented in the Mid–City neighborhood of LA, the young men walked out onto Norton Street looking for something to eat. They spotted a newspaper boy who looked a lot like Bradbury. And then Schwartz realized there was a reason for that.

Schwartz walked up to his client and told the 20-year-old writer the best news the young man had ever heard up to that point in his life: Ray Bradbury had just sold his first story. *Super Science Stories* published "The Pendulum" on August 22, 1941, Ray's 21st birthday. The rookie author celebrated by treating himself to a red car ride "way up to Forum" to find a store where he could buy a copy.[1] No matter that he was only paid half a penny per word, and he had to split even that with Henry Hasse, with whom he'd written the story, so that he only got a quarter of a penny per word. Ray Bradbury was a professional writer now.

After years of trying, Bradbury's momentum was finally building. Next Schwartz sold "Gabriel's Horn," then negotiated the sale of "The Piper," the ex–*Futuria Fantasia* story that was also the first of Bradbury's stories set on Mars and not co-authored with Hasse (Bradbury ended his partnership with Henry Hasse shortly thereafter). Being represented by Julius Schwartz, he sold half a dozen stories in 1942 and a dozen in 1943. By 1944 Bradbury was done selling newspapers. He later said that he stopped selling papers at $10 a week when his writing began earning $11 a week.[2] Bradbury earned somewhere between $15 to $25 for each story. When he published his first book, *Dark Carnival*, in 1947, he sent a signed copy to Julius Schwartz. The inscription began "For Julie, in fond remembrances of Norton Street."[3]

Bradbury's stories at this time trended toward more fantasy and supernatural, and most of the sales would go to *Weird Tales*. The young author was thrilled at being published in a magazine he used to read at his grandma's house. He did manage to expand genres and made sales to some of the detective magazines as well. The editor of *New Detective*, W. Ryerson Johnson, agreed to publish "The Long Night" and wrote to Julius Schwartz, "This Bradbury is beyond question the most promising writer I have ever read. He's going places."[4]

The Other Ray

At the same time, Ray Harryhausen, who would later jokingly refer to himself as the "Other Ray," was breaking into films. Harryhausen had been trying since finishing high school to work in the movie business, somehow. He applied for a job at Disney, among other studios, and finally found work through George Pal. A Hungarian Jew fleeing Hitler, Pal first made forays into Hollywood with his "Puppetoon" shorts, small 3-D animated films.

Harryhausen helped Pal animate some of the immigrant's earliest projects in America, including a series of 10-minute films about a Black boy named Jasper, politically incorrect shorts that often come with disclaimers now (the most stomach-churning title: *Jasper and the Watermelons*). Racist though they are, the Jasper short films are nevertheless impressive—the piano sequence from *Jasper and the Haunted House* is an especially fascinating coordination of stop-motion with music. Other Pal works Harryhausen lent his skilled hands to were the Jim Dandy series (about a bumbling music-prone man) and a short movie called *Tulips Shall Grow*, a less-than-subtle propaganda piece about the Nazi invasion of Holland.

Briefly, Harryhausen worked with his hero, Willis O'Brien, on one of Pal's films, but the animator of *King Kong* fame soon quit. Harryhausen himself was not always happy to be under Pal's tutelage. The films were less than 10 minutes long and took months to make. In one year, Harryhausen recalled making all of six short films, often animating until two in the morning. Frequently Harryhausen wasn't technically animating. Instead, Pal cut the same character from wood, each doing a progressive motion. "Twenty-five separate figures had to be made to assemble one complete step in the animation procedure," Harryhausen recalled in his book *Ray Harryhausen: An Animated Life*. "Words would be formed by the succession of heads to synchronize with the dialogue." Harryhausen didn't care for the assembly-line style of the process, but working for Pal did teach him the basics.

When he wasn't working for Pal, Harryhausen began taking classes on being a combat cameraman. He knew, as did most other young men of the era, that he would be putting on a uniform sooner or later. If he had to be a soldier, he wanted to put his expertise to use.

32

The First Clubroom

"Gone are the days!" began an announcement that ran in the LASFS club zine *Shangri-L'Affaires* in December 1942. It continued: "—when Thursday nights meant Clifton's, 7th & Broadway. Now the address is on fashionable Wilshire Boulevard— our own meeting chamber, where fans may come any day of the week." In late 1941, LASFS realized their dream of getting their own clubroom. The fans rented space at 1055 Wilshire Boulevard in the fall of 1941 and declared it their official headquarters.[1] They soon met at Clifton's less often and instead used their clubhouse, where they could store books, papers, and other items crucial to fans. The room housed their library of primarily fanzines and prozines, said to be 1,000 pieces, plus their own mimeograph machines, which they could use to churn out their latest publications.

The clubroom was also bedecked with original pulp art, most of it Forry's. This description ran in their fanzine, *Shangri-L'Affaires*, in January 1943:

> Originals from various collections were tacked on the walls. Items are: Morey, interior from "Mochanica"; Paul, interior from "Taa the Terrible"; Forte, interior from "Touching Point"; Paul, "Man from Saturn" back cover from Fantastic Adventures; Morey, black-and-white "Mechanica" cover; Cartier, interior from "The Exalted"; Paul, cover from June 1940 SCIENCE FICTION; Fuqua, cover, "The Man from Hell"; Paul, interior, "Beyond the Great Oblivion"; Wexler, interior, "Bon Voyage!"; Cover-Photo from June 1938 Amazing Stories; an original, "Witchfinder," by Roy Hunt, and two original cartoons by Guy Gifford.

On one bizarre occasion, at the second LASFS clubroom (more on that later), a pair of paintings were mysteriously dropped off. The story, outlined in *Shangri-L'Affaires*, went like this: "Art enthusiasts were flabbergasted to walk into the clubroom and find a classic Finlay on display, attached to it a note." The note explained that the person who left the painting wanted to join LASFS but couldn't afford the 50-cent dues, so he was dropping off this painting instead, an original work by Virgil Finlay. A few weeks later, another painting—this time a St. John original sketch from *The Devil's Planet*—was left at the club, evidently by the young man's sister. Affixed to it was the following note: "TO THOSE INTERESTED: I AM NO SUCKER LIKE MY BROTHER ... I WANT $5.00."[2]

Groups of fans had rented a place together before. As fans clustered in the '30s, they began to form bonds so close that they moved in with one another and used their shared living arrangements as an unofficial HQ. The Futurians rented a series of dwellings in New York, with names like Michel Manor, Ivory Tower, and the Futurian Embassy. There, Wollheim, Michel, and other members of the Futurian movement lived together, cooked for one another, and fought about who did the dishes.[3] The boys also published together, having their own mimeographs and other printing equipment. The presence of so much paper and printing in a private home made neighbors curious; the Futurians found one of their compounds raided by G-men from the Treasury Department on suspicion of counterfeiting. They also were raided by the NYPD, who suspected they were homosexual. The policemen were convinced otherwise after finding a stack of female nudes, "evidence" that they seized.[4] The Futurians would go on to write a combined 129 stories together (plenty of these short tales were collaborations) and many would edit pulp magazines. According to Damon Knight, the Futurians had at one point controlled over half of the magazines in the science fiction field.[5]

Arthur C. Clarke and fellow writer William F. Temple lived in a home known simply as the Flat, near the British Museum, for 18 months before World War II. The Flat became the base for British science fiction writers and the British Interplanetary Society.[6]

In 1943 a group of fans in Battle Creek, Michigan, moved into an entire house together and dubbed it the "Slan Shack," which soon became the general nickname for any house or apartment where fans roomed together. (In 1940 A.E. van Vogt published a novel called *Slan*. The Slans are a superior race who are persecuted for their intelligence. Science fiction fans soon identified with a group of mutants who are vilified for being smarter than average, leading to the common refrain "fans are Slans!")

The LASFS clubroom was unique in that it was a place of business instead of a shared apartment. After America entered the war, fans who were now servicemen made it a point to call on the clubroom, some even leaving their own collection behind for safekeeping. These young men often contacted members via postcard ahead of time, to set up a visit. One example of such a visit was reported in *Shangri-L'Affaires* in September 1943: "Latest servifan to reach Shangri'la is Cpl. Henry Golman, former Pittsburg fan, who came to our club in response to a telegram dispatched to him at Camp Haan, California, in answer to his inquiry. Astonishing coincidence developed whom Pvt Dal Coger, ex–Michifan, met Goldman in the clubroom, and they learned they wore both stationed in the same Battalion at Haan!" The current LASFS website describes the clubroom during the war as "a major embarkation center for soldiers and sailors shipping out into the Pacific … [where] members were always ready to stop fighting long enough to greet and play host to fans in uniform passing through LA to the front."[7]

In the February 1942 issue of *Shangri-LA* it was reported that business was booming, and that several members were checking out the mags. It was also described in the pages of that same fanzine (July 1942) as a "cluttered little room."

The LASFS clubroom was also the longest lasting of the sci-fi clubs. Whereas as other "slan shacks" died off as its members grew up and moved on, LASFS would have a series of official clubhouses for decades and only closed its most recent spot due to COVID.

Chapter 4's Official Library

One of the key reasons Chapter 4 decided to rent a space was to find a home for its library.

When a fan read a favorite tale in a borrowed magazine, it was not always a given that he or she would see it again. Science fiction anthologies were rare. Without an internet, finding old copies of *Astounding* or *Wonder* publications could be tricky and haphazard, mixed in with a blend of fun in tracking down that holy grail of an issue a fan had been craving for years. Individual fans had to make do, like Ray Bradbury getting his hands on copies left behind by boarders who rotated through his grandmother's house in Waukegan, or Frederik Pohl unearthing a stash of magazines in the attic of his uncle's barn: "I remember a hot summer in my uncle's attic, smelling of salt and curing tobacco, where I found a treasure trove, 20 back years of *Argosy* and *Weird Tales*."[8] Fan and author Robert Bloch described in his memoir *Once Around the Bloch* hitting the one shop in Milwaukee where he knew he could buy a copy of *Weird Tales*, always on the first of the month, and he had to hit the store as soon as it opened because it only stocked two copies. The 25-cent cover price was no meager sum for a teen who only got a dollar per month from his parents. Fans scoured used book shops or magazine stores (stores that sold nothing besides old magazines) for back issues of science fiction pulps or other general fiction magazines that might have an occasional fantasy or stf piece. There were reports of finding a box of science fiction magazines in the back of a shop seemingly dumped there with contempt and being able to buy the entire run of a pulp for less than five bucks. Arthur C. Clarke found a British Woolworth's that sold back issues of pulps for three pence. Other readers literally picked issues out of the trash, and it is said that American pulps first came to Britain as ballast in cargo ships.

Getting together to exchange and/or sell one another back issues of *Weird Tales* or *Amazing Stories* was part of the reason fans gathered to begin with. Many of the Depression-era lads simply read these magazines on the spot of wherever they gathered with other fans, unable to shill out a few coins to just buy the issue. One study found that over half of all readers didn't get their magazines from newsstands, but secondhand for free, at barber shops, beauty salons, and other gathering places.[9] In Los Angeles a key place to get science fiction was the very store where Ray Bradbury saw the poster advertising the Science Fiction League, Shep's Shop.

Public libraries didn't always stock "lowbrow" fare such as Jules Verne or Edgar Rice Burroughs, and they certainly would not sully their shelves with *Amazing* or *Weird* or *Wonder* tales. Realizing that the patchwork of magazine stores and swapping issues with friends was inadequate, the first fans began to form special libraries of their own, some quite well put together.

It is not surprising that LA's chapter of the Science Fiction League was on the forefront of creating a fan library, given that their leader, Ackerman, had a literal garage-full of magazines. Chapter 4 had been reporting organizing their own library as far back as 1936. A typical meeting of Chapter 4 included a report from the league librarian, a job that at different times was filled by T.B. Yerke, Roy Test, Ray Bradbury, Morojo, and Forry Ackerman. It was considered an important job, right up there with president and treasurer. Seemingly every long-term member of Chapter 4 took a turn as the official librarian at some point.

According to issue #1 of *Imagination*, published in 1937, Chapter 4's library consisted of donated materials and had "almost every issue of every stf mag ever published."[10] On one occasion, Chapter 4's minutes recalled a fan donating more than 500 magazines. Later, the league enjoyed a rare windfall when a fan named Lew

Torrance donated his entire personal library—a "200-pound collection of over 400 magazines," including complete sets of *Science Fiction Digest* and *Fantasy Magazine*—to the league.[11] The league library was organized at the behest of 30-year-old director Russell J. Hodgkins, whose home boasted 300 books and more than 800 fanmags. According to his own biography published in *Imagination* #4 (January 1938), Hodgkins had hoarded hundreds of back issues of science fiction magazines, some of which he had professionally bound, a collection that took up "40-odd feet of cupboard space."[12] He organized and indexed this collection with all the professionalism of a librarian, with a file of *Weird Tales* going back to 1925.

In #16 of the Chapter 4 publication *Voice of the Imagination*, the back page advertised that the league library had a complete collection of all prozines issued since April 1926. Fans of the era would have understood why that year was significant; it was the first time *Amazing Stories* was printed. Chapter 4 later reported that their library was kept in the home of member Al Mussen,[13] this being before the clubhouse. Members were free to use it; nonmembers could access the stacks "by arrangement."

Other science fiction libraries grew organically from their cliques and clubs. In the pages of *Thrilling Wonder Stories* the director of the Yorkshire (England) chapter of the league announced plans to build a "laboratory-library hut."[14] He further reported: "We have, like most chapters, a library—rather modest, yet to us of great value and interest ... but up to now we are each taking care of his own collection and hope to have them altogether in the near future." The nearby Nuneaton branch of the Science Fiction League had a library of 130 books, along with several magazines.[15] The International Cosmos Science Club, run by the Futurians, also boasted a lending library for dues-paying members, primarily consisting of back issues of the pulps.[16] Dick Wilson claimed that their Futurian House had the greatest "collection of science and fantasy fiction extant."[17] The Science Fiction Advancement Association lent out back issues of *Amazing Stories* from its science fiction retail library via mail. Its members could borrow issues for 12 cents each, 17 cents if the issue still had its cover.[18] In 1946 a group of fans that included Ackerman collectively published indexes and checklists chronicling every stf magazine in English ever printed. The lists were imperfect, but their very existence, accomplished only after countless hours of unpaid labor and printing, is itself impressive.

33

The War Comes Home

In 1940 America wasn't officially in the greatest conflict the world had ever seen, yet. But the rest of the world was at war, and fandom wasn't immune. Chapter 4 had always published correspondence from British and other European fans. Now, these overseas letter writers brought the war to their Yank friends.

Prominent British fan and author Ted Carnell wrote in: "I have already lost three local friends. Two killed in action and the other posted 'Missing.'"[1] In another issue of *VoM* Carnell commented, with admirable bravery and humor, on the daily occurrence of getting bombed: "It is a job to find a Londoner who isn't nearly missed." He went on to explain why he and his wife chose to sleep in their house, instead of a shelter: "If one is destined for us, then we'll be waiting for it in comparative comfort."[2]

Another fan wrote:

> Our pub where we used to hold our SFA [Science Fiction Association] meetings regularly and drink quarts of beer accompanied by sausages, has been demolished in a recent raid. How manyhappy evenings I had spent there with Ted Carnell, Bill Temple, Arthur Clarke, Ken Chapman, Wally Gillings, and many others. All these people are now scattered over different parts of the country....[3]

Arthur C. Clarke, showing classic British wit and grace, submitted this letter to the *Voice of the Imagination*: "Spies from the ministry of rubbish reported me the other day and my typewriter was removed in a raid." Clarke went on to say that the war brought an oddly surreal beauty, with blackouts making it possible to do stargazing hitherto inconceivable in London. The zeppelins now floating everywhere above gave the skies a futuristic glow: "Looking up at their glistening teardrops, one can dream that the centuries have rolled by, and that some great fleet from beyond is coming in across the skies of the Earth."[4]

One European fan even wrote about getting a letter smuggled out of occupied France: "My letter of November 19th ... was sent through an American friend going to Switzerland." He also described escaping the occupied zone with his wife: "We slipped through the 'line' in the wee hours of the morning helped by a peasant guide."[5]

Anti-war rants could still be found in the pages of fanzines during the war, even in those published in Britain, where Hitler's bombs were falling: "The pals of Adolf and the buddies of Winston would like the armed support of America's youth. To some of these prosperous cadaver-wholesalers, you are just a commodity."[6] The pacifists were by no means a solid majority. Another fan wrote in to Ackerman and Morojo's *VoM* (*Voice of the Imagination*) and sarcastically asked if they would "perhaps make a clever and/or amusing pun on the day the statue of Admiral Nelson climbs down from Trafalgar Square, and, goose-stepping to Buckingham Palace, begins singing 'Deutschland uber Alles.'" Ackerman and other fans tried to get whatever pulps they could across the Atlantic. Ackerman sometimes published the addresses of fans in England, France, and elsewhere, advertising that he would send them pulps, and encouraged others to do the same.

While there had always been a pacifist bend to early fandom, by 1941 the young men who made up the vast majority of American fans accepted that they would be drafted, with the exception of those unfit to serve, of which there were more than a few. Many of these boys became fans due to unhealthy childhoods. H.G. Wells, Ray Bradbury, Frederik Pohl, Donald A. Wollheim, and Raymond A. Palmer are but a few of the science fiction pioneers who spent months, sometimes years in bed or at home, a not uncommon way to spend a late nineteenth or early twentieth-century childhood. Lots of time convalescing meant exclusion from sports and plenty of time to read. Two of Bradbury's siblings died as toddlers, meaning his mother panicked whenever he was ill and kept him indoors. Bradbury, as autobiographical as a writer gets, wrote more than one story about a sickly boy, such as "The Emissary" and "The Halloween Tree."

Still, when the time came, most of the fans would serve, and some made the ultimate sacrifice.

But first, the fans threw one last party in Denver.

34

Denvention

Denver hosted the third World Science Fiction Convention, organized by the ad hoc Colorado Fantasy Society. The con, named the Denvention, was held over the 4th of July holiday of 1941 at the Shirley-Savoy Hotel. Heinlein was the guest of honor, after much campaigning from Forry Ackerman. Walter J. Daugherty oversaw much of the ceremony, although local fan Olon F. Wiggins was the official chairman (he will be remembered as one of the fans who rode the rails all the way from Denver to Chicago to attend the second Worldcon). The society was promised they would get the hall free if 100 people stayed at the hotel, but only 90 attended.[1] The objections that Denver would be too hard for fans to get to proved not totally without merit. That, and the draft began claiming more and more of the young male fans. To quote writer E. Everett Evans: "Every time someone absent was mentioned someone else says 'oh, he was drafted.'"[2] America had not yet declared war, but by now the country had assumed it would be getting involved sooner or later, causing Roosevelt to invoke a peacetime draft for the first time in US history. Fans Robert A. Madle and Milt Rothman, in a sign of the times, registered for the draft en route to Denver.

Denver was so difficult to reach that the fanzine *The Comet* offered a $25 prize for whoever made the greatest sacrifice to attend, and there was fierce competition. The aforementioned Madle and Rothman crammed into a car with four other fans.[3] Yerke, Freehafer, and Morojo drove 36 hours straight from LA, and Daugherty drove the Heinleins all the way from LA as well.[4] Erle Korshak and Mark Reinsberg bought a car for $35 that blew out in Nebraska. They scrapped the car for $25 and hitchhiked the rest of the way. A group of Minnesota fans, unable to attend, sent a record they had made to be played at the Denvention. Allen Class won the greatest sacrifice award, having hitched all the way from Ohio. Once there he supported himself by working as a dishwasher while renting a room, having arrived a month before the con started, but he would win the $25 award.[5] By the time of the actual convention *The Comet* had folded, so the prize was paid by Robert Heinlein. Denvention was also the first con anyone reached via airplane. Fan John Bell flew home after it was over, having declined an offer from other fans to carpool.

Denvention didn't officially kick off until July 4, but by July 2 dozens of fans were already in town. Robert Heinlein's hotel room became a meeting place. Walter J. Daugherty came on his honeymoon, with his bride, Eleanor O'Brien, in tow. There were two days of partying, since the Denvention was the first where most of the fans were old enough to drink. A group of fans got drunk and tried to steal a hotel carpet. Other fans locked hotel room doors from the outside, locking other fans in.

T.B. Yerke attended and sent a postcard to Bradbury after the first day: "Everybody is drunk and coming and going at all hours ... fans are riding up and down 17th st. all night in street cars."[6]

July 4

Denvention began in earnest on Independence Day, 1941. As the guest of honor, Heinlein gave the keynote address, called "The Discovery of the Future."[7] After his speech, he answered written questions. When asked about conscientious objectors, he replied that America and her freedoms were worth fighting for.

Heinlein's speech was saved for posterity by Daugherty, who put a recording record player near the podium. Daugherty recorded a total of 65 discs at Denvention, with nine alone devoted to Heinlein. "Few Fans escape with their voices unrecorded," one fan noted.[8] Fans were free to step up to the recorder and have their thoughts cut into the album for posterity. Daugherty later recalled that he had just bought a machine called a Recordio Pro and with it dozens of discs flawed on one side that he got for a nickel apiece. He claimed he recorded the entire convention.[9]

Ackerman later transcribed a recording of Heinlein's opening address and sold copies of the speech for a dime apiece, without Heinlein's permission or blessing. Here is how Heinlein began Worldcon 1941:

> I have been reading science fiction as long as I could get hold of it; and I probably experienced much the same process that most of you did: Parental disapproval, those funny looks you get from friends, etc. for reading "that kind of junk." Well, we here, the science fiction fans—we are the lunatic fringe. We are the crazy fools who read that kind of stuff; who read those magazines with the covers with the outlandish machines and the outlandish animals on it, etc. You leave one around loose in your home. Your friends will pick it up, those who are not fans, ask you if you really read that stuff, and from then on they look at you with suspicion.
>
> There won't always be an England—nor a Germany, nor a United States, nor a Baptist Church, nor monogamy, nor the Democratic Party, nor the modesty tabu, nor the superiority of the white race, nor aeroplanes—they will go—nor automobiles—they'll be gone, we'll see them go. Any custom, technique, institution, belief, or social structure that we see around us today will change, will pass, and most of them we will see change and pass.[10]

The Denvention Costume Ball

That night fans held the costume ball, the outfits being the most elaborate at any con so far. E.E. Evans took the $5 first prize as the birdman from Rhea, evidently inspired by a Paul painting. Fans were awed at the feathers attached to his costume (each one he sewed on separately) and the eyes on stalks. Morojo bought the costume at auction the following day. Daugherty came in second at $3 as a "Venusian space pilot" with his helmet made from parts salvaged from the airplane factory where he was working. (According to one source, he wore a "$500 space pilot costume which incorporated a plastiglass helmet, shoulder guards, ray gun and a protuberance on the headpiece which was purported to be a means of thought expression."[11])

Ackerman won third place ($2) as the hunchback of Notre Dame, wearing a mask on loan from Harryhausen. Other costumes were Damon Knight as John Star (one of the "Cometeers" created by author Jack Williamson); Cyril Kornbluth as a mad scientist; Robert Lowndes as a zombie; and Leslyn Heinlein as Queen Niphar, a character from James Branch Cabell's novel *Figures of Earth*. Robert Heinlein hung a sign around his neck that said "Adam Stink, the World's Most Life–like Robot" and wore normal clothes.[12] Morojo wore a Harryhausen-made mask as Akka, a frog-like creature from the A. Merritt story "The Moon Pool"[13]; Art Widner was Old Granny from A.E. van Vogt's *Slan*; Erle Korshak was a ghost, complete with sheet and skeleton head.[14]

The costume ball was followed by a screening of *The Lost World* and, according to one report, a showing of "a couple of scientific shorts that were very good."[15]

The next day various issues were brought up and voted on. The fans passed a measure to send zines and magazines to fans in war-ravaged Britain. Ackerman already had been shipping paper and magazines to English fans, who were suffering chronic shortages due to the war. In gratitude, he was later made an honorary member of the British Science Fiction Association.

Daugherty handed out medals he cast himself; to be given out to the best fans, actually "Daugherty picked the winners without help from others."[16] The awards were as follows: Best Humor (Damon Knight, for his work on the zine *Snide*), Best Fan Artwork (Roy Hunt), Best Zine (Olon F. Wiggins), and Best News Magazine (Julius Unger). Forry Ackerman got a medal for being the Best Fan Number One, the first of many awards he would get throughout his life.

The Denvention Auction

On that second evening there was an art auction, with Erle Korshak at the reins again. The buildup to World War II had created jobs, and many of the attendees had considerable cash on hand. And this time Palmer did not send a cartload of originals as he did at Chicon, so more money was bid on fewer items. Bok, Paul, and Finlay works went for nine, even 10 dollars.[17] Fans sold items to one another. E. Everett Evans paid another fan $15 for the Finlay "Metal Monster." (Evans bought the painting from the young men because, in his words, "the boys needed some cash in a hurry Friday night.") After Korshak sold his ghost skull for $1, it changed hands a couple more times before being given to Daugherty's new wife, Eleanor, as a wedding gift.

The following day fans voted on where to have the next con. Los Angeles was chosen, mostly due to the lobbying of Daugherty. Earlier that day there was a fan softball game. The third Worldcon ended with a banquet that attracted 40 people. Daugherty did a Roosevelt impersonation; Willard Hawkins made a speech in which he said, "It's the world that's out of step, not science fiction fans."[18] The evening ended with a rendition of "Auld Lang Syne." July 7 happened to be Robert Heinlein's birthday, so there was also a rousing chorus of "Happy Birthday." He was gifted a stack of books signed by the fans.

It would be the last Worldcon until 1946.

35

The Fans Go to War

On December 7, 1941, fan and writer Arthur Louis Joquel II burst into the LASFS clubroom and announced the news to the other fans: the Japanese had just bombed Pearl Harbor.

"Who's she?" replied one of the fans.[1]

Most of the fans knew nothing about Pearl Harbor, but the war's impact would be felt immediately. The city swung into action. In a sign of bad times ahead, the FBI detained 300 Japanese-Americans the very next day.[2] Fearing the Emperor's Imperial Navy would appear on the horizon any moment and that Hollywood would soon fall prey to Japanese Zeros (and the Japanese did sink a few tankers off the West Coast in the next few weeks and months), the harbor area of Los Angeles experienced its first blackout. The denizens of the clubroom saw stars over downtown LA for the first time in their young lives.

Before America officially declared war, some fans ranted against any military involvement while others, like Heinlein, insisted that military service was every young American's duty. While many fans had assumed they would apply as conscientious objectors, most would end up serving. As one fan put it: "In the event of an Axis victory, there would be no freedom of any kind in the world that would follow—and certainly no fandom."[3] Only one prominent fan, Charles D. Hornig, specifically refused to serve, and instead declared a status of conscientious objector. He worked at a forestry camp in Oregon, but was later jailed after leaving the camp in 1943, insisting he was an *absolute* objector. Michel and Wollheim and a couple of their like-minded fans were found to be 4-F, while most of the able-bodied Futurians would join the service. Hitler did, after all, attack their beloved Comrade Stalin.

Many of the first fans would even be helped by the war. As fan historian Art Widner wrote, "the intellectual nature of fans led them into safe, and even relatively pleasant, nooks and crannies of the military."[4] Also, as Harry Warner, Jr., stated in his fan history *All Our Yesterdays*, "the sedentary nature of fandom attracted a fair proportion of physical wrecks."[5]

This is not to say fans shirked their duty. Russell J. Hodgkins, former LASFS president, worked as a mechanic for the Army Air Corps. Roy Test, Jr., the 14-year-old in whose garage the first meeting of Chapter 4 was held, flew 32 missions over Europe on a B-17 called the "Bad Penny." Frederik Pohl, one of the banned Futurians, served as a weather observer in Italy after unsuccessfully volunteering for service in either the Arctic or Antarctic, seemingly wanting to see the ice worlds he'd read about in stories such as *Who Goes There*. L. Ron Hubbard briefly commanded a submarine chaser.⁶ Heinlein, through his old connections in the navy, managed to secure a civilian position as an engineer at the Naval Aircraft Factory in Philadelphia and got his buddy Isaac Asimov a job as a chemist there. Towards the end of the war, Heinlein assembled a group of science fiction writers, including John W. Campbell, Jr., L. Sprague de Camp, Theodore Sturgeon, and L. Ron Hubbard, to brainstorm ideas for fighting off kamikaze attacks. The navy didn't take any of their ideas seriously.⁷

Some fans made the ultimate sacrifice. Alvan W. Mussen, one of the founding members of LASFS in 1934 who housed the LASFS library for a time, went MIA in the Philippines. Blaine Dunmire of Pennsylvania, assistant director of the Pennsylvania Science Fictioneers, was aboard a transport that went down in the Mediterranean. Harvey Greenblatt, who may have attended the first Eastern Science Fiction Convention in Philadelphia on October 22, 1936, was killed in France after having received the Bronze Star.⁸ Earl Kay, who helped edit the fanzine *Fanews*, was killed in Germany on May 2, just days before Germany's surrender.⁹

Bradbury, Ackerman, and Harryhausen would put their unique skills to work.

Harryhausen Goes to War

"Animation: An Accurate Science for Precise Army Instruction. This picture proves the possibilities of three dimensional animation as a medium of visual education…. This would reduce learning time to a minimum without impairing the method's high degree of accuracy."

So began the Star Wars scroll that introduced the Harryhausen short, *How to Bridge a Gorge*.

Aware that he would be drafted, Harryhausen took night courses in combat photography at Columbia Studios while working for George Pal during the day. Harryhausen later joked, "I thought I wanted to be a combat cameraman, I didn't realize they were shot like clay pigeons."¹⁰ Hoping to make films for the army, he created two military stop-motion animation films, *How to Bridge a Gorge* and *Guadalcanal*. His 3-D animation skills would never be used in service of his country, but they would help him land a job in military filmmaking. While he was initially given standard training in the Army Signal Corps (earning a marksman badge), he would eventually get transferred to the Special Services Division after showing his footage to superior officers. The Special Services Division was the section of the army responsible for creating propaganda and training films (John Wayne was also an employee). Harryhausen would work underneath Frank Capra, serving in roles from assistant cameraman to "clapper boy," most notably on Capra's *Why We Fight* series. Harryhausen reached the rank of sergeant third grade.

He also sculpted 3-D models for Ted Geisel, before that artist was better known as Dr. Seuss. The cartoonist was at work creating a series of *Snafu* cartoon films, about a soldier forever screwing up. Harryhausen created 3-D models of Private Snafu for Geisel's cartoonists. A couple of Harryhausen's Snafu models were featured on covers of *Yank* magazine.

While traveling in Europe and on shore leave in New York, which he described as an "Aladdin's cave of antiquarian bookshops,"¹¹ he managed to procure first edition books he had always admired, including those by H.G. Wells and an edition of

Dante's *Inferno* illustrated by Gustave Doré, along with original engravings by that same French artist. He collected the Doré books *The History of the Crusades* and *Roland the Furious*.

Ackerman Goes to War

Over the years, Ackerman would waver on how many pen pals he had as a young man—sometimes he said 114, sometimes 117—and on how many movie stills he owned. Was it 50,000 or 100,000? One number he never got wrong was how long he was in the army. Ackerman served exactly three years, four months, and 29 days. He repeated that exact amount of time in every interview he ever gave on the subject. Not that he was counting.

Initially Ackerman hoped his unique skills as a varitypist for the Fluor Drafting Company would spare him military service. He was no longer working at The Academy, where he described his boss as a petty tyrant. He and a group of other employees agreed to all quit on the same day as an unofficial strike, but on the day of the "strike" only he and one other employee actually quit.

He next tried his luck at self-employment. The name of Ackerman's company was Assorted Services, which he founded with fellow LASFS member Ted "Teddy" Emsheimer and advertised in the pages of *VoM*. What services he provided were as varied as the title suggested. He found lodging for out-of-town fans, provided movie stills for a fan in France,[12] did everything from returning a book to reminding people about birthdays. He also did a fair amount of printing, mimeographing, and lithography, using his skills to create zines, posters, and other paper materials for other fans who didn't have the equipment, knowledge, or time to run their own copies. Ackerman was putting his already considerable experience with typing and mimeographing to use.

Heinlein was so amused by his friend's business

Forry Ackerman in uniform, 1942 (Forrest Ackerman Papers, 2358, American Heritage Center, University of Wyoming).

organization that he wrote a story, titled "We Also Walk Dogs," in Ackerman's honor. After Assorted Services didn't quite work out, he once again worked as a varitypist, this time for the Fluor Drafting Corporation. But after Fluor trained a woman on the machine and freed him up to fight, Forry had to go.

As he wrote in one of his zines, "Cpl Forry the 'Ack-Ack' has been very active lately.... It seems the #2 face was subjected to live fire from machineguns and crawled about 60 yards in and out of shell holes and under barbed wire and around exploding land mines."[13]

Forry would later say he wept on the day his induction papers came. As the years to the war built up, Ackerman had always thought he would file as a conscientious objector. He even joked that he and all other science fiction fans should be exempt, since they were obviously insane. When the time came, however, Ackerman changed his tune: "I had no objections to killing anybody who had intentions of bothering me."[14]

Initially Forry was denied entry into the navy because of, in his own words, "fizikal deficiency."[15] According to his draft card he was 6'1" and all of 135 pounds; he was initially rejected for being too thin. ("Not for mental reasons, scums!" he reassured his fellow fans, in *VoM* #17.) He wound up in the army, where he went from "puns to guns."

In the September 1942 issue of the Chapter 4 zine *Shangri-LA* it was reported that Ackerman was inducted on August 7, 1942. The editing of *VoM* and other zines was turned over to Morojo and another female fan, Barbara Bovard. In that same issue of *Shangri-LA* they reported that if Forry "was carried into actual combat and thereby liquidated" $1,000 and his garage-full of science fiction memorabilia would be turned into an "embryo of a foundation" devoted to the preservation of science fiction. In preparation for this, the zine continued, Forry, Morojo, and other fans spent a weekend organizing his garage-sized collection; they "put the garage-full of duplicates in order and excerpted piles of old Argosies and All Storys, etc." Ackerman also typed and printed a checklist of his library of roughly 1,300 books.

Before going off to boot camp, Forry gathered his parents, his grandmother, his Aunt Louise, and Morojo and explained that in the event of his death, the money was to go to the establishment of a science fiction foundation. His entire collection would go to this foundation, with Morojo as the executor of his wishes.

This was his contribution to an idea called the National Fantasy Fan Foundation (eventually to be known as the National Fantasy Fan Federation), an idea first suggested by author Damon Knight. Since New Fandom's decline, the clique of fans nationwide called for some sort of national fan front. Ackerman wanted the foundation to fund his concept, a museum/library devoted to nothing but science fiction. The little clubhouse on Bixel Street was fine, but Ackerman wanted something bigger. Huge, in fact, a Library of Congress of science fiction, with branches in multiple cities and overseas. After the war, he attempted to garner funds for a museum and archive for all fans of science fiction and fantasy. About 20 or so fans said they would pay for the space if he would provide his materials, but the project never materialized. When the time came, there were "only 19, then 18, then 17," and the project eventually fizzled.[16]

Still, it was not a total loss. His pursuit of the idea got him several new pieces for his collection. He wrote fellow fans and explained that if they couldn't donate money (few did) these individuals could contribute books, manuscripts, maybe a movie prop or two, knowing they would be looked after and part of the only and greatest museum devoted to science fiction memorabilia. In a form letter he explained who had contributed what: "Isaac Asimov, $150...Ray Bradbury (numerous manuscripts, inscribed works).... HUGO GERNSBACK (artwork).... RAY HARRYHAUSEN (motion picture models).... DON POST STUDIOS (life masks) ... art by BOK, PAUL, FINLAY, BONESTELL, BRUNDAGE."[17] Derleth of Arkham House donated a first edition of every book his company published, which included the earliest books of Lovecraft and Bradbury. Ackerman would eventually, gradually, build the world's greatest horror/sci-fi/fantasy museum, if not in the way he initially imagined. In any case, the National Fantasy Fan Foundation would, after fits and starts, eventually launch, one of its first projects being the first *Fancyclopedia*, a book containing definitions of fan terms and personalities.

On September 6, 1942, Ackerman was back in town, in uniform. Over dinner at Clifton's, Forry explained to his fan friends that he had landed an office job at Fort MacArthur, after a brief stint making dog tags (he even is said to have somehow published a zine using the machine meant for imprinting the tags, a project he called a "Metalomag"). He would spend the war editing *The Alert*, a section within the camp's newspaper, the *Ft. MacArthur Bulletin*, that related the happenings at the post and had Ackerman's puns all over it (*Alert* #51, Dec. 10, 1943, page 5: "A gift of free tickets to the War Theatre was to be made to all PPs as a kind of bonus for good behavior. Ticket or leave it!"). As he would explain himself in the pages of the *Bulletin*: "This is me—Sgt. Forrest J Ackerman—'Ack-Ack'— ....I have long maintained that the pun is mightier than the sword.... I'm one of that growing group of starry-eyed guys known as 'scientifiction fans'—interested in the literature of the Atomic Age, interplanetary exploration, and the like."

Fort MacArthur (named after the general's father) was two hours south of LA in San Pedro and key in defending Los Angeles during the war. It was also a recruit reception and training center, a place to turn civilians into soldiers. As the war wound down it served the opposite purpose of discharging more than 150,000 soldiers.[18]

The Bulletin reported what was going on at the base: recent scores from base teams, who won the Medal of Honor, birthdays, brief biographies of some of the men, always with a dash of Ackerman's trademark humor (the Friday the 13th edition printed the "3" backwards, with the caption "Will it Beat Jinx?"[19]). Not surprisingly, Ackerman was keen on reporting which Hollywood entertainers dropped in to do shows. He personally met then-famous actresses, including Carole Landis and Dorothy Tuomi. His friend Daugherty was then working in Hollywood and introduced Ackerman to Ginger Rogers and Ackerman's personal crush, French star Simone Simon, best known for her lead role in *Cat People* and *Curse of the Cat People*. Ackerman would end up being just one of many notables on the *Bulletin/Alert* staff, which included future screenplay writer Bob Schiller (he worked for *I Love Lucy*), sportswriter Lupi Saldana, and cartoonist Zeke Zekley.[20] One of his cohorts, Will Gould, was already established, drawing the newspaper strip *Red Barry* before the war.

The paper was a hit, judged second most popular out of 2,000 military publications. It was during this time that Ackerman achieved his signature pencil mustache, modeled after one of his favorite actors, Warren William.

Forry also began his career as a bit actor. When Columbia decided to make a film version of *Hey Rookie!* (previously it had been a play), they used the fort for a few key moments. In a scene shot at the base's recreation room, Forry is seen reading his own camp newsletter.

It was also the first time he struck up a friendship with Fritz Lang, the director who made Ackerman's favorite film of all time, *Metropolis*. Ackerman managed to catch up with the Austrian and his girlfriend after the two were leaving a private theater together that had just shown a film of his (Lang had fled to America from the Nazis). Ackerman learned of this private screening and had to secure leave to go off base. He wasn't allowed into the small theater where the private screening was. Instead he nervously tapped Lang on the shoulder as he and his secretary Lily (later his wife) walked down Hollywood Boulevard. Ackerman showed Lang the signed photo of himself Lang had shipped to Forry over a decade earlier. After wholeheartedly shaking his hand, Lang said he was glad to finally meet Forry in person. They would become lifelong friends. Lang invited Forry and Morojo to visit him on the set of his film, *The Woman in the Window*. Decades later, at a film festival that screened *Metropolis*, members of the audience wanted Lang to take to the stage and field questions about the film. Instead Lang put a hand on Forry's shoulder and explained, "Anything you want to know about Metropolis, ask my friend Forry Ackerman."[21]

Shortly after meeting for the first time, Fritz Lang and Lily Latte visited Forry at his New Hampshire Street home and perused the young man's collection of books and magazines. Forry was impressed; Lang took genuine interest in his collection, pulling down books and talking at length about them. "So he called for the first Weird, the Annual, Strange Tales, first Finlay portfolio, everything he had been wanting to see...," Forry wrote in the pages *Shangri-L'Affaires* in an article he called "Lang is a Fan!"[22]

Ray Bradbury Goes to War

Ray Bradbury was visiting a friend in Hollywood when he first heard the news about Pearl Harbor, and, like almost every other American, he spent December 7 glued to the radio. The next day the headline of the newspaper he sold at his trusty corner on Norton and Olympic blared, "WAR DECLARED BY U.S."

Unlike many young men of his generation, Bradbury was not exactly eager to serve. He had literal nightmares of going to war and being killed before he had a chance to make it as a writer. ("I used to have nightmares of a giant bulldog grabbing me in the middle of the night, chewing me and eating me alive," Bradbury is quoted recalling in *Surround Yourself with Your Loves and Live Forever*. "That was the dream of war.") It was a moot point, as his eyesight was terrible and the military of World War II rejected young men for far less (his brother was not allowed to serve for a broken eardrum and being overweight). When he went in for his physical exam he was told to take off his coke-bottleglasses and read the letters off of the chart. Bradbury replied, "What chart?" This was no dodge—Bradbury was all but blind without his glasses, though decades later he would have his vision corrected by LASIK (he continued to wear glasses anyway, as they were part of his look). As a young man, he attempted to correct his vision via a method endorsed by Aldous Huxley called the

Bates Method, which required him to spend two to three hours per day with exercises, relaxation, and sunning.[23]

Having a background in radio, Bradbury wrote ads for the Red Cross encouraging people to donate blood, and for the LA Department of Civil Defense.[24] ("My present RED CROSS schedule, for which I work gratis, keeps me damnably busy," Bradbury wrote in a letter to Derleth.[25]) Otherwise, he did what he had been doing before, selling newspapers and writing. His apparent relief at not having to serve thoroughly unimpressed Heinlein, the ex-military man who moved to Philadelphia to work for the Navy Yard. It is not known exactly why the two had a falling out. The general consensus is that Bradbury was not at all disappointed to be 4-F, and that this disappointed Heinlein, who felt it every young man's duty to serve, somehow.

Heinlein, by the same reasoning, was very proud of Ackerman's service in the army, and helpfully gave his young friend about 50 snapshots of nude women that Heinlein had personally taken himself. One out of every two girls were willing to pose if approached "deferentially," Heinlein explained. During basic training, Ackerman plastered his bunk at the barracks with these photos, winning over his fellow soldiers.[26]

In 1942 the Bradbury family moved to Venice Beach, after Leo was transferred by his employer, the Bureau of Power and Light. The Bradburys settled into a rental house next to a power substation. Ray soon set up an office in the family garage, with the sound of the power station forever humming while he typed away. He also spent as many as eight hours a day writing at his friend's mother's apartment building. Grant Beach's mom owned the tenement building at the corner of Figueroa and Temple that she rented mostly to Mexicans. Inspiration for stories with Latinos—such as "The Wonderful Ice Cream Suit" and "I See You Never"—sprang from this time and place. ("I See You Never" was based on an incident Bradbury personally witnessed, an illegal immigrant being hauled off by immigration officials. The title was derived from what the man said in his broken English as he was being taken away.) He worked there so often, writing and revising a story a week and then sending it off to the various pulps, that he soon began getting his mail there. He sometimes spent the night either at the Beach residence or his Aunt Neva's in Hollywood.

He had a falling out with Beach so that, by late 1946, the office in the garage next to the substation became his primary writing home. The home and substation are gone now; in its place stands a building with a plaque that proudly claims to be the site where Bradbury wrote *The Martian Chronicles*. This is accurate enough: many of the stories he wrote in '46 would end up woven into the tapestry that became *The Martian Chronicles*, though Bradbury initially published the stories as individual pieces. As he would later say, "I'd written a novel but didn't know it."

36

The Second Clubroom

Ackerman continued to go to meetings of LASFS, commuting from Fort MacArthur, often spending the night on Morojo's couch, her apartment being across the street from the second LASFS clubhouse.

The first clubroom on Wilshire didn't last long: the fans were evicted in March of 1943, due to noise and rowdiness. The clincher came when a group of them late at night desperately shrieked that one of their cars was on fire. They filled trashcans with water and frantically ran outside, buckets in tow, only to "put out" a steaming radiator. "That she lost five tenants the next day was considered oddly coincidental," one of the fans insisted.[1]

In April of 1943, the LASFS crew first moved into its new clubroom on 637½ South Bixel Street. They found the onetime beauty parlor to their liking, especially because of the multiple outlets for their printing equipment. Their first official meeting at the new clubhouse was on June 5, 1943. In *Fantasy Fiction Field* #128, published in June 1943, the clubroom was described as "decorated with original illustrations by Paul, Finlay, Bok, Cartier, Dold, Wright, Hunt, Brown, Magarian, Krupa, and others." Ninety dollars would be raised by auctioning off some of these works to pay for the move. Most of the Pauls and Boks went for less than $10, but someone did pay an astonishing $25 for a Finlay cover.[2] They painted their emblem with their motto ("de profundis ad astra"—from the depths to the stars) on the glass front door.

Bixel Street became a legendary address in the world of 1940s fandom. Not only was South Bixel the location of Chapter 4's clubhouse, but Morojo lived across the street at 628 South Bixel. A visitor described her apartment as "a small room ... in front, street-side, with piano, a double-bed, and one wall lined with magazines on loan from Ackerman."[3] About a dozen or so fans lived in an apartment building called the Tendril Towers at 643 South Bixel Street. Tendril Towers was not a towering structure but a two-story rooming house with a long set of stairs going up to the adobe-looking home. More than a dozen fans lived and rotated through the rooming house during the war and for a few years after. Some fans spent more time at the towers than in the official clubroom. The fans began referring to this collection of dwellings as "Bixelstrasse" (*Strasse* is German for "street"). LASFS moved to another clubhouse in 1948, when the original building was torn down. None of the original Bixel Street fan locations remain.

This description of the second clubhouse was printed in the April 1944 issue of *Shangri-L'Affaires*:

36. The Second Clubroom

> A plate glass door and a large display window with two small side windows and a glass transom make up the frontal appearance of the local Society. Altheda Slate, sister of former member Eleanor O'Brien, has painted the club emblem, our name, and list of activities on our large display window. The fact that the room was formerly a beauty shop is advantageous one way. There are twelve electric plug-ins and sockets around the room at even intervals. A large closet houses the mimeograph and the mimeograph supplies. Out of the treasury, we purchased some venetian blinds for the door and the window, plus a large rug for the floor and twenty metal chairs. A large day couch with mattress has been donated and blankets have been loaned for same to house and bed any fan who arrives from out of town, and needs a place to stay for a day or so. Many local fans as well as out-of-towners have taken advantage of this convenience. Three large book-cases, built by Daugherty, adorn one side of the room.... The room is about twenty feet wide and thirty feet long, with a high ceiling. The floor is painted grey, with a cream-colored wall and blue trim. Blue molding, about eight feet high around the room, supports a large variety of science fictional original illustrations and covers. Well represented are the works of Dold, Cartier, Paul, Hunt, Wasso, Krupa, and Tom Wright.... Recent installation of a telephone has been a great convenience to the club for outgoing calls, as well as for members outside to contact the club at any time of day or night. Many types of queer calls have been made and received. The biggest surprise call of them all was the Thursday night meeting that was interrupted (pleasurably) by a phone call from Slan Shack, in Battle Creek, Michigan. The phone is one of the wall types and hangs in the rear of the room with an imposing list of local fans' numbers slightly over it. The activity, I should say "THE ACTIVITY" of the group has reached a new high lately. Publications literally keep the mimeograph humming and hardly an evening passes but what the club is a veritable bee hive of one activity or another.

A less flattering, maybe more honest description came from Francis T. Laney, in his memoir of early fandom, *Sweet Idiocy* (page 33):

> The room is a blend of pigsty and monk's cell. When i first saw it, it was even worse than it is now, since many of the members were using the place as an office, and their personal papers and other impedimenta were strewn around in careless abandon. There was an austere and extremely dirty couch in one corner, and a rickety old square table covered with typewriters and loose papers. A large mimeograph sat on an upended fibre barrel, and another similar barrel was packed to the bursting point with wastepaper. A couple or three ramshackle home-made bookcases filled with tattered magazines, and 25 or 30 uncomfortable folding chairs comprised the remainder of the furnishings. The shortcomings of the room and contents were made even more apparent by the pitiless glare of six or eight naked light bulbs set in sockets around the wall. The floor was a welter of cigarette butts and other trash, not the least of which was the filthiest and most badly worn out rug I have ever seen.

But even Laney had to acknowledge the place was a sinkhole of activity: "The evenings especially saw the premises crowded; many of the members were actively engaged in publishing, kept their typewriters and other equipment right there in the room; there was usually someone reading something out of the club library..."

In *Shangri-L'Affaires* it was reported that the clubhouse was brimming with equipment, including three typewriters and a mimeograph. The bookshelves were overflowing "into every corner of the clubroom."[4] In the August 1943 edition of *Voice of the Imagination*, Ackerman reported that the clubhouse hung a flag with the names of 18 members now in the service.[5] Stateside LASFS fans arranged to have both prozines and fanzines shipped to fans now serving overseas, although wartime secrecy and other restrictions hindered this. ("Dear Ghoulss, First, thanks very much... for sending the Shangri-L'Affaires by first class mail," read a letter to *Shangri-L'Affaires* #27 from fan and serviceman Bob Hoffman. "It took 23 days, but at least it got here...."[6]) In the January '45 issue of *Shangri-L'Affaires*, a soldier reported that he used to send fanmags overseas until regulations banned the practice, to save on shipping.

Another issue of *Shangri-L'Affaires* summed up a typical night at the clubroom:

> Walt was deep in the mimeoing of VENUS, and the floor was studded with piles of the same. Alva was sitting over on the couch, reading, Forry was at the table, doing something at the typewriter. Walt's secretary (ahem) was working away in the middle of the floor. Walt's typewriter is one of those elaborate affairs that opens up into a table, and she was stenciling the Hasse stories for Walt's new mag. Walt was at the mimeograph and I was reading a story in the latest WEIRD TALES.[7]

Fan boys in the military who had only read about the clubroom in a variety of mimeographed pages now could see it in person (example: "Cpl. Douglas Blakely, former Minnefan, arrived here a few Sundays ago and was enthusiastically welcomed by his former pals"[8]). Servicemen and fans gathered there, then headed over to the nearby professional building for dinner or coffee, an evening often ending with a round of miniature golf. The names and addresses of nearby fans were posted on the clubroom door, in case an out-of-towner should visit at a time when no one was at the clubhouse.

A much sought-after address was Ackerman's legendary home on New Hampshire. Soldiers and sailors who were fans often made it a point to see the collection of the world's greatest collector. A Lt. Earl D. Leeth once dropped by the clubhouse, then made his way to Ackerman's free museum, where, according to Ackerman, he made "the sacred pilgrimage to the garage by the dark of the moon; and, due to (cunningly contrived) poor nite-lites, forty-four mags were palmed off on him for the preposterous total of $16."[9]

Christmas with LASFS

Members of Chapter 4 who weren't sent overseas still had their meetings, and they continued to party, if not without sacrifice (their annual beach party had to be cut short due to a wartime curfew). They continued with different projects. At one point, LASFS devoted $10 to making screen tests of various members, hoping to get someone interested in bankrolling a film about fandom.

And they still had their annual holiday parties,[10] trading and giving away gifts that would one day make collectors drool. At the Christmas party of '43, the gift exchange was summed up this way: "Presents, such as toy telescopes/AMAZING QUARTERLIES (the really amazing ones—Ziff-Davis, not Gernsback) and other equally valuable things were exchanged. Several horrible originals were also gotten rid of by their various owners."[11]

At the 1944 LASFS holiday party, Forry Ackerman dressed as Santa Claus and handed out presents, such as a Buck Rogers spaceship and an original Frank Kramer painting, along with the inevitable books and magazines.[12] Earlier that night, fans auctioned books and original illustrations to each other. At Christmas '45 the presents included several original interior illustrations and the Bok "powers" lithographs. These were a series of Bok prints, black and white, abstract illustrations of nude figures, each of which had "powers" with a color in the title ("The Black Powers," "The White Powers," etc.). Five of these "Powers" by Bok would end up in the Bradbury estate.[13]

37

The War on Bixelstrasse

But not all was well on Bixelstrasse. The type of feuding that had been prevalent on the East Coast reared its ugly head at the clubroom. Many found Ackerman arrogant and more than a bit prudish. 4SJ (one of his many nicknames) banned ashtrays from the clubroom in a doomed attempt to get other members to quit smoking. The upshot was a floor littered with cigarette butts. A lifelong teetotaler, he also banned drinking from the premises. The March 11, 1944, issue of the zine *Fantasy Fiction Field* was almost wholly devoted to lambasting Ackerman and his clique, Morojo and Walter J. Daugherty. A group of fans complained that the "Great God Ackerman" was a dictator who insisted on molding all fans to his ideals and that "to some of us Ackerman holds a deep personal grudge" for going out, drinking, and partying, rather than hanging around the musty clubroom. The eight undersigned (including T.B. "Tubby" Yerke) went on to say that they tired of his "campaign to mold each and every newcomer into his own concept of the new fan." They also pointed out his "unending insistence on simplified spelling, his often obnoxious craving for nudes, his tacit disapproval of smoking and normal hell-raising." The eight announced they were resigning and forming their own club.[1]

They weren't the last to resign. According to *Fancyclopedia*, a dictionary of fan terms edited as a partnership between Jack Speer, LASFS, and the National Fantasy Fan Foundation, reasons for defecting from LASFS were legion: "dislike of Ackerman personally; Ackerman's objections to the intrusion of drinking, wenching ... on LASFS affairs; belief that the Society was becoming a collection of psychologically maladjusted people; and discontent with the accomplishments of the LASFS as compared to its possibilities."[2]

The *Fancyclopedia* is by no means an official reference book. It was really more of set of terms for people in the world of Fandom, and most of the readers were people already familiar with Ackerman, Daugherty, and the rest of the LASFS crowd (its clarification of the abbreviation "LA"? "Los Angeles, dummkopf"). Nevertheless, it does give insight into what were commonly held beliefs regarding fandom at the time.

Various members of LASFS broke off, started their own groups, and dissipated. In March of 1945 a group formed calling itself the Futurian Society of Los Angeles, which counted Morojo as a charter member but fizzled when a few members moved to New York.[3] Another group of former league members formed the Knaves, also known as the Knanves because of a typo (pronounced nanveehs), but this organization too was short-lived. (Laney in his memoir *Sweet Idiocy* had this to say about the meetings of the Knaves: "There was no gavel, no chairman, no formality."[4]) One of the defectors to join the Knaves was T.B. Yerke, the young man who had introduced Bradbury to LASFS. Ackerman was so bitter about the defection that he bad-mouthed Yerke in his own zine, claiming that Yerke now walked across the street to avoid Bradbury and also that Yerke was 4-F due to manic depression not hypertension as Yerke insisted.[5] Another group of ex–LASFS members, including Yerke and T. Laney, formed the Outsiders. Initially the Outsiders had no constitution and were meant to be a little less formal and more fun than LASFS (Yerke would eventually draw up a constitution). While the Outsiders did a fair amount of publishing, the group had died out by the fall of 1944.

Yerke would end up leaving fandom altogether, or "gafiating," a fan acronym for "getting away from it all." Fed up with the fighting, he surrendered his entire collection, a situation Ackerman was more than happy to exploit. As Ackerman reported in the November 1944 *Shangri-L'Affaires* under the headline "YERKE GOES BERSERKE," Yerke came to the clubroom (sometimes called the "crudroom") and wanted to spread the word that his entire collection was free to anyone who had a car. "To be sure, Honest Acky spread the word ... with the subdued whisper of a centenarian turtle with laryngitis," Ackerman boasted. He now had another haul of fanzines and prozines to add to his garage. "Haul's well that ends well," Ackerman concluded.

Ackerman's obsession with fandom may have been maddening, but it was also likely why LASFS continued when so many other groups came and went. It may have been his "fanatical puritanism," in the words of Laney,[6] that saved the society. The original league at times seemed to fade—at one 1945 meeting only Ackerman and one other member were present—but LASFS would weather these times, unlike their rivals.

The Existence of Homosexuality

Some bitter defectors also claimed that many members of Chapter 4 were homosexual, an accusation that could tarnish any organization in these times. In the October 1941 issue of *Shangri-L'Affaires*, Ackerman himself laughingly reported that Morojo and Pogo dressed the boys up in their dresses for Halloween, and that Bradbury was voted "prettiest girl." As Warner points out in his book *All Our Yesterdays*, "survivors of the era contradict one another about how many fairies were members."[7] Francis T. Laney wrote in his memoir *Sweet Idiocy*: "The club had from two to four active homosexuals in its membership at all times, ... one of the most active members of the club was also the most vocal homosexual, and ... he was continually bringing other fags around the club."[8] In 1947, Laney caused a stir in #36 of *Shangri-L'Affaires* by claiming that 50 percent of LASFS members were gay, after a bitter ex-member put that number at 80 percent. Laney arrived at this number after he led an investigation that included consulting with other members, asking known homosexuals about certain members, and remembering which members tried to "make" him and others. As a rebuttal, fan Dale Hart asserted that while LASFS "had several people who might dilate the eyes of Dr. Kinsey," they "betrayed no index to their suspected-by-few character."[9] Hart also wrote that he had never "been met with a flutter of butterfly hands, the patter of softly-running words, of the felicitous falling of Bobby Pins."[10]

However many there were, no one seemed to dispute that Chapter 4 had more gays than most, probably more than any other fan group. Tendril Towers, the rooming house where several members lived, was sometimes nicknamed the "Bixel Street Fairy Palace."[11] One member, E.E. Evans, was jailed for "lewd acts" but claimed he was framed.[12]

Chapter 4 once made homosexuality a topic of discussion at one of their meetings, as transcribed in *Shangri-L'Affaires*:

> After a long moment of dead silence, the club recovered enough from the shock of hearing such a topic mentioned in public to discuss some of the theories which have been advanced to explain the existence of homosexuality. The majority of those present seemed to agree that inversion was usually due to maladjustment in infancy, but Joquel steadfastly maintained that the "third sex" was the most prominent example of human mutation now extant.[13]

However crude their language, the fans tolerated homosexuality as much as any organization of that era. Even Laney, who led the investigation to figure just how many gays were in the group, gave the usual claim that he didn't mind homosexuals as long as they didn't "try anything" with him.

38

Goodbye, Morojo; Hello, Tigrina

LA resident and fan Alva Rogers excitedly watched as Forry Ackerman opened his ever-present attaché case. This was the great Forry Ackerman, after all, Mr. Science Fiction himself, a young man who already had the largest collection of science fiction ephemera. What would he pull out of his case? A first edition Edgar Rice Burroughs? A sketch by Frank Paul or Virgil Finlay? A rare fanzine?

Forry took out a bottle of bourbon. Is this a good brand, Forry asked? It was Thanksgiving weekend, 1944, and he and Morojo had just split up. For the first and last time in his life, Ackerman wanted to get good and drunk. The boys were taking a red car to Francis T. Laney's house. Laney was throwing a party for author A.E. van Vogt, who had been hanging around the clubroom, and Ackerman wanted to be tipsy before they pulled in.[1]

This is how Francis Laney described Ackerman's first and last encounter with booze:

> Forrest J Ackerman had decided to prove to himself that he was right in frowning on the use of alcoholic beverages, and showed up with a pint. I had intended to mix his drinks personally, to make sure that he did not get too stiff—having some vague idea that if he were properly guided-guarded he might find the release of a moderate amount of alcohol sufficiently desirable to wish to try it again. However, someone (Rae Sischo, I believe) started mixing doubles and gave one to the Ack. He sat there looking like the wrath of God, and waiting for something horrible to happen. It commenced to hit him a little, the old frozen repression started to slough off, and first thing you knew, the boy was having a good time. Then, all of a sudden, he realized that he felt the liquor, and collapsed moaning in a heap, spending the remainder of the evening stretched out on the bed. Most of us felt at the time that the deal was pretty much put on, but of course we may have been mistaken. At any event, he proved to himself that liquor and Acks didn't mix—which was about all he had in mind.[2]

It is not known why Forry and Morojo broke up, only that Ackerman was devastated when it happened. According to Laney's memoir *Sweet Idiocy*, Ackerman had initially split up with Morojo due to her habit of smoking in the LASFS clubroom. He sent 50 postcards to fans announcing the breakup, then sent another 50 postcards to the same fans when Morojo gave in on the smoking.[3] The messages from both of these postcards were printed in the zine *Fantasy Fiction Field*, #159. (Quote from the first postcard: "Forry once was her mentor; finally became her tormentor. Their affinity for one another wore thinity to infinity: Now these 2 entites go their separate ways...") There is no disputing that Ackerman was staunchly opposed to drinking, smoking, and later in life, drugs. He once remarked that editing *Famous Monsters* allowed him to influence kids away from drugs and booze. To quote Ackerman, "I wish to God that society were rid of smoking, drinking and drugs."[4]

Ironically, for all of his abstaining from smoking, drugs, and booze, Ackerman still had a heart attack at age 50, an event he blamed in part on the stress of working for *Famous Monsters of Filmland*. Before then he was known for long, night-after-night birthday parties. After the heart attack he celebrated his birthday by parceling out the celebrations, no more than 60 guests per party. His birthday could thus go on for weeks.

So why did she part with him? Maybe Morojo had had enough of the unpaid labor, as she clearly did the bulk of the stenciling and editing while Ackerman was in the service. Maybe she was finished with the constant fan feuding and fighting. In 1944 Morojo stepped down from being treasurer of LASFS, a job she'd held since 1937, only to get elected director. She resigned this post after a week. Or maybe she was done with Ackerman trying to get her to quit smoking and was still bitter about the postcards. In any case, the two were finished. She would later remarry but only had the one son from her first marriage. She died in 1964, at 60 years old. Upon her death Ackerman wrote that he had barely spoken to her in the 20 years since their breakup. He submitted a three-page essay to a zine in which he said she was a "real science fiction fanne" (underline in the original) and "the greatest female fanne who ever lived." But it wasn't the most heartfelt of eulogies. As evidenced in this paragraph, he was still quite angry at his ex (and a few other people):

> Perhaps no one would be more surprised than Myrtle that I am contributing to a memorial about her because I had scarcely spoken to her for about 20 years and I stayed that way. I got mad at her about half my life ago (for purely personal reasons, nothing to do with fandom) the way I stayed with Laney till the time of his death. The way I expect to stay with Mel Hunter and Scott Meredith. Altho it is not impossible for me to overcome an old enmity: in times past I have had bitter feuds with Wollheim, Moskowitz, & Pohl, and today we get along famously. But I doubt that time will ever come with Judith Merril; and it did not come with Morojo.[5]

Ackerman was crestfallen by the breakup. It would not be easy to find another girl as enthusiastic about the fantastic. He did, however, soon find someone new, maybe even better.

He had known her for years. Petite and pretty, Edythe Eyde had done some modeling and was a poet, musician, and active fan who always, at least in fan circles, called herself Tigrina. In his memoir *Sweet Idiocy*,[6] Laney described her as "a rather handsome young lady" who "took a genuine interest in weird fiction and cinema, was a not incompetent poet and, in a pedantic sort of long-winded way, a pretty good fan writer."

> She was rather short, neatly built, and with a whooping laugh that sometimes embarrassed her. Everyone around the club seemed to like Tigrina, and she managed to stay around for close to two years without becoming embroiled in any fusses, apart from one memorable occasion when E. Everett Evans unadvisedly patted Tigrina's little posterior one night after the meeting, and came within a hairsbreadth of having his face slapped as T told him off in a way I hugely loved. Right there in the clubroom, too.

After having corresponded with her through fanzines, Ackerman met up with Tigrina in San Francisco on his way back from the Denvention in '41. This is his account of their first encounter, in the October 1941 issue of *Voice of the Imagination*: "I follow'd, heart in my mouth, I don't mind tellingU...all humanity seemd to cease to exist as my attention was focust on the flower-skirted girl in front of me." He was still dating Morojo at the time. He later offered to print a photo of Tigrina dressed in "exoticostume" in the next issue of *VoM* if anyone was willing to send $5 for about 150 prints.

Tigrina had been contributing to various zines since 1941 and was so obsessed with the occult that one of her catchphrases was "Thank Satan." To the chagrin of some purists, she was more interested in witchcraft and black magic than in science fiction. Ackerman, however, could accept her not being a "pure" fan. She was beautiful, loved the fantastic, edited zines, was blonde and ... perfect.

After his relationship with Morojo ended, Forry grew more infatuated with Tigrina. Eventually, Ackerman did what made the most sense to him: he proposed to her in the pages of a fanzine. In the June 19, 1945, of issue of *FANEWS*, under the headline "An Open Heart Letter to Tigrina," he wrote the following, in his flowery original handwriting: "U are a beautiful phantasy treasure.... U could bring a lasting source of happiness into my life."

Tigrina published a lengthy response in *FANEWS* #170 (June 1945) where she hemmed, hawed, and more or less said no. She was flattered, especially since Ackerman had a reputation in fan circles as being somewhat aloof, but the long distance between them would pose a problem. ("Have you ever tried, f'rinstances, throwing a kiss 400 miles?") She ended her essay: "Let's keep the rest of the fen guessin, shall we?" Ackerman understood, almost. She had politely declined his offer. What was not reported in the zines, what she herself didn't fully understand, was that she was homosexual.

The first time a lesbian asked her if she was gay, Tigrina didn't quite grasp what the woman meant, but she and Forry would both gradually come to terms with who she was. There had been hints. Forry noticed that she seemed as interested in Marlene Dietrich as he was. In an open letter to one of the many zines Ackerman edited, Tigrina asked a few questions regarding some of the women he had been photographed with (Forry's answers are in italics): "Also, I noticed that in the picture that Fojak gave me of Morojo and him in Chicago (or was it New York?) (*Chi*) at the Fantasy Convention, there was another girl in that picture. Who is she? (*Pogo*) She certainly is attractive. I would like to meet both Morojo and her some time."[7] After she came out to him, they still spent plenty of time together—among their dates was seeing Boris Karloff in a live play and getting the man's autograph afterwards[8]—and they would be friends for life. He later often joked that he had an affair with a lesbian.

He was more than accepting, if not flat out enthusiastic, about her lifestyle. In 1947 he contributed to a zine she edited called *Vice Versa*, the first devoted to lesbians ("America's Gayest Magazine"). In the opening issue she wrote that her paper was for "those of us who will never quite be able to adapt ourselves to the iron-bound rules of convention."[9] She typed each individual issue twice on carbon paper for five copies each, printing only 10 copies of each issue.

"Every time I buy a copy of *Weird Tales*, for example," she wrote in the August 1941 edition of *Voice of the Imagination*, "I get an exclamation of horror and disgust from my mother and a frown and a shake of the head from my father and a l—o—n—g lecture on why I should not fill my so-called mind with such 'childish fancy and degrading filth.'" One could only imagine the response if her parents had seen an issue of *Vice Versa*. In the first issue, she wrote about Halloween as "an appropriate day for those of us who must masquerade the other 364 days of the year."[10] She followed this essay with a short fiction piece in which a straight woman at a Halloween party is seduced by a "Dracula" who isn't quite what he seems.

She published poetry, essays, and reviews of any film, novel, or stage play that implied lesbian love. Her good buddy Forry Ackerman would always take credit for publishing the first lesbian science fiction story, called "World of Loneliness." He published another lesbian piece, "Kiki," which ran in the seventh issue. It should be remembered that what they were doing was illegal, since in this America, one could go to jail for sending "obscene" materials through the mail, which was often defined as anything that deviated from the heterosexual norm. She sent her zines out in sealed envelopes sans return address. Later she would publish articles under the name "Lisa Ben."[11]

Ackerman himself was fined in 1960 for correspondence with a straight male friend of his. The men had been exchanging letters, pretending to be a lustful lesbian couple. When his friend's wife found the letters, Forry was charged with and convicted of mailing letters on five separate occasions that were "obscene, lewd, indecent, lascivious and filthy."[12] He was fined 50 dollars per letter and told to have no further correspondence concerning lesbians.

He also befriended a group of lesbians called The Daughters of Bilitis, the first lesbian rights group in America (Tigrina was a member). They made him an "honorary lesbian" and, he claimed, invited him to parties where he observed all of the "happy girls" making out with each other. One naked woman was exciting, but "two together was even better," he later quipped.[13] Tigrina and Fojak platonically dated for a couple of years, until Forry met the woman he would spend his life with.

39

Victory

The end of the war changed the world of science fiction fandom. Elevated it, it could be said. Far-fetched ideas once forecast by H.G. Wells, Jules Verne, and others—wars fought from the air, drones, rockets, atomic weapons—were now a reality. While most of the public still looked down on science fiction fans as harmless kooks, the world was starting to concede that these space age fans might not be so crazy after all.

Or at least they were, as Douglas Adams would say, mostly harmless. A few years after the war, LASFS was surveilled by the LAPD vice squad, evidently suspecting the fans of illegal activity until the officer in charge concluded they were just a bunch of "crackpots."[1] LASFS was also investigated by the FBI as being a possible den of Communism. It would eventually come out that active fan Sam Russell (he published *The Acolyte* with Laney) had secretly spied on LASFS and sent reports to the FBI. He testified under oath that LASFS was not affiliated with the Communist party and had no interest in politics.[2]

One of the side effects of the war was the death of the pulps. Many titles were killed off by war-era paper rationing and simply never came back, and television finished them off for good. Some pulps converted to slicks and others switched to tiny digest-sized magazines, but most died off. Street & Smith, the "grandaddy of pulps," ceased printing both pulps and comics in 1949.[3] The Shadow and Doc Savage may have survived countless death traps and villains in the '30s and '40s, but they could not outwit modern market forces.

The Return of Fandom

LASFS celebrated the end of the war in a big way, by hosting a major convention. Pacificon, or the fourth Worldcon, had been planned for 1942 but was delayed due to the war. Walt Daugherty and his wife Virginia (he and Eleanor, the bride he brought with him to the Denver convention, had split up), Forry Ackerman, and Paul Freehafer were the key organizers of the event that took place over the July 4 holiday, 1946. Paul Freehafer was the treasurer of Pacificon but unfortunately would die before seeing it come to fruition. About 120 fans were in attendance, most from California. Some fans even flew.

Pacificon, as it was called, was held in a hall across from MacArthur Park. Canadian-born writer A.E. van Vogt and his wife, E. Mayne Hull, were equal guests of honor (decades later, Ackerman claimed he had lobbied for a sole woman to be the guest of honor, either M. Brundage or C.L. Moore, but he was outvoted). In his opening address van Vogt gave a speech, called "Tomorrow on the March," in which he argued, "Of course, we shall have another war, because human beings have not yet learned to understand themselves."[4] Ray Bradbury was supposed to do a humorous sketch with Daugherty but forgot his lines. Robert Bloch talked about a radio show he was launching, *Stay Tuned for Terror*, and played recordings of it.

Ackerman hoped to use Pacificon to sell the concept of the Fantasy Foundation, but he was too ill to proceed and eventually Tigrina persuaded him to leave. He was gifted a free Paul painting as a consolation prize. Ackerman did not mention his early departure in his own reporting of the event in his latest fanzine, *Glom*,[5] but simply claimed that he had been on hand to report the goings-on of the National Fantasy Fan Foundation, and that he was willing to donate his entire collection of 1,300 books and 1,400 magazines to the cause. He sold 80 foundation memberships. His sickness kept up a strange tradition since Chicon, where one of the organizers fell ill, seemingly the victim of stress. For a while the not-so-funny joke went that every con claimed one victim.

Once again, Korshak auctioned off original art from various publications, such as *Planet Stories*, *Famous Fantastic Art*, *Startling Stories*, and *Thrilling Wonder Stories*, paintings and sketches that had been taped to cardboard and put on display. Among the more unique items up for grabs were copies of *Rhode Island on Lovecraft*, a slim volume of neighbors' recollections of the late Lovecraft, who had lived in Providence, Rhode Island. Korshak sold copies for 50 cents. Francis T. Laney, in his zine *Fan-dango*, balked at the "utterly unjustifiable prices" and raged: "The reserve figures on most lots were at least twice what I would have considered paying for them. But no blame can really be attached to Daugherty and the convention committee for pegging them so high, in light of the fact that the suckers present consistently bid far beyond them. Barnum was right."[6]

Tigrina helped sell Pacificon by getting on the *Queen for a Day* radio show and telling the whole country about the event. She also ran, along with Virginia Daugherty, the third masquerade ball, which took place during the evening of the third day, Thursday, July 6. Once again cosplayers topped the last convention. Actress Cay Forrester, the all–American girl of 1946, was in attendance for publicity reasons (the fans voted Ms. Forrester as "the girl we would most want to be stranded on the moon with"), and was terrified by a Frankenstein (Bob Hoffman) who been made up by an industry professional. Hoffman's costume consisted of "thick-soled shoes, shabby too-short coat, and the rod sticking through his neck."[7] Ackerman reported that another young woman was dressed as the Snake Mother, a character from a story by A. Merritt. Her costume was "a large headdress and nothing in particular from there down to the scales that began at her waist."[8] The costume was partly out of necessity, the girl evidently having a broken leg—Ackerman referred to her as being "temporarily invalided."[9] Though Ackerman did not give the woman's name, she was none other than Morojo, who came with her new boyfriend and fellow fan, Dale Hart, who was dressed up as the character the Gray Lensman, a sort of intergalactic patrolman created by E.E. Smith. The costume was created by his girlfriend, the founding mother of cosplay.

Another male cosplayer dressed so convincingly as a female that when a couple of other men entered the room he was changing in, they instantly backed out, thinking they'd stumbled into the ladies' room.

Tigrina once again showed off her love of black magic, dressed as the made-up character of Dracula's daughter. Here's a description of her costume from the *Shangri-L'Affaires* (September 1946) report: "It was all black, spangled with black sequins. A headpiece like Batman's was at first accompanied with a black eyemask, the only mask at the masquerade. Elbow length gloves, bra, and tights from waist to ankle, with over all a peekaboo cloak."

Other costumes included male and female vampires, the birdman from Rhea, a Tibetan Buddhist, Cthulhu, and someone dressed as a "future cowboy."[10] At the end of the evening, Tigrina sang a song she wrote, "The Sabbath Summons." A screening of the movie *1,000,000 B.C.* followed.

The last day concluded with the fan banquet, or "fanquet." All told, it was a successful con, although Francis T. Laney—he'll be remembered as the fan who tallied just how many members of LASFS were gay—raged that "he had seen ten fairies"[11] and that another fan left after a man made a pass at him in an elevator. It was one of the last cons attended mostly by insiders and professionals, such as Ackerman, Daugherty, Bradbury, and Leigh Brackett.

The fourth Worldcon proved that fandom was back, and for good this time. The postwar years saw an explosion in cons across the country, some attracting as many as 800 people.[12] (It should be noted that conventions did go on during the war, but they were much smaller in size, many of them really just fans gathering at someone's house. For example, Ackerman hosted "Staplecon" at his parents' house on Staples Avenue in San Francisco during the war years. He produced a special Staplecon pamphlet with original artwork by Harryhuasen and Bok. During the 1943 Staplecon original works by Wesso and other artists were sold off to pay for the pamphlet.) While small in size compared to today's conventions that attract thousands, the postwar cons proved that the conventions would be a permanent force. In 1948 Worldcon went international for the first time; the Toronto gathering, where someone paid $76 for an original Finlay, was known as "Torcon." The auction raised over $400, a Worldcon record. In 1949 the so-called Cinevention was held in Cincinnati. Local TV station WLWT gave the event a half-hour of coverage, and there was also reporting on the event from the *Cincinnati Post* and *Cincinnati Enquirer*. According to Fred Patten's excellent synopsis of the convention, the TV coverage consisted of a panel of the some of the best-known fans of the time, including "(David) Kyle, Fritz Leiber, Jr., E.E. Evans, Judy Merril, E.E. Smith, Jack Williamson, Hannes Bok, John Grossman, Forrest Ackerman, Ted Carnell, Bob Tucker, Erle "Mel" Korshak, Lloyd Eshbach, James A. Williams, and Dr. C.L. Barrett, representing the authors, artists, publishers, and bibliophiles." The televised discussion was the most publicity any convention had gotten so far. Cinevention raised over $1,300, $980 of which came from the auction. Two Lovecraft poems and his autograph sold for a combined $13, the tally of original cover art added up to just shy of $50, and six bound volumes of Tarzan originally cut and scrapbooked from the papers sold for $13. The costume ball (which had not happened at Torcon) was a bit toned down, with one of the participants actually a model hired by someone else. About 175 people attended.[13]

Chapter 4 soon launched its own con. Westercon started in September 1948 and continues to this day. Initiated by Walt Daugherty and other members of the Los

Angeles Science Fantasy Society, Westercon (official name: The First Annual West Coast Scienti-Fantasy Conference) was initially meant to be a science fiction convention for fans on the West Coast who couldn't make it to Worldcon. The event attracted at least 73, with Ray Bradbury and Forry Ackerman in attendance, Bradbury being a featured speaker. Still the funnyman, he took to the podium carrying a 500-page speech, but gave a speech that was "somewhat briefer."[14] At the 1952 Westercon, in San Diego at the Grant Hotel, Ray lost a contact lens, which was covered in crud and unusable by the time he found it. He wore glasses, a look he maintained ever since.

Westercon is still held every year and is sponsored by LASFS. Though it is not always in LA, it is always in the western US or Canada, the rule being that it must be west of the 104th meridian.[15]

40

Significant Others

Both Ackerman and Bradbury met their life partners shortly after the war. Both men met the women they would spend their lives with in bookstores.

Ackerman and Wendy

Mathilde "Tilly" Porjes immediately noticed the tall, handsome young man in the May Company's book section. Ackerman was there to buy remainder books, which were on sale for 29 cents. Forry took an armload. "He's mine," Tilly told the other sales girls, and stepped up to ask if she could help him. "She's been helping me ever since," Forry would always joke.

Like his previous girlfriend Morojo, Tilly was an older young woman and a mother, having been married and now with a son. Her birth name was Mathilde Wahrman, Porjes being the name she took after she married. Born in Poland and raised in Germany, the young Jewish woman fled to England, where she survived the Blitz. She'd lived in Cuba and Israel before settling in LA.[1]

Their first date was at Clifton's. Forry thought she seemed like a nice girl, someone to see movies with; once her husband came back, he would get out of the way. But her husband never came over from Israel. Before their marriage she was known as Wendayne Mondelle, an Ackerman creation. She eventually legally changed her name to Wendayne when she became a citizen, and typically went by "Wendy." They married in 1949. Besides English, she spoke fluent French, German, Italian, and Hebrew and would lend her unique talents to fandom, most notably translating the Perry Rhodan series (which is hundreds of volumes long) from the original German. A med school student in Germany before being dismissed for being Jewish, she taught French and German at a local college.

Ray Bradbury and Maggie

Fowler Brothers bookstore opened in 1888 and would stay in business for over 100 years. The store had a guest registry for visitors to sign. So we know that John Philip Sousa, Zane Grey, Charles Lindbergh, Robert Kennedy, and silent stars Tom Mix and Douglas Fairbanks all passed through its doors. The store gained notoriety in 1922 as the last place director William Desmond Taylor was seen before he was found murdered.[2] It was part of the legendary Booksellers Row, a lineup on and around Sixth Street, in the same neighborhood as Clifton's. Not for nothing, the only remaining bookstore in that neighborhood today is called The Last Bookstore.

Fowler Brothers was also the place where Ray Bradbury met his wife.

One April day in 1946, Bradbury walked into Fowler Brothers bookstore. The young woman behind the counter, Marguerite McClure, was suspicious of the young man's military overcoat with infinite pockets, not to mention the briefcase he carried. She had been told to be on the lookout for anyone suspicious, as there had been a rash of thefts. She asked the young man if she could help him. He asked if they had a copy of the anthology *Who Knocks?* He was a writer, and one of his stories was in it. Intrigued, Marguerite would take a copy of *Who Knocks?* home and read his story in the collection, "The Lake." She was dazzled.

A few days later Ray returned and asked her out for coffee.

Marguerite McClure was more than Bradbury's intellectual equal. The daughter of a wealthy restaurateur from the Leimert Park area, she loved the European classics and preferred history to all other forms of reading. After that fateful encounter at the bookstore they next moved on to beach trips, riding the merry-go-round at Griffith Park, seeing *The Postman Always Rings Twice* at Loew's State Theatre. They went for long walks on the beach where Maggie read him poetry, stanzas that would pop up again in Bradbury's writing (such as in the titles "And the Moon Be Still as Bright," "There Will Come Soft Rains," etc.). And they went to bookstores, lots of them. Besides her employer, they hit the May Company, the Satyr Book Shop, Bullock's, Martindale's in Santa Monica, Pickwick Books in Hollywood.

Bradbury called her Peg or Peggy but eventually settled on Maggie. By June 20, not quite two months after he convinced Maggie he wasn't a shoplifter, he wrote in the back of a book (*The Unquiet Grave*, by Cyril Connolly) "Maggie and Ray engaged."[3] The first person he introduced her to was Ray Harryhausen.

Ray and Maggie married on September 30, 1947.[4] Ray Harryhausen was their best man. The minister actually gave Bradbury the $5 fee back, saying, "You're a writer aren't you? ... You're going to need this." Bradbury eventually paid him back, years later.[5] After this small civil ceremony at Mount Calvary Church (Ray Harryhausen and Maggie's witness, a gay man named John Nomland, were the only two guests), Harryhausen bought the couple dinner and drove them to their small bungalow at 33 Venice Boulevard. For the first time at age 27, Bradbury was about to spend the night at a home not owned by his family. He'd been sharing a bed with his brother Skip until now. The low-rent apartment didn't have a phone, but across the street from the $30-a-month bungalow was a gas station with a phone booth.[6] Ray left an apartment window open so he could hear the phone ring. He'd dash outside and pick it up, usually fielding a phone call from a producer he'd been in touch with or sometimes his new agent, Don Congdon, who would represent him for the next 54 years. He told Congdon and others to only call him during his "office hours" so he wouldn't always have to listen so intently.

41

Dark Carnival

Julius Schwartz would sell a total of 69 of Bradbury's stories (about 30 of them to *Weird Tales*) before giving up agenting to become an editor at DC Comics. Bradbury arguably had outgrown Schwartz, as his own star was rocketing. In 1945, his story "The Big Black and White Game" was chosen for the anthology *Best American Short Stories*. He soon "graduated to the slicks," getting published in better-paying, more mainstream publications like *Charm, Collier's*, and *Mademoiselle*. (A young editor named Truman Capote decided to publish the tale "Homecoming" in *Mademoiselle*'s October issue. This story was illustrated by Charles "Chas" Addams, whose cartoons were the basis for the hit show *The Addams Family*.) In 1947, "Homecoming" was chosen as one of the O. Henry Award prize stories of 1947. But the biggest development for Bradbury of 1947 was the publication of his first book, *Dark Carnival*, at the behest of his good friend August Derleth.

Derleth and Bradbury had been corresponding for years, with Derleth often recommending authors to Bradbury.[1] Before publishing Bradbury's first book, Derleth helped rescue Lovecraft from obscurity by publishing the first-ever collection of that late writer's stories. When Lovecraft died in 1937, his passing was noted in the fanzines (a zine called *Amateur-Correspondent* devoted its May–June 1937 issue to him) and almost nowhere else; Lovecraft was neither rich nor famous. He died of cancer, not starvation, as is sometimes reported, but that rumor shows just how destitute he was. Julius Schwartz reported that Lovecraft was so broke that he often corresponded using penny postcards with tiny writing (Schwartz: "You almost needed a magnifying glass to read them").[2] Under no copyright protection, Lovecraft's work continued to pop up in fanzines years after he died.

Much has been said about Lovecraft's inherent racism. He harbored a fear of anyone or anything different, which was seemingly everything and everyone. He is said to have not left his home in Providence, Rhode Island, where he was cared for by various elderly relatives, until age 30. After his mother died, Lovecraft married a Sonia H. Greene and moved in with her in Brooklyn near Prospect Park. Described as attractive and intelligent, she was the breadwinner while her husband continued to write. Lovecraft, away from his beloved Providence, detested the "alien hordes" of New York. He eventually moved back in with his aunts in Rhode Island and continued his relationship with his wife by correspondence.[3]

While he wrote prolifically, he did not get paid for a work of fiction until 1922, and then would appear regularly in the pulps of the day, most notably in *Weird Tales*. Between 1923 and 1926 *Weird Tales* published 19 of his stories, all of them written years earlier. He continued to publish, off and on, in the pages of the pulps for the rest of his life.[4] He is best known for a series of stories that were expanded upon by other writers, including August Derleth, which together became known as the Cthulhu Mythos. (How do you pronounce Cthulhu? There's a debate. The most common pronunciation is *koo-too-loo*. It has also been pronounced *cul-lall-loo*, which some purists say is how Lovecraft himself pronounced it. Ackerman once said that he heard Lovecraft somehow say it with a whistle. Others have said it should be spoken with a guttural sound.)

As he aged, Lovecraft lived on a combination of a family trust fund that earned somewhere between 10 and 15 dollars per week, some work here and there, and occasional checks from editors when he had something published. He is said to have had zero tolerance for cold and would spend entire winters shuttered in his Rhode Island home.

After his passing, Derleth and friend Donald Wandrei—both pulp writers who had corresponded with Lovecraft often—attempted to publish a collection of Lovecraft's short stories, called *The Outsider and Others*, only to be rebuffed by publishers who saw no value in the project. The only option was to found their own company, Arkham House, the name derived from a fictional locale created by Lovecraft, and pay out of pocket to finance the book (they also had to promise the printer they would buy a certain number of copies). Their company was based in Sauk City, Wisconsin (where Derleth lived in a house designed by Frank Lloyd Wright). It was considered to be the first small press to specialize in science fiction and fantasy, their first editions (Arkham typically doesn't publish reprints) often commanding hundreds of dollars. *The Outsider and Others* was never reprinted and had a one-time run of fewer than 2,000 copies. These first and only editions now start at about $4,000. Derleth never personally profited from the inflation of his own book, having sold most of his copies before the boom hit. *The Outsider and Others* was an early example of small press science fiction books being artificially inflated. The niche dealers buying science fiction refused to buy a book on release. When the remainders then turned up in bookstores for less than a dollar, the dealers snatched them up and flipped them for between one and five dollars. In 1945 Sam Moskowitz reported that dealers were selling copies of *The Outsider and Others* for $50.[5]

Bradbury was a 19-year-old newsie in 1939 when he first mailed a letter to Derleth, congratulating the young editor on his Lovecraft publication. Bradbury and Derleth had a mutual love of Lovecraft and other weird writers, along with poetry and newspaper comics (Derleth scrapbooked comics as well). Bradbury explained in his first letter that he bought a copy of *The Outsider* from Ackerman, but that Ackerman planned to buy another copy, assuring Derleth that his buying a secondhand copy in no way dug into sales. He then went on to praise Derleth for his book: "I make only ten dollars a week. But I will give up half of my salary any day to buy such a book as this Memorial Volume." He said of Lovecraft, a man he regretted never meeting: "I shall never ascend to his literary heights, try as I may, but the memory of H.P.L. and his stories will make me write the harder and try to educate myself to the intricacies of weird masterpieces."[6]

As Bradbury's star rose in the pulps, Derleth took notice. He initially asked Bradbury to contribute to an anthology he was putting together called *Who Knocks? Who Knocks?* was, remember, the book Bradbury asked for on that fateful day when he met his soul mate at Fowlers. Eventually, he asked if Bradbury would be interested in publishing his own collection of short stories. The upshot was *Dark Carnival*, published by Arkham House in 1947 after endless meddling and tweaking on Bradbury's part.

Bradbury was forever pushing back the manuscript, first due in April of 1946, then June, and so on. In November of 1946 he mailed a copy of his short story "The Coffin" and insisted that it replace a different story, "The Poems" ("a horribly bad story.... Yes, THE POEMS has been advertised everywhere, but how many people remember titles?"). As late as March of 1947 he was tinkering with the galleys, insisting on words and/or paragraphs being changed. In a letter dated March 12, 1947, he wrote, evidently in reference to a previous letter:

> I understand very well your attitude when you say that of the 30 books you have published before DC [*Dark Carnival*] you have had fewer changes in the lot than in DC alone so far. My only defense is that in the time of rewriting a book for publication, a writer becomes so blind to his work, so exhausted of critical faculty, that he lets a lot of things slip through...

In a following letter, he again sent in still more blue-penciled corrections he wanted made.[7] Acknowledging that it would be costly to make changes to a book in the final stages of being printed and that many copies had already been ordered, Bradbury said he would be willing to pay out of pocket for the changes, explaining, "I didn't sign a contract with Arkham House to make money—I signed to have a good book put out."[8] (Ackerman ordered 25 copies of *Dark Carnival* but asked if Derleth could sell them to him at a discount, so that he in turn could sell copies with a markup. Both Derleth and Ackerman were among the first generation of fans, as Ackerman reminded Derleth in a letter: "We've met since time immemorial, and I never miss."[9]) Finally Derleth had to cut him off.

Dark Carnival had an initial run of 3,000 copies, 1,000 more than Arkham House normally printed; Derleth was confident Bradbury had a greater ability to move books than most of his other writers. One of the people Bradbury sent a copy of this book to was Hal Foster, the *Prince Valiant* artist whose works he had obsessively scrapbooked as a boy. He signed it, "You're one of the greatest artists of the 20th century. I love your work and I love you."[10]

Dark Carnival remains a highly collectible book, since it was almost never reprinted. A British edition was released with fewer stories due to lingering wartime paper shortages, and in 2001 Bradbury published a limited-edition reprint, with new material and a cover that Bradbury had painted himself when he was a young man. Recently, HarperCollins issued a reprint available in Britain. Sixteen of the 27 stories in *Dark Carnival* had been published in the pulps but were altered from how they originally appeared in the magazines.[11] Bradbury bought the rights to *Dark Carnival* and reprinted many, but not all, of those stories in the collection *The October Country*, but the *October* stories from *Dark Carnival* he altered further still. As Bradbury once explained, "You age between publications of a story. You have to go over everything very carefully and make sure it's the way you want."[12] Most, if not all, of the stories were written in his father's garage in Venice Beach in 1947, next to the humming powerhouse.

42

The Beast from 20,000 Fathoms

After the war, Ray Harryhausen struck out on his own to make it as a 3-D animator. One of his first stateside projects was a commercial using Lucky Strikes, an ad that ended with a batch of dancing cigarettes spelling out "Lucky Strikes Means Fine Tobacco." He used the project to convince advertisers of his ability, but it was not meant to be an actual ad that aired. (When this experiment was released to the DVD *The Early Ray Harryhausen*, it was preceded by several disclaimers insisting Harryhausen did not, in fact, back tobacco.) He later complained that the commercial was "borrowed" without his permission.[1] He next produced a series of commercials for the Los Angeles Lakewood Real Estate company. He dreamt up the character "Kenny Key," a dancing key sporting a derby hat, bowtie, cane, and cigar, an endeavor that took eight weeks to shoot. He made other commercials that paid little and "didn't inspire" him.[2] He needed a project that he both loved and would display his talent.

At war's end he got ahold of 1,000 feet of 16 mm Kodachrome stock that the navy was just going to throw away. (Kodachrome was such high quality that decades later, when the academy worked to preserve his early works, they were able to make film negatives directly from Harryhausen's original prints, then almost 50 years old.) He used this trove to animate classic fairy tales and nursery rhymes, starting with Mother Goose, then Little Red Riding Hood, Rapunzel, Hansel and Gretel, and King Midas. Both of his parents helped build the sets, with his mother baking and decorating the actual gingerbread home for Hansel and Gretel (tragically, this piece of cinema history was lost to the hungry mice of Harryhausen's garage). Martha also sewed costumes, tiny curtains, and any other fabric needed, while his father helped build miniature sets. His parents appear in the credits as Fred Blasauf and Martha Reske.

Sometimes Ray bought props, little pictures, and furniture, at a shop on Olvera Street, a then Mexican part of LA. He wrote in his book *The Art of Ray Harryhausen* that while his parents had been more than supportive, "I couldn't expect them to keep me all my life."[3] He referred to these fairy tales as his "teething rings." To emote the characters, Harryhausen created a series of heads to show characters smiling, grimacing, etc. He displayed these heads in his London office for decades.[4] He sold the fairy tale films to schools across the country. Most schoolchildren of the '40s and '50s saw at least one of Harryhausen's originals flickering from the back of a classroom.

A golden opportunity came when his mentor Willis O'Brien contacted him about working on another gorilla picture. Harryhausen enthusiastically agreed to help with *Mighty Joe Young*, not only designing the armatures of the title gorilla, but also doing about 90 percent of the actual animation work. Ray worked quickly but effectively, earning the nickname "One Take Harryhausen." O'Brien later hired him to animate the dinosaur sequences for *The Animal World* (1956), a nature documentary that otherwise had real footage of living creatures. Nevertheless, O'Brien's dinosaurs (he built them, Harryhausen animated them) were featured on the poster of the film, even though they were only in the movie for about 10 minutes. The fighting monsters even got a second life as a View-Master sequence and also popped up in a few films and TV shows that needed a dinosaur sequence but couldn't afford to make their own.

The Two Rays Work Together

By 1953 both Rays were professionals, busy in their respective fields, Harryhausen with his monsters, Bradbury with his typewriter. Not only was Bradbury enjoying accolades as a fine short story writer and getting his works published as collections (*Dark Carnival*, *The Martian Chronicles*, *The Illustrated Man*), but he also was writing for early television. His works were adapted for the earliest of thriller TV shows, such as *Lights Out* (originally a radio series, where Bradbury stories also appeared), *Out There*, and *Suspense*, shows so early (1951–52) that there are no existing prints. He also worked closely with EC to have dozens of his stories adapted for their line of mystery and science fiction comics. In 1951 he wrote a short novella called *The Fireman*. His agent and publisher both agreed the work could be expanded into a novel. One day, while typing in his garage, he saw a ray of sunshine stream onto a book, making him wonder at what temperature paper burns. The title *Fahrenheit 451* was born.

He also wrote the screenplay for the film *It Came from Outer Space*, credited as the first major 3-D film.

Nevertheless, the Rays had time to visit bookstores, see films, and otherwise spend a lot of time together. Because Bradbury never learned to drive, Harryhausen often drove his pal to important, life-altering events. It was Harryhausen who chauffeured newlyweds Ray Bradbury and Marguerite McClure to their new home in Venice after their wedding and supper afterwards. It was coming home from a bookstore with Harryhausen that Bradbury got the message that director John Huston had called, asking if the aspiring screenwriter would be interested in living in Ireland for a few months to work on his screenplay of *Moby Dick*. Then it was Harryhausen who saw the Bradbury family off to Ireland. Once, Harryhausen drove Bradbury to meet Aldous Huxley, an incident that did not go well for the animator. In 1951 Bradbury was invited to have tea at Huxley's home, a meeting that also included Gerald Heard and Christopher Isherwood. Bradbury got Harryhausen to give him a ride, but once there, the British author of *Brave New World* explained that Harryhausen wasn't invited and so would have to wait outside. Bradbury apologized to his friend, then went inside, leaving his best friend to spend the afternoon sitting on Huxley's front steps.[5]

Bradbury's favorite memory of Harryhausen took place at a Halloween party in 1950, a small gala at the Bradbury house that included Bradbury, Maggie, Fritz Lang with Lily Latte, and Ray Harryhausen and his marionettes. It was not uncommon for Harryhausen to bring puppets and/or dinosaurs with him to different gatherings so he could entertain, stowing his creations in a suitcase. On this Halloween, Harryhausen brought a doll that looked like Bette Davis. They put on a record and he made the marionette walk like the actress. "Ray's creative energy and humanity came down through those strings into the body of that marionette," Ray recalled. "Fritz Lang and I were stunned, because what he was doing was impossible—impossible, that is unless you're Ray Harryhausen, and you were born to perform that certain kind of magic."[6]

When Harryhausen was tapped to make his first independent monster movie, he called on his buddy Bradbury to do the writing. It seemed that after a decade of dreaming and talking, the two Rays were finally going to make their great dinosaur movie.

The Beast from 20,000 Fathoms is one of the most important if not the most important monster movie ever made. It was the first time Harryhausen had complete control of a project; it was his introduction of the technique he would call Dynamation; it began the monsters-on-a-rampage craze of the '50s, the *Beast* being the first time a nuclear explosion brought a creature to life; and *Beast* was the closest the two Rays came to doing a film together.

Origins of the Beast

Bradbury and Maggie were strolling down Venice Beach when they saw scraps of a roller coaster rusting in the ocean, remnants of an amusement park that had been there in better times. (Elsewhere in Venice, old circus lion cages had been left to rot in the ocean, the inspiration for the opening scene in Bradbury's *Death Is a Lonely Business*.) The long metal and knotted track reminded Bradbury of a dinosaur skeleton. What's a dinosaur doing in Venice Beach? Later, in the middle of the night, he heard a foghorn sound off. Of course. The dinosaur, last of its kind, rose from the deep after hearing the foghorn, thinking he'd finally found a companion. Bradbury wrote "The Fog Horn" the following morning.

The story would appear in the *Saturday Evening Post* under the much punchier title "The Beast from 20,000 Fathoms" (it would always, in every Bradbury collection, be titled "The Fog Horn"), accompanied by a beautiful two-page illustration by James R. Bingham of a dinosaur attacking a lighthouse.

At the same time, the producing team of Jack Dietz and Hal Chester had contracted Harryhausen to make a monster for the film they were calling simply *Monster from the Sea*. *King Kong* had recently been re-released and again packed movie houses, convincing the pair of producers that monsters were star attractions. According to Harryhausen, producer Jack Dietz went into his office, threw down the two-page spread of the dinosaur attacking the lighthouse from the *Saturday Evening Post*, and said, "That's the beast we want."[7] Harryhausen recommended his pal Bradbury to write the project (whether or not Harryhausen noticed that Bradbury's name was attached to the story in the *Post* isn't known). Hal Chester called on Bradbury to critique the script so far and provide professional feedback.

Bradbury read the screenplay and pointed out the similarity between *Monster* and his own story. According to Bradbury, Hal Chester's jaw dropped when he explained that the "beast" looked a lot like a creature the fantasy writer had created for the *Saturday Evening Post*. Chester, for his part, would always say he'd gotten the idea from different articles about the depths of the ocean and recent discoveries of frozen woolly mammoths.

However the idea came about, Chester soon realized the value in having Bradbury's name attached to the film and wrote him a royalty check. He also bought the rights to the title; *The Monster from the Sea* would now be known as *The Beast from 20,000 Fathoms*.

Bradbury's involvement never went beyond allowing Universal to use his idea. His name would be displayed prominently on the posters, and one of the trailers ran, "The Importance and Impact of the *Saturday Evening Post* Thriller that Held Millions Spellbound." The opening credits would say that the film was "suggested by" a story by Ray Bradbury. Bradbury always insisted that he had wanted to work on the film further but that no one called him back.

In any case, the young screenwriter soon got an offer he couldn't refuse, working for the legendary director John Huston on an adaptation of *Moby Dick*. Bradbury spent four in months in Ireland in 1953–54 working on the project. Like every other aspect of his life, Bradbury's time in Dublin would inspire him. He wrote a series of one-act plays, short stories, and eventually a novel, *Green Shadows, White Whale*, about his time on the Emerald Isle. John Huston would later tell Bradbury that "The Fog Horn" convinced him Bradbury was the man for the adaptation.

The *Beast* cost about $200,000 to make and raked in millions, making it one of the most profitable films of 1953.[8] It is full of personal touches from Harryhausen. In the scene where the two lead men are looking through drawings of dinosaurs, most of the artwork is by Charles R. Knight, who had a huge influence on Harryhausen and is considered the best dinosaur artist of all time. The animator's beast is more thoughtful and detailed than most giant monsters of the era. Instead of simply squashing a car underfoot, it steps on a car, does a double take, and swipes it away; such little details added hours of work. (Harryhausen would always insist, however, that it was a coincidence that the first two letters of the fictional dinosaur's name—rhedosaurus—were his initials.) Sadly, the eponymous beast no longer survives; Harryhausen, ever pragmatic, pillaged the rhedosaurus for the dragon sequence in *The 7th Voyage of Sinbad*.

Like all success stories in Hollywood, *20,000 Fathoms* birthed many imitators. In the '50s, drive-ins seemingly hosted another monster every week, where giant spiders/crickets/lizards sacked a different city, keeping the National Guard busy through the decade. The best and most famous imitation of Harryhausen's creature was Godzilla. Lest there be any doubt about what inspired the most famous of Japanese monsters, the working title for *Godzilla* was *The Big Monster from 20,000 Miles Beneath the Sea*.[9] (Note: It is not possible to go 20,000 miles or 20,000 fathoms below the ocean. A fathom is equal to six feet, so 20,000 fathoms would be 120,000 feet or a little over 22 miles. The deepest point of the ocean is the bottom of the Mariana Trench, not quite 36,000 feet, about seven miles.)

The Beast from 20,000 Fathoms also brought about Harryhausen's efficient Dynamation technique. He realized that if he were to continue to make monster movies, he needed to find a way to make them more affordable. The extensive matte paintings, dozens of models, and elaborate miniature sets of his hero, Willis O'Brien, were dazzling but simply more than what producers were willing to pay for. Unless all future dinosaurs were to be stuntmen in costumes or lizards with fins glued to their backs (several iguanas and gila monsters were hurt—or at least humiliated—in the making of monster movies in the '50s and '60s), he needed to find a way to do it cheaper.

The result was Dynamation, the revolutionary technique where his creations reacted to actors, rather than the other way around. Simply put, he would first film actors responding to whatever creature was the star of a particular scene, be it a skeleton or a beast from another planet. He would then rear-project (meaning the projector is behind the screen instead of in front) this footage onto a screen with his miniature standing in front. Advancing the film one frame at a time, he would move the creature in conjunction with the action behind it, shoot one frame, then forward the film another frame and move the creature slightly, and so on. The creature was sandwiched between this rear-projected screen and a piece of glass. On the glass Harryhausen blacked out—matted—what was to be in front of the creature, plus whatever he didn't want to appear in the final film, such as the table the monster was standing on. After filming he would rewind the film and shoot again, the creature and animation table cleared away. A different piece of glass, the counter-matte, was inserted, this time blacking out what was clear and vice versa, completing the image.

Complicated as this sounds, Dynamation meant reduced costs, due to being able to use smaller models and not needing to create elaborate miniature worlds. This was far more efficient than the techniques of his mentor O'Brien, who created dozens of different models of Kong, everything from the giant hand that Fay Wray sat in to the mini version that scaled the Empire State Building. O'Brien designed 25 different models for *The Lost World*, along with many miniature sets.

Impressive as this was, his labor was simply beyond the reach of what studios could afford.

Harryhausen was passionate but also pragmatic, and all about efficiency. The reason the Ymir (pronounce *e-meer*) and the Cyclops both walk with their elbows bent, as if ready to pounce, was to save money. Doing away with the need to make their arms swing reduced animation time. Medusa's snake body was not an accurate portrayal of mythology, but it did save Harryhausen the trouble of having to animate more limbs. He used narration in the fairy tales so he wouldn't have to sync dialogue. Harryhausen's methods breathed new life into stop-motion animation.

None of this is to say that Harryhausen was lazy. He would consider it a good day if he could shoot 400 frames, or 30 feet of film, about 16 seconds. His most famous scene, the five-minute skeleton sequence from *Jason and the Argonauts*, took four months. He painstakingly moved each skeleton separately, alone. He sometimes did as little as 16 frames per day, less than a second of footage. It took him and his crew four days to film the destruction of the Supreme Court in *Earth vs. the Flying Saucers*, a sequence that lasts seven seconds.

It is rumored that producer Charles Schneer insured Harryhausen's hands for a million dollars.

As the decades ticked by Harryhausen felt that Hollywood would not accommodate him. He was originally approached to do the *King Kong* remake in the '70s, only to have producers walk away when he explained he would need about two years to complete the film, not really that much time to make a feature length stop-motion animation movie. Having done almost all of the animation of every film himself for his 16 features, his last film would be *Clash of the Titans* in 1980. As he aged he increasingly didn't care for modern movies, saying he was so sickened by *The Silence of the Lambs* he had to walk out. In a letter to Ray Bradbury dated November 14, 1973, he wrote that he expected the public to enjoy his latest effort, *The Golden Voyage of Sinbad*, assuming the public was "fed up with sex, sadism and blood and guts." He could care less for CGI, explaining in an interview, "If you make it too realistic, you bring it down to the mundane level."[10] Stop-motion animation had a surreal quality that he preferred.

In 1986 he established the Ray and Diana Harryhausen Foundation as an organization to look after and take care of his models. In 2008 he had his daughter Vanessa investigate the contents of a garage on his property in California. There she and a team of men (her husband, Kenny; special effects artist Randy Cook; and filmmaker Jim Danforth) discovered a total of 14 boxes of material they shipped back to London. The trove included test footage from *20 Million Miles to Earth* and the 7th *Voyage of Sinbad*; models from his fairy tales, like Little Miss Muffet (somewhat worse for the wear as she'd been stashed in the bottom of a box), the spider that scared her, and the Queen of Hearts; an early King Kong puppet he'd made as a boy; a woolly mammoth and T.rex armature from his early *Evolution* project; a plethora of sketches; the cave bear model (albeit missing its head) that Harryhausen created from his mom's old fur coat; the bottom half of one of the saucers from *Earth vs. the Flying Saucers*; and his first skeleton. They found additional footage of Harryhausen and his dad walking, running, or otherwise reacting to unseen monsters, footage young Harryhausen no doubt planned to use in future projects. This early film is now stored at the custom-built archive for WingNut Films in New Zealand, which is owned by Peter Jackson.

As for the two Rays making a film together, Harryhausen later explained that Bradbury wasn't so sure that was such a great idea after all: "Ray pointed out that it might be dangerous to work together because we might lose our friendship. These businesses are crazy and the very essence of it can sometimes antagonize friendships."[11]

Perhaps Bradbury was thinking about his strained relationship with Huston that came about when they were working on *Moby Dick* together. Maybe, but Bradbury doesn't appear to have ever given up on working with Harryhausen completely. In a letter from Harryhausen to Bradbury, the animator explains that he will not be able to work on a filmed version of Bradbury's novel *The Halloween Tree*, as Bradbury had suggested. It's tantalizing to think about what might have been.

43

Forry Ackerman's Agency

On January 1, 1945, Forry Ackerman's younger brother, Alden, was killed at the Battle of the Bulge. He was all of 20.

Forry published a eulogy in the January 1945 *Voice of the Imagination* that at times could be underwhelming: "There is, at the present time, not one person living that I know of who would say 'Forry, hop to it; you've carte blanche with me; I'm behind you 100%.' So it works out this way, that I say 'OK, I'll dedicate myself to humanity thru my brother.'" Writing eulogies would never be Forry's forte.

The death of his brother did not sell Forry on military service; he would later have nightmares about his time in the army even though he stayed close to home, rose to the rank of staff sergeant with five people working beneath him, and never saw combat. His nightmares always involved him somehow getting drafted back into the army. He had dreams of someone giving him a "little card to carry that says Ackerman ain't in the Army anymore and I carry that around in case of emergency, that if something comes up they try to tap me and I say Nope! Nope! I got my card."[1] Later in life, at one of his many auctions of some of his own memorabilia, he offered up his old army uniform for exactly one dollar.

After the war, Ackerman was determined to somehow, someway, earn a living with his love of all things science fiction and the fantastic. He tried his hand at writing and got some stories published. For the most part, though, he wanted to work in the world of science fiction rather than creating new works. In 1947 Ackerman, following the advice of his good friend and writer Henry Kuttner, established the Ackerman Agency International (a.k.a. the Science Fantasy Agency, also sometimes called the Ackerman Authors Agency).

He represented, among others, L. Ron Hubbard, one of his friends from his LASFS days. Forry was one of the first people Hubbard revealed his newfound knowledge to, revelations that eventually led to the religion of Scientology. Hubbard told Forry about a manuscript he'd written, *Excalibur*, so profound that it drove anyone who read it insane, to the point of suicide. The last person who'd read it jumped out a window, Hubbard insisted. Forry never saw it.

Forry was willing to give Scientology a chance, but became disillusioned with this new religion when a young woman who was supposed to be Scientology's first "clear"—meaning, among other things, that she would remember everything that had happened up to that point in her life—got up on stage at a conference and could not repeat words that had just been read to her from a dictionary.[2] But Ackerman never gave up on Scientology completely, saying that Dianetics helped him deal with his

FORREST J ACKERMAN

Sci-Fi/Imagi-Movies
Author • Editor • Actor • Agent
**FAMOUS MONSTERS OF FILMLAND
WONDERAMA**

2495 Glendower Avenue
Horrorwood, Karloffornia 90027
Fon: 213-MOONFAN
Fax: 213-664-5612

One of Forry Ackerman's many business cards (from the collection of John L. Coker III).

brother's death and that Hubbard's treatment got him over his fear of dogs. Another "religion" of sorts he tinkered with was cryogenics, or being frozen and then revived in the future. In an interview he claimed to be present within 48 hours of the first human being cryogenically frozen[3] and speculated that he might choose to undergo the procedure when facing death's door, joking that he just might make a comeback decades in the future.

He continued to attend every World Science Fiction Convention. The 1953 Worldcon was the first where the "Hugos"—the Oscars of science fiction—were handed out, named after Hugo Gernsback. Ackerman received the very first Hugo (one of six that year), handed to him by none other than toastmaster Isaac Asimov. The award was for #1 Fan Personality. Ackerman "re-warded" the award to another fan in England who he earnestly felt deserved it more, Kenneth F. Slater.

In the end, his three main contributions to science fiction fandom all stemmed from his habits as an early 20-something: his tinkering with language, which led to the invention of the phrase "sci-fi"; giving fans free tours of his collection, spawning the Ackermansion; and his love of publishing, leading to the highly influential cult magazine, *Famous Monsters of Filmland*.

Science Fiction versus Sci-Fi

For all of his attempts to "improve" English, Ackerman's one lasting contribution to the language would be shortening science fiction to "sci-fi." Ackerman always said the idea came to him while driving with Wendy in 1954, when an ad came over the radio advertising hi-fi stereo. On the spot, he swapped out "hi-fi" with "sci-fi" (Wendy thought it would never catch on). Or so Ackerman says—Heinlein claimed to have used the phrase five years earlier. The phrase was not popular with everyone. Writer

Harlan Ellison—among his several contributions to science fiction are classic episodes of *Star Trek*—especially hated the phrase, claiming that "sci-fi" was "the sound of two crickets screwing." To which Ackerman replied, "You must really have your ear down in the dirt to hear two crickets screwing." Ellison found the phrase derogatory, the equivalent of calling women "broads" or "chicks." Ackerman claimed he'd never heard Ellison call women anything but "chicks."[4] Ellison lectured entire audiences about why they must never use the phrase. His campaign against the phrase wouldn't succeed, though plenty of purists still loath the shortening.[5]

The Origin of Famous Monsters of Filmland

In September of 1957 Ackerman was staying at the Hotel Chesterfield in Manhattan when he heard a knock on the door. Instead of the male magazine publisher he was expecting to see, he found himself looking at a stunning young blonde. "You must be James Warren's girlfriend," was all he could say. Soon Warren himself popped into view from his hiding spot. It turned out Ackerman had unintentionally stopped a prank cold; the girl, Phyllis Farkas, was to rip off her blouse and scream rape, and then Warren would barge in and confront Ackerman. The joke foiled, the two men soon got down to business (Phyllis Farkas would help edit *Famous Monsters*).[6]

Ackerman and Warren had been corresponding for years. Warren was one of the many publishers Ackerman contacted in hopes of selling works of the talent he represented as a literary agent, a stable that housed the likes of L. Ron Hubbard, Isaac Asimov, and Ed Wood. (He met Ed Wood, who tried to get him to sell some of his stories, at a party. Wood supplied him with a few "fantasy stories," but that was as far as their relationship went, besides a few drunken phone calls late at night. Ackerman would later joke that he was Ed's "illiterary agent." Decades later, after the legendarily bad director had passed, Ackerman finally published one of Ed Wood's stories, complete with misspellings, such as a woman being tied up, "bound and gaged." He said Ed was "really in earnest" and always did his best.) By his own recollection, Ackerman was representing about 150 writers, including handling the foreign rights for his old buddy Ray Bradbury. The phone number Ackerman had as a literary agent began with 666.

James Warren was the publisher of a short-lived magazine called *After Hours*, described as a poor man's *Playboy*. Each issue had a different theme, and, at Ackerman's suggestion, Warren decided to make the fourth a science fiction issue, devoted to the girls of tomorrow. Ackerman contributed both stories and nonfiction pertaining to science fiction. He mined his collection for images of curvy, semi- or totally nude women from sci-fi and fantasy to run alongside his writing. These pictures included covers from M. Brundage, whose bound nudes looked totally at home in a pornographic magazine. For some reason and related to nothing else in the contents, this issue also printed a few photos of legendary pinup Bettie Page, complete in her jungle girl outfit.

This would turn out to be the last issue of *After Hours*. The publication was hardly the only *Playboy*-imitation on the market, and Warren faced legal troubles as part of an anti-smut campaign then sweeping through his native Philadelphia. The charges were dropped, but not until after he had been arrested.[7] He needed something new, ideally a publication that would turn a profit fast.

Warren's next venture was one that would cash in on the monster craze dominating the youth market of the time. Universal had recently rolled out Shock Theatre, a package of pre-war horror films (including *Dracula*, *Frankenstein*, and *The Wolfman*) to be shown in syndication on local stations. With many of the movies only an hour to an hour and a half long, a horror host introduced each movie and added bits of commentary along the way to make these programs fill air time.[8] Most major cities had their own version of Shock Theatre with an accompanying host (and occasional hostess), from the "Cool Ghoul" Roland of WCAU-TV in Philadelphia to Dr. Meridian of WPTA in Fort Wayne, Indiana. As Ackerman put it, the old films were "exhumed like a mummy for individual telecasting."[9] Meanwhile, new B-horror films dominated the theaters, as they were cheaply made with mostly unknown actors (e.g., Michael Landon played the title character in *I Was a Teenage Werewolf*). Horror was everywhere, fueled by the Baby Boom generation now entering its teen years. The time was ripe for *Famous Monsters of Filmland*.

In 1957 Ackerman was visiting Paris on the way home from the 15th World Science Fiction Convention in London (Loncon—the first Worldcon held other than in North America) when he picked up a magazine devoted to classic monsters. There on the cover of *Cinema 57* snarled the Werewolf of London. In between the pages loomed Dracula, Frankenstein, and other heroes of his youth. Ackerman bought six copies.[10]

Ackerman showed Warren one of these editions, and Warren realized a publication devoted to classic monsters could turn a profit. Initially the plan was to simply translate *Cinema 57* and reprint the photos, a one-shot printing that would earn some fast money. Like most get-rich-quick schemes, this plan was far easier said than done. After having the text translated into English, Warren found the writing too esoteric for the teen and young adult audience his magazine would be aimed at. He also found that the stills from the magazine were in the hands of private collectors and that tracking them down would be quite the chore and involve legal hassles. Forry assured Warren he could replicate most if not all of the images from his own personal collection of stills, clippings, and pressbooks. At this point Ackerman had about 35,000 pictures, the collection he'd been building since he was a 10-year-old buying lobby cards from movie theaters.

Decades later Forry recalled, "This will be just one opportunity in my whole life to get my best stills out of my files and present them in a magazine."[11] Both men went into the project seeing it as something they would do once and move on. Warren certainly needed the money. When he first "flew" to LA to meet Ackerman, he had actually hopped on a Greyhound to Vegas, then flew into LA from there, giving the appearance of having more money than he really did.

Ackerman printed a quick mock-up of the magazine he was calling "Wonderama." Warren shopped the idea around to numerous New York publishers only to be rebuffed every time. A total of 13 distributors passed.[12] Salvation came from *Life* magazine, which happened to publish a piece on the monster craze currently raging through the American teen culture. It was a brief paragraph titled "Ghastly Look of Film Fad" surrounded by still images and posters of then hits like *I Was a Teenage Werewolf* and *The She-Creature*. "Ghastly sights are now in darkened movie theaters everywhere," the article explained, seemingly not approvingly. "Horror films as a group are the biggest profit makers in the business today."[13] It was this article that convinced the Kable News Company to back the project.[14]

Soon, Jim Warren and Forry J were working long hours putting together the issue. Ackerman's intention was a single publication with stills from what he felt were the most important films of the 1920s and '30s—that period he defined as the best era of cinema—with accompanying text. *Phantom of the Opera, Things to Come, The Mystery of the Wax Museum*, and, naturally, *King Kong* were among the films to be profiled. He would use a total of 75 stills from his private collection in the first issue of *Famous Monsters of Filmland*, a title Forry hated. He wanted to call it "Wonderama" because he was always a fan more of science fiction than horror, and the idea of a magazine specifically for horror initially had limited appeal. "Monsters were a very minor part of the publication as far as I was concerned,"[15] Ackerman later recalled in an interview. "He [Warren] said, 'I don't think you're going to like the idea, but you are going to be the editor of a magazine called—are you ready for this—Famous Monsters of Filmland.' And indeed I let out a shriek heard round the world."[16] But with Kable writing the checks he had to compromise. "That's the way the mummy crumbles," he quipped. Warren designed the *Famous Monsters* logo on a cocktail napkin, a signature that has been practically unchanged over the decades.

It was Warren's idea to give the magazine a childish, humorous lean. He had noticed that films that would have terrified children a generation prior were mostly drawing giggles. According to Ackerman, Warren would hold up a sign saying, "I am 11 and a half yours old, and I am your reader. Make me laugh." Forry was not keen on laughing at the legends he had admired his whole life, but Warren had invested $30,000 in the project.

The two men put in 20-hour days assembling *Famous Monsters*, Warren staying at a nearby hotel. "I would turn out copy till 3 or 4 in the morning," recalled Ackerman. "Then we would drive over 3 blocks to Ships 24 hour restaurant ... after which I left Jim off at a nearby motel, went home to bed and 4 hours later picked him up again and we were off and running."[17]

Ackerman could use the distraction; unbeknownst to Warren, Wendy was drawing up divorce papers. Ackerman had been planning to file himself, but she hit first. The issue was her son Michael, with whom Forry didn't want to be weighed down. Her lawyer threatened to take half of his collection. They divorced but remarried in 1972 and would be companions for life.

For the cover, James Warren himself dressed up as Frankenstein, a smiling girl named Marion Moore (a local waitress Warren recruited) in a low-cut top looking up at him. This first issue had "Collector's Edition" printed on the cover, which is exactly what it became. It's one of the few items stamped as "collectible" that would actually turn out to be valuable.

Ackerman's prints were all over the first run of *Famous Monsters*, an issue that would define the magazine. Much of what would make *Famous Monsters* famous is right there, such as his whacky puns and silliness seemingly lifted from the pages of *Imagination!*, starting with the very first sentence:

"You're stuck! The stuff this magazine is printed on ... is actually glue. YOU CANNOT PUT THIS MAGAZINE DOWN!" The introductory article ended with Forry's suggestion at a new insult: "When your best friend starts giving you a hard time ... just shrug your head nonchalantly and stop him cold in his cracks with, 'Well, that's how the monster mumbles.'"

That phrase never caught on, but the magazine did, and the first issue set a precedent for what would become typical of *Famous Monsters*. Articles like "Alice in Monsterland" and "Monsters Are Good For You." All of Forry's favorites are there, as he really did think there wouldn't be a second issue. (He later said in an interview that if he'd had his way, not an issue would go by without Lugosi, Karloff, and Lon Chaney, Sr. That was almost the case.[18]) He devoted considerable space to Lugosi, Karloff, King Kong, and his all-time favorite, Lon Chaney Sr., all of them accompanied by his stills. Forry also ran the illustrated story "Frank and Humbug."

Ackerman also wrote an article on special effects, called "How Hollywood Makes a Monster." Here he profiled the husband-and-wife monster-making team Paul and Jackie Blaisdell, who created such beasts as the She-Creature and the Puppet-People. Forry's focus on filmmaking techniques is what would make *Famous Monsters* a must for little boys like Steven Spielberg and George Lucas. Magazines about Hollywood have been published since its earliest days, but Ackerman was the first to focus on the "Backroom Boys," the special effects wizards behind the camera. These articles sometimes gave intricate details about how the Hollywood makeup artists created their monstrous creations. The very second page of the first issue shows an actress having monster makeup applied for the lead role in *Ape Girl*.

 The first issue of *Famous Monsters of Filmland* was a runaway success, selling about 150,000 copies in spite of it hitting magazine stands in New York during a devastating blizzard. The magazine garnered 75 fan letters the day after it first went out, a total of 300 in its first four days of existence.[19] Warren had shrewdly advertised in high school newspapers across the country and also sent color proofs of the cover to TV stations hosting Shock Theatre in hopes they would promote the magazine. Warren asked Forry if he had enough stills for another issue. Forry said he could supply *FM* with enough images "until [his] dying day and 17 reincarnations beyond that."[20]

The second issue triumphantly declared on the cover, "First issue sold out!," once again displaying Warren in a monster mask. Issue #2 also points out that someone can be seen reading the first issue of *FM* in the film *Earth vs. The Spider*, the film's producer being an early fan. It was to be the first of many endorsements from Hollywood insiders. Published in issue #2 would be a picture a fan sent in of himself dressed up as the Creature from the Black Lagoon, which began a trend of publishing photos of fans disguised as their favorite famous monster. Issue #2 also wrote up about upcoming scary movies, "More than you could shake a broomstick at!" Summing up current horror and fantasy while advertising any and all upcoming horror films, a TV Guide for horror fans would also become a staple of *Famous Monsters*. (Ackerman listed every film absolutely regardless of quality. In the second issue he mentions the Ed Wood film *Graverobbers from Outer Space*, better known as *Plan 9 from Outer Space*.) The same fan who meticulously published lists of any and all imagimovies as a teenager in the early '30s was now putting this seemingly useless talent to use. He even mentioned LASFS briefly in the second issue, when he wrote how "the world's oldest science fiction club turned out en masse" to see *Son of Frankenstein* when it was released.

And there was still more of Lon Chaney Sr., Bela Lugosi, and Boris Karloff.

Issue #2 ("The only magazine banned in Transylvania!") introduced two new revenue streams. One was a mail-order section in the back that would balloon to include all sorts of playful terrors. To name but a random few, any 11-year-old with a paper route or who sold enough issues of *Grit* could order a six-foot Frankenstein pin-up, a Dracula kite, rubber bats (of course), a variety of monster masks (sometimes with accompanying claws), makeup kits to transform yourself into any number of creatures, little coffin-shaped boxes in which to save previous issues, genuine soil from Castle Dracula,[21] Venus flytraps, shrunken heads, and even a squirrel monkey ("Live delivery guaranteed"). Many of the offerings from the back pages of *Famous Monsters* have become collectibles in their own right. The glow-in-the-dark toys, Pez dispensers, and Aurora plastic model kits of classic Universal monsters command respectable sales on eBay.

For more adult subscribers, they sold both projectors and 8 mm reels of classic films, marketing to the first generation of fans to enjoy their favorite movies at home, pre–VCR. If a reader hoarded his pennies he just might have been able to afford an 8 mm projector for a mere $9.98, plus postage and handling ("Portable! Lets you show monster movies anywhere—any time!"). The projector could show 200-foot wonders that included Lugosi and Karloff movies, along with Harryhausen classics like *Mighty Joe Young* and *Earth vs. the Flying Saucers*.

The second new source of income was for boys (and some girls) to join the Famous Monsters Club. In the back pages of issue #2, between a hairy gorilla's arms, ran an ad explaining to kids that for 75 cents they would receive an official Famous Monsters badge (sporting Lon Chaney Sr. as Phantom of the Opera), a certificate, and a membership card.

To save money (sales of issue #2 were not nearly as good as those for #1), Warren painted the cover of #3 himself, a headshot of Lon Chaney's Phantom of the Opera. From that point on and for decades to come, each cover of *FM* would be graced with an original painting, starting with artist Albert Nuetzell, who would be replaced in November of 1960 (#9) by Basil Gogos. Gogos's bright, colorful portraits displayed the likes of Karloff and Lugosi in all of their bloody beauty. His first portrait was of Vincent Price.

Ackerman used his vast collection of stills to reply to fan requests for photos from various horror and sci-fi films, in a feature he called "You axed for it!" Before the internet, Forry Ackerman could dig out a photo of that one actor from that one obscure horror film.

He also published a pen pal section. Just as Gernsback created a letters section for fans to get in touch with one another, Ackerman created a pen pal section where fans could leave their names, addresses, and interests. "I am 15 years old and would like to hear from serious animation fans to exchange ideas and techniques," wrote one fan, then left his name and address. "I am a Trekkie. I do monster makeup. I would like to hear from high schoolers," ran another. At times the letters read like singles ads: "Interested in Gothic horror, fantasy. Would like to write girls 16 and up" ran one ad, followed by a male name and British address. "I'm 19 and would like to write to a girl between 14 and 19 who is a Bela Lugosi admirer," went another.[22] Forry also created a swap section, where fans could write in advertising what they were willing to sell or looking to buy, such as one fan who said he was keen to buy anything related to Flash Gordon "such as props, belts, ray guns, etc."[23]

There were imitators almost immediately following *Famous Monsters* #1, with Warren going as far as to unsuccessfully sue the publishers of *World Famous Creatures*, which came out sometime between *FM* #2 and #3. (Forry recalled that *WFC* imitated his puns and even a few facts that he had made up as a joke, meaning they couldn't have gotten these "facts" from anywhere else.) There would be other knock-offs, such as *Castle of Frankenstein*, *Mad Monsters*, and *Monsterscene*, but *Famous Monsters of Filmland* would stay on top and have the greatest impact.

In spite of its success, *Famous Monsters* didn't pay Ackerman as well as it should have. Still, he hung on, maybe hoping for more money down the road or that he could monetize the success of *FM*, somehow.

Or maybe he was just having too much fun. Here, finally, was validation for the crazy kid who had spent hours hoarding movie stills, writing about movies, compiling lists of any and all horror, fantasy, and science fiction. He was finally sharing the useless knowledge he'd been amassing since he was nine, and the world wrote back. He received hundreds of letters every week, and replied to as many as he could (he claimed he replied to all of them). "Dr. Acula"—one of his many self-assigned nicknames—hated Sundays and holidays because the mail didn't come. He published fan letters in a column, Fang Mail (his mother managed the hundreds of daily Fang Mail letters for years). Readers sending in a picture of themselves saw their own photos published alongside their letters, especially if in the photos they donned fangs or a cape. In the early sixties, in the pages of *Famous Monsters*, he explained that he would be doing a tour of the country, and if a fan wrote in, he or she may just get a visit from Dr. Acula himself. More than 8,700 fans, mostly young adults and children, wrote in. In 1964 he and his wife embarked on the promised trip, meeting some 1,300 fans.[24]

Adults often disapproved of *Famous Monsters* and its imitators. Martin Powell writes about going to the drugstore with his dad just to buy comics and *Famous Monsters of Filmland*. "Predictably, the sour-faced little old lady at the cash register never failed to give me a surly frown, along with my change, whenever I plunked down for the latest issue Famous Monsters of Filmland on her counter." More than one young fan of *Famous Monsters* recalled hiding the magazine under a bed or floorboards, like so much porn. James Van Hise, a close friend and biographer of Forry's, said that his first purchase of *Famous Monsters* so shocked his mother that he wouldn't be able to buy another copy until he was an adult. Forry hated the self-righteousness of parents and teachers and dubbed the PTA the "Peasants of Transylvania."

Ackerman and Warren teamed up to do almost 200 issues together, running sometimes quarterly, other times bimonthly. They experimented with other specialty magazines, but neither *Famous Westerns of Filmland* nor *Spacemen* caught on. It was *Famous Monsters* that would play the greatest role in raising the next generation of filmmakers.

44

The Ackermansion

> "Saturdays, Sundays and holidays don't mean a thing to me.... One day is much the same as the other. It's go, go, go, from the time I roll out of bed.... Life constantly revolves around some aspect of science fiction and fantasy."
> —Forrest Ackerman

In 1951 Ackerman moved out of the seven-room apartment that he'd been renting from his grandmother, which by now was full of memorabilia, and into a house proper. The first Ackermansion was on 915 Sherbourne Drive, which his father had bought for him, an address Ackerman inevitably referred to as "Scarebourne." On moving day he used the help of 13 friends—eager fans he paid with pieces of his own collection, mostly duplicates—to make repeated trips with a two-ton truck.

Briefly his wife managed to keep the collection in the basement, but it grew like so much science fiction kudzu, so that, within 10 years, the Ackermans would need to get a separate apartment, the house unlivable.

The collection continued its inexorable, blob-like growth, forcing the couple to move yet again in 1973. The Son of Ackermansion at 2495 Glendower Avenue in the Griffith Park area was located on a hill below the Wright-designed home that had the title role in the *House on Haunted Hill*, a domicile Forry always pointed out to his countless visitors. His 17-room Ackermansion once belonged to former film star Jon Hall, best known as Ramar of the Jungle.

The Ackermansion: A Tour

The walls of every room of the Son of Ackermansion were covered in art, including original *Famous Monsters* covers by Basil Gogos and Albert Nuetzell; original pulp art by Frank R. Paul, M. Brundage, Virgil Finlay, and old league member Hannes Bok, the artist Bradbury made famous; cover art replicas by Anton Brzezinski; lobby cards, movie stills, and posters, many of them ones that Forry had bought for a dime at local theaters as a child; and the painting Forry commissioned Frank Ron Paul to paint for him, recreating that first cover painting Ackerman stumbled across in a drugstore at age nine. Forry's recreation depicted himself standing in for the intergalactic explorer, and the title "Amazing Forries" in place of *Amazing Stories*. The living room housed a bookcase including rare first editions by H.P. Lovecraft and a piano

Top: Ray Harryhausen and Forry Ackerman (shown here circa 1965) bond in the Ackermansion over the creature that spawned their 70-year friendship. *Bottom:* Another photograph of Ray Harryhausen and Forry Ackerman at the Ackermansion circa 1975 (from the collection of John L. Coker III).

covered with Forry's own awards, such as a Nebula Award, various Hugo Awards, and the Saturn Award originally presented to Frank R. Paul (a ringed planet on a pedestal). In the living room Forry often sat in a stately wooden chair he claimed had once seated Lincoln as his great grandfather took a photograph of the president.

Next, into the dining room, where another bookcase stood with more than 500 different editions of *Frankenstein* and *Dracula*, including a first-edition *Dracula* signed by Bram Stoker, Bela Lugosi, Christopher Lee, and several other performers involved with their own versions of the vampire king. Different monster toys and heads, mostly of Frankenstein, stood atop this case. A larger-than-life wax figure of Frankenstein loomed in one corner.

Other rooms he devoted to his lifelong favorites. The Lon Chaney Sr. Room was just off the "kitchen" (so full of loot it's unlikely any cooking went on in there). In the Chaney Room he stored, among other treasures, Lon's beaver hat and fangs worn in the lost horror film *London After Midnight*. The Karloff/Lugosi room he decorated with old stills, posters, and paintings pertaining to both men, along with an original Bela Lugosi cape (from his last film, *Plan 9 from Outer Space*) as well as one of Lugosi's rings and bowties. A coffin lay in front of the sofa. The *Metropolis* Room, dedicated to Forry's favorite film, housed Fritz Lang's monocle along with other personal items of the Austrian-born director. The silver-painted walls were covered with rare *Metropolis* posters and artworks. Forry later claimed to have seen *Metropolis* 105 times, no small accomplishment in the time before VCRs.[1]

In various display cases he kept a collection of Harryhausen original models and miniatures, like the elephant who fought the Ymir of *20 Million Miles to Earth*, the model Embarcadero tower from *It Came from Beneath the Sea*, the US Capitol and saucers from *Earth vs. the Flying Saucers*, the miniature temple from *Jason and the Argonauts*, the centaur from *The Golden Voyage of Sinbad*, the lighthouse destroyed by *The Beast from 20,000 Fathoms*. Forry also owned some of Harryhausen's earliest creations, like the brontosaurus made with lamps and stockings. In Seattle, Ackerman picked up a replica that someone somehow made of the Martian Harryhausen created for a few minutes of a never-realized project, another film version of *War of the Worlds*. How this ended up in a Seattle flea market is anyone's guess.[2] By far his most unique Harryhausen item was the life mask the animator made of Ackerman when Ackerman was 24.

Besides Harryhausen's monsters, Ackerman collected the creations of the legendary stop-motion animator's lifelong mentor, Willis O'Brien. He owned O'Brien's brontosaurus from *The Lost World*, one of the original armatures of *King Kong*, and a menagerie of extinct animals from Skull Island, like the styracosaurus, the brontosaurus that ate a sailor in a tree, the stegosaurus, and the pteranodon who kidnapped Fay Wray (this flying beast was mailed to him in a shoebox, courtesy of Rod Serling's brother). Decades later, at a 50th anniversary screening of *King Kong* at Grauman's Chinese, he was on hand to show off these originals.

The "Garage Mahal," built to hold four cars, instead housed thousands of pulps, monster magazines, and books. These were spares; original copies he stored in the basement called "Grislyland," along with the thousands of stills, press clippings, posters, and childhood scrapbooks, as well as the replica of the Ultima Futuria "robotrix" from *Metropolis* commissioned by Forry and built at Don Post Studios. Forry loved this statue so much that he decorated her in lieu of a Christmas tree every December.

(He had been wanting to build a replica of that robot since at least the war. In the June 1944 issue of *Shangri-L'Affaires* he speculated on having Harryhausen make it.)

And then there was everything else. Entire books have been devoted to Ackerman's collection. Here is an abbreviated list of the items once in his museum of a home: the head and claws of the title character of *Creature from the Black Lagoon*; Captain Kirk's chair; Spock's ears; a Star Trek phaser; a hand-written screenplay of *The Wizard of Oz*; Claude Rains's cape from *Phantom of the Opera*; one of the hands from the original *The Thing*; possibly, one of the saucers from *Plan 9 from Outer Space* (some say Ackerman was duped into buying just an ordinary pie pan); a life mask of Bela Lugosi made for *The Return of the Vampire*; a Cylon from *Battlestar Galactica;* Lon Chaney Sr.'s fishing pole; the trophy head from 1932's *The Most Dangerous Game*; the arm and three-fingered hand from a dying alien at the end of *The War of the Worlds*; the only King Kong jigsaw puzzle known to still exist (these were sold as a promotional item to promote *King Kong* when it was released in 1933, one of the first examples of movie merchandising); an edition of *Frankenstein* signed by Mary Shelley to her goddaughter; numerous books autographed by Edgar Rice Burroughs, whom he'd met three times; most of Heinlein's books, autographed by the man himself; and drawings of Martians and Martian cars from his grandfather, George Herbert Wyman. In a 1988 interview with Eastern New Mexico University, he claimed to have 125,000 films.[3]

It was said that any random box in Ackerman's house was better than almost any individual collection anyplace else.

He had papers crucial to the history of science fiction, items thought lost that resurfaced after his death, including an early draft of a Stanley Weinbaum story, original manuscripts of L. Ron Hubbard and Bradbury (including an early version of *Fahrenheit 451*), a copy of the speech Heinlein gave at the 1941 Worldcon, and countless letters to and from countless fans, some famous, some who remained unknown. He got the final autograph of Bela Lugosi, Vincent Price, A.E. van Vogt, and others in the business. (He inherited many of Lugosi's personal possessions, simply because Forry had been his friend for years. Later in life, he would drive Bela to film premieres, often sitting with the legendary actor on the balcony, where Bela would chain smoke. Ackerman completely despised the depiction of Bela in *Ed Wood*. Bela was a gentleman who would never have called Karloff a "cocksucker." Forry's Lugosi collection included one of Dracula's capes, his ring, and a collection of sound discs from Lugosi's films. He once played these records back to an elderly Lugosi, who sat transfixed to hear his own voice again. Ackerman insisted he was the 99th person to walk past Lugosi's casket and said he half expected Bela to rise from the grave.)

What is most amazing is that most of these items Ackerman procured for almost nothing. Directors and propmen did not always treasure what they had and were willing to give items to the eccentric Forry for free. By the 1970s, with Ackerman's status as an expert and collector established, many of the directors who read *Famous Monsters* as kids now gave their props and other memorabilia to Forry free of charge, knowing they would be treasured. Hence Forry received the puppet of Stripe, leader of the eponymous creatures from the 1984 movie *Gremlins*. Director Joe Dante had been a fan.

Other items he got through sleuthing and searching, using techniques that would make Indiana Jones proud. The Gill-man costume of *Creature from the Black*

Lagoon fame, assembled by gluing foam rubber scales to a latex suit, was mostly thrown out. Forry got the head and claws of the Creature from a boy who had gotten them from another boy, who was the son of the janitor sweeping up the set after filming was completed. The janitor thought the costume pieces looked forgotten and figured they might make fun toys for his son to play with, which the boy did for years before selling them to another boy for $5. Forry somehow tracked down the second boy and asked if he would like to double his money, offering to buy the head and claws for $10. The boy—now old enough to drive—piled the head and claws into a rental car, drove to Forry's house, found no one home, and later returned the rental, forgetting the head and claws in the trunk. Luckily the young man retrieved both from the rental agency and handed them over to Ackerman, no harm done.[4]

Most amazingly of all, essentially anyone could see this collection, free of charge.

Not long after moving in to his first house in 1951, Ackerman began allowing people to view his collection. By his own reckoning, he hosted more than 50,000 visitors throughout his life.[5] Fritz Lang, Christopher Lee, Vincent Price, Bela Lugosi, and Barbara Steele are among the thousands who signed the guestbook. Later famous guests included Penn and Teller, Leonardo DiCaprio, and Steven Spielberg. Director John Landis and special effects master Rick Baker came to the Ackermansion together as a pair of unknown 21-year-olds and repeatedly visited after they had both made names for themselves.

One didn't need to be famous. Any determined enough reader of *Famous Monsters* could visit the Ackermansion so long as they planned accordingly. Forry hosted visitors, free of charge, every Saturday when he was home. If one was in LA, all he had to do was dial 213 MOON-FAN and he would be talking to the Ackerman himself. Even if a fan didn't phone ahead, odds were that if you saw his red Cadillac (the car was a gift from *Famous Monsters* publisher James Warren) parked in the driveway with the "SCI-FI" plate—he never parked in the garage, stuffed to the rafters with books and magazines—he'd be willing to give you a tour. You rang the bell, and a voice would answer, "Who dares disturb the sleep of the vampire?" He would come to the door wearing a Hawaiian shirt, more often than not also donning Bela Lugosi's cape, his hand boasting the ring Lugosi wore and also the scarab-beetle ring that had once been on Boris Karloff in *The Mummy*.

If a fan didn't live in California and lacked the funds to fly out there, there was just a chance a fan could win an all-expenses-paid trip to the sacred house on 2495 Glendower Avenue. *Famous Monsters* sponsored filmmaking contests, monster making contests, and other competitions where creatives sent in their material. Winners sometimes were rewarded with free flights to the Ackermansion.

In 1964 *Famous Monsters* sponsored a contest where fans could send in photos of their own monster disguise, done up in horror with an official *Famous Monsters* makeup kit (buying the kit was one of the conditions of entry). Runners up got trophies and their beautifully terrifying pictures in *Famous Monsters*. The overall winner of the contest, Val Warren, was awarded the role of "Teenage Werewolf Monster" in the 1964 film *Bikini Beach*, along with a trip to California that included a visit to the Ackermansion, where young Mr. Warren got to try on the head of the Creature from the Black Lagoon, among other treasures. Val also met writer Robert Bloch, Bela Lugosi's last wife, Hope, and writer Fritz Leiber, among other Hollywood royals.

Issue #32's cover featured the winning entry of a model making contest, depicting King Kong forcing a train from an elevated track. The 16-year-old creator and his mother were flown out to Hollywood and, besides being given a tour of the Ackermansion, met Fred Gwynne (Herman Munster), Natalie Wood, Tony Curtis, and other VIPs.

Dennis Muren, who would later head Industrial Light and Magic, was a frequent Saturday visitor to the Ackermansion. He and his teen friends would show their homemade films to Forry and other frequent visitors, including Bradbury and Harryhausen (Dennis would eventually meet Harryhausen simply by looking him up in the phone book). Ackerman was a sort of Willy Wonka of horror, the avuncular hero who allowed random fans a tour of his house as part of a trip they would never forget.

Thanks to its owner's ever-trusting nature, security was all but nonexistent at the Ackermansion, and theft was a problem. Even before either Ackermansion, someone swiped an early Hannes Bok from Forry's apartment. He openly admitted that people touring his home had "sticky fingers." In an interview he recalled that a 19-year-old somehow walked away with more than 400 pieces valued at $4,000, although most of what the young man took was eventually recovered.[6] Among the items the man is said to have stolen was one of Bradbury's earliest editions of *Fahrenheit 451*, called *Long After Midnight*, and copies of *Futuria Fantasia*, along with works by van Vogt and stills of *Dracula* and *King Kong*.[7] Items that vanished for good include the mask of Glenn Strange as Frankenstein; half of the submarine from George Pal's *Atlantis, the Lost Continent* that he had sitting in the backyard (the prop was so large it must have taken four men to haul it out of his garden, Forry reckoned); one of the guest books signed by numerous VIPs; the statue of Talos from *Jason and the Argonauts*; and the set of sound discs from the movie *Frankenstein* Carl Lammle sent him as a teen. Someone would later call Forry claiming he had owned a set of sound discs from *Frankenstein* and was willing to sell them to him for $7,500. Forry knew he was talking to the thief and hung up.[8]

The Son of Ackermansion was open from 1973 to 2002.

45

Harryhausen Moves to London

Ray Harryhausen moved to England in 1959 to take advantage of a special effects technique called sodium backing that was only available, or at least more affordable, in Great Britain's Rank Laboratory. The process made it easier for him to make the traveling mattes he needed. He also preferred filming in Europe, with its easy access to genuine ruins. For scenes in *Clash of the Titans*, he shot footage at both an ancient Roman amphitheater and the 5,000-year-old Greek temple at Paestum. Madrid, Barcelona, and the Caves of Artà are but a few places where he filmed on location.[1]

He was not necessarily planning to stay in London permanently, but after meeting the love of his life he would become a permanent resident.

Harryhausen met Diana at a function neither wanted to attend. Diana Livingstone was the great-granddaughter of explorer David Livingstone, as in "Dr. Livingstone, I presume?" (Ray Harryhausen later designed a sculpture of Dr. Livingstone being attacked by a lion, a statue based on a family legend. It still stands in the Livingstone Center. Harryhausen made the original mold for the sculpture out of beeswax.) The pair hit it off, she invited him over to her flat that very night for scrambled eggs, and they never looked back. Ray Harryhausen moved to the Holland Park area of West London.

Diana signed onto a busy lifestyle consumed by passion. Earlier on the same day that he met his soul mate, Harryhausen bought a dead crab to be used in the film *Mysterious Island* for the sequence in which a giant crab attacks a couple of lead characters. He stuck an armature (skeleton) inside the crab's body instead of creating a crustacean from whole cloth.[2] Harryhausen was in the middle of filming *Jason and the Argonauts* when they married in October of 1962. On their wedding day, they received this telegram from the crew: "Heartiest Congratulations Stop Urgent Stop Please Advise Seeding Time Hydra Jason Cutting Room."

Diana was getting an inkling of what she was in for.

The Harryhausen home in Holland Park would end up decorated with his various creations, including a bronze lamp he made depicting the lighthouse being set upon by the rhedosaurus. The couple had one daughter, Vanessa. Among her favorite "toys" as a little girl was the model of Gwangi, the eponymous dinosaur from *The Valley of Gwangi*, and the alligator from *The 3 Worlds of Gulliver*. She used to push Gwangi around in her baby stroller.

46

The First Comic-Con

Ackerman claimed that in one year, there were no fewer than 49 conventions in LA, sometimes two or three happening at once. Ackerman loved these cons, loved meeting his fans and being in the thick of things. There was hardly a conference he didn't like, regardless of how big or small. He organized his own event, the first *Famous Monsters* convention, in 1974. He signed so many autographs at this event that his arm was sore.

In 1970, he agreed to go to a tiny gathering in San Diego, organized by a group of teen and pre-teen boys.

Shel Dorf moved to San Diego in 1969 from Detroit, where he ran something called the Triple Fan Fair, so-named because it covered fantasy comics, films, and books. He wanted to set up a similar con in San Diego, but wasn't sure if the con should focus on comics or expand to include films, literature, and any other industry where fantasy and science fiction were represented.

Dorf and his friends—none of them older than 19 (Mike Towry was 14, Barry Alfonso only 12)—sought advice from the great comic book artist Jack Kirby, who had just moved to Irvine. Do it all, Kirby advised: comics, movies, wherever and whenever our loves are represented. It will bring in more people and be more fun.

Dorf had heard through a friend that Ray Bradbury was planning on giving a talk at the University of California at San Diego. After Bradbury was done with his lecture, called "The Creative Impulse in Apollo Year One," Shel and fellow planner Richard Alf approached Bradbury. Knowing Bradbury was a longtime fan of comic strips, Shel wisely brought along one of his own comic-strip scrapbooks. Ray asked if he could keep them. The young men gently told him no, then went on to describe a convention they were planning in San Diego.

Ray Bradbury had been a comics collector before comic books existed. As a boy growing up in Waukegan, he daily excised Flash Gordon, Buck Rogers, and Prince Valiant from local papers, and would always say that the sound of the paper thudding onto the front porch was the most beautiful he'd ever heard. His collecting stopped briefly as a nine-year-old after schoolyard bullies taunted him as a weirdo who hoarded comic strips. As he wrote in the San Diego Comic-Con brochure in 1980:

> Kids made fun, I took on embarrassment, and tore up the strips. A month later, empty, I burst into tears, asked myself what was wrong. The answer: Buck Rogers was gone, and life not worth living.
>
> Damn! I must have cried. Or darn, anyway.

And I started collecting Buck Rogers all over again.
Since that day I have never listened to anyone about my tastes.

It was a turning point for the future fantasy writer. He would always follow his heart and do what he loved, whatever the world thought. Decades later, the writer Robert Bloch recalled visiting Bradbury at his LA home and poring over his collection of comic strips. Bradbury kept these dozen or so scrapbooks of newspaper strips his whole life. They are now housed at the Center for Ray Bradbury Studies in Indianapolis.

As Ray looked at the comic strips and they talked, Shel invited him to be the first guest at San Diego's Golden State Comic-Con. Ray was agreeable provided that the con pay for his train fare and a hotel room, along with his customary speaking fee of roughly $3,000. Accounting for inflation, that would be anywhere from $20,000 to $35,000 in today's dollars.

Shel was devastated. There was simply no way he and his cluster of teen boys could come up with that kind of money. Then and there it hit Shel to explain that they were a nonprofit attempting to put on an educational event for the public good. If that was the case, Bradbury answered, he would be happy to attend for free. Before this conversation, the nitty gritty details about the financial organization of the conference had not occurred to the boys. Comic-Con San Diego is a nonprofit to this day.[1]

In March of 1970, Shel and his crew organized a "Mini-Con" to help pay for the larger comic book convention in San Diego later that same year, an event they were calling the Golden State Convention. Forry Ackerman was one of the guests of honor at the March Mini-Con, the event held in the basement of the Grant Hotel. The program listed his talk as a "Sci-Fi panel discussing Karloff, new trends, Moon landing, etc." This small gathering laid the groundwork for the Golden State Comic Book Convention a few months later.

Forry Ackerman's endorsement helped convince Bradbury that this larger event was worth attending. By 1970 Bradbury was a living legend, his book *Fahrenheit 451* already a mainstay of high school English classrooms across the country. Ackerman, while not as famous as Bradbury, was a rock star in the world of horror and science fiction fandom. For these two to forgo payment and attend a little-known convention reflects generosity and devotion on their part. Neither one had any way of knowing what Comic-Con would one day become.

"Comics Connoisseurs Here for Golden State Convention." So began the only article written about the first comic book convention in San Diego. "More than 200 persons who take their funnies seriously gathered in the US Grant Hotel yesterday for the start of the first San Diego Golden State Comics Convention," reporter Andrew Makarushka explained.[2]

The article appeared in the back pages of the *San Diego Union*, squeezed between a story about testing the exhaust of cars and above an ad for a furniture sale. The ad took up most of the page. The journalist covering the event, Andrew Makarushka, had to convince his editor that the story was even worth doing. Without the promise to get an interview with Ray Bradbury, the *Union* may not have bothered covering it (incredibly, Makarushka never went to Comic-Con again). About 300 fans and professionals packed into the basement conference room of the US Grant Hotel to listen to Bradbury talk for about 45 minutes, following Jack Kirby. (Jack Kirby would later immortalize the five boys who made up the first Comics Convention San Diego committee in the 1970 comic book *Superman's Pal Jimmy Olsen,* as a group of boys called the Five String Mob.) Writer A.E. van Vogt was also in attendance, along with Forry Ackerman. Bradbury and Ackerman both went to almost every subsequent Comic-Con San Diego for the rest of their lives. Neither of them could have imagined a day when this humble afternoon would sprout into the largest gathering in the world, attracting upwards of 150,000 fans.

47

Passing the Torch

> "Without Ray Bradbury, there is no Stephen King."
> —Stephen King

> "Some say *Citizen Kane* is the best movie ever made. I say no, it's *Jason and the Argonauts*."
> —Tom Hanks

> "In 1965 I started my own fan magazine ... the high point of my career came when Forrest J Ackerman sent for 50 copies."
> —John Carpenter[1]

In the '60s and '70s the fanboys became men and then elder statesmen, inspiring the next generation behind them just as they had been inspired by Jules Verne and Boris Karloff. The team of Ray, Forry, and Ray were easily accessible, friendly to presidents and anonymous 12-year-olds alike, helping the next generation make their dreams a reality.

Passing the Torch: Forry Ackerman

Forry wasn't sure if he wanted to see a film called *Schlock*, a low-budget horror film about a gorilla "banana monster" no one would likely care about. Ultimately though, Forry was a purist, determined to see every horror, fantasy, or science fiction movie ever made. He was pleasantly surprised. *Schlock* was no *Frankenstein*, but it was not exactly *Plan 9 from Outer Space* either. Clearly, it had been made by someone with talent.

As he was leaving the theater (other versions say this happened a week later at the airport), a young man tapped him on the shoulder and explained that he was the director of the film, and that there were only three people in the world whose opinion mattered to him: "Alfred Hitchcock, Orson Welles, and you." Forry was flattered to be in such company, even if, he joked later, he was at the bottom of the pile. The young man was named John Landis. He'd made the film after borrowing $60,000 from his uncle. As a boy, Landis had to smuggle copies of *Famous Monsters* into his home, past the disapproving eyes of his mother.[2]

A distributor paid Landis to make his opus longer, and the young director gave his idol a bit part; Forry can be seen in the final cut eating popcorn, next to the title character in a gorilla suit, who is Landis himself. Landis would recast Ackerman in a similar scene in the *Thriller* video; Ackerman is sitting behind Michael Jackson in the Palace Theatre. Later, at a much more established point in his career, Landis cast Ackerman as a bar patron in *Beverly Hills Cop III*, where he is seen sitting next to another childhood idol of his, Ray Harryhausen. Landis would be one of the most frequent celebrity visitors at the Ackermansion, but when he first visited he was an unknown 21-year-old, as was the buddy who went with him that first time, Rick Baker.[3] Baker would one day make a name for himself in special effects, but one of his first gigs was as designer of the Schlock monster's costume. The team of Baker and Landis would go on to create *American Werewolf in London* and Michael Jackson's *Thriller* video.

Joe Dante sent a long letter to *Famous Monsters* at age 13, about the 50 worst horror films ever made. After doing some editing and throwing in a few verses of his own, Ackerman published the piece as "Dante's Inferno." This began a lifelong friendship. (Dante's article actually caused a surprising storm of controversy, since American International Pictures, which owned the distribution rights to several items on Dante's list, felt that the piece would hurt their profits.) As an adult and director, Dante asked Forry to do a cameo in his film *Piranha*, where Forry would get eaten by the title creatures. Ackerman declined, but Dante did gift him paraphernalia from the movies *Innerspace* and *Gremlins*. Dante also gave him a cameo in *The Howling* (he's seen with a copy of *Famous Monsters* in a bookstore).

As his star rose, Forry never forgot that fans were what made him, and he paid them back. In 1962 after meeting 18-year-old Don Glut at a convention, Forry agreed to do a bit for the teen boy's film, in which Forry is seen ripping up a copy of *Horror Monsters #1*, *Horror Monsters* being one of his many copycat competitors. (Actually, he tore it in such a way that it could be readily put back together. Forry was a collector, after all.[4]) This bit can be seen in Glut's DVD *I Was a Teenage Movie Maker*. Filmmaker and actor Kenneth J. Hall convinced Uncle Forry to do a cameo in the low-budget film *Evil Spawn*.[5] On more than one occasion, Forry played roles that buried him under mounds of monster makeup, such as his role as a "special zombie" in *The Return of the Living Dead Part 2*. By the time of his death at 92, he had had cameos in about 112 films,[6] mostly bit parts in films like *Dinosaur Valley Girls*, *Bikini Drive-In*, and *Attack of the 60 Foot Centerfold*.

As a 12-year-old, Peter Jackson wrote a will where he left everything he had, whatever that might have been, to Forry Ackerman. Later in life, when Jackson was a young filmmaker shooting the movie that would eventually be titled *Dead Alive* (in New Zealand it was called *Braindead*), he learned Forry was at a con in New Zealand. The unknown persuaded Forry to don a fedora and shoot a few minutes of reaction shots to monsters yet unseen. All of this was filmed at the Wellington Zoo with no one's permission; the pair were chased out by security.[7]

Others who were inspired by Ackerman before making names for themselves were John Carpenter, who as a teen sent Ackerman copies of his zine, and then Ackerman requested 50 more copies; Billy Bob Thornton, who as a boy entered a *Famous Monsters* model-making contest (using the Aurora kits sold in the back pages); Kiss guitarist Gene Simmons, who said that "Forrest J Ackerman invented Gene Simmons"[8]; Steven Spielberg, who as a legendary director took a tour of the Ackermansion and then called his youngest son over to tell him, "Meet Forry Ackerman. This man and your grandfather are the reason I make movies"; Skip Smith, makeup artist at CNN for 25 years, who said he started out making monsters for a live haunted house using techniques he'd learned from *Famous Monsters*; Guillermo del Toro, who as a child wrote to Ackerman, asking to be adopted and to live with him in the Ackermansion; and Kirk Hammett, lead guitarist of Metallica, who bought several original cover art paintings by Basil Gogos.

In 1961 Ackerman launched *Spacemen*, essentially a sci-fi version of *Famous Monsters*. (Ackerman printed an ad in *Famous Monsters* where he encouraged readers to send in 35 cents for a "collectible" first issue of *Spacemen*. The first issue of *Spacemen* did indeed become a collectible.) Billed as the "World's Only Space Movie Magazine," it did not take off, in spite of having articles by Bradbury and about Harryhausen. Ackerman also sold 8mm home versions of his old friends' films, Bradbury's *It Came from Outer Space* and Harryhausen's *One Million Years B.C.*, in the back pages. The magazine quickly folded, but not before a hopeful, unknown 14-year-old mailed in a story. Ackerman didn't print the boy's early effort, a story called "The Killer," but he didn't throw it away, which is how Stephen King's first manuscript found its place in Ackerman's house of horrors.[9] Ackerman later published the one-page opus in *Famous Monsters* #202 in 1994, when King was well established.

King remembered his first issue of *Famous Monsters* as lovingly as Ackerman recalled losing his virginity to *Amazing Stories*. The future horror writer grew up in the small hamlet of Durham, Maine, and was the only fan in a town of 900 people. One day, while shopping in the nearby city of Freeport, he spied a copy of *Famous Monsters* in a magazine store. The neon-glowing cover depicted Claude Rains as the Phantom of the Opera, painted by Basil Gogos. The rest, as they say, is history. "I took it down with a hand that was almost trembling; I really could not believe such a thing," Stephen King wrote in his introduction to Christopher O'Brien's *The Forrest J Ackerman Oeuvre*.[10] The boy ignored the sneers of the clerk as he made change. The adults in his life disapproved of him reading the "junk" that he kept hidden behind a loose baseboard in his bedroom.

Ackerman, remembering his own young days as the editor of fanzines hardly anyone noticed, gave considerable ad space in *Famous Monsters* to countless clubs—groups with colorful names like The Coffin Bangers, the Classic Horror Club, and The Cyclops Club (one to keep an eye on)—and amateur publications in a section called the Haunt Ads.

The first time Stephen King met Steven Spielberg, they discussed *Famous Monsters*.

Passing the Torch: Ray Harryhausen

Ackerman once received a letter from an 11-year-old boy asking that he forward it to Ray Harryhausen. This was not an uncommon request. One of the services Ackerman provided for fans was passing on mail to Karloff, Lugosi, Christopher Lee, and numerous other horror and fantasy stars whose contact information he kept in a top-secret Rolodex at the Ackermansion (he claimed to always change one digit of each contact, lest anyone glance at his Rolodex to contact these people). Whenever one of these legends passed into old age and began to decline, Forry appealed to his readers to send letters of appreciation. Fans simply mailed their thanks to *Famous Monsters*, and he would see to it that the terrors and scream queens of yore got their tokens of appreciation.

This time, the request was from a boy asking to contact the current star Ray Harryhausen. The pre-teen boy's name was John Landis. Landis was mesmerized by Harryhausen's *The 7th Voyage of Sinbad*, so much so that after his parents took him home from the film, he asked his mom, "Who does that? Who makes the movie?" His mom explained that filmmaking involves a lot of people, but that ultimately the director was responsible. The eight-year-old decided that movie director would be his career. Sinbad inspired him the way Kong had inspired Harryhausen. Landis and Rick Baker both treasured the letters they got from him, a correspondence starting long before either had careers in Hollywood. Decades later, as one of the top names in Hollywood, Landis gave Harryhausen cameos; the tall, bald animator can be seen sitting next to Forry Ackerman in a hotel bar in *Beverly Hills Cop III*. He's also one of the doctors in the "doctor, doctor, doctor" scene in *Spies Like Us* (along with Bob Hope, Derek Meddings, and Terry Gilliam). John Landis also cast Harryhausen in his film *Burke and Hare*, playing the role of "distinguished doctor." Other works Harryhausen appeared in under other directors include a spot in the remake of *Mighty Joe Young* along with the female lead of the original, Terry Moore. At one point Harryhausen tells Charlize Theron that she reminds him of Moore when she was younger, a reference to Moore's role in the original film. A restaurant in the animated film *Monsters, Inc.* is named after Harryhausen.

Randall William Cook saw *7th Voyage* when he was seven and instantly fell in love with Harryhausen's unique stop-motion approach. Then, when he was 19, he met Harryhausen:

> Ray's mother lived in Los Angeles and her number was in the phone book. I called her up to get his address in London, and Ray happened to be visiting at the time. I didn't have anything to show except for a couple of drawings and a little makeup thing I'd done, but I wanted to meet and get a sense of him because his work meant so much to me. Somewhere along the line Ray saw the work I did for *Caveman* and other projects, and we became friends.[11]

Film students and fans called Harryhausen all the time, and, to their amazement, he not only answered but sometimes even invited them to his London house. "Why he didn't know his name was in the London phonebook I do not know," his daughter, Vanessa, explained in a documentary. "He was the only Harryhausen in it."[12]

In the early '90s, dozens of Hollywood elites wrote to the Academy of Motion Picture Arts and Sciences in a successful campaign to get Ray Harryhausen an award for lifetime achievement. Phil Tippett, the visual effects genius behind the first three *Star Wars* films and *Jurassic Park*, wrote in that Harryhausen had inspired him as a kid and that "Harryhausen and Charles Schneer single-handedly kept the fantasy and science fiction genre alive through the 1950s, 60s and 70s."[13] Elsewhere Tippett said that he knew what he wanted to do with his life after seeing the *7th Voyage of Sinbad*. Other dignitaries to mail in letters of support included Burgess Meredith, Joe Dante, Rick Baker, John Landis, Barry Levin, Randall William Cook, and George Lucas.[14]

Peter Jackson sent Harryhausen a poster of *The Fellowship of the Ring* and signed it, "Hi Ray! Without you none of this would have happened!"[15] Tom Hanks would always say that the skeleton fighting sequence from *Jason and the Argonauts* made him want to make movies.

Landis frequently visited Harryhausen in his London home, often bringing cake or hamburgers and other foods he liked. He once brought a bag of marbles to Harry, saying, "See Harry, you haven't lost your marbles." John Landis hosted the 2010 BAFTA awards ceremony where Harryhausen was presented with a special Lifetime Achievement Award, at the British Film Institute Southbank Theatre in London. It was his 90th birthday, and it was a surprise party; he thought he was just going to be doing a regular talk. Instead, John Landis hosted a tribute to him that included Peter Jackson, Rick Baker, and other wizards of Hollywood, along with Vanessa Harryhausen. Steven Spielberg, George Lucas, Tim Burton, and James Cameron were among the VIPs who taped video messages of congratulations shown at the gala (along with his good friend Ray Bradbury, of course, who signed off from his wheelchair in California with "I love you"). The event ended with Peter Jackson personally screening the Harryhausen-inspired films he made as a teenager. The 14-year-old can be seen slaying a cyclops and fighting an army of invisible skeletons—he never figured out how to animate his own skeletons, so he's seen swinging a sword at thin air. After screening this early effort to his mentor and everyone else at the ceremony, Peter Jackson then presented Harryhausen with the BAFTA award.

Passing the Torch: Ray Bradbury

> "My muse for the better part of my sci-fi career."
> —Steven Spielberg

> "The man who took the idea of the American Midwest and made it magical and tangible."
> —Neil Gaiman

The number of people inspired by Ray Bradbury could fill up a book on its own. Sufficient to say, he was one of the most important writers of the twentieth century, and also surprisingly approachable. Endless numbers of fans have told "I met Ray" stories. He was as easy to get an autograph from as the movie stars of his roller-skating boyhood days.

Besides being laid back and easy to talk to, he also mentored a decent number of authors before they themselves became professionals. More than one amateur mailed him a story and was flabbergasted when he not only replied, but sent back their typed works with extensive commentary. Bradbury didn't forget how Heinlein and Brackett and other established authors took him under their wings, back when he was a hopeful teen with a lot of enthusiasm but little ability. Now it was time to return the favor to the next generation.

LASFS member Craig Miller remembered reaching out to Ray Bradbury in 1967 at 13 years old. Bradbury replied that he could give him a half-hour on a certain date. When Miller and his two cousins came to visit, they spent hours talking, with Miller taping the interview onto his reel-to-reel recorder.[16]

As a seventh grader, Dan Chaon sent a few stories to Ray Bradbury "which were basically Bradbury fanfic." Bradbury wrote back with critiques and suggested the boy submit his writing to professional journals, beginning a correspondence that lasted years. Bradbury only balked when his protégé went off to college ("What can you learn in college that you can't get from your library?"). Dan Chaon is now an acclaimed author who teaches creative writing.[17]

Keith Feller, by his own admission a "goofy kid in the early 60s," was editing a zine called *FANTI*. He got permission from Bradbury to print one of his stories, "Here There Be Tygers," in his amateur publication. The writer only asked that the boy gift him three free copies. Feller also got in touch with Forry Ackerman, who granted him free ad space in *Famous Monsters*.[18]

Before Jonathan Maberry was the acclaimed author of *Rot & Ruin*, he was a teenager with dreams. One of them—which came true at age 14—was to meet Ray Bradbury: "It was amazing," Maberry remembered. "He took so much time to talk with me and offer advice about writing. That Christmas he gave me a signed copy of *Something Wicked This Way Comes*."[19]

For decades starting in the early 1970s, Bradbury was the keynote speaker at the Santa Barbara Writers Conference, a gathering of both established authors (other speakers have been Maya Angelou, Clive Cussler, and cartoonist Charles M. Schulz) and also young, unknown writers. These anonymous scribes found Bradbury easy-going and easy to approach and came out with a book, *A Tribute to Ray Bradbury: Thirty-Three Years of Inspiration at the Santa Barbara Writers Conference*, where they recalled their encounters. "The students met a totally approachable, loving and lovable human being," said one of the organizers of the conference, Barnaby Conrad. One young woman recalled being so inspired by Bradbury's words that she went back to her dorm room and cried.

In 2012 a group of writers published a book and also a series of comics (later gathered into a graphic novel), all under the name of *Shadow Show*. This anthology, edited by Mort Castle and Bradbury biographer Sam Weller, was devoted to Ray Bradbury, with a total of 26 different writers contributing short stories based on the themes found in his works. The lineup included Neil Gaiman, Joe Hill, and Margaret Atwood.

Amanda Gorman is the youngest person ever to read an original poem at a presidential inauguration, at age 22. She named Bradbury's *Dandelion Wine* as the book that most influenced her as child. "It was the first time I'd heard a metaphor in such a way, and my mind was blown," she explained. "It was a watershed moment for the way I viewed the power of language."[20]

48

Growing Old, Never Growing Up

> "It's rare in the history of motion pictures or any other art form that two young men meet and promise themselves a lifelong friendship."
> —Ray Bradbury, on presenting Ray Harryhausen with the Academy of Motion Picture Arts and Sciences Gordon E. Sawyer Award, March 7, 1992

Once, Ray Bradbury and Forry Ackerman were drinking at the Musso & Frank Grill in LA when a group of star-struck Goth teens recognized Ackerman right away, asked for his autograph, and talked to him at length. Finally, one of them noticed Ray Bradbury and asked for his signature too.

"It's about time!" Bradbury joked. It was not often that this most famous of fantasy writers was overshadowed.[1]

Ray, Forry, and Ray were friends for life. The two Rays were frequent guests at the Ackermansion. Bradbury often attended Ackerman's days-long birthday parties, and Ray and Forry enjoyed attending various conferences in and around the LA area, including attending every Comic-Con for as long as they could. Ackerman wrote about both Rays often in the pages of *Famous Monsters* and dedicated issue #118 to Harryhausen, on the occasion of his old friend's 55th birthday. ("Your lifetime friend Ray Bradbury leads all the rest in wishing you a happy birthday and not far behind is another lifetime friend, the man your daughter Vanessa calls 'Uncle Forry.'"[2]) Harryhausen's creatures frequently appeared on the cover of *Famous Monsters*.

In 1991 Ray Bradbury was among the Hollywood VIPs who lobbied for Harryhausen to get an award for lifetime achievement: "If you should decide to award him this special Oscar, I would be honored and overjoyed to be the Presentor on that night."

Ray Bradbury presented Ray Harryhausen with the Gordon E. Sawyer Academy Award (with Tom Hanks hosting) on March 7, 1992, over 50 years after their first fateful encounter at Clifton's. "I think if it's possible, I'm more excited about this than Ray is," Bradbury began. He then told the world of the pact the two men made: "That we'd grow old but never grow up."

Naturally, Bradbury cried all night.

Harryhausen wrote to Bradbury often, beginning with "Dear Brother Ray" in crystal clear handwriting.[3] Other times Harryhausen signed off as "the Other Ray."

After Harryhausen moved to England he still visited California often, and the trio that Forry dubbed the "Bat Pack" went to Disneyland together, families in tow. As a little girl, Vanessa Harryhausen referred to Bradbury and Ackerman as "Uncle Ray" and "Uncle Forry." In turn, Harryhausen was godfather to the four Bradbury daughters, who all called him "Uncle Ray" and his wife "Aunt Diana." Vanessa Harryhausen read *Famous Monsters* while eating breakfast, and Bradbury's daughters mailed in letters to Ackerman's magazines. Susan Bradbury Nixon had fond memories of Uncle Ray coming to visit and taking them to the alligator farm in Thousand Oaks, California. Later as an adult she visited the Harryhausens in London, where they would take walks through Kensington Gardens and watch Laurel and Hardy movies. Ray and Ray would get hamburgers at the Spaghetti House whenever Harryhausen came to town.

Decades later, the three boys would be invited to a 50th anniversary screening of *Kong* at Grauman's Chinese, where they met and were kissed by Fay Wray.

In the '90s and 2000s the trio attended reunions at Clifton's Cafeteria with old-timers from LASFS. In a letter dated from 1999, Ackerman invited Bradbury to one of these gatherings, reminding his old friend, "We owe it to Bruce Yerke, Paul Freehafer, Morojo, Pogo, E. Everett Evans, Daugherty."[4] (Forry once wrote Bradbury a letter on some of Bradbury's stationery, which had "The Illustrated Man" on the letterhead. Forry altered it so it now said "The Illustrated Ackerman.") The Bat Pack were interviewed at Clifton's in 2004, in the Little Brown Room. When the interviewer, Mark Cotta Vaz, broke out the original armature (skeleton) of Mighty Joe Young, 84-year-old Harryhausen began moving the limbs. "Some people gotta dance. I gotta animate," Harryhausen explained.[5]

Over 70 years after first bursting into the Little Brown Room, Ray Bradbury

(From left) Ackerman, Harryhausen, Bradbury, and Daugherty, at a '90s reunion at Clifton's Cafeteria (from the collection of John L. Coker III).

celebrated his 89th birthday—one of his last—at Clifton's. Ackerman and Harryhausen both attended. The staff of Clifton's gifted him an authentic Clifton's lunch tray.[6]

Ray, Forry, and Ray appeared on panels together at Comic-Con San Diego in the mid- and late 2000s. Their very last meeting together was at the Bookfellows bookshop, in Glendale, California, on February 25, 2008.

Forry died on December 4, 2008.

The "Bat Pack" one last time, at Bookfellows Fine & Rare Books in Glendale, California, 2008 (photograph courtesy of John Sasser).

49

The End of the Ackermansion and *Famous Monsters*

"Life has not rewarded me financially as much as it has Arthur C. Clarke, Ray Bradbury, Robert Heinlein, L. Ron Hubbard, Steven Spielberg, Stephen King, George Lucas, Larry Niven, Robert Silverberg, Frank Herbert, et al...."

—Forry Ackerman[1]

The last issue of the initial run of *Famous Monsters* that Ackerman edited was #190, with him resigning in August of 1982. He had been disgruntled for years, complaining about unreturned phone calls and the fact that James Warren was often MIA at the office. It turned out Warren had been hoping to retire from the magazine and publishing world at age 50, and that birthday was approaching, so he was gradually losing interest and backing away from the publication. Ackerman finally decided to call it quits when Warren offered the job of chief editor to someone younger, demoting Ackerman to the title of "Editor Emeritus."[2] There is a photo of the two smiling together at a '90s Comic-Con, evidently having forgiven each other. Ackerman would later say in an interview that he didn't hate Warren so much as he was "baffled" by him.

Ackerman finished his career with a letter, a goodbye that ended with one of his trademark puns: "Forry get me not."[3] It never saw the light of day. Instead, the current staff published a sunny article explaining that "Forry has decided to move onto other things." It would be the last issue of *Famous Monsters'* initial run of 24 years. All of Warren's remaining publications—*Eerie, Vampirella,*[4] and *Creepy*—folded as well. In August of 1983 a bankruptcy auction was held to help pay off Warren's creditors. Almost everything Warren had ever published—a copy of almost every issue of every magazine—he stored in warehouse the size of six basketball courts, almost one million separate books or magazines.[5] The auction catalog was 29 pages long. Ackerman complained bitterly that some of his stills were sold without his permission or compensation.

But it was not the end of *Famous Monsters*. Like the creatures profiled in its own pages, *Famous Monsters of Filmland* would continue to lumber from the dead and has existed in one reincarnation or another for the past 40 years.

Shortly after leaving, Ackerman edited a magazine called *Forrest J Ackerman's Monster Land*, later shortened to simply *Monster Land*, which ran until 1987. In 1993, photographer Ray Ferry found that the title *Famous Monsters of Filmland* had fallen out of copyright. He decided to bring it back, hiring Ackerman as the chief editor, under issue #200. Ultimately the two men had a falling out, with Ackerman fighting a long, protracted suit against Ferry. The gist of Ackerman's complaint was that Ferry wanted Ackerman the brand but not Ackerman the man. Ferry was, Ackerman argued, using "Dr. Acula's" name and brand without his permission, implying that Ackerman was still on board when in fact Ferry had edged him out. John Landis and Ray Bradbury both served as character witnesses during his suit, with Bradbury explaining that Ackerman had been known as "Dr. Acula" since at least the '40s. (Bradbury also testified, "Forrest J Ackerman ... he's my life. I wouldn't be sitting here today if it wasn't for him."[6]) Ackerman eventually won after a ruling from the Los Angeles Superior Court on May 11, 2000, awarding him $342,000 in punitive damages and $382,500 in compensatory damages, but Ferry then declared bankruptcy. While the courts held his bankruptcy in contempt, the fact remained that he never paid Ackerman.

The End of the Ackermansion

As Forry aged, he tried finding a permanent home for the Ackermansion. He attempted a deal with the city of LA (there was talk of an "Ackerman wing" of the LA Public Library); the idea of housing the entire collection on the decommissioned cruise ship the *Queen Mary* was floated (pun intended, in honor of Forry). He fielded offers from Monterey, Cleveland, Texas, Berlin, Disneyworld, and others, but found nothing feasible. He unsuccessfully applied for a Ford Foundation grant. The Ackermonster appealed to friends, both famous and anonymous, to get the funds needed to make sure his mansion outlived him, but found it no easier to raise money in the '80s and '90s than in the '40s and '50s, when he tried to get funds for his National Fantasy Fan Foundation. He would also be bitter that no one, not Spielberg or Lucas, simply put up the money to make his amateur museum a professional one.

In April of 2002, Ackerman had a stroke and drifted in and out of a coma. Fearing the worst, his attorney began selling off pieces of the collection, convinced the end was near and that Forry would die before being able to pay legal fees. By the time he recovered his strength, Forry decided to let the sale continue, plagued as he was with both legal and medical bills. In September of 2002 an estate sale was held at the legendary mansion, presided over by Ackerman himself, before the home itself was sold. "The artwork was generally sold for 100 dollars a painting, magazines and fanzines were fifty cents, paperbacks were a dollar and hardcovers were two dollars," recalled Ackerman's friend and biographer James Van Hise. The furniture and glassware went, too. When a fan asked how he felt about this Ackerman replied, "It's 75 years of my life down the drain!"[7]

He soon moved into a modest bungalow on Russell Avenue, keeping somewhere between 100 and 200 pieces of a collection that once numbered more than 300,000 items. His last remaining bits included his first letter from Burroughs when he was 11, the King Kong models, and Stephen King's first story. And, of course, that first issue of *Amazing Stories* that he bought instead of the medicine that would cure his cold. He still let visitors drop in for free at his "mini-mansion." His last home was demolished in 2019, after a failed attempt to declare it a historic site.

49. The End of the Ackermansion and Famous Monsters

In 2007 investor and publisher Philip Kim purchased *Famous Monsters* and arranged with Ackerman to legally relaunch the magazine, one of Ackerman's last acts before his death in 2008.

In the weeks before he died Forry knew the end was near and many visitors called on him, with Ray Bradbury being one of the last. The two men were alone, so it is not known what was discussed when Hollerbochen came to visit Fojak. We can assume *King Kong* came up at least once.

Forry Ackerman died at three minutes to midnight on December 4, 2008. In a coincidence right out the movies he loved so much, a painting of himself that he commissioned years earlier also depicts him pointing to a clock showing what would turn out to be the exact time of his death, 11:57 p.m.

On March 8, 2009, his caretaker, Joe Moe, organized a tribute to him at The Egyptian,[8] the cinema where Forry spent so many afternoons with his grandparents. The theater was packed. Ray Bradbury, John Landis, documentarian Paul Davids, and special effects master Rick Baker were among those who spoke. (Bradbury: "I had a chance to visit Forry about two weeks before he passed away. I was able to sit with him and hold his hand, and look into his face and tell him how he changed my life. Back when I was 17 years old, he took me into his life.") At the end of the tribute, a filmed goodbye of Forry's was shown, his ghostly head looming on the screen, oxygen tube keeping him alive. "Hello fans, wherever you are, treasures of my life," he began, softly. "And this is, Uncle Forry saying so long, and thanks for everything." He ended with the phrase he'd always said he wanted to be his last words, "Sci-fi."

An auction the following April of Ackerman's few remaining pieces netted over a quarter of a million dollars. Among the items sold were Bela Lugosi's ring worn in *Abbott and Costello Meet Frankenstein* ($46,000); the edition of *Dracula* signed by Bram Stoker, Bela Lugosi, Christopher Lee, and John Carradine, among others ($25,000); the top hat worn by Lon Chaney in *London After Midnight* ($27,500); and the nude statue of Marlene Dietrich Forry commissioned ($9,000).[9]

50

Afterlife

> "How many friendships have you known in your lifetime lasted so long?"
>
> —Ray Bradbury, at the ceremony placing Ray Harryhausen's star on the Walk of Fame[1]

The Los Angeles Science Fantasy Society still meets every Thursday. As of this writing they are at 4,380 consecutive meetings, currently being done via Zoom. They begin by reading the meeting minutes from the previous week. They then auction off the naming rights to those minutes, the winner typically paying five or six dollars. They sound off on developments in science fiction and science ("moments of science"), update current members on the lives of past and current members, and read the "patron saints," in which they bestow honors on past and current members. Each patron saint naming ends with a rousing "hip hip hooray!"—the very words with which Forry ended his first letter to *Amazing Stories*.

True to form, there are word plays galore, and whoever makes a pun has to pay a fine. At a recent meeting, talk about the Mars rover's vibrations led to a joke about the Beach Boys (think about it, you'll get it). They discuss horror and science fiction, and give weekly birthday and death updates of anyone who was ever involved in those genres, mostly celebrities only diehard fans are likely to know.[2]

The Bixel Street clubroom was vacated in April of '49 and moved to 1305 West Ingraham Street. The clubhouse would then relocate to different locations many times (Clubhouse 3 was sold and became the investment fund), including a 30-year stint on Burbank Boulevard in North Hollywood from 1973 to 2011, followed by a stretch in Van Nuys. As of this writing, there is no official clubhouse, due to COVID and other factors.[3]

In an interview, Bradbury biographer Sam Weller asked Ray what it felt like to visit his future gravesite, a plot alongside his wife's in Los Angeles's Westwood Memorial Park. "I'd much rather be buried on Mars," he replied.

> Put my ashes in a tomato soup can, because that's all I ate when I was a child. Bury me on the red planet. Place a tombstone there with my name and a listing of my most well-known books, *Fahrenheit 451*, *The Martian Chronicles*, *The Illustrated Man*, *Dandelion Wine*, and *Something Wicked This Way Comes*. And at the top of the tombstone I'd like there to be a little hole and underneath that it should read, "Place only dandelions here."[4]

From left: Forrest J Ackerman, Ray Harryhausen, Ray Bradbury, Julius Schwartz, Archon 20, October 1996, Collinsville, Illinois (photograph by John L. Coker III).

Instead, Bradbury is buried in a simple plot, next to his wife, in a cemetery also populated by Natalie Wood, Marilyn Monroe, his old friend and partner Gene Kelly, and plenty of other notables. The small stone marking his grave states only his name, the years of his birth and death, and that he was the author of *Fahrenheit 451*. People have been known to leave dandelions, in honor of his novel *Dandelion Wine*. Once, somebody left behind a belt-changer, something he used as a teen to make change for people buying papers.

After Ray Bradbury passed, the first person his daughter Susan Nixon called was Ray Harryhausen, because "I didn't want him to hear the news from radio or television."[5]

Ray Bradbury's star is on the Hollywood Walk of Fame, appropriately enough just outside of a bookstore (Larry Edmunds). His good buddy Harryhausen's star is just down this famed road in front of the legendary El Capitan Theatre, across the street from Grauman's Chinese, where he first saw *King Kong* all those years before. Both Ackerman and Bradbury turned out for the ceremony dedicating Harryhausen's star ("Kong-gratulations!" Forry quipped). Bradbury joked that, someday, he would dig up his star and place it next to Harryhausen's. Ackerman has yet to get a star, in spite of a furious campaign from his fans.

Forry Ackerman died on December 8, 2008, age 92. He is entombed in Forest Lawn Memorial Park behind a plaque that says, "Sci-Fi was my high." (The marker for his wife, Wendy, states, "Beloved wife of Mr. Science Fiction.") A lifelong atheist, he did not believe in heaven, ghosts, UFOs, or anything supernatural. As he once told an interviewer, "I don't expect to survive in any way, shape, or form."[6] But some say he has.

The Ackermansion has since been purchased, emptied of all signs of its past life. New tenants have reported hearing footsteps, seeing an old man pacing, a "shadow person" moving across the wall, a woman floating above a bed, and a woman with a young boy. None of these witnesses knew anything about the house's unique past. It is hard to imagine a more fitting afterlife for the lifelong fan of all of things magical and terrifying than to spend eternity as a poltergeist.[7]

Joe Moe, Ackerman's caretaker, helped organize the tribute at the Egyptian Theatre. He reported having an extremely lucid dream, in which Forry visited him and told him what a good job he'd done.

A fan of Forry's had a collection of plastic model monsters bought from the pages of *Famous Monsters* (Dracula, the Wolfman, Frankenstein, Creature from the Black Lagoon). On the day of Forry's death, they fell, one by one, from his shelf. As he checked on one that fell, another fell, and then another and another.[8]

Ray Harryhausen died on May 7, 2013. His wife Diana was unable to attend the funeral due to her own poor health. When Harryhausen's daughter, Vanessa, came home from the service, she was working on summoning the courage to tell her mom that she had just buried their beloved Ray. But Harryhausen's widow spoke first. "Mum greeted me with a beautiful smile and said: 'Hello darling! Guess who I've just seen?'" Diana Harryhausen went on to explain that she had just seen her dearly departed husband. Ray stood in the doorway, waved goodbye, and left.[9] Diana followed her husband to the other side a few months later.

On Bradbury's last night on Earth (June 5, 2012), Venus transited across the sun, an occurrence that happens only once every 100 years.

Whatever one's beliefs, there's no doubt that Ray, Forry, and Ray would be thrilled to know their deaths added a little more mystery and imagination to the world.

Chapter Notes

Prologue

1. Ray Bradbury, "Yestermorrow and Beyond; an Evening with Ray Bradbury," lecture at the University of North Alabama, May 22, 2000, reprinted in *Famous Monsters* no. 365 (January/February 2013).

1. When this author attended Comic-Con in 2018, he was charged more than $3,000 for a three-night stay in a single bed motel room with a stand-up shower. Luckily someone else paid the bill.

2. L. Weisberg, "San Diego's Hotel Tax Hike Measure Failed to Pass. Or Did It?" *San Diego Union-Tribune*, April 8, 2020, www.sandiegouniontribune.com/business/tourism/story/2020-04-08/san-diegos-hotel-tax-hike-measure-lost-or-did-it.

3. L. Weisberg, "Comic-Con is staying in San Diego—at least through 2024," *San Diego Union-Tribune*, July 5, 2019, https://www.sandiegouniontribune.com/business/tourism/story/2019-07-05/comic-con-is-staying-in-san-diego-at-least-through-2024.

Chapter 1

1. Ray Bradbury, *Greentown, Tinseltown* (Stanza Press, 2012), unnumbered page after the introduction.

2. In November of 1945 Bradbury had just sold a few stories to some well-paying magazines and went on a trip with his good friend Grant Beach. While staying in a guest home in Mexico City, Bradbury saw Steinbeck eating breakfast but was too nervous to approach. Steinbeck was drunk, accusing a female photographer of blackmail. He then staggered off to observe the filming of the Spanish-language version of *The Pearl* (so Bradbury recalled in his intro to the reprint of *Dark Carnival*, 2001). In a letter to August Derleth (dated December 10, 1945), Bradbury had this to say about his encounter with Steinbeck: "When I was in Mexico City I had breakfast with John Steinbeck several mornings; a very big, shy, good-humored person with, unfortunately, a great love of liquor which made some of his conversations a bit fuzzy." Bradbury later learned that Steinbeck read Bradbury's stories to his own children.

3. Ray Bradbury, *A Graveyard for Lunatics: Another Tale of Two Cities* (William Morrow Paperbacks, 1st edition, 2001), 19.

4. Sam Weller, *Listen to the Echoes: The Ray Bradbury Interviews* (Hat & Beard Press, 2017), 35.

5. David Kipen, *The WPA Guide to the City of Angels* (University of California Press, 2011), 3.

6. Ibid., 229.

7. Ibid., 3.

8. Ibid., 108.

9. Ibid.

10. Sam Weller, *The Bradbury Chronicles: The Life of Ray Bradbury* (Harper Perennial, Annotated edition, 2006), 38.

11. Ibid., 49.

12. Ibid., xi.

13. Ray Bradbury, "Buck Rogers in Apollo Year 1," in *The Collected Works of Buck Rogers in the 25th Century*, ed. Robert C. Dille (Chelsea House Publishers, 2nd printing, 1970).

14. Terry Pace, "Ray Bradbury's Earliest Influences," *Monsters from the Vault* 16, no. 30 (Spring 2012): 51.

15. Ray Bradbury, diary entry for August 22 to August 27, 1940, in *Greentown, Tinseltown* (Stanza Press, 2012).

16. Weller, *Bradbury Chronicles*, 80.

17. William F. Nolan, *The Ray Bradbury Companion: A Life and Career History, Photolog, and Comprehensive Checklist of Writings with Facsimiles from Ray Bradbury's Unpublished and Uncollected Work in All Media* (Gale Research, 1975), 41.

18. Jonathan R. Eller, *Becoming Ray Bradbury* (University of Illinois Press, 2011), 14.

19. Ted Dikty, *The Who's Who in Fandom* (self-published, 1940), accessed at Fanac.org.

20. Weller, *Bradbury Chronicles*, 82.

21. Eller, *Becoming Ray Bradbury*, 18.

Chapter 2

1. Kipen, *WPA Guide*, 80.
2. Victoria Dailey, "How LA Became a Destination on the Book Trail," *Literary Hub*, June 8, 2018, lithub.com/how-la-became-a-destination-on-the-rare-book-trail/.
3. Kipen, *WPA Guide*, xxvii.
4. *Imagination!* 1, no. 1 (October 1937).
5. *Imagination!* 1, no. 5 (February 1938).
6. T. Bruce Yerke, *Memoirs of a Superfluous Fan, Vol. 1* (Southern California Institute for Fan Interests, 1922), 6.
7. Gary K. Wolfe, *How Great Science Fiction Works*, episode 6, "The Rise of the Science Fiction Pulps," from the Great Courses Series, The Teaching Company, LLC, 2016.

Chapter 3

1. *The AckerMonster Chronicles!*, directed by Jason V. Brock, JaSunni Productions, October 31, 2012.
2. Hugo Gernsback, *The Perversity of Things: Hugo Gernsback on Media, Tinkering, and Scientifiction*, ed. Grant Wythoff (University of Minnesota Press, 1st edition, 2016), https://manifold.umn.edu/read/the-perversity-of-things-hugo-gernsback-on-media-tinkering-and-scientifiction/section/71ba6e6b-b4b2-40a2-bdb1-af133fc6b93b).
3. Ibid.
4. Hugo Gernsback, ed., *Modern Electrics* 2, no. 9 (December 1909).
5. Hugo Gernsback, ed., *The Experimenter* 1, no. 4 (November 1924).
6. Hugo Gernsback, ed., *Electrical Experimenter* 7, no. 2 (June 1919).
7. Mike Ashley, *The Gernsback Days* (Wildside Press, 2004), 121.
8. Hugo Gernsback, "A Gyro-Electric Destroyer," *Electrical Experimenter* 5, no. 58 (February 1918). Painting by George Wall.
9. Hugo Gernsback, "The Automatic Wireless Soldier," *Electrical Experimenter* 6, no. 6 (October 1918): 372.
10. Ibid.
11. Hugo Gernsback, ed., *Science and Invention* 4, no. 23 (August 1923): 319.
12. Hugo Gernsback, "Science Fiction vs. Science Faction," *Wonder Stories Quarterly* 2 (Fall 1930): 5.
13. Hugo Gernsback, ed., "The Electric Duel," *Amazing Stories* 2, no. 6 (September 1927).
14. Hugo Gernsback, ed., "The Magnetic Storm," *Electrical Experimenter* 6, no. 4 (August 1918).
15. Charles S. Wolfe, "The Educated Harpoon," *Electrical Experimenter* 7, no. 84 (April 1920): 1256.
16. Hugo Gernsback, ed., *Amazing Stories* 1, no. 1 (April 1926): 3.
17. Sam Moskowitz, "The Origins of Science Fiction Fandom: A Reconstruction," in *Science Fiction Fandom*, ed. Joe Sanders (Greenwood Press, 1994).
18. Hugo Gernsback, *Amazing Stories* 1, no. 10 (January 1927): 974.
19. John Cheng, *Astounding Wonder: Imagining Science and Science Fiction in Interwar America* (University of Pennsylvania Press, 2013).
20. For example: "T. Alan Koss, 389 St. Kilda Rd. Melbourne, S.C. 2, Australia, Member Number 497, welcomes correspondence with other members of the League. Here is a chance for those who wish over-seas pen pals." Another: "Eugene K. Dildine 134 N. Wayne Ave, Columbus, OH, would like to write to those interested in chemistry, biology, bio-chemistry, physics, and radio-activity, also hypnotism of which he is a profound student. He is confined permanently to bed and promises to answer all correspondence."—From *Wonder Stories* 6, no. 7 (1934): 877.
21. Hugo Gernsback, ed., The "Swap" Column, *Thrilling Wonder Stories* 11, no. 1 (December 1934).
22. David Ritter and Daniel Ritter, *The Visual History of Science Fiction Fandom: Volume One—The 1930s* (First Fandom Experience, LLC, 2020).
23. Hugo Gernsback, "$500.00 in Prizes," *Science Wonder Quarterly* 1, no. 1 (Fall 1929): on verso of cover.
24. Hugo Gernsback, ed., *Wonder Stories* 3, no. 11 (April 1932).
25. One interesting fact about the Scienceers is that their first meeting was in Harlem, at the apartment of rocketry enthusiast Warren Fitzgerald. Warren has been described by early fans as a "light-skinned negro," but there is some confusion about this. While Moskowitz, in his history *The Immortal Storm: A History of Science Fiction Fandom*, refers to him as "James Fitzgerald" and a "colored fan" and Allen Glasser (in his early memoir *History of the Scienceers: The First New York City Science Fiction Club, 1929*) described him as "a light-skinned Negro—amiable, cultured, and a fine gentleman in every sense of that word," the census records him as white. There doesn't seem to be any doubt he was married to a Black woman, Gertrude. It may be that the other Scienceers made an assumption based on the race of his wife. Or maybe it was the census taker who was wrong. In any case, Warren is also remembered as being in his early thirties, about 15 years older than the other Scienceers. Fitzgerald appears to have dropped out of the fan scene altogether, becoming more involved in rocketry. The only other active African American fan may have been in Maine. A Russell Harold Woodman published four issues of a zine called *Triton* before quitting. In May 1949 he wrote a letter to fellow fan Harry Warner (published in Warner's book *All Our Yesterdays*): "Perhaps a storm wave would sweep certain frontiers of the fan world if I had stayed in publishing

long enough to reveal that I am a Negro. " This is not to say that African Americans didn't write science fiction. W.E.B. Du Bois himself wrote a short story called "The Comet" about a poor Black man and rich white woman who are the only survivors in a post-apocalyptic New York.

26. Hugo Gernsback, ed., *Wonder Stories* 3, no. 11 (April 1932).

27. Hugo Gernsback, "The Science Fiction League, an Announcement," *Wonder Stories* 5, no. 9 (April 1934): 933.

28. Hugo Gernsback, *Wonder Stories* 5, no. 10 (May 1934): 1062.

29. Hugo Gernsback, ed., *Thrilling Wonder Stories* 8, no. 3 (December 1936): 114.

30. Frederik Pohl, *The Way The Future Was* (Ballantine Del Rey, 1979), 18.

31. Ray Bradbury, "How to Become a Sci-Fi Fan," *Imagination!* 1, no. 9 (June 1938).

32. Gary Westfahl, *The Rise and Fall of Science Fiction, from the 1920s to the 1960s* (McFarland, 2019).

33. Ashley, *The Gernsback Days*, 238.

34. Yerke, *Memoirs*, 4–5.

35. *Fantasy Magazine* 5, no. 2 (July 1935): unnumbered last page.

Chapter 4

1. Ray Bradbury in an interview dated April 16, 2004, at Clifton's Cafeteria with Forry Ackerman and Ray Harryhausen. *Ray Harryhausen: The Early Years Collection,* Disc 1, featurette, "Interview at Clifton's Cafeteria," directed by Ray Harryhausen, Global Entertainment, February 22, 2005.

2. Eller, *Becoming Ray Bradbury*, 18.

3. There is some debate about which group is the oldest. The Philadelphia Science Fiction Society also claims to title of earliest science fiction group, having first begun meeting in December of 1934. The debate could be dependent on one's definition of "continuous." Philadelphia's society has its roots in Bob Madle's Boys Science Fiction Club, which began in 1934. Then there's the fact that it has been officially called The Philadelphia Science Fiction Society since 1935, whereas LASFS didn't officially adopt its current name until 1940. Best to say that both organizations spawned in 1934 and still exist today.

4. Kipen, *WPA Guide*, 160.

5. *Ibid.*, xlvi.

6. Edmond J. Clinton III, *Clifton's and Clifford Clinton: A Cafeteria and a Crusader* (Angel City Press, Illustrated edition, 2015), 58.

7. Dartnell Corporation, *Sales Management* 41(July 1937).

8. Russell Hodgkins, "Way out West!" *Imagination!* 1 (October 1937).

9. Yerke, *Memoirs*.

10. Ray Bradbury in an interview dated April 16, 2004, at Clifton's Cafeteria with Forry Ackerman and Ray Harryhausen. *Ray Harryhausen: The Early Years Collection,* Disc 1, featurette, "Interview at Clifton's Cafeteria," directed by Ray Harryhausen, Global Entertainment, February 22, 2005.

11. Yerke, *Memoirs*, 11.

12. Ray Bradbury in an interview dated April 16, 2004, at Clifton's Cafeteria with Forry Ackerman and Ray Harryhausen. *Ray Harryhausen: The Early Years Collection,* Disc 1, featurette, "Interview at Clifton's Cafeteria," directed by Ray Harryhausen, Global Entertainment, February 22, 2005.

13. Yerke, *Memoirs*, 11.

14. Walter Sullivan, "Visit to LASFL," *Spaceways* 2, no.4 (April 1940): 12.

15. Jerry Weist, *Bradbury, An Illustrated Life: A Journey to Far Metaphor* (William Morrow & Co., 2002).

Chapter 5

1. Ray Bradbury, as quoted in Terry Pace, "Witness and Celebrate," *Famous Monsters of Filmland* no. 265 (Jan/Feb 2013): 55.

2. There is some controversy about Ackerman's middle name. Early photos of him as a small child record his name as Forrest Clark Ackerman. However, author and filmmaker Paul Davids bought several of Ackerman's personal papers including his birth certificate, which recorded Ackerman's middle name as being "James." Also, his birth certificate records his first name as being spelled simply "Forest," but since he and almost everyone else spelled his name with two r's, this author is doing so as well.

3. Transcript of an interview with Mark McGee, October 3, 1982, University of Wyoming, American Heritage Center, Forrest J Ackerman Papers, 1920–1987, 02358, Box 3, Folder 9.

4. Forry J Ackerman, "The Forrest of Prime Evil," *Famous Monsters of Filmland* no. 104 (January 1974): 39.

5. "FJA," *Gosh Magazine*, reprinted in *Ackermansion Memories* 8 (March 2019).

6. Forrest J Ackerman, "Close Encounters of the Weird Kind: Auctions Speak Louder than Weirds," *Famous Monsters of Filmland* no. 169 (November 1980): 38.

7. Forrest J Ackerman, as quoted by Christopher O'Brien, *The Forrest J Ackerman Oeuvre: A Comprehensive Catalog of the Fiction, Nonfiction, Poetry, Screenplays, Film Appearances, and Other Works, with a Concise Biography* (McFarland & Co., 2012), 16.

8. Forrest J Ackerman, letter published under "The Reader Speaks," *Science Wonder Quarterly* 1, no. 1 (Fall 1929): 136.

9. Hugo Gernsback, *Wonder Stories* 6, no. 7 (December 1934): 887.

10. This figure comes from superfan R.D. Swisher. He worked as an organic chemist by

day but enjoyed indexing things at night. By the outbreak of the war he had indexed more than 6,000 cards of facts regarding fanzines, prozines, authors, stories, and writers of letters. According to Warner in his history of fandom, *All Our Yesterdays* (p. 65), "his wife did a lot of the clerical work."

11. At that time the technology of imprinting the soundtrack onto film did exist, but studios mostly opted for the sound-on-disc system from Vitaphone. This was a projector hooked up to a record player, mechanized so the film and record would play in sync. Most talking pictures during the late '20s and early '30s came with a set of records, or sound discs, to be played with the reels of film. Each reel had an accompanying record, plus one extra for the overture. Ackerman would eventually collect the original discs from Karloff's *The Mummy, Frankenstein, The Murders in the Rue Morgue,* and *Dr. Jekyll and Mr. Hyde,* among others. At a time when movies came and went and there was no promise of seeing them again, he could at least play the sound back. Decades later, Ackerman would have the pleasure of playing one of these discs from *Rue Morgue* back to Bela Lugosi himself. The hearing-impaired Lugosi was thrilled to hear his old voice again.

12. Forry J Ackerman, "My Science Fiction Collection," *The Fantasy Fan* 1, no. 2 (October 1933): 20.

13. Letter from Forry J Ackerman to Charles R. Tanner, dated December 13, 1930, University of Wyoming, American Heritage Center, Forrest J Ackerman Papers, 1920–1987, 02358, Box 10.

14. Forry recalled later: "In 1929, I was living in San Francisco, and there was the Daily Chronicle magazine that had a Sunday section, with one page devoted to kids. You could send in a little poem or drawing or something of that sort. They had a contest and two hundred youngsters, including my thirteen year-old self, wrote a short story. Out of the two hundred, mine won the first prize, which was a stamp album. The story was called 'A Trip to Mars.'"—From "Another Part of the Forrest," a presentation by Ackerman at DragonCon, Atlanta, GA (June 1997) that was recorded and transcribed by John L. Coker III.

15. Transcript of an interview with Mark McGee, October 3, 1982, University of Wyoming, American Heritage Center, Forrest J Ackerman Papers, 1920–1987, 02358, Box 3, Folder 9.

16. O'Brien, *The Forrest J Ackerman Oeuvre,* 18.

17. Forrest J Ackerman, "Through Time and Space with Forrest J Ackerman, Part 1," *Mimosa Online,* by Nick and Richard Lynch, www.jophan.org/mimosa/m28/forry.htm.

18. Unpublished interview, September 29, 1974, reprinted in *Ackermansion Memories* 9: 79.

19. Julius Schwartz and Brian M. Thomsen, *Man of Two Worlds: My Life in Science Fiction and Comics* (Harper Paperbacks, 2000), 20.

20. *Ibid.,* 36.

21. Jerry Siegel, "The Reign of the Super-Man," *Science Fiction: The Advance Guard of Civilization* 1, no. 3 (January 1933), accessed at fanac.org.

22. Julius Schwartz, "The Science Fiction Eye," *The Science Fiction Digest* (August 1933): 9, accessed at fanac.org.

23. Comic Connect, The World's Premier Online Comic Marketplace & Auctioneer, https://www.comicconnect.com/item/739916?tzf=1), accessed on June 1, 2021.

24. Brad Ricca, *Super Boys* (St. Martin's Press, 2013), 56.

25. *Science Fiction Digest* 1, no. 12 (August 1933): inside front cover, accessed at fanac.org.

26. *Wonder Stories* 7, no. 8 (April 1936): 1008.

27. "Chapter News and General Activities–Los Angeles," *Thrilling Wonder Stories* 10, no. 3 (December 1937): 116.

28. NLK, unpublished interview, dated September 29, 1974, reprinted in *Ackermansion Memories* 9 (September 2019).

29. "Doc" Ackerman, "Stick out Your Tongue," reprinted in *Ackermansion Memories* 9 (September 2019).

30. Warner, *All Our Yesterdays,* 111.

Chapter 6

1. Eller, *Becoming Ray Bradbury,* 18.

2. "Thrilling Wonder Stories," *Chapter News and General Activities: Los Angeles* 8, no. 2 (October 1936): 127.

3. *Imagination!* 1, no. 2 (November 1937): 4.

4. Gernsback put 17-year-old Hornig in charge of *Wonder Stories* after seeing the boy's work on the fanzine *The Fantasy Fan.* Hornig was so young he needed his parents' permission, which they granted after he agreed to finish his education by attending night school.

5. Arthur J. Burks, "What a Writer Thinks of S-F Fans," *Thrilling Wonder Stories* 9, no.3: 118.

6. Russ Hodgkins, "Way Out West," *Imagination!* 1, no. 1 (October 1937): 7.

7. Yerke, *Memoirs,* 4.

Chapter 7

1. Not paying the author was unfortunately a common practice of the time. Writers obviously balked, but there was little to be done—they knew there were thousands of other dreamers willing to take their place. Obviously there could be no magazine without the writer, but the writer was at once the most important and most expendable. Editors had to pay the writers eventually, but the printers and distributors had to be paid now, or the magazine wouldn't exist. As Frederik Pohl wrote in *The Way The Future Was*: "When you can't pay all the bills, which bills do you pay? ... You pay the printers, because if you

don't they won't print your next issue, and then you're out of business. You pay your paper supplier, because if you don't he won't give the printer any paper to print your next issue on. Out of what's left you pay at least enough of your taxes, rent and utilities to keep things from being turned off. And then you start to think about the writers." If the writer never got a check, he still saw his name in the pulpy pages, something he'd been dreaming about for years. When Bradbury got published for the first time in *Script* he didn't receive a dime, and literally jumped for joy. The writers who made more made more because they wrote more, period. Most authors were hacks; a few were gifted. Writers who at least occasionally published in the pulps include the likes of Theodore Dreiser, Sinclair Lewis, F. Scott Fitzgerald, Tennessee Williams, Upton Sinclair, along with virtually all science fiction writers, since there was almost no other place for them to get published.

2. F.M. Busby, "Fan Clubs: An Example," in *Science Fiction Fandom*, ed. Joe Sanders (Greenwood Press, 1994), 143.

3. Sam Moskowitz, "The Origins: A Reconstruction," in *Science Fiction Fandom*, ed. Joe Sanders (Greenwood Press, 1994), 30.

4. Allan Glasser, ed., *The Planet* 1, no. 1 (July 1930), accessed at fanac.org.

5. Allan Glasser, ed., *The Planet* 1, no. 3 (September 1930): 5, accessed at fanac.org.

6. Harry Warner, Jr., *All Our Yesterdays* (Advent Pub Inc., 1970).

7. Arthur Jean Cox, "Is There a Fan in the House?" *Shangri-LA* no. 8 (September 1948), reprinted in Rob Hansen's book *Bixelstrasse* (Ansible Editions, 2022), 390.

8. Warner, *All Our* Yesterdays, 176.

9. Damon Knight, *The Futurians: The Story of the Science Fiction Family of the 30's that Produced Today's Top SF Writers and Editors* (Day, 1977), 11.

10. Warner, *All Our* Yesterdays, 177.

11. *Ibid.*, 179.

12. *Ibid.*, 176.

13. *SunT(r)ails* 1, no. 1 (October 1, 1941): 2, accessed at fanac.org. Quotes in the original.

14. "The Boiling Point," *The Fantasy Fan* 1, no. 2 (October 1933): 27.

15. Quoted by John L. Coker III in *David A. Kyle: A Life of Science Fiction Ideas and Dreams* (Days of Wonder Publishers, 2006).

16. Forrest J Ackerman, "Wither Ackermankind," *Novae Terrae* 1, no. 9 (December 1936): 4, published by Chapter 22 of the Science Fiction League, Nuneaton, England.

17. Sam Moskowitz, *The Immortal Storm* (Hyperion Press, 1974), 18.

18. One might wonder why a top-tier writer like Lovecraft even bothered with a kid like Ackerman. But Lovecraft was not well known in his time. He was, however, a prolific letter writer. According to Harry Warner, Jr.'s book on early fandom, *All Our Yesterdays*, Lovecraft wrote more than 100,000 letters in his lifetime, averaging eight to 12 per day. All of them were handwritten, and some were as long as 60 pages. He had 50 to 100 correspondences going at any one time and wrote a letter a week to one individual for 12 years.

19. David and Daniel Ritter, ed., *The Earliest Bradbury* (First Fandom Experience, 2020), 117.

20. T. Bruce Yerke, ed., *Imagination!* 1, no. 1 (October 1937): 1.

21. Arthur Louis Joquel II, *SunT(r)ails* 1, no. 1 (October 1, 1941): 2, accessed at fanac.org.

22. Bob Madle, "Fandom up to WW2," in *Science Fiction Fandom,* ed. Joe Sanders (Greenwood Press, 1994), 48.

23. Forrest Ackerman, "I Remember Morojo," reprinted in *Ackermansion Memories* 2.

24. According to Charles D. Hornig, several male fans were infatuated with Pogo, including himself. He published a one-shot flyer called *Hornig's Bulletin #1* in which he half-heartedly apologized for making unwanted advances: "I have a list of some of Fandom's most active who have experienced the misfortune to 'fall' for Pogo. ... I had a particularly bad case of it. ... Several others have been through the same mill." This eight-page rant ended by explaining, "The next Bulletin will contain a further analysis of this situation," but fortunately, there does not appear to have been a "next."

25. Francis T. Laney, *Ah! Sweet Idiocy! The Fan Memoirs of Francis T. Laney* (self-published, 1948).

26. "Myrtle Rebecca Douglas, an Appreciation," reprinted in *Ackermansion Memories* 2 (2006): 4.

27. Warner, *All Our* Yesterdays, 26.

28. T.B. Yerke, *Imagination!* 1, no. 1.

29. Forry Ackerman, *Imagination!* 1, no. 2: 18.

30. Erdstelulov, "Onward Esperanto," *Imagination!* 1, no. 1: 8.

31. Russ Hodgkins, "Ye Ed Say," *Imagination!* 1, no. 1 (October 1937).

32. Russ Hodgkins, "Way Out West," *Imagination!* 1, no. 5 (February 1938).

33. Forrest J Ackerman, "Wither Ackermankind," *Novae Terrae* 1, no. 9 (December 1936), issued by Chapter 22 of the Science Fiction League, Nuneaton, England, accessed at fanac.org.

34. Sam Moskowitz, *Seekers of Tomorrow* (World Publishing Company, 1966), 355.

Chapter 8

1. Jon Eller interview with Ray Bradbury, October 12, 1998.

2. *Imagination!* 1, no. 1 (October 1937): 6.

3. *Imagination!* 2, no. 22 (November 1937): 12.

4. Ritter, *The Earliest Bradbury*, 17.

5. Ray Bradbury, "My Friend Forry," in *Tales*

of the Time Travelers: Adventures of Forrest J Ackerman and Julius Schwartz, ed. John L. Coker III (Days of Wonder Publishers, 2009).
  6. *Imagination!* 1, no. 2: 3.
  7. Yerke, *Memoirs*, 12.
  8. Yerke, *Memoirs*, 13.

Chapter 9

  1. Henry Kuttner, "Writers of the Future," *Imagination!* 1, no. 4 (January 1938): 8. Kuttner would partner with his wife, Catherine, a rare husband-and-wife team in the Golden Age of science Fiction. Kuttner met his wife through his good friend, H.P. Lovecraft. Lovecraft sent Kuttner a batch of unpublished stories and asked for his opinion. Lovecraft then requested Kuttner send these stories on to C.L. Moore, another friend of Lovecraft's who had been publishing her own yarns for years. Kuttner had been wanting to write Moore anyway, as he had always been a fan, so he forwarded these pieces with a letter of praise to "Mr. C.L. Moore," not yet realizing her gender. They would soon collaborate on dozens of projects together, spawning a romance and marrying in 1940. They worked together on stories so much that, they claimed, they couldn't remember who had written what. In his memoir *Man of Two Worlds: My Life in Science Fiction and Comics*, Julius Schwartz tells the tale of staying at their house and falling asleep while Kuttner was writing. Kuttner stopped typing at 4 a.m., but then Schwartz heard typing again. He turned to see Moore now at the typewriter, picking up where Kuttner had stopped. After Kuttner's untimely death in 1958, Moore stopped writing fantasy fiction altogether.
  2. Nolan, *The Ray Bradbury Companion*, 42.
  3. Nolan, *The Ray Bradbury Companion*, 51.
  4. Weller, *The Bradbury Chronicles*, 86.
  5. Eller, *Becoming Ray Bradbury*, 19.
  6. Ray Bradbury, "Hollerbochen's Dilemma," *Imagination!* no. 4: 6.
  7. Jack Speer, "Letter to Imagination!" *Imagination!* 1, no. 5 (February 1938): 17.
  8. Ray Bradbury's diary entry for Thursday, January 6, 1938. Reprinted in *Greentown, Tinseltown*, ed. Ray Bradbury and Don Albright (Stanza Press, 2012).
  9. T. Bruce Yerke, *Mikros* 1, no. 3 (November 1938), accessed at fanac.org.
  10. Bradbury and Albright, *Greentown, Tinseltown*, 141.
  11. For example, in a letter from Ackerman to publisher August Derleth dated December 29, 1945, August William Derleth Papers, Wisconsin Historical Society, Division of Library, Archives, and Museum Collections, Box 1, Folder 1.
  12. Forry Ackerman, "Burn, Witch, Burn," *Sex and Censorship* 1, no. 2, reprinted in *Ackermansion Memories* 4 (2017).
  13. Alan White, "Mr. Monster: Another Time, Another Place," 39, https://efanzines.com/MrMonster/Mr.Monster.pdf.
  14. *Fantast* 13 (April 1942): 13.
  15. Forry Ackerman and Morojo, ed., *Voice of the Imagination* 19 (November 1941): 1.
  16. Letter from the secretary treasurer of the American Fantasy Association, published in *Imagination!* 1, no. 9: 16.
  17. Edgar Rice Burroughs, *Imagination!* 1, no. 6 (March 1938): 19.
  18. "Elmo Lincoln, Biography," Internet Movie Database, https://www.imdb.com/name/nm0511104/bio/?ref_=nm_ov_bio_sm.
  19. Moskowitz, *Seekers of Tomorrow*, 179.
  20. Douglas Ellis, Ed Hulse, and Robert Weinberg, *The Art of the Pulps* (National Geographic Books, 2017), 22.
  21. Forry Ackerman, "Tarzan with a French Accent," *GLOM* no. 8 (July 1947).
  22. Letter from Wollheim to Ackerman dated March 20, 1938, reprinted in *Ackermansion Memories* 1 (2014).
  23. Donald A. Wollheim, "In Defense of Progress," *Imagination!* 1, no. 9 (June 1938): 9.
  24. Erik Freyor, "Debunking of 'Progress,'" *Imagination!* 1, no. 9 (June 1938): 10.

Chapter 10

  1. *LA Evening Citizen News*, March 29, 1933, 6.
  2. Ray Morton, *King Kong: The History of a Movie Icon from Fay Wray to Peter Jackson* (Applause Theatre & Cinema Books, 2005), 78.
  3. Richard Schickel, dir., *The Harryhausen Chronicles*, Rhino Theatrical, July 9, 2002.
  4. Charles Beardsley, *Hollywood's Master Showman: The Legendary Sid Grauman* (Cornwall Books, 1st Edition, 1983), 73.
  5. Ray Harryhausen and Tony Dalton, *Ray Harryhausen: An Animated Life* (Billboard Books, 2004), 9–10.
  6. Ray Harryhausen, as quoted by Ray Bradbury in "The Man Who Lives to Create Monsters," *The LA Times*, August 14, 1977, 45.
  7. Harryhausen and Dalton, *Ray Harryhausen*, 9–10.
  8. *Ibid.*, 18.
  9. Ray Harryhausen and Tony Dalton, *A Century of Stop Motion, From Melies to Aardman* (Watson-Guptill, 2008), 63.
  10. Alec Nevala-Lee, *Astounding: John W. Campbell, Isaac Asimov, Robert A. Heinlein, L. Ron Hubbard, and the Golden Age of Science Fiction* (Dey Street Books, 2018), 3.
  11. Vanessa Harryhausen, *Ray Harryhausen, Titan of Cinema* (National Galleries of Scotland, 2020), 37.
  12. "Cashing in on a Fantasy," *Popular Mechanics* 75, no. 4 (April 1941): 568–69.
  13. O'Brien, *The Forrest J Ackerman Oeuvre*, 24.

14. Ray Bradbury, "The Man Who Lives to Create Monsters," *The LA Times,* August 14, 1977, 45.
15. "Meeting of June 2, 1938,"*Thrilling Wonder Stories* 12, no. 2 (October 1938): 114.
16. Weller, *The Bradbury Chronicles,* 91.

Chapter 11

1. Ray Harryhausen, foreword to *Dinosaur Tales* by Ray Bradbury (Bantam Books, 1983).
2. Ray Bradbury, as quoted in *Tales of the Time Travelers: Adventures of Forrest J Ackerman and Julius Schwartz,* ed. John L. Coker III (Days of Wonder Publishers, 2009).
3. *Ibid.*
4. Barbara Lewis, "Ray Bradbury: The Martian Chronicler," *Starlog* no. 25 (August 1979): 29.
5. Ray Bradbury, Introduction, *Futuria Fantasia* (Graham Publishing, 2007).
6. John L. Coker III, ed., *Tales of the Time Travelers: Adventures of Forrest J Ackerman and Julius Schwartz* (Days of Wonder Publishers, 2009).
7. Ray Harryhausen and Ray Bradbury, 2003 interview at the Warner Bros. Studios in Burbank, released on the DVD *The Beast from 20,000 Fathoms,* Warner Home Video, October 21, 2003.
8. Ray Bradbury, as quoted by Terry Pace, "A Certain Kind of Magic," *Famous Monsters of Filmland* no. 271 (January/February 2014), 56.
9. *Ibid.*
10. Harryhausen, *Ray Harryhausen,* 184.
11. Weller, *The Bradbury Chronicles,* 90.

Chapter 12

1. Russ Hodgkins, "Way Out West," *Imagination!* 1, no. 9: 2.
2. Sam Moskowitz, *The Immortal Storm* (Hyperion Press, 1974), 39.
3. Knight, *The Futurians,* 13.
4. Warner, *All Our Yesterdays,* 29.
5. "Leeds Chapter, England," *Thrilling Wonder Stories* 11, no. 1 (February 1938): 118.
6. Cheng, *Astounding Wonder,* 252.
7. *Ibid.,* 266.
8. *Ibid.,* 276.
9. *Ibid.,* 202.
10. Ritter, *The Visual History,* 229.
11. Davis Publications, *Analog,* March 29, 1982, 46.
12. Amy Teitel, *Breaking the Chains of Gravity: The Story of Spaceflight Before Gravity* (Bloomsbury Sigma, 2018), 18.
13. "Rocketry's First Martyr," *Wonder Stories* 10, no. 3 (December 1937).
14. Cheng, *Astounding Wonder,* 291.

Chapter 13

1. Ray Bradbury, Introduction, *Futuria Fantasia* (Graham Publishing, 2007).
2. Weller, *The Bradbury Chronicles,* 89.
3. *Thrilling Wonder Stories* 11, no. 1 (December 1938).
4. Terry Pace, "Ray Bradbury's Earliest Influences," *Monsters from the Vault* 16, no. 30 (Spring 2012).
5. Maria A. Slowinska, "Consuming Illusion, Illusions of Consumability: American Movie Palaces of the 1920s," *Amerikastudien/American Studies* 50, no. 4 (2005): 575–601.
6. *Ibid.,* 575.
7. Ben M. Hall, *The Golden Age of the Movie Palace* (C.N. Potter, 1975), 5–10 and 26.
8. *Ibid.,* 140.
9. The five grand movie palaces of Racine, Wisconsin, were the 1,800-seat Majestic, built with apartments to house the traveling vaudevillians who performed there before or after picture shows; the 1,800-seat Venetian, decorated with a Renaissance motif of tapestries and silk-embroidered hangings, all beneath a domed ceiling dotted with twinkling lights as stars; the 1,258-seat Rialto, which was right next door; the 1,170-seat RKO Theatre, which at one point hung a sign that loomed seven stories above downtown Racine while flashing lightning bolts; and the 1,000-seat Rex Theatre, a former opera house. Source: *Historic Movie Theatres of Wisconsin,* by Konrad Schiecke.
10. The most famous of the movie palace organists was Jesse Crawford. He started his career playing in Seattle and was good enough to be bought by Sid Grauman to play at the Million Dollar Theatre in LA. New York poached Crawford next, where he played at the Tivoli until he moved to the Windy City to play at the aptly named Chicago. Adolph Zukor hired him to return to New York to work at his palace, The Paramount. Crawford was famous enough that his name often popped up in newspaper ads for the films.
11. Hall, *The Golden* Age, 21.
12. Coker, *Tales of the Time Travelers.*

Chapter 14

1. Deborah Painter, *Forry: The Life of Forrest J Ackerman* (McFarland, 2010), 31.
2. Author listed only as AZSHYGOUS. *Imagination!* 2, no. 1 (October 1938): 1.
3. Yerke, *Memoirs,* 24.
4. Yerke, *Memoirs,* 25.
5. "Los Angeles Chapter Meeting of January 19th, 1939," *Thrilling Wonder Stories* 13, no. 3 (June 1939): 122.
6. Ray Bradbury, Introduction, *Futuria Fantasia* (Graham Publishing, 2007).
7. Eller, *Becoming Ray Bradbury,* 58.

8. Mark Reinsberg, ed., *Ad Astra* 1, no. 5 (January 1940): 14.
9. Ray Bradbury, "Ain't He Cute," *Voice of the Imagination* no. 11 (January 1941): 5.
10. Forry Ackerman and Morojo, ed., *Voice of the Imagination* no. 4 (December 1939): 13.
11. Forry Ackerman and Morojo, ed., *Voice of the Imagination* no. 6 (April 1940): 12.
12. T. Bruce Yerke and Russ Hodgkins, "Reply to Lowndes," *Mikros* 1, no. 6 (September 1939): 5.
13. Ron Reynolds (Ray Bradbury), "Don't Get Technatal," *Futuria Fantasia* no. 1 (Summer 1939): 5.
14. Eller, *Becoming Ray Bradbury*, 35.
15. Ibid.
16. Ibid., 38.
17. Moskowitz, *Seekers of Tomorrow*, 368.
18. Eller, *Becoming Ray Bradbury*, 34.

Chapter 15

1. *Army Ordnance* 26, no. 146 (September/October 1944): 198.

Chapter 16

1. Ray Bradbury, *Futuria Fantasia* no. 2 (Fall 1939).

Chapter 17

1. Robert A. Madle, "Science Fiction Fandom up to WW2," in *Science Fiction Fandom,* ed. Joe Sanders (Greenwood Press, 1994), 45.
2. Lew Wolkoff, ed., *Phoxphyre: The World's First Science Fiction Convention*, November 24, 1983, https://fanac.org/conpubs/Early%20Conventions/First%20Convention/Phoxphyre.pdf.
3. D.W.F. Mayer, "The British Science Fiction Conference," *Novae Terrae* 1, no. 8 (November 1936): 3, 19. Rob Hansen, "The First Convention (1937)," http://www.fiawol.org.uk/fanstuff/THEN%20Archive/1937con.htm.
4. Ritter, *The Visual History*, 220.
5. Moskowitz, *The Immortal Storm*, 82.
6. Madle, "Science Fiction Fandom," 47.
7. Ritter, *The Visual History*, 338.

Chapter 18

1. Eller, *Becoming Ray Bradbury*, 28.
2. Weller, *The Bradbury Chronicles*, 94.
3. Coker, *Tales of the Time Travelers*, 108.
4. Ibid., 109.
5. Ibid.
6. Ibid.
7. Andrew Liptak, *Cosplay: A History* (Saga Press, 2022), 18.

Chapter 19

1. Schwartz and Thomsen, 50.
2. Richard Ketchum, "The World of Tomorrow: The 1939 New York World's Fair," in *The 1930s*, ed. Louise I. Gerdes (Greenhaven Press, Inc., 2000), 335.
3. Ibid.
4. Ritter, *The Visual History*, 408.
5. Ketchum, "The World of Tomorrow," 335.
6. James Mauro, *Twilight at the World of Tomorrow: Genius, Madness, Murder and the 1939 World's Fair on the Brink of War* (Random House, 2010), 28.
7. "Life Goes to the New York World's Fair," *Life,* July 3, 1939, 55.
8. Mauro, *Twilight at the World of Tomorrow*, 292.
9. Forry Ackerman, as quoted in *Surround Yourself with Your Loves and Live Forever*, ed. John L. Coker III (Days of Wonder Publishers, 2008), 110.
10. Weller, *The Bradbury Chronicles*, 95.
11. Eller, *Becoming Ray Bradbury*, 30.
12. Quote from Julius Schwartz, *Tales of the Time Travelers: Adventures of Forrest J Ackerman and Julius Schwartz*, ed. John L. Coker III (Days of Wonder Publishers, 2009).
13. Warner, *All Our Yesterdays*, 120.
14. Moskowitz, *Seekers of Tomorrow*, 367.
15. Ray Bradbury, "Off the Cuff," *Shangri-L'Affaires,* August 1959.
16. Nevala-Lee, *Astounding*, 182–183.
17. Forry J Ackerman, *Fantasy Times* no. 169 (December 1952), reprinted in *Ackermansion Memories* 4 (March 2017): 42.
18. Ray Bradbury, "I Am Positively Not Robert Bloch," *The Alchemist* 1, no. 5: 21. Reprinted in *The Earliest Bradbury*, ed. David and Daniel Ritter (First Fandom Experience, 2020), 125.

Chapter 20

1. Knight, *The Futurians*, 108.
2. Nevala-Lee, *Astounding*, 105.
3. Ashley, *The Gernsback Days*, 140.
4. Moskowitz, *The Immortal Storm*, 50.
5. Knight, *The Futurians*, 12.
6. Ibid., 96.
7. Ritter, *The Visual History*, 424.
8. Sam Moskowitz, *New Fandom* 1, no. 6 (January 1940), as reprinted in Ritter, *The Visual History*, 420.
9. Moskowitz, *The Immortal Storm*.
10. Jonathan Eller, "Ray Bradbury: One Story at a Time," *Comic-Con Souvenir Book*, July 2020, 18.
11. Ray Bradbury, *Surround Yourself with Your Loves and Live Forever*, ed. John L. Coker III (Days of Wonder Publishers, 2008), 89.
12. Charles G. Martignette, "Where Have All the Paintings Gone?" in Robert Lesser, *Pulp Art* (Sterling Publishing, 1997), 136.

13. Lesser, *Pulp Art*, 6.
14. Lesser, *Pulp Art*, 7.
15. Charles G. Martignette, "Where Have All the Paintings Gone?" in *Pulp Art* by Robert Lesser (Sterling Publishing, 1997), 136.
16. Ritter, *The Visual History*, 227.
17. *Thrilling Wonder* 9, no. 1 (February 1937): 116.
18. Forry Ackerman, "The Precificon," July 1946, reprinted in Rob Hansen, *Bixelstrasse* (Ansible Editions, 2022), 297.
19. Barbara Bovard, "Ten Nights in a Madhouse," *Shangri-L'Affaires* no. 11B (August 1943): 8.
20. *Ad Astra* no. 5 (January 1940): 13.
21. Allen Class, letter to *Voice of the Imagination* no. 18 (October 1941): 10.
22. FANAC Fan History, "Erle Korshak—A Fan History Zoom Session with Joe Siclari and Stephen Korshak (Part 2)," May 5, 2021, YouTube video, 1:11:20, https://www.youtube.com/watch?v=0PE8pcwolOo.
23. Eller, *Becoming Ray Bradbury*, 30.
24. Sam Moskowitz, *New Fandom* 1, no. 6 (January 1940): 29.
25. Ritter, *The Visual History*, 423.
26. *Ibid.*, 407.

Chapter 21

1. Sam Moskowitz, *New Fandom* 1, no. 6 (January 1940): 7.
2. *Ibid.*
3. David Saunders, "Frank R. Paul," *Field Guide to Wild American Pulp Artists*, https://www.pulpartists.com/Paul.html.
4. Erle M. Korshak, "The Early Days," *First Fandom Annual* (2021): 4.
5. Weller, *The Bradbury Chronicles*, 97.

Chapter 22

1. Eller, *Becoming Ray Bradbury*, 30.
2. *New Fandom* 1, no. 6: 22. Also, excerpt from Ray Bradbury's 1939 Diary for Friday, July 7 (from the collection of John L. Coker III): "Big day... went to Farnsworth Wright's...showed him Hans' [sic] drawings...he will let hans [sic] do an illustration for Weird. Yahee! Got to [insert "see"] Virgil Finlay's drawings. Then over to see Erisman... talked...told us to come back at four-thirty...met Finlay at American Weekly...back to Erisman... big argument over Paul cover...which Wollheim finally won in drawing..."
3. Eller, *Becoming Ray Bradbury*, 31.
4. Letter from Ray Bradbury to *Fantastic Novels*, January 1941. Reprinted in Robert Lesser, *Pulp Art*, 160.
5. Knight, *The Futurians*, 122.
6. Letter from Bok to Derleth, dated March 9, 1963, August William Derleth Papers, Wisconsin Historical Society, Division of Library, Archives, and Museum Collections, Box 6, folder 5.
7. Letter from Bok to Derleth, dated July 28, 1946, August William Derleth Papers, Wisconsin Historical Society, Division of Library, Archives, and Museum Collections, Box 6, folder 5.
8. Stephen Korshak, ed., *A Hannes Bok Treasury* (Underwood Books, 1993).

Chapter 23

1. Ritter, *The Visual History*, 407.
2. "Amazing! Astounding!" *Time* XXXIV, no. 2 (July 10, 1939).
3. Sam A. Moskowitz, *New Fandom* 1, no. 6 (January 1940), reprinted in Ritter, *The Visual History*, 418.
4. *Ibid.*
5. Frederik Pohl, *The Science Fiction Roll of Honor* (Random House, Inc., 1975), 223.
6. Eller, *Becoming Ray Bradbury*, 42.
7. Ray Bradbury, "Local League Life," *Futuria Fantasia* 1, no. 2 (Fall 1939): 20.
8. Jack Erman, "Farwest Facts," *Ad Astra* no. 5 (January 1940): 13–14.
9. Ray Harryhausen, *The Art of Ray Harryhausen* (Billboard Books, 2006), 31–32.
10. Forrest Ackerman, "Ackorns by Acky," *Shangri-L'Affaires* no. 20 (November 1944).

Chapter 24

1. Coker, *Tales of the Time Travelers*.
2. Nevala-Lee, *Astounding*, 111.
3. *Ibid.*, 112.
4. *Ibid.*, 113.
5. Schwartz and Thomsen, 60.
6. *Ibid.*
7. *Ibid.*
8. *Ibid.*, 56.
9. Ray Bradbury, as quoted in *Surround Yourself with Your Loves and Live Forever*, ed. John L. Coker III (Days of Wonder Publishers, 2008), 61.
10. Eller, *Becoming Ray Bradbury*, 66.
11. Weller, *The Bradbury Chronicles*, 105.
12. Eller, *Becoming Ray Bradbury*, 65.
13. "Henry Kuttner," *Thrilling Wonder Stories* 8, no. 3 (June 1939, 10th anniversary issue): 87.
14. Weller, *The Bradbury Chronicles*, 103.
15. *Le Zombie* no. 2 (February 1940): 2.
16. *Ad Astra* no. 5 (January 1940): 12.
17. Eller, *Becoming Ray Bradbury*, 68.
18. Ray Bradbury, as quoted in Coker, *Surround Yourself*, 62.
19. Eller, *Becoming Ray Bradbury*, 68.
20. Forry Ackerman, *Famous Monsters of Filmland* no. 265 (January/February 2013).

Chapter 25

1. T. Bruce Yerke, *Shangri-LA* 1, no.1: 5. Also, "LASFS History" by the LA Science Fantasy Society, accessed at LASFS site, http://www.lasfsinc.info.
2. Emily Welly, "Walter Daugherty, King Tut Expert, Dies at 90," *Santa Maria Times*, June 16, 2007, http://santamariatimes.com/articles/2007/06/16/news/centralcoast/news05.txt.
3. Forry Ackerman, "OFF THE RECORD," *Voice of the Imagination* no. 11 (January 1941): 10.
4. Forrest Ackerman, "Ackorns by Acky," *Shangri-L'Affaires* no. 20 (1944), reprinted in *Ackermansion Memories* 5: 18.
5. Bob Tucker, letter to *Voice of the Imagination* no. 14 (May 1941): 10.
6. Warner, *All Our Yesterdays*, 249.
7. T. Bruce Yerke, *Mikros* 1, no. 6 (September 1939): 3.
8. *Ad Astra* 5 (January 1940): 11.
9. Yerke, 4–5.

Chapter 26

1. Eller, *Becoming Ray Bradbury*, 41.
2. Sarah Stewart Johnson, *The Sirens of Mars: Searching for Life on Another World* (Crown, 2021), 13.
3. Ibid., 18.
4. Warner, *All Our Yesterdays*, 248.
5. Forry Ackerman and Walt Daugherty, "NEWS NOTES OF SHANGRI-LA BY ACKERMAN AND DAUGHERTY," *Shangri L'Affaires* no. 12 (September 1943): 8.

Chapter 27

1. FANAC Fan History, "Erle Korshak—A Fan History Zoom Session with Joe Siclari and Stephen Korshak (Part 2)," May 5, 2021, YouTube video, 1:11:20, https://www.youtube.com/watch?v=0PE8pcwolOo.
2. Warner, *All Our Yesterdays*, 93.

Chapter 28

1. Allied Authors, "History Milwaukee Fictioneers and Allied Authors," allied-authors.org/, accessed January 25, 2022.
2. "Roger Sherman Hoar is Dead," *New York Times*, October 18, 1963, 24.
3. Richard Toronto, *War Over Lemuria: Richard Shaver, Ray Palmer, and the Strangest Chapter of 1940s Science Fiction* (McFarland & Company, 2013), 41.
4. Ibid., 48 and 47, respectively.
5. Ray Palmer, "Guest Editorial #1," *Ad Astra* 1, no. 3 (September 1939): 12.
6. Toronto, *War Over Lemuria*, 43.
7. "Milwaukee Youth Writes Horror Tales, Sells 'em," *Milwaukee Journal*, April 5, 1935.
8. Gerry de la Ree and Sam Moskowitz, "After Ten Years: A Tribute to Stanley G. Weinbaum, 1902–1935," November 1945, 15.
9. Ray Palmer, "Stanley Grauman Weinbaum," *Fantasy Magazine*, January 1936, reprinted in *Ackermansion Memories* 3 (September 2016): 61.
10. *Le Zombie* 2, no. 23 (February 10, 1940): 4.
11. Isaac Asimov, "The Second Nova," introduction to *The Best of Stanley G. Weinbaum* (Random House, 1974).

Chapter 29

1. Freehafer tragically died of a bad heart at age 27. Francis T. Laney remembered him in his memoir *Sweet Idiocy*: "One of the most sunny natures I've ever encountered. His health was atrocious, and his personal appearance showed it, but though doomed from childhood to a very short life, he had resolved to make the best of it and live it fully." Every meeting hall in every LASFS clubroom has been named Freehafer Hall in his honor.
2. Knight, *The Futurians*, 81.
3. Erle Korshak, "The Third WorldCon—Denvention 1941," *First Fandom Annual* (2016): 29.
4. Forry J Ackerman, "Behold Margaret Brundage," *The Alchemist* 1, no. 5 (February 1941): 13–15.
5. Lesser, *Pulp Art*.
6. Walt Liebscher, "Rite Hook" (letter), *Voice of the Imagination* no. 16 (Special Denvention Issue, 1941): 7.
7. Warner, *All Our Yesterdays*, 98.
8. Forrest J Ackerman, *Tales of the Time Travelers: Adventures of Forrest J Ackerman and Julius Schwartz*, ed. John L. Coker III (Days of Wonder Publishers, 2009).
9. Bob Tucker, "The First ChiCon," self-published essay, 1965, 9.
10. "Chicon History," https://chicon.org/home/about-worldcon/about-us/chicon-history/.
11. Forry Ackerman, "Forrest J Ackerman's Chicon I Reminiscence," fancyclopedia.org/Chicon_I_Reminiscence_(Ackerman).
12. Warner, *All Our Yesterdays*, 96.
13. David Ritter and Daniel Ritter, *The Visual History of Fandom, Volume Two: 1940* (First Fandom Experience, LLC, 2022), 50.
14. Email from Eric Grayson, dated May 4, 2022.
15. Tucker, "The First ChiCon," 9.
16. Ritter, *The Visual History of Fandom, Volume Two*, 66.
17. This author was lucky enough to speak to Korshak via Zoom just a few months before he died. When I asked the 97-year-old Korshak why he simply threw the paintings out into the crowd, he explained, "What else were we gonna

do? There were piles of them." FANAC Fan History, "Erle Korshak—A Fan History Zoom Session with Joe Siclari and Stephen Korshak (Part 2)," May 5, 2021, YouTube video, 1:11:20, https://www.youtube.com/watch?v=0PE8pcwolOo.
    18. Ritter, *The Visual History of Fandom, Volume Two*, 68.

Chapter 30

1. Tucker, "The First ChiCon," 9.
2. Warner, *All Our Yesterdays*, 97.
3. Ibid., 99.
4. Forry Ackerman, "Early Sf Fans Recall the Third WorldCon," *First Fandom Annual* (2016): 25.
5. Warner, *All Our Yesterdays*, 99.

Chapter 31

1. Ray Bradbury, diary entry for August 21, as reprinted in *Greentown, Tinseltown* (Stanza Press, 2012).
2. Barbara Lewis, "The Martian Chronicler," *Starlog* no. 25 (August 1979): 55.
3. Moskowitz, *Seekers of Tomorrow*, 366.
4. Ibid., 362.

Chapter 32

1. The earliest mention this author found of the clubroom was in the October 1941 issue of *Shangri-L'Affaires*: "This is being typt direct on stencil in the LASFS Clubroom."
2. Forry Ackerman, "Corn-fetti by Ack-Ack," *Shangri-L'Affaires* no. 18B (September 1944): 9.
3. Warner, *All Our Yesterdays*, 219.
4. Knight, *The Futurians*, 136 and 117.
5. Ibid., 12.
6. Warner, *All Our Yesterdays*, 158.
7. "LASFS History," Official site of the LA Science Fantasy Society, www.lasfsinc.info, accessed July 14, 2021.
8. Michael R. Page, *Frederik Pohl: Modern Masters of Science Fiction* (University of Illinois Press, 2015), 14.
9. Cheng, *Astounding Wonder*, 68.
10. Russ Hodgkins, "Way Out West," *Imagination!* 1, no. 1 (October 1937): 4.
11. *Thrilling Wonder Stories* 13, no. 2 (April 1939): 127.
12. "Biografys." *Imagination!* 1, no. 4 (January 1938): 4.
13. "Chapter News and General Activities—Los Angeles," *Thrilling Wonder Stories* 10, no. 2 (October 1937): 124.
14. *Thrilling Wonder Stories* 9, no. 3 (June 1937).
15. M.K. Hanson, ed., "Nuneaton Branch," *Novae Terrae* no. 12 (May 1937): 15.
16. John B. Michel, *The International Observer*, March 1936, 2.
17. Dick Wilson, letter to *Voice of the Imagi-Nation* no. 4 (December 1939): 5.
18. "SFAA Library; Bargains in Back Numbers," *Tesseract*, May 1937, 12.

Chapter 33

1. Ted Carnell, letter to *Voice of the Imagination* no. 8 (special Chicon issue, August 1940): 13.
2. Ted Carnell, letter to *Voice of the Imagination* no. 11 (January 1941): 8.
3. Jon Craig, letter to *Voice of the Imagination* no. 17 (August 1941): 18.
4. Arthur C. Clarke, letter to *Voice of the Imagination* no. 6 (April 1940): 9.
5. Letter to *Voice of the Imagination* no. 14 (May 1941): 10.
6. "Fantasy show-downby Januarius," *Fantast* 2, no. 5 (December 1941): 12.

Chapter 34

1. Rob Hansen, *Bixelstrasse: The SF Fan Community of 1940s Los Angeles* (Ansible Editions, 2022), 18.
2. Ibid.
3. Robert A. Madle, *First Fandom Annual* (2016): 31.
4. Coker, *Tales of the Time Travelers*, 111.
5. Hansen, *Bixelstrasse*, 22.
6. Postcard from Yerke to Bradbury, reprinted in *First Fandom Annual* (2016): 30.
7. Warner, *All Our Yesterdays*, 103.
8. E. Everett Evans, "July 1941: Denvention Dope," reprinted in Hansen, *Bixelstrasse*, 18.
9. Walt J. Daugherty, *First Fandom Annual* (2016): 27.
10. Robert Heinlein, "Discover of the Future," speech at third World Science Fiction Convention, transcribed by Forry Ackerman, accessed at Fanac.org.
11. Rusty Hevelin, "Denvention Report," fanac.org/Denvention3/denvention1report.
12. Warner, *All Our Yesterdays*, 137.
13. "Cos Story Transcript: Morojo," *The Cosplay Journal*, thecosplayjournal.com/cosstory/episode-2-morojo, accessed on August 29, 2022.
14. E. Everett Evans, "July 1941: Denvention Dope," reprinted in Hansen, *Bixelstrasse*, 19.
15. Ibid.
16. Warner, *All Our Yesterdays*, 104.
17. Hansen, *Bixelstrasse*, 21.
18. Warner, *All Our Yesterdays*, 107.

Chapter 35

1. Forry Ackerman, as quoted in Hansen, *Bixelstrasse*, 34.

2. "Round of Japanese Aliens in Southland Begun by F.B.I.," *The LA Times*, December, 8, 1941, F1.
3. L.R. Chauvenet, "President's Report," *Bonfire* 1, no. 3 (December 1941).
4. Art Widner, "Wartime Fandom," in *Science Fiction Fandom*, ed. Joe Sanders (Greenwood Press, 1994), 56.
5. Warner, *All Our Yesterdays*, 160.
6. Nevala-Lee, *Astounding*, 160.
7. *Ibid.*, 201.
8. Wolkoff, *Phoxphyre*, 8.
9. Warner, *All Our Yesterdays*, 161.
10. Scott Essman, "Ray Harryhausen: In His Own Words," *Famous Monsters* no. 271 (January/February 2014): 39.
11. Ray Harryhausen, *The Art of Ray Harryhausen* (Billboard Books, 2006), 19.
12. Forry Ackerman, *Voice of the Imagination* no. 15 (June 1941): 3.
13. *Shangri-L'Affaires* no. 13 (April 1944): 2.
14. Warner, *All Our Yesterdays*, 150.
15. Forry Ackerman, *Open Letter to Anglofans*, September 1, 1941. This was a one-time publication about his efforts to send materials to England during the war.
16. Sam Sackett, "The Ackerman Story," *Fantastic Worlds* no. 2952, reprinted in *Ackermansion Memories* 9 (September 2019): 52.
17. Forry Ackerman, letter as reprinted in *Amazing Forries: This Is Your Life Forrest J Ackerman* (Metropolis Publications, 1976).
18. California Center for Military History, California Military Department, "Fort MacArthur History," www.militarymuseum.org/FtMacArthur.html.
19. *Ft. MacArthur Bulletin/Alert* 3, no. 26 (Friday, April 13, 1945).
20. Email exchange with Stephen Nelson, June 3, 2021.
21. Interview, Eastern New Mexico University, Roosevelt County Oral History Project, February 13, 1988, https://library.biblioboard.com/anthology-collection/28fd5bd2-49d5-4491-8dc6-9b9730b6399b/20e3b58d-82f9-4e41-afd2-9dd745af2221.
22. Forry Ackerman, "Lang is a Fan!," *Shangri-L'Affaires* no. 21 (December 1944): 5.
23. Letter from Ray Bradbury to August Derleth, dated August 3, 1945, August William Derleth Papers, Wisconsin Historical Society, Division of Library, Archives, and Museum Collections, Box 6, Folder 8.
24. Nolan, *The Ray Bradbury Companion*, 54.
25. Letter from Ray Bradbury to August Derleth, dated January 31, 1946, August William Derleth Papers, Wisconsin Historical Society, Division of Library, Archives, and Museum Collections, Box 6, Folder 8.
26. *The AckerMonster Chronicles!*, directed by Jason V. Brock, JaSunni Productions, October 31, 2012.

Chapter 36

1. Rob Hansen, "The LASFS Clubroom," accessed at http://www.fiawol.org.uk/.
2. Hansen, *Bixelstrasse*, 60.
3. "Myrtle Rebecca Douglas, an Appreciation," *Ackermansion Memories* 2 (2016): 4.
4. Walt Daugherty, "NEWS NOTES OF SHANGRI-LA BY ACKERMAN AND DAUGHERTY," *Shangri-L'Affaires* no. 12 (September 1943), 9.
5. Hansen, *Bixelstrasse*, 73.
6. Rob Hoffman, letter to *Shangri-LA* no. 27 (October 1945): 17.
7. Forry Ackerman, "Slobber by Yobber," *Shangri-L'Affaires* no. 19 (October 1944): 19.
8. "Late News Flashes from Shangri-LA," *Shangri-LA* no. 11 (August 1943): 3.
9. Forry Ackerman, "Rum, Little Chillun," *Shangri-L'Affaires* no. 22 (January 1945): 3.
10. They didn't just celebrate Christmas. In the January 1941 issue of LA-based zine *Ad Astra*, it was reported that on the fifth Thursday of November 1940, members of LASFS gathered for Thanksgiving: "Twas on the 5th Thursday of November—how well we remember—all thru the land there was turkey on hand! & the imaginatives of LA did indeed have something to be thankful for that holiday-, for our-'mems were invited to the home of Secy Yerke for a real old fa'shiond Thanxgiving Turkey Dinner Delux (with all th' trimmin's), hospitably prepared & 'served by Bruce's Mother & 'Grandmother. Have Hodgkins, Pogo, Bradbury, Paul Freehafer, 4e, Morojo, Yerke, Daugherty & other stfans together in one gathering & U'r bound to have a greatime!"
11. Jike and Aloojo, "Shangri-LA Inside Out," *Shangri-L'Affaires* no. 13 (April 1944): 4.
12. "Xmas at the LASFS," *Shangri-L'Affaires* no. 21 (December 1944): 10.
13. Nate D. Sanders Auctions, "Lot #92: Collection of Five Hannes Bok Lithographs Personally Owned by Ray Bradbury," November 20, 2014, http://natedsanders.com/collection_of_five_hannes_bok_lithographs_personal-lot32732.aspx.

Chapter 37

1. *Fantasy Fiction Field* 10, no. 5 (March 11, 1944).
2. John Bristol Speer, *Fancyclopedia* (self-published in collaboration with the National Fantasy Fan Foundation, Forry Ackerman, and the Los Angeles Science Fantasy Society, 1944), 52.
3. Warner, *All Our Yesterdays*, 251.
4. Laney, *Ah! Sweet Idiocy!*, 75.
5. *Ibid.*, 60.
6. *Ibid.*, 64.
7. Warner, *All Our Yesterdays*, 252.

8. Laney, *Ah! Sweet Idiocy!*, 51.
9. Hansen, *Bixelstrasse*, 375.
10. *Ibid.*
11. Laney, *Ah! Sweet Idiocy!*, 92.
12. Hansen, *Bixelstrasse*, 361–363.
13. Jikè and Alojo, "Shangri-LA Inside Out," *Shangri-L'Affaires* no. 13B (April 1944): 3.

Chapter 38

1. Alva Rogers, "Fran the Iconoclast," *Innuendo* no. 11 (December 1960).
2. Laney, *Ah! Sweet Idiocy!*, 101.
3. *Ibid.*, 56.
4. Arnie Katz, "Mr. Monster: Another Time, Another Place," self-published zine, https://efanzines.com/MrMonster/Mr.Monster.pdf, 2.
5. Forry Ackerman, "Myrtle Rebecca Douglas: An Appreciation --520 07 0328/I Remember Morojo," self-published, February 11, 1965, posted at efanzines.com/Morojo/.
6. Despite what one might guess from the title, Laney took his memoir very seriously. This is how he described the process for printing his own book: "Published by Francis T. Laney and Charles Burbee for FAPA at Los Angeles, Anno Domini 1948. This book is hand-set in Underwood Pica and printed on special sulfite base paper with little or no rag content. Like the fine books of the 18th and early 19th centuries, it is published unbound, so that gentlemen may have it embellished to match their libraries."
7. Tigrina (with responses to her questions from Forry Ackerman), letter published in *Voice of the Imagination* no. 17 (August 1941): 21. In that same letter, Tigrina objected to Forry's use of nude drawings. Under the headline "Damsels Dressed Only in Sandals are Scandals" she complained about "the pulchritudinous lovelies wearing smiles but nothing much else."
8. "LASFS," *STEFNEWS* no. 68 (November 17, 1946).
9. *Vice Versa* 1, no. 1 (June 1947): 1. Accessed at queermusicheritage.com/viceversa.
10. *Vice Versa* 1, no. 5 (October 1947): 6. Accessed at queermusicheritage.com/viceversa.
11. Eric Marcus, "Lisa Ben 'Gay Girl,'" Gay Today: Diverse News for the LGBTQ Community, September 8, 1997, http://gaytoday.badpuppy.com/garchive/p eople/090897pe.htm.
12. "On March 16, 1960, the Grand Jury for the Southern District of California returned a five-count indictment against the appellant, charging in counts 1 through 5, respectively, that appellant on five separate occasions mailed letters which were obscene, lewd, indecent, lascivious and filthy in violation of Title 18, United States Code, Section 1461." Forrest James Ackerman v. UNITED STATES of America. No. 17252, United States Court of Appeals Ninth Circuit, August 18, 1961, accessed at law.rescource.org.
13. *The AckerMonster Chronicles!*, directed by Jason V. Brock, JaSunni Productions, October 31, 2012.

Chapter 39

1. Warner, *All Our Yesterdays*, 253.
2. Hansen, *Bixelstrasse*, 418.
3. Cheng, *Astounding Wonder*, 302.
4. Forry Ackerman (as Weaver Wright), "Pacificon Report" *Glom* no. 6 (January 1947): 2.
5. *Ibid.*
6. Francis T. Laney, "Pacificon Diary," *Fandango* 4, no. 1 (Fall 1946): 6.
7. Hansen, *Bixelstrasse*, 318.
8. Warner, *All Our Yesterdays*, 261.
9. Forry Ackerman (as Weaver Wright), "Pacificon Report," *Glom* no. 6 (January 1947): 3.
10. Warner, *All Our Yesterdays*, 262.
11. *Ibid.*, 263.
12. Harry Warner, Jr., "Fandom Between WW2 and Sputnik," in *Science Fiction Fandom*, ed. Joe Sanders (Greenwood Press, 1994).
13. Fred Patten, "Cinvention," CFG History, http://www.cfg.org/history/.
14. Len Moffatt, "Partial Recall: The Fan Memoirs of Len Moffatt, Part Five," LA Science Fantasy Society, http://www.lasfsinc.info/index.php?option=com_content&task=view&id=258&Itemid=564).
15. "Westercon," https://fancyclopedia.org/Westercon.

Chapter 40

1. Coker, *Tales of the Time Travelers*, 2009.
2. Larry Gordon, "Final Chapter at Oldest L.A. Bookstore," *The LA Times*, March 23, 1994, https://www.latimes.com/archives/la-xpm-1994-03-23-me-37466-story.html).
3. Eller, *Becoming Ray Bradbury*, 131.
4. *Ibid.*, 157.
5. Ray Bradbury, *Dark Carnival* (Gauntlet Press, 2001), xx.
6. Coker, *Tales of the Time Travelers*.

Chapter 41

1. When this author went to the Wisconsin Historical Society to access August Derleth's papers, I found myself thumbing through a file that also included correspondence between Derleth and Forry Ackerman, Robert Bloch, Hannes Bok, etc. That was just in the A–B file.
2. Schwartz and Thomsen, 37.
3. Sam Moskowitz, *Explorers of the Infinite* (Fantasy Home, Inc., 1957), 251.
4. *Ibid.*, 252.
5. Warner, *All Our Yesterdays*, 89.
6. Letter from Bradbury to Derleth, dated November 23, 1939, August William Derleth

Papers, Wisconsin Historical Society, Division of Library, Archives, and Museum Collections, Box 1, Folder 1.

7. Letter from Bradbury to Derleth, dated March 17, 1947, August William Derleth Papers, Wisconsin Historical Society, Division of Library, Archives, and Museum Collections, Box 1, Folder 1.

8. *Ibid.*

9. Letter from Ackerman to Derleth, dated January 29, 1947, August William Derleth Papers, Wisconsin Historical Society, Division of Library, Archives, and Museum Collections, Box 1, Folder 1.

10. Ray Bradbury, "SDCC 2002 Julius Schwartz & Ray Bradbury Panel," reprinted in *Ackermansion Memories* 7 (2018): 11.

11. Bradbury, *Dark Carnival*, xii.

12. Ray Bradbury, "Off the Cuff," *Shangri-LA* no. 45, reprinted in *Ackermansion Memories* 5 (2017): 44.

Chapter 42

1. Harryhausen, *The Art of Ray Harryhausen*, 37.

2. *Ibid.*, 49.

3. *Ibid.*

4. Harryhausen, *Ray Harryhausen: Titan of Cinema*, 59.

5. Email exchange with Jon Weller, July 12, 2019.

6. Ray Bradbury, as quoted by Terr Pacce, "A Certain Kind of Magic," *Famous Monsters of Filmland* (January/February 2014).

7. Mike Hankin, *Ray Harryhausen: Master of the Majicks, Vol. 2, The American Films* (Archive Editions LLC, 2008), 73.

8. Warner Brothers publicity for *The Beast from 20,000 Fathoms* included the "first and only animated lobby and front display ever created!" This lobby display that theater owners could buy for $16.95 was animated: "The Crimson tongue darts up and down! The glaring eye moves back and forth! And the display includes a motor and battery! IT ROARS!" Plus, "IT'S IN COLOR!" (Caps in the original, of course). The publicity team also encouraged owners to hire a plasterer to make giant dinosaur prints, to be displayed out front. Source: Hankin, *Ray Harryhausen, Master of the Majicks*, 102.

9. Danny Peary, *Cult Horror Movies: Discover the 33 Best Scary, Suspenseful, Gory, and Monstrous Cinema Classics* (Workman Publishing Company, 2014).

10. Ray Harryhausen. *Ray Harryhausen: The Early Years Collection*, Disc 1, featurette, "Interview at Clifton's Cafeteria," directed by Ray Harryhausen, Global Entertainment, February 22, 2005.

11. Don McGregor, "From a Compassionate Gorilla to a Venusis Monster to Mythological Titans: An Interview with Ray Harryhausen," *Starlog* no. 51 (October 1981): 24.

Chapter 43

1. Transcript of an interview with Mark McGee, October 3, 1982, University of Wyoming, American Heritage Center, Forrest J Ackerman Papers, 1920–1987, 02358, Box 3, Folder 9.

2. Keeping.Skepticism.Working, "Forrest J Ackerman—L Ron Hubbard's Literary Agent—Secret Lives—Scientology," January 7, 2015, YouTube video, 24:57, https://www.youtube.com/watch?v=uhl2bE-1LiA.

3. Typed transcript of Forry Ackerman with John Mansfield of Canada, circa 1966.

4. Forry Ackerman, unpublished interview, dated November 22, 1974, printed in *Ackermansion Memories* 9 (September 2019): 2, 83–84.

5. Paul Markey, "Harlan Ellison Remembered—the Greatest Writer You've Never Read," Rte.re, Ireland's National Public Media, June 30, 2018.

6. Bill Schelly, *James Warren, Empire of Monsters: The Man Behind Creepy, Vampirella, and Famous Monsters* (Fantagraphics Books, 2021), 42.

7. *Ibid.*, 38.

8. Bill Newcott, "Night of the Horror Hosts," *Saturday Evening Post*, September/October 2022, 24.

9. Forry Ackerman, "TV Means Terryfying Vampires," *Famous Monsters* no. 1 (1958): 60.

10. Schelly, *James Warren*, 42.

11. Mansfield transcript.

12. Bob the Caretaker, "Pre-Historic Famous Monsters," Astounding Horrors: Nightmares From the Golden Age of Cinema, April 18, 2018, www.astoundinghorrors.com/post/pre-historic-famous-monsters.

13. "Speaking of Pictures: Ghastly Look of a Film Fad," *Life* 43, no. 20 (November 11, 1957): 16.

14. O'Brien, *The Forrest J Ackerman Oeuvre*, 36.

15. Mansfield transcript.

16. *Ibid.*

17. Forrest J Ackerman, *Forrest J Ackerman: Famous Monster of Filmland* (Imagine, 1986).

18. Forry Ackerman, interview with Mark-Sielski, "Master of Monster Memories," *Magick Theatre* 8 (1986), reprinted in *Ackermansion Memories* 2 (2016).

19. *Science Fiction Times* no. 294 (May 1958), reprinted in *Ackermansion Memories* 11 (January 2020).

20. Mansfield transcript.

21. Lest one accuse Ackerman and Warren of literally selling dirt to gullible preteens, according to the book *Empire of Monsters*, a biography about James Warren, Warren did in fact pay a stewardess to scoop up a few pounds of dirt

from the earth surrounding Vlad the Impaler's castle. He then sold the soil in little coffins that could be worn as pendants for a mere $9.95, not counting shipping and handling. The FBI briefly questioned Warren about selling this "questionable substance" before letting him off with a warning.

22. Correspondence from *Famous Monsters of Filmland* no. 126 (July 1976): 4.

23. Correspondence from *Famous Monsters of Filmland* no. 118 (August 1, 1975): 71.

24. *Rue Morgue Magazine* no. 83 (October 2008): 17.

Chapter 44

1. Coker, *Tales of the Time Travelers*.

2. "A Conversation with Forrest J Ackerman and Ray Harryhausen," interview by John Coker III, *Archon 20, Collinsville, IL, October 4, 1996*.

3. Interview, Eastern New Mexico University, Roosevelt County Oral History Project, February 13, 1988, https://library.biblioboard.com/anthology-collection/28fd5bd2-49d5-4491-8dc6-9b9730b6399b/20e3b58d-82f9-4e41-afd2-9dd745af2221.

4. Deborah Painter, *Forry: The Life of Forrest J Ackerman* (McFarland, 2010), 86.

5. Joe Moe et al., *House of Ackerman: A Photographic Tour of the Legendary Ackermansion* (Midnight Marquee Press, 2010), 9.

6. Mansfield transcript.

7. Andrew Porter, "Pickering Blows His Cool; The Great Scienti Claus Robbery," *DEGLER!* 13, no. 164 (January 1967): 49, reprinted in *Ackermansion Memories or When Monsters Were Famous*, ed. James Van Hise (self-Published, 2014).

8. Ackerman, *Forrest J Ackerman*.

Chapter 45

1. Harryhausen, *Ray Harryhausen*, 99.
2. Ibid., 101.

Chapter 46

1. Email from Mike Towry, "Ray Bradbury and the first Comic-Con," April 26, 2021.

2. Andrew Makarushka, "Comics Connoisseurs Here For Golden State Convention," *San Diego Union*, August 2, 1970.

Chapter 47

1. Scott Eyman, "Forry Ackerman's Fantastic, Horrific Museum," *Cleveland Plain Dealer*, December 16, 1980, reprinted in *Ackermansion Memories* 6 (2018).

2. Martin Booe, "The Monster Maven," *The Washington Post*, May 28, 1993.

3. In an interview, Forry Ackerman's assistant and caretaker in later years, Joe Moe, said that John Landis was the most frequent celebrity guest at the Ackermansion. He also said of Landis: "Through thick and thin he was there. Unconditionally. Always bringing other fascinating people to meet his favorite Uncle. Always sending toys and postcards from his world travels…. Stars and fans alike became 14-year-olds once they crossed the threshold into 'Forryworld.'" Heather Buckley, "Moe, Joe, Friend of Forry Ackerman," Dread Central.com, February 22, 2009.

4. Don Glut, as quoted by Jessie Lilley, "FJA Invades Chicago," *Famous Monsters of Filmland* no. 250 (A Special Issue-Length Tribute to A Famous Monster in Filmland, June 2010): 8.

5. Kenneth J. Hall, as quoted by Jessie Lilley, "The Ackermonster Meets the Evil Spawn" *Famous Monsters of Filmland* no. 250 (A Special Issue-Length Tribute to A Famous Monster in Filmland, June 2010): 25.

6. Joe Moe, *Famous Monsters of Filmland* no. 250 (A Special Issue-Length Tribute to A Famous Monster in Filmland, June 2010): 5.

7. Jessie Lilley, "Braindead," *Famous Monsters of Filmland* no. 250 (A Special Issue-Length Tribute to A Famous Monster in Filmland, June 2010): 29.

8. Gene Simmons, "Monster of Rock," *Rue Morgue* no. 83 (October 2009): 20.

9. O'Brien, *The Forrest J Ackerman Oeuvre*, 38.

10. Stephen King, "The Importance of Being Forry," introduction to O'Brien, *The Forrest J Ackerman Oeuvre*, 9.

11. Adam Eisenberg, "Randall William Cook: An Oscar Winner's Journey from Harryhausen to Hobbits," *VFXV: The Magazine of the Visual Effects Society*, January 10, 2022, https://www.vfxvoice.com/randall-william-cook-an-oscar-winners-journey-from-harryhausen-to-hobbits/.

12. Becky Manson, dir., *Ray Harryhausen: Titan of Cinema*, National Galleries of Scotland, 2020.

13. Letter from Phil Tippett to the Academy of Motion Pictures Arts and Sciences, dated October 17, 1991, accessed at Center for Ray Bradbury Studies, School of Liberal Arts: IUPUI, Indianapolis, IN.

14. "Every person at Industrial Light and Magic has been inspired by his imagination and his artistry." So wrote George Lucas to the board of governors of the Academy of Motion Picture Arts and Sciences on December 2, 1991. He also argued that without Harryhausen, there would be no *Star Wars*. Harryhausen's influence on Lucas is apparent. The scene where Luke Skywalker and Princess Leia swing across the broken bridge in the Death Star was clearly inspired by a key moment from *The 7th Voyage of Sinbad*. The city of Petra plays a key role at the end of *Indiana*

Jones and the Last Crusade and also in Harryhausen's *Sinbad and the Eye of the Tiger*.

15. Harryhausen, *Ray Harryhausen*, 188.
16. FANAC Fan History, "Death Does Not Release You - LASFS (pt1 of 2)—Craig Miller-Tim Kirk—Ken Rudolph—Bobbi Armbruster," March 1, 2022, YouTube video, 48:35, https://www.youtube.com/watch?v=YkNzGdFZE6o.
17. "By the Book: Dan Chaon Doesn't Want to Hear About Your Middle-Class Norwegian Life," *New York Times*, June 2, 2022, https://www.nytimes.com/2022/06/02/books/review/dan-chaon-by-the-book-interview.html.
18. Keith Feller, "Bradbury, Ackerman & Me," *Scary Monsters Yearbook* no. 2016 (1993).
19. Jonathan Maberry, "Sci-Fi Scribes on Ray Bradbury: 'Storyteller, Showman and Alchemist,'" *Wired*, https://www.wired.com/2012/06/ray-bradbury-writer-memories/.
20. Amanda Gorman, "Amanda Gorman: 'I wanted my words to re-sanctify the steps of the Capitol': The youngest presidential inaugural poet in U.S. history on Toni Morrison, the power of language and her debut children's book," *The Guardian*, September 25, 2021, www.theguardian.com/books/2021/sep/25/amanda-gorman-i-wanted-my-words-to-re-sanctify-the-steps-of-the-capitol.

Chapter 48

1. Email exchange with John Sasser, dated May 26, 2021.
2. Forrest J Ackerman, *Famous Monsters of Filmland* no. 118 (August 1975): 4.
3. Letter from Harryhausen to Bradbury, dated November 14, 1973, accessed at Center for Ray Bradbury Studies, School of Liberal Arts: IUPUI, Indianapolis, IN.
4. Letter from Forry Ackerman to Ray Bradbury, dated May 21, 1999, accessed at Center for Ray Bradbury Studies, School of Liberal Arts: IUPUI, Indianapolis, IN.
5. *Ray Harryhausen: The Early Years Collection,* Disc 1, directed by Ray Harryhausen, Global Entertainment, February 22, 2005.
6. Alysia Gray Painter, "Foodie Find: Own a Vintage Clifton's Cafeteria Tray," NBC Los Angeles, December 9, 2020,https://www.nbclosangeles.com/the-scene/foodie-find-own-a-vintage-cliftons-cafeteria-tray/2481234.

Chapter 49

1. Forry Ackerman, "Open Letter to the Science Fiction and Fantasy World," May 1981, reprinted in *Ackermansion Memories* 4 (2017).
2. Schelly, *James Warren*, 299.
3. *Ibid.*, 300.
4. Warren and Ackerman teamed up to create the sexy, semi-nude (sometimes totally nude—Forry was still Forry) female heroine Vampirella. Forry got the name from the recent film *Barbarella*. Vampirella hails from the planet Drakulon, a realm where their water is the same substance as human blood, hence Earthlings have nourishment flowing through their veins. Vampirella is both a character and also serves as a Cryptkeeper-style hostess of other terrifying tales. Vampirella's first outing displayed one of Forry's trademark puns ("You won't have died in vein!"). The title character is first seen taking a shower.
5. Schelly, *James Warren*, 306.
6. Caitlin Liu, "Author Ray Bradbury Gives Testimony on 'Dr. Acula,'" *LA Times*, May 2, 2000, https://www.latimes.com/archives/.
7. James Van Hise, "The End of the Ackermansion," in *Ackermansion Memories or, When Monsters Were Famous*, ed. James Van Hise (self-published, 2014), 54.
8. O'Brien, *The Forrest J Ackerman Oeuvre*, 64.
9. Mike Glyer, "Ackerman Auction Takes in Quarter Million," Posted May 3, 2009, file770.com/ackerman-auction-takes-in-quarter-million/.

Chapter 50

1. *Ray Harryhausen: The Early Years Collection,* Disc 1, featurette, "Ray Harryhausen, The Hollywood Walk of Fame," directed by Ray Harryhausen, Global Entertainment, February 22, 2005.
2. This author virtually attended a meeting where they noted the passing of Peter Palmer, best known for playing the title role in *Li'l Abner*. He was also in the TV version of *Superboy* and in *Edward Scissorhands*, among many other films. While discussing this, another member pointed out that Palmer got the role of Li'l Abner because he played it on stage, but that it wasn't the first time Li'l Abner had been filmed; that was in 1940. This information was pulled from a viewing of the virtual LASFS meeting on September 23, 2021.
3. "LASFS Clubhouse," Fancyclopedia 3, https://fancyclopedia.org/LASFS#LASFS_Clubhouse.
4. B.J. Hollars, "Live Forever," *The Rumpus*, June 7, 2012, therumpus.net/2012/06/live-forever/.
5. Harryhausen, *Ray Harryhausen*, 182.
6. Transcript of an interview with Mark McGee, October 3, 1982, University of Wyoming, American Heritage Center, Forrest J Ackerman Papers, 1920–1987, 02358, Box 3, Folder 9.
7. Paul Davids, *An Atheist in Heaven* (Yellow Hat Productions, Inc., 2016), 451.
8. *Ibid.*, 313.
9. Harryhausen, *Ray Harryhausen*.

Bibliography

Ashley, Mike. *The Gernsback Days*. Wildside Press, 2004.
Bradbury, Ray. *Dark Carnival*. Gauntlet Press, 2001.
Bradbury, Ray. *A Graveyard for Lunatics: Another Tale of Two Cities*. William Morrow Paperbacks, 1st edition, 2001.
Bradbury, Ray. *Greentown, Tinseltown*. Stanza Press, 2012.
Clinton, Edmond J., III. *Clifton's and Clifford Clinton: A Cafeteria and a Crusader*. Angel City Press, Illustrated edition, 2015.
Coker, John L., III, ed. *David A. Kyle: A Life of Science Fiction Ideas and Dreams*. Days of Wonder Publishers, 2006.
Coker, John L., III, ed. *Surround Yourself with Your Loves and Live Forever*. Days of Wonder Publishers, 2008.
Coker, John L., III, ed. *Tales of the Time Travelers: Adventures of Forrest J Ackerman and Julius Schwartz*. Days of Wonder Publishers, 2009.
Eller, Jonathan R. *Becoming Ray Bradbury*. University of Illinois Press, 2011.
Hansen, Rob. *Bixelstrasse: The SF Fan Community of 1940s Los Angeles*. Ansible Editions, 2022.
Harryhausen, Ray, and Tony Dalton. *A Century of Stop Motion, From Méliès to Aardman*. Watson-Guptill, 2008.
Harryhausen, Ray, and Tony Dalton. *Ray Harryhausen: An Animated Life*. Billboard Books, 2004.
Harryhausen, Vanessa. *Ray Harryhausen: Titan of Cinema*. National Galleries of Scotland, 2020.
Kipen, David. *The WPA Guide to the City of Angels*. University of California Press, 2011.
Knight, Damon. *The Futurians: The Story of the Science Fiction Family of the 30's that Produced Today's Top SF Writers and Editors*. Day, 1977.
Laney, Francis T. *Ah! Sweet Idiocy! The Fan Memoirs of Francis T. Laney*. Self-published, 1948.
Lesser, Robert. *Pulp Art*. Sterling Publishing, 1997.
Liptak, Andrew. *Cosplay, a History: The Builders, Fans, and Makers Who Bring Your Favorite Stories to Life*. Saga Press, 2022.
Mauro, James. *Twilight at the World of Tomorrow: Genius, Madness, Murder and the 1939 World's Fair on the Brink of War*. Random House, 2010.
Moe, Joe, et al. *House of Ackerman: A Photographic Tour of the Legendary Ackermansion*. 2010.
Morton, Ray. *King Kong: The History of a Movie Icon from Fay Wray to Peter Jackson*. Applause Theatre & Cinema Books, 2005.
Moskowitz, Sam. *The Immortal Storm: A History of Science Fiction Fandom*. Hyperion Press, 1974.
Moskowitz, Sam. *Seekers of Tomorrow*. World Publishing Company, 1966.
Nevala-Lee, Alec. *Astounding: John W. Campbell, Isaac Asimov, Robert A. Heinlein, L. Ron Hubbard, and the Golden Age of Science Fiction*. Dey Street Books, 2018.
Nolan, William F. *The Ray Bradbury Companion: A Life and Career History, Photolog, and Comprehensive Checklist of Writings with Facsimiles from Ray Bradbury's Unpublished and Uncollected Work in All Media*. Gale Research, 1975.
O'Brien, Christopher. *The Forrest J Ackerman Oeuvre: A Comprehensive Catalog of the Fiction, Nonfiction, Poetry, Screenplays, Film Appearances, and Other Works, with a Concise Biography*. McFarland, 2012.
Painter, Deborah. *Forry: The Life of Forrest J Ackerman*. McFarland, 2010.
Pohl, Frederik. *The Science Fiction Roll of Honor*. Random House, Inc., 1975.
Pohl, Frederik. *The Way the Future Was*. Ballantine Del Rey, 1979.
Ritter, David, and Daniel Ritter. *The Earliest Bradbury*. First Fandom Experience, LLC, 2020.
Ritter, David, and Daniel Ritter. *The Visual History of Science Fiction Fandom, Volume One: The 1930s*. First Fandom Experience, LLC, 2020.

Ritter, David, and Daniel Ritter. *The Visual History of Fandom, Volume Two: 1940*. First Fandom Experience, LLC, 2022.
Sanders, Joe, ed. *Science Fiction Fandom*. Greenwood Press, 1994.
Schelly, Bill. *James Warren, Empire of Monsters: The Man Behind Creepy, Vampirella, and Famous Monsters*. Fantagraphics Books, 2021.
Toronto, Richard. *War over Lemuria: Richard Shaver, Ray Palmer, and the Strangest Chapter of 1940s Science Fiction*. McFarland, 2013.
Van Hise, James, ed. *Ackermansion Memories*, No. 1–12, series of self-published zines.
Warner, Harry, Jr. *All Our Yesterdays*. Nesfa Press, 2nd edition, 2004.
Weist, Jerry. *Bradbury: An Illustrated Life; A Journey to Far Metaphor*. William Morrow & Co., 2002.
Weller, Sam. *The Bradbury Chronicles: The Life of Ray Bradbury*. Harper Perennial, Annotated edition, 2006.
Weller, Sam. *Listen to the Echoes: The Ray Bradbury Interviews*. Hat & Beard Press, 2017.
Westfahl, Gary. *The Rise and Fall of Science Fiction, from the 1920s to the 1960s*. McFarland, 2019.
Yerke, T. Bruce. *Memoirs of a Superfluous Fan, Vol. 1*. Southern California Institute for Fan Interests, 1944.

Index

Numbers in ***bold italics*** indicate pages with illustrations

Abbott and Costello Meet Frankenstein 201
A.C. McClurg 53
Academy of Motion Picture Arts and Sciences 81–82, 193; Gordon E. Sawyer Award 196
Ackerman, Alden 172
Ackerman, Carroll Cridland *see* Wyman, Carroll Cridland
Ackerman, Forrest "Forry" J 44, 71, ***87***, 141, 173, 181, ***197***, 203; abbreviation of "scientifiction" 20; and the Academy of Motion Picture Arts and Sciences 81–82, 141; and Ackerman Agency International 172–173, 175; and Ackermanese 46, 50; Ackermansion 180–185; adolescent years 33; afterlife, alleged 204; and alcohol 152, 153; and *Amazing Stories* 30, 95; and art 97; and Assorted Services 141; atheism 29, 36; birth 28; and Bradbury, Ray 7, 196–198, 201; Bradbury, first meeting of 27; as Bradbury's agent 175; and Bradbury's early writing 51–52, 109; and Brundage, M. 122; and Burroughs, Edgar Rice 42, 52–53; and Campbell, John W., Jr. 90; and Chapter 4 of the Science Fiction League, founding of 36, 39; and collecting, early years 31, 106, 112, 142, 148, 151; and Comic-Con San Diego 187; and cosplay 83, 87; and cryogenics 173; and Daugherty, Walter J. 111; and death 198, 201, 203–204; and Derleth, Auggie 164, 165; "Dr. Acula" 199; and Douglas, Myrtle 43, 87–88; and Douglas, Myrtle, breaking up with 152, 154; and Douglas, Myrtle, death 154; and Ellison, Harlan 173–174; and Esperanto 13, 36–37, 46; and *Famous Monsters of Filmland* 174–179; and *Famous Monsters*, quitting 199; and fanzines 42; and Ferry, Ray 199–200; and Flagg, Francis 33, 48; at Ft. MacArthur 143; and *Futuria Fantasia* 77–78, 80; and Harryhausen, Ray 63, 64, 104–105, 196–198; and Heinlein, Robert A. 106, 145; and Hubbard, L. Ron 172–173; and Hugos 173; and *Imagination!* 45, 65, 72; influence on younger fans 190–192; and Landis, John 190–191, 193, 219; and Lang, Fritz 144; and LASFS infighting 150–151; and LASFS Thanksgiving 216; and League Librarian 132; and lesbians 156; and letters to *Famous Monsters* 179, 192; and letters to pulp magazines 31–32, 33; and Lovecraft, H.P. 42; and *Metropolis* 63, 144; middle name 207; and *Monsters of the Moon* 124; and Moore, Catherine L. 33; and movie stills 30; and movies 29–30, 72, 73; and moving to Los Angeles 36; and The National Fantasy Fan Foundation 143; and nudity 52, 145, 150; and office worker 81; and pulp art 98, 100, 125; recordings 112; in San Francisco 22, 31–33; and "sci-fi" 173–174; and science 53; and the Science Fiction League 24, 36, 111; and scientology 173–173; Shep's Shop 13; short stories by ("Cosmic Report Card: Earth" 33; "Earth's Lucky Day" 33; "The Hazy Hord" 48, 50; "Kiki" 156; "Nymph of Darkness" 33; "A Trip to Mars" 33, 208; "World of Loneliness" 156; "World War Three" 33); and soil from Dracula's castle 218; and *Spacemen* 192; and Superman 35; and Tigrina 155–156; and *The Time Traveller* 40; and *Voice of the Imagination* (aka *Vom*) 77; and Warren, James, first meeting 174; and Weinbaum, Stanley 119; and Wollheim, Donald 92; and the World Science Fiction Convention, general 17; at World Science Fiction Convention (1st; WorldCon), 84–87, 94, 99, 100, 116; and World Science Fiction (2nd; ChiCon), 121, 123–124; and World Science Fiction Convention (3rd; DenVention) 136–138; and World Science Fiction Convention (4th; PacifiCon) 158; and World Science Fiction Convention (6th; Cinevention) 159; and World War II 133–35, 141–142, 146–147, 172; and Wright, Weaver 48, 50; and Yerke, T.B. "Tubby" 22
Ackerman, Wendy (aka Porjes, Mathilde "Tilly"): burial 203; divorce 176; first meeting Forry Ackerman 161
Ackerman, William 28, 60

223

Index

The Ackermansion: end 200–201; Scarebourne (first Ackermansion) 180; security 185; Son of Ackermansion 180
The Ackermonster Chronicles 29
The Acolyte 157
Acres of Books 108
Action Comics 35
Ad Astra 97, 118
Adams, Douglas 157
Addams, Charles "Chas" 163
Addams Family 163
The Adventures of Superman 59
Aelita, Queen of Mars 29
African American fans 206
After Hours 175
Ah! Sweet Idiocy 42, 214
Air Wonder Stories 32
Al Ringling Theatre 74
Aladdin and the Wonderful Lamp (film) 85
The Alchemist 91
The Alert 143
Alf, Richard 187
Alfonso, Barry 187
All American Comics *see* DC Comics
All Our Yesterdays 41, 43, 69, 101, 139, 151, 206
All Quiet on the Western Front (film) 59, 81
All-Story Magazine 53
Allen, Gracie 9, 10
Amazing Stories 30, 32, 33, 40, 106, 122, 133; Ackerman's love of 30, 31, 180; and artwork 95; founding 20–21; Gernsback loss 23; letters to 22, 60; and Mars 115; and rocketry 68; and World Science Fiction Convention (2nd; ChiCon) 121
American International Pictures 191
American Interplanetary Society 69
American Museum of Natural History 65
American Rocket Society 69
American Weekly 100
American Werewolf in London 191
Amory, Guy 78, 83
And So Died Riabouchinska (TV adaptation) 8
Angelou, Maya 195
The Animal World 167
Antiques Roadshow 11
Ape Girl 177
Argosy 30, 132

Arkham House 143, 164, 165
Armstrong, Robert 55
Aroturus 92
The Art of Ray Harryhausen 166
Ashley, Mike 24
Asimov, Isaac 22, 91, 93, 95, 107, 143, 173, 174; and pulps 101; and Weinbaum, Stanley 120; and World War II 139
Associated Oil Company 77
Astonishing Stories 103, 107
Astounding Science Fiction 23, 50, 91, 92, 108, 109; and Heinlein 106, 107
Astounding Stories 30, 37
Astronautics 69
The Atom (superhero) 90
Atwood, Margaret 195
Audubon Junior High 58
Aurora kits 191
Australia 69
Austria 70

Bach, Johann Sebastian 101
BAFTA 194
Baker, Rick 164, 191, 193, 194, 201
Balboa High School 33
Baldwin Hills 59
Balter, Elsie 121
Baraboo, WI 74
Barcelona 186
Barnes, Arthur K. 38
Barrett, C.L. 159
Barrymore, John 71
"The Bat-Pack" 64, 197
Bath, England 115
Batman 90
Battle Creek, MI 131, 147
Battlestar Galactica 183
Baum, L. Frank 10
Baumhofer, Walter 97
Beach, Grant 145
Beast from 20,000 Fathoms 168–171; publicity for 218
Bell, John 136
Bellamy, Edward 28
Ben-Hur 7
Benny, Jack 10, 51
Berkeley, University of California 35
Best American Short Stories 163
The Best of Stanley G. Weinbaum 120
Beverly Hills 72, 108
Beverly Hills Cop III 191, 193
Beyond the Pole 30, 95
The Big Sleep (film) 12, 109
Binder, Jack 97
Bixel St. 44, 146
"Bixelstrasse" 146, 150

Blackstone the Magician 74
Blaisdell, Jackie 176
Blaisdell, Paul 176
Blasauf, Fred 166
A Blind Bargain 29
Bloch, Robert 118, 119, 132, 188; and Weinbaum, Stanley 120; at the World Science Fiction Convention (4th; PacifiCon), 158
Blue Book 30
The Blue and White Daily 11, 51
Bok, Hannes 16, 78, 80, 83, 100–102, 107, 114, 138, 143, 146, 180; and Ackerman 159; and Bradbury 149, 213; theft 185; at World Science Fiction Convention (4th) 159
Bonestell, Chesley 143
Bookfellows bookstore 198
bookstores 12, 162, 198; *see also* Shep's Shop
Boucher, Anthony 108
Bovard, Barbara 141
Boys Scientifiction Club 35
Brackett, Leigh 108, 109
Bradbury, Esther 5, love of films 7
Bradbury, Jane 5
Bradbury, Leonard 5–6, 8, 10, 60
Bradbury, Leonard, Jr., "Skip" 5, 7, 10. 60
Bradbury, Marguerite "Maggie" (aka McClure, Marguerite) 167, 168; brief biography 162; first meeting Ray Bradbury 162
Bradbury, Neva 10, 66, 145
Bradbury, Ramona 105
Bradbury, Ray: **2, 6, 65**, 84, *197*, 203; and Ackerman, Forry 28, 114, 143, 17, 196–198; and "Ackermanese" 46; at Ackerman's memorial tribute 201; and Ackerman's suit against Ray Ferry 199–200; and *Amazing Stories* 95; autographs, collecting 9–10; and Bloch, Robert 119; and Bok, Hannes 100–102; and *Buck Rogers* 122, 187; and Burroughs, Edgar Rice 52; chapter 4 of the Science Fiction League 38–39; and childhood sickness 135; Comic-Con San Diego, 2008 4, 187; and comics, collecting 187–188; *Dark Carnival*, publication 163, 165; death 204; and Derleth, Auggie 163–165; diary entry 213;

dinosaurs, love of 7, 64–65; and *Fahrenheit 451* 167; first writing of 50–52, 114; and *Futuria Fantasia* 77–79, 83, 103, 114; and Harryhausen, Ray 63–67, 71, 104–105, 166–168, 194, 196–198; and Heinlein, Robert 107–108, 109–110, 114, 145; and Huston, John 167, 169; and *Imagination!* 45–50, 78; and LASFS infighting 151; and LASFS Thanksgiving 216; and Latinos 145; as League librarian 132; and Los Angeles, moving to 5; and the Los Angeles Science Fantasy Society (LASFS) 115; and Mars, the planet 114; as movie fan 7; and movie theatres 73; as newspaper salesman 64–65, 72; novels and stories ("Among the Metal Gods" 50; "And the Moon Be Still as Bright" 162; "The Big Black and White Game" 162; "Black Symphony" 108; "The Coffin" 165; *Dandelion Wine* 7, 51, 195, 203; *Dark Carnival* 114, 119, 128, 163, 165; "Death's Voice" 50; "Don't Get Technatal" 79; *Fahrenheit 451* 167, 183, 185, 203; "The Fireman" 167; "The Fog Horn" 168, 169; "Gabriel's Horn" 128; "Green Shadows, White Whale" 169; "The Halloween Tree" 171; "Here There Be Tygers" 195; "Hollerbochen Comes Back" 51; "Hollerbochen's Dilemma" 50–52; "Homecoming" 16; "I See You Never" 145; "IF" 72; *The Illustrated Man* 167; *It Came from Outer Space* (film) 167; "It's Not the Heat, It's the Hu—" 109; "The Lake" 162; "The Laurel and Hardy Love Affair" 9; "The Long Night" 128; "Lorelei of the Red Mist" (with Leigh Brackett) 109; "Mars Is Heaven" 91; *The Martian Chronicles* 145, 167; "Million Year Picnic" 91; "The Night" 51; "The Pendulum" 83, 128; "The Piper" 114, 128; "The Poems" 165; *Something Wicked This Way Comes* 7, 11, 195, 202; "Space" 80; "There Will Come Soft Rains" 162; "Truck Driver After Midnight" 50; "Tyrannosaurs Rex" 66; "The Whole Town's Sleeping" 51; "The Wonderful Ice Cream Suit" 145; "Zero Hour" 91); and pulp art 97, 98, 99, 100; and pulps 97, 131; recordings 112; as Reynolds, Ron 78, 79, 114; and the Santa Barbara Writers Conference 195; and Schwartz, Julius 34, 90, 128; and the Science Fiction League 23–25; and *Spacemen* 192; and technocracy 78–80; and television 167; and typewriters 78; and wedding 162; and Weinbaum, Stanley 119; at Westercon 160; at the World Science Fiction Convention (WorldCon) 84–86, 91, 99, 100; and World Science Fiction Convention (4th; PacifiCon) 158; and World War II 144

Bradbury, Samuel 5
Bradbury, Susan *see* Nixon, Susan Bradbury
Bradbury Building 28, 29
Brady, Frank 54, 98
Bride of Frankenstein 32, 72
Brief Candle 101
British fandom 22, 33
British Film Institute Southbank Theatre 194
British Interplanetary Society 70, 131
The British Museum 131
British Science Fiction Association 138
The Brown Derby 10, 71
Brundage, M. 122–123, 143, 158, 175, 180
Brzezinski, Anton 180
Buck Rogers 8, 32, 84, 187
The Bulletin of the American Interplanetary Society 69
The Bullock's bookstore 162
Bureau of Power and Light 145
Burke and Hare 193
Burks, Arthur J. 37
Burns, George 9, 10
Burroughs, Edgar Rice 10, 21, 44, 52–53, 132, 183; and Ackerman, Forry 32, 35; and Bradbury, Ray 52, 53
Burton, Tim 194
Busy Bodies 59

Cabell, James Branch 138
Cabot, Bruce 55
Cage, Nicolas 35
Cagney, James 36

California: Bradbury's move to 5, 10
Calkins, Dick 121
Cameron, James 194
Campbell, John W., Jr. 59, 91, 92, 101; and Heinlein 107; and World War II 140
Canada 33, 34
Cantor, Eddie 74
Capote, Truman 163
Capra, Frank 140
Caravan Hall 93
Carnell, Ted 134, 159
Carpenter, John 190, 191
Carradine, John 201
Carter, John 8, 53
Cartier, Edd 130, 146, 147
Castle, Mort 195
Castle of Frankenstein 179
The Cat and the Canary 7, 104
Center for Ray Bradbury Studies Indianapolis 188
Chandler, Raymond 12
Chaney, Lon, Jr. 72
Chaney, Lon, Sr. 7, 29, 177, 178, 182, 201
Chaon, Dan 195
Chaplin, Charlie 56
Chapman, Ken 134
Chapter 4 of the Science Fiction League 37, 38, 109; Ackerman joins 36; art auctions 97; Bradbury's first meeting 37; and changing name to the Los Angeles Science Fantasy Society 110; first meeting 36; and league library 132; and parties 72, 77, 115; pulp magazine trading 39; speaker of the week 39; and zines 78; *see also* Los Angeles Science Fantasy Society
Charm 163
Chester, Hal 168–169
Chicago 36, 53, 74, 84, 136; and the World Science Fiction Convention (2nd) 98, 115
Chicago *Herald-American* 123
Christmas 148
Cincinnati 159
Cincinnati Enquirer 159
Cincinnati Post 159
Cinema 57 175
Cinevention *see* the World Science Fiction Convention (6th)
The Circus 56
Civilian Conservation Corps 10
Clairvoyant 72

Clarke, Arthur C. 43, 70, 84, 131, 132, 134; and *Amazing Stories* 95; and World War II 134
Clash of the Titans 171, 186
Class, Allan 98, 136
Classic Horror Club 192
Cleveland Rocket Society 69
Clifton's Cafeteria: 11, 25–27, 36, 44, 47, 49, 64, 71, 97, 109, 115, 130, 143, 162; Ackerman and Wendy's first date 161; Bradbury's birthday at 98; reunion at 197
Clinton, Clifford 25–26
The Coffin Bangers 192
Collecting Monsters of Film and TV 30
Collier's 163
Colorado Fantasy Society 136
Columbia Pictures 81, 140, 143
The Comet 41, 118, 136
Comic-Con San Diego, 2010 1–3, 187–189, 196, 205
comics: 96; Bradbury's collection of Sunday comics 8
Communism 54, 79, 80, 157
Conan the Barbarian 43
Condé Nast 96
Coney Island 99
Congdon, Don 162
Conrad, Barnaby 195
Cook, Fred 96
Cook, Randy 171, 193
"Cool Ghoul" Roland 175
Cooper, Arthur Melbourne 57
Cooper, Gary 10
Coriell, Vern 74
Corvais, Antony 83
Cosmic Stories 35, 41, 104
Cosmos (book) 101
cosplay 87–88, 126, 137–138, 158–159
Coward, Noël 10
Cowboys Vs. Aliens 1
Craig, Daniel 1
Crawford, Jesse 210
Creation (unfinished film) 58, 59
Creature from the Black Lagoon 177, 183–184
Crime of Dr Crospi 72
cryogenics 36
Cthulhu 164
Cuba 161
Culver City 59
Cummings, Ray 16, 20
Cumnock, Bob 13, 25
Cunningham, Cecil Claybourne 78
Cunningham, E. 78
Curtis, Tony 185
Cussler, Clive 195
Cyclops 170
The Cyclops Club 192
Czechoslovakia 90

The Damn Thing 43
Dandelion Wine 7, 51, 195
Danforth, Jim 171
Dante, Joe 183, 191, 193
Dante's Inferno 29
Dark Carnival 114, 119
Daugherty, Virginia 157, 158
Daugherty, Walter J. 49, 111, 143, **197**; and the LASFS Clubhouse 147; and LASFS infighting 150; and LASFS, Thanksgiving 216; and recording fan voices 137; and Westercon 159–160; and World Science Fiction Convention (3rd; Denvention) 136–138; and World Science Fiction Convention (4th; PacifiCon) 157–158
A Daughter of Uncle Sam 16
Davids, Paul 201, 207
The Dawn of Flame and Other Stories 120
Day, Laraine 71
A Day with Jack Dempsey 74
DC Comics 22, 34, 37, 50, 90, 163
Dead of Night 29
de Camp, L. Sprague 140
Delgado, Marcel 57
del Toro, Guillermo 192
Deluge 72
Denvention *see* the World Science Fiction Convention (3rd)
Derleth, August "Auggie" 102, 119, 143, 145, 163, 205; and Bradbury's first book 163–165; and H.P. Lovecraft 163–164; private papers 217
The Devil's Planet 130
Dianetics 172
DiCaprio, Leonardo 184
Dickinson, Emily 108
Dietrich, Marlene 9, 10, 29, 201
Dietz, Jack 168
Dilly Company 121
The Dinosaur and the Missing Link 57
Disney 129
Disney, Walt 7
Disneyland 197
Dr. Acula 199
Dr. Jekyll & Mr. Hyde (film) 81
Dr. Meridian 175
Dr. Seuss *see* Geisel, Theodore
Dold, Elliott, Jr. 32, 146, 147
Don Post Studios 143
Doré, Gustave 58, 141
Dorf, Shel 187–188
Doubleday 90
Douglas, Myrtle (aka "Morojo") 36, 44–45, 52, **87**, 142, 195; and Ackerman, Forry J, breaking up with 153, 154; and art collecting 97, 125; and Bixel St. 146; and cosplay 87, 138; death 154; and *Imagination!* 45, 49; and LASFS infighting 150, 154; as league librarian 132; as a nudist 52; recordings 112; and *Voice of the Imagination* (aka *Vom*) 77, 83; and the World Science Fiction Convention 87–88, 99; and World Science Fiction Convention (2nd; ChiCon), 121, 123; and World Science Fiction Convention (3rd; Denvention), 136–138; and World Science Fiction Convention (4th; Pacificon) 158
Douglas, Virgil 44, 45
Downey, Robert, Jr. 1
Dracula (book) 182, 201
Dracula (film) 29, 56, 72, 175
Dracula (play) 29, 30
Dreiser, Theodore 209
drones 15
Du Bois, W.E.B. 206
Dunmire, Blaine 140
Dweller in the Martian Depths 42
Dynamation 169–170

Earth vs. the Flying Saucers 61, 170, 171, 178
Earth vs. the Spider 177
Eastbay Science Correspondence Club 22
Edison, Thomas 57
Egyptian Theatre 29, 75, 201, 204
El Capitan Theatre 10, 203
Eldred, Brian 78
The Electrical Experimenter 15, **17**, 18, 95
Electro Importing Company Catalog 14
Elizabeth, New Jersey 86
Ellison, Harlan 173–174
Empire of Monsters 218
The Empire Strikes Back 109
Emsheimer, Ted "Teddy" 141
The Enchanted Toymaker 57
End Poverty in California (EPIC) 106

England 34, 46, 84, 134, 138, 161
England, George Allan 16
Eshbach, Lloyd 159
Esperanto 36, 44, 46
Evans, E.E. 137, 138, 152, 154, 159, 195
Evolution of the World 61, 171
The Excluded Six 93
Explorers of the Infinite 33

Fahrenheit 451 167, 183, 185
Fairbanks, Douglas 7, 36, 162
Famous Fantastic Art 158
Famous Monsters Club 178
Famous Monsters of Filmland 30, 34, 104, 111, 154, 196; and contests 184; convention 187; and Haunt Ads 192; and King, Stephen 192; origins 174–179; pen pal section 179; toys 178
Famous Westerns of Filmland 179
Fancyclopedia 143, 150
Fanews 42, 155
Fantasia 61
Fantast 52
Fantasy Advertiser 42
The Fantasy Fan 32, 40, 42
Fantasy Fiction Field 107, 146, 153
Fantasy Magazine 24, 33, 34, 90, 101, 133
fanzines 40–42
Farkas, W. Phyllis 174
Farley, Ralph Milne 117
Fascism 54
Faulconer, Kevin 3
Faulkner, William 12, 109
Favreau W., Jon 1
FBI 157
Feller, Keith 195
Ferry, Ray 199–200
Fields, W.C. 9
The Figueroa Street Playhouse 9
Fine Arts Theatre 72
Finlay, Virgil 32, 96, 97, 100, 125, 130, 138, 143, 146, 180, 213
First Men on the Moon 61
The First National Convention 84
Fitzgerald, F. Scott 12, 209
Fitzgerald, Warren 206
Fitzmaurice, George 56
Flagg, Francis 33, 36, 50
The Flash 90
Flash Gordon 8, 38, 40, 122, 187
The Flat 131
Flushing Meadows 89

Fonda, Henry 10
Fontaine, Joan 10
Ford, Harrison 1
Ford Foundation 200
Forman, Ed 37, 68
The Forrest J Ackerman Oeuvre
Forrest J Ackerman's Monster Land 199
Forrester, Cay 158
Ft. MacArthur 143, 146
Ft. MacArthur Bulletin 143
Ft. Wayne, IN
Forte, John 130
The Forum 73
Foster, Hal 165
Fowler Brothers bookstore 161–162, 165
Fox (movie studio) 73
France 70, 134, 140, 141
Frank, Rich 121
Frank and Humbug 177
Frankenstein (book) 182
Frankenstein (film) 29, 32, 56, 72, 175
Freehafer, Paul 13, 121, 136, 157, 197; death 214; and LASFS, Thanksgiving 216
Freehafer Hall 214
Freyor, Erick 54, 83
Frontier (fanzine) 43
Future Fiction 83
Futuria Fantasia 77–79, 83, 101, 107, 185
The Futurian Society of Los Angeles 150
The Futurians 22, 54; at the first World Science Fiction Convention (WorldCon) 92–94; and the library 134; shared living space 130–131; World Science Fiction Convention (2nd; ChiCon) 121; and World War II 139
The Futurians (book) 94, 101

Gable, Clark 9
Gabriel Over the White House 72
Gaiman, Neil 194, 195
Galactic Patrol 37
Gandy, Joseph Michael 59
Garbo, Greta 10
Garland, Judy 10
Gein, Ed 119
Geisel, Ted 140
The General Cable Company 10
General Motors 89
Germany 69, 70, 140
Gernsback, Hugo: 49, 53, 143; biography 14; coining of phrase "Science Fiction" 20; early publications 15; and

films 16; and the Futurians 92–93; and Mars 115; military inventions 16; and Paul, Frank 95; rocketry 69; *A Romance of the Year 2660* 19–20; science fiction clubs 22; and the Science Fiction League 111; "scientifiction" 16; work in radio 15; work in television 15
The Gernsback Days 24
Getty Oil 28
Ghost Stories Magazine 28, 30
Ghoul 72
Gifford, Guy 130
Gillespie, Jack 93
Gilliam, Terry 193
Gillings, Wally 22, 134
Giordano, Luca 73
Glasser, Allen 34, 40
Glazner, David 3
Glendale, CA 198
Glom 158
Glut, Don 191
Goddard, Robert 68
Godzilla 169
Gogos Basil 178, 180, 192
The Golden Voyage of Sinbad 171, 182
Gone with the Wind 59, 73, 82
Gorman, Amanda 195
Gottliffe, Harold 69
Gould, Will 143
Grant, Cary 29, 71
Grant Hotel, San Diego 160, 188
Grapes of Wrath (book) 101
Grauman, Sid 55–56, 75, 210
Grauman's Chinese Theatre 55–56, 59, 75–76, 197, 203
A Graveyard for Lunatics 5, 67
Gray, Mary Corinne "Patty" (aka "Pogo") 44, 121, 155, 197, 209; and LASFS Thanksgiving 216
Grayson, Eric 124
Green Lantern 90
Green Shadows, White Whale 10
Green Town, IL 7
Greenblatt, Harvey 140
Greene, Sonia H. 163
Grey, Zane 162
Griffith Park 162, 180
Grossman, John 159
Gumm Sisters 10
Gwynne, Fred 185

Hall, Jon 180
Hall, Kenneth J. 191
Hamilton, Edmond 20, 21, 24, 108, 127
Hammett, Dashiell 12

Hammett, Kirk 192
Hanks, Tom 190, 196
Hansen, Lucile Taylor (aka "L. Taylor Hansen") 109
Harkins, Donald 9
Harlow, Jean 9, 55
Harper's Magazine 72
Harryhausen, Diana 86, 97, 204
Harryhausen, Frederick 58, 59, 166
Harryhausen, Martha 58, 166
Harryhausen, Ray 54, **56**, 66, 77, *181*, 191, *197*, 203; and Ackerman, Forry 143, 159, 182, 196–198; Ackerman, Forry, first meeting with 63; Ackermansion 182; and Baker, Rick 193; Bradbury, Ray and Maggie, wedding 162, 167; Bradbury, Ray, death 203; Bradbury, Ray, first meeting of 64–65; Bradbury, Ray, friendship with 66, 166–168, 171, 194, 196–198; Bradbury, Ray, writing about Harryhausen 66–67; and commercials 166; death 204; and dinosaurs 59; Dynamation 169; early film-making 60–61, 81; early life 56–59; early model-making 60; early reading habits 58; European locations 186; and fairy tales 166; and *Imagination!* 72; and *King Kong* 56–59, 62–63, 67, 81, 171; and Kong, his dog 61, 104; and Landis, John 193, 194; and Livingstone, Diana 186; at Manual Arts High School 62, 81, 104; and mask making 104, 138; and *Mighty Joe Young* 166–167; and military service 129, 140; and O'Brien, Willis 61–62, 81, 166–167; and Pal, George 129; in *Popular Mechanics* 62; and Ray and Diana Harryhausen Foundation 171; and *Spacemen* 192
Harryhausen, Vanessa 171, 186, 193, 194, 196, 197
The Harryhausen Scrapbook 60
Hart, Dale 98, 151, 158
Hasse, Henry 83, 107, 114, 128
Hawkins, Willard 138
Hawthorne Theatre 63
Hazy Hord 48, 50
He Who Gets Slapped 7
hectograph 43

Heeley, Bill 69
Heinlein, Leslyn 106, 108, 138
Heinlein, Robert A. 43, 91, 98, 183; and Ackerman, Forry 106, 141, 145; biography 106–107; and Bradbury, Ray 107–108, 145; and the Mañana Literary Society 107–108; and pulps 101; recordings 112; works by ("For Us, the Living 107; "Life-Line" 107; "Misfit" 107; "The Moon Is a Harsh Mistress" 106; "Requiem" 107; "Starship Troopers" 106; "Stranger in a Strange Land" 106); and the World Science Fiction Convention (3rd) 136–138; World War II 139
Hell's Angels 55
Herald Examiner 71
Herald-Express 71
Herschel, William 115
Hey Rookie! 143
Heylandt, Paul 69
Hill, Joe 195
Hitler, Adolf 70, 124, 129, 139
Hoar, Roger Sherman *see* Farley, Ralph Milne
Hodgkins, Russell J. 25, 46, 50, 52–53; and director of Chapter 4 of the Science Fiction League 49, 111; and LASFS Thanksgiving 216; and the league library 133; and World War II 139
Hoffman, Bob 147, 158
Hog Wild 59
Hogenmiller, Linus 33
Holland 129
Holland Park 186
Hollywood: Bradbury's love of 7; population growth 6; writers in 12
Hollywood Bowl 71
Hollywood Cemetery 9
Hollywood Walk of Fame 203
Holm, Eleanor 89
homosexuality 131; and LASFS 151–152, 155, 159
Hope, Bob 104, 193
Hornig, Charles D. 37, 40, 47, 49, 83, 97, 111, 209; and the first World Science Fiction Convention 84, 86, 100; and formation of the Science Fiction League 22–23; and the Futurians 93; and World War II 139; at the World's Fair 90
horror hosts 175
Hotel Chesterfield 174
Hotel Chicagoan 121, 123

House on Haunted Hill 180
Housh, Snow Longley 11
Howard, Robert E. 43
Howitt, John Newton 96, 97
The Howling 191
Hubbard, L. Ron 48, 71, 108, 183; and Scientology 172–173; and World War II 139–140, 174
Hugo Awards 80, 173
Hull, E. Mayne 157
The Humpty Dumpty Circus 56
The Hunchback of Notre Dame (film) 7, 72
Hunt, Roy 97, 130, 138, 146, 147
Hunter, Mel 154
Huston, John 167, 169
Huxley, Aldous 12, 144, 167

I Love Lucy 143
I Was a Teenage Movie Maker 191
I Was a Teenage Werewolf 175
The Ilford Science Literary Circle 22
Illini Fantasy Fictioneers 116
Imagination! (zine) 25, 36, 39, 43, 44, 46, 47, 50, 68, 72, 77–78, 83, 132, 133; and Michelism 54; relationship to Shep's Shop 13
The Immortal Storm 42, 93
Innes, David 53
International Scientific Association 22, 68, 69, 93, 118
The Invisible Man (film) 8, 72, 97
The Invisible Man Returns 72
Invisible Ray 72
Ireland 167, 169
Israel 161
It Came from Beneath the Sea 82
It Came from Outer Space 167, 192
It's a Wonderful Life 71

Jackson, Michael 191
Jackson, Peter 171, 191, 194
Jackson, Samuel L. 1
Japan 139
Jason and the Argonauts 170, 182, 186, 194
Jasper and the Haunted House 129
Jasper and the Watermelons 129
Jet Propulsion Laboratory 68
Jim Dandy 129
Johansson, Scarlett 1
John Carter of Mars 32

Johnson, Jennet 11
Johnson, Lyndon B. 115
Johnson, W. Ryerson 128
Jolson, Al 9, 29, 55
Joquel, Arthur Louis II 42, 139
The Jungle 106
Just Imagine 30

Kable News Company 175
Karloff, Boris 36, 155, 177, 182, 184, 192
Kay, Earl 140
Keaton, Buster 71
Keller, David H. 35
Kelly, Gene 203
Kennedy, Robert 162
KGAR radio station 8
Kim, Philip 201
King, Stephen 190, 192
King Features Syndicate 122
King Kong (comic strip) 8
King Kong (film) 8, 29, 31, 55–56, 58, 67, 72, 75, 176, 182,183, 197; influence on Ray Harryhausen 56–59, 62–63, 81; remake 171, 177
The King of Kings 7, 59
Kippin, Leonard A. 22
Kirby, Jack 187, 188
Kirk, James T. 183
The Knaves 150
Knight, Charles 58, 169
Knight, Damon 41, 92, 101, 112, 131, 138, 142
Kornbluth, Cyril 87, 121, 138
Korshak, Erle M. 22, *85*, 99, 116; and pulp art 98, 123, 125, 214; and World Science Fiction Convention (2nd; ChiCon) 121, 123–124; and World Science Fiction Convention (3rd; Denvention) 136–138; and World Science Fiction Convention (4th; Pacificon) 158; World Science Fiction Convention (6th; Cinevention 159)
Korshak, Stephen 98
Krupa, Julian 97, 121, 146, 147
Kuttner, Henry 38, 49, 50, 108–109, 114; marriage to Moore, C.L. 210
Kyle, David 44, 89, 110

La Brea Tar Pits 56, 59
The Lad and the Lion 52
Lake Michigan 7
La Marr, Barbara 10
Landis, Carole 143
Landis, John 184, 190–191, 193, 194, 200, 201, 219
Laemmle, Carl 32

Landon, Michael 175
Laney, Francis T. 44, 146, 152, 153, 154, 157; and Freehafer, Paul 214; and homosexuality 151–152; and LASFS infighting 150–151; and Sweet Idiocy, publishing of 217; at World Science Fiction Convention (4th; Pacificon) 159
Lang, Fritz 32, 36, 59, 70, 167–68, 182, 184; and Ackerman, Forry 144
LAPD 157
Larry Edmunds bookstore 203
The Last Bookstore 162
The Last Days of Pompeii 66
Latinos 145
Latte, Lilly 144, 168
Laurel and Hardy 9, 59, 197
Lee, Christopher 182, 184, 192, 201
Leeds, England 24, 69, 84
Leeds Rocket Society 69
Leeds Science Fiction League 84
Leiber, Fritz, Jr. 159
Leimert Park 65
The Lensman 124
Lesser, Robert 98
Lessons in Love 74
Levin, Barry 193
Lewis, Perry 78
Lewis, Sinclair 209
USS *Lexington* 106
Ley, Willy 70, 99
libraries: Los Angeles Public Library 12, 200; private science fiction clubs 132–133; Waukegan Public Library 7, 10
Liebscher, Walter 123
Life Magazine 115, 175
Light from Beyond 42
Lights Out (radio) 8
Lights Out (television) 167
Lincoln, Elmo 53
Lindbergh, Charles 162
Lippert, Brandon 67
Little Brown Room 25, 27, 36, 37
The Lives of a Bengal Lancer 10
Livingstone, Diana *see* Harryhausen, Diana
Lloyd, Harold 10, 55
Loew's State Theatre 162
London 84, 171, 176; Harryhausen in 186, 194, 197
London After Midnight 182, 201
Long Beach 108

Looking Backward 28
Lorre, Peter 72
Los Angeles: bookstores 12; Bradbury's arrival 5–6; diverse population 6; movie theatres 72, 74; population growth 6
Los Angeles City College 36, 62
Los Angeles County Museum 59, 60
Los Angeles High School 10, 11, 51; *Anthology of Student Verse* 11, 50
Los Angeles Science Fantasy Society (LASFS) 111, 201; and clubroom, first 130, 139, 146; and clubroom, 1949–present 202; and clubroom, second 146–149, 215; and the FBI 157; and infighting 150–151; and the LAPD 157; and the library 132; and publishing 112, 114
Los Angeles Superior Court 200
The Los Angeles Theatre 75
Los Angeles Times 115
The Lost Continent 67
The Lost World (film) 7, 29, 56, 57, 59, 85, 115, 138, 170, 182
Lovecraft, H.P.: 43, 50, 120, 159, 180, 209; and Ackerman, Forry 35, 209; and Bloch, Robert 119; death 163; and Schwartz, Julius 163
Lovell, Tom 97
Lowell, Percival 115
Lowndes, Robert A.W. 24, 93, 121
Lucas, George 177, 193, 194, 219–220
Lugosi, Bela 29, 31, 36, 72, 177, 182, 183, 184, 192, 201
Luxembourg 14, 15

M 72
Maberry, Jonathan 195
MacArthur Park 157
MacDermott, Aubrey 22
Mad Monsters 179
Mademoiselle 163
Madle, Robert 43, 100, 136
Madrid 186
Magarian, Albert 146
Makarushka, Andrew 188
The Maltese Falcon 72
Man of Two Worlds 108, 210
The Man Who Lived Again 72
Mañana Literary Society 107–108
Manchester Interplanetary Society 69

Index

Manual Arts High School 62, 81
Margulies, Leo P. 85
Mariner 4 115
The Mark Strand Theatre 74
Mars (planet) 40, 114–115
Martian Chronicles (book) 90
A Martian Odyssey 119, 120
Martignette, Charles G. 96
Martin, John 59
Martin, Lew 121
The Martindale's bookstore 162
Marvel Comics 37, 50
Mata Hari 56
Matches: An Appeal 57
May, Leonard 22
May, Lillie 111
May Company bookstore 161
The Mayan Theatre 75
McClary, Thomas 92
McClure, Marguerite *see* Bradbury, Marguerite "Maggie"
Meddings, Derek 193
Medusa 170
Méliès, Georges 56–57
Memoirs of a Superfluous Fan, Vol. 1 22, 25, 42, 113
Meredith, Burgess 10, 193
Meredith, Scott 154
Merril, Judith 154, 159
Merritt, A. 100, 138
The Meteor 34
Metropolis 32, 56, 63, 144, 182; at the first World Science Fiction Convention 94
Mexico City 205
MGM Studios 9, 73
Michel, John 41, 54, 79; and the World Science Fiction Convention 93–94, 121, 130; and World War II 139
Michelism 53–54, 79
Mid-City 44
Mighty Joe Young 166–167, 178; remake 193
Mikros 51, 112
Miller, Craig 194
The Million Dollar Theatre 75
Milwaukee 43
Milwaukee Fictioneers 34, 117–120
Milwaukee Journal 119
Miracle Science and Fantasy Stories 32
Mix, Tom 162
Moberg, Inar 5
Moberg, Vivian 10
Moby Dick (film) 167, 169, 171
Modern Electrics 14, 18, 95
Moe, Joe 201, 204, 219

Mondelle, Wendayne 161
Monroe, Lyle *see* Heinlein, Robert
Monroe, Marylin 52, 203
Monster Land see Forrest J Ackerman's Monster Land
Monsters, Inc. 193
Monsters of the Moon 124
Monsterscene 179
The Moon Is a Harsh Mistress 106
Mooney, Jim 37, 50
Moore, Catherine L. (aka C.L. Moore) 33, 50, 108, 109, 158; marriage to Kuttner, Henry 210
Moore, Marion 176
Moore, Terry 193
Morey, Leo 130
Morning Song 50
Morojo *see* Douglas, Myrtle
Moskowitz, Sam: 33, 46, 154, 164; and the Futurians 93; and pulp art 98; and Tigrina 155; and Weinbaum, Stanley 120; and World Science Fiction Convention (1st) 84, 92–94, 96, 99, 103, 119
The Most Dangerous Game 67, 183
Motion Picture News 74
movie theatres 72–75
The Mummy 8, 29, 72, 84
Murders in the Rue Morgue (film) 32
Muren, Dennis 185
Museum of Arts and Sciences at Exposition Park 59
Mussen, Al 133, 140
Mussolini, Benito 124
The Mysterious Island 8, 29, 186
The Mystery of the Wax Museum 8, 176
The Mystery Ship 16, **19**

Napier, Carson 53
NASA 115
National Fantasy Fan Federation (aka National Fantasy Fan Foundation) 142, 150, 158, 200
National News Syndicate of America 122
National Screen Service 30
Naval Academy 91
Naval Aircraft Factory 140
Nazis 70, 89, 144
Nebula Award 182
Nevala-Lee, Alec 93
New Detective 128
New Fandom 92, 93
New York 36, 73, 84; and the first World Science Fiction Convention 84–90
The New Yorker 71
New Zealand 171
Newark, New Jersey 84
Nias Island 60
Nicholson, Jim 34
Nixon, Susan Bradbury 97, 203
North Hollywood 201
Novae Terrae 46
Nowlan, Phil 122
Nuetzell, Albert 178, 180
Nuneaton, England 133
NYPD 131
NYU 70

Oakland, CA 22
O'Brien, Christopher 192
O'Brien, Eleanor 136, 138, 147, 157
O'Brien, Willis 7, 57, 58, 63, 170, 182; Harryhausen, Ray, first meeting with 61–62; Harryhausen, Ray, working with 81, 129, 166, 167; and Pal, George 129
Of Mice and Men (film) 72
Old Dark House 97
Old Man River 74
Olsen, Bob 33, 38
Once Around the Block 119, 132
One Glorious Day 29
1,000,000 B.C. 158, 192
Orban, Paul 97
Der Orchideengarten 31
Orpheum Theater 29
Oscar the Obscene Octopus 89
Out There 167
The Outsider and Others 164
The Outsiders 151

Pacific Electric Building 24
Pacific Western Oil Corporation 28
PacifiCon *see* World Science Fiction Convention (4th)
Page, Bettie 175
Pal, George 129, 140
Palmer, Ray: 22, 34, 35, 44, 90, 97, 135, 138; *Amazing Stories* 34, 118; biography 117–119; and pulp art 98; and Weinbaum, Stanley 120; and World Science Fiction Convention (2nd; ChiCon) 121
Paramount Studios 9, 10, 72, 81
Paris 175
Parkhurst, Harry 97
Parsons, Jack 37, 68

Pathé Lot 59
Patten, Fred 159
Paul, Frank R.: 30, 32, 97, 101, 121, 123, 125, 130, 138, 143, 146, 147, 180, 182; and Bradbury 213; and the first World Science Fiction Convention 94, 99; and Gernsback, Hugo 95–96
Pearl Harbor 139
Peckinpah, Sam 71
Penn and Teller 184
Pennsylvania Science Fictioneers 140
Peoria Rocket Society 69
Perry Rhodan 161
Petaja, Emil 101, 107
The Phantom of the Opera (film) 7, 29, 176, 178, 183
Philadelphia 84, 140, 145, 175
Philadelphia Science Fiction Society 207
Philbin, Mary 29
Philippines 34
Photoplay 32
Pickford, Mary 12
Pickwick Books 162
The Pickwick Theatre 67
Plan 9 from Outer Space 177, 182, 183
The Planet (fanzine) 41
Planet Stories 109, 158
Playboy 175
Pluto (planet) 115
Poe, Edgar Allan 10, 20
Pohl, Frederik 22, 23, 91, 93, 103, 110, 132, 135, 154, 208; and World War II 139
Poland 36
Polaris 112
Pope, Alexander 108
Popular Publications 96, 97
Porjes, Mathilde "Tilly" *see* Ackerman, Wendy
Porjes, Michael 176
The Postman Always Rings Twice 162
Powell, Martin 179
Price, Vincent 178, 184
Prince Valiant 8, 165, 187
Providence R.I. 158, 163
Psycho (book) 119
pulp magazines: 13, 38; artwork 96–97, 125, 130; end 157; letters to 21; and writers 208
Puppetoons 129

Queen for a Day 158
Queen Mary 200
Queens, New York City 89
Queens Science Fiction League 68, 93

Racine, WI 74, 210
radio: Bradbury stories adapted for 8; Bradbury's job at a radio station 8; Gernsback work in 14–15; LA's early radio stations 7
A Radio-Controlled Television Plane 15
Radio News 15
Rains, Claude 8, 183, 192
Ralph 124c 41+; A Romance of the Year 2660 19–20
Ramar of the Jungle 180
Rank Laboratory 186
The Raven (film) 72
The Ray Bradbury Theatre 28, 29
Ray Harryhausen: An Animated Life 129
RCA 89
Reagan, Ronald 71
Red Barry 143
The Red Cross 145
Reed, Donna 71
Reeves, Judson W. *see* Septama, Aladra
Regina Theatre 72
Reinsberg, Mark 116, 121, 124, and the World Science Fiction Convention (3rd; Denvention) 136
Reske, Martha 166
The Return of the Vampire 183
Reynolds, E.C. 24
Reynolds, Ron *see* Bradbury, Ray
Rhode Island on Lovecraft 158
Ringling Brothers 74
Rio Bravo 109
RKO 73, 74, 81
Robbins, Trina 52
Roberds, Sully 124
Robeson, Paul 74
rocketry 68–70
Rocklynne, Ross 100, 107, 123
Rogers, Alva 153
Rogers, Buck 121
Rogers, Doug 78, 83
Rogers, Ginger 143
Rogers, Will 11, 29, 50
Roosevelt, Franklin D. 89, 136, 138
Roswell, New Mexico 5
Rothman, Milt 136
The Roxy 55, 73–74
Ruppert, Conrad 34, 40, 90
Russell, Sam 157
Russia 70

St. John, J. Allen 98, 130
Saldana, Lupi 143
San Diego 187

San Diego Convention Center Corporation 1
San Diego's Golden State Comic-Con *see* Comic-Con San Diego
San Fernando Valley 53
San Francisco 22, 31–33, 155, 159
San Francisco Chronicle 34
San Pedro 36, 144
Santa Barbara Writers Conference 195
Santa Claus (film) 57
Santa Fe 121
Santa Monica 109
Saturday Evening Post 60, 71, 168–169
Saturn Award 182
Satyr Book Shop 162
Sauk City, Wisconsin 164
Saunders, Norman 97
Sayers, Jo Ann 10, 71
Schiller, Bob 143
Schlock 190
Schneer, Charles 170, 193
Schulz, Charles M. 195
Schwartz, Julius 22, 34, 35, 40, 89, 108, 109, **203**; as Bradbury's agent 34, 90, 127, 163; and the Futurians 93; and the Kuttner-Moore partnership 210; and Weinbaum, Stanley 120; at the World Science Fiction Convention (WorldCon) 100; at the World's Fair 90
Science and Invention 15, 20
Science Correspondence Club 22, 41; *see also The Comet*; International Scientific Association
Science Fiction (pulp magazine) 83
Science Fiction (zine) 34–35, 118
The Science Fiction Advancement Association 133
Science Fiction Association 84
science fiction conventions: early years 84; first World Science Fiction Convention 84–99
Science Fiction Digest 34, 40, 118, 133
Science Fiction League: Bradbury's first encounter 11, 13, 25, 27; creation 21–24; meetings 25; name change 111, 207; *see also* Chapter 4 of the Science Fiction League; The Los Angeles Science Fantasy Society

Science Fiction Quarterly 83
The Science Fiction Writers of America 120
The Science Fictioneers 111
Science Wonder Quarterly 22, 31
The Scienceers 22, 41, 206
Scientific Detective Monthly 30
Scientology 172–173
Scott, Howard 79–80
Scott, Ridley 53
The Scoundrel 72
Screen Writers Guild 12
Script Magazine 109
Seattle 101, 182
Second Eastern Science Fiction Convention 84
The Secret in the Tomb 120
Seekers of Tomorrow 46
Selenites 60
Septama, Aladra 33
The 7th Voyage of Sinbad 169, 171
Shadow Show 195
Shakespeare, William 108
Shangri-LA Record 112
Shangri-L'Affaires 80, 97, 104, 111, 115, 130, 131, 141, 144, 183; and homosexuality 151–152; and LASFS infighting 151; and World Science Fiction Convention (4th) 159; and World War II 146, 147
Shaver, Richard 118
Shaver Mystery 118
She 66, 72, 81
The She Creature 176
Shelley, Mary 183
Shepherd, Lucie 13, 36
Shep's Shop 11–13; 36, 46, 106, 131
The Shirley-Savoy Hotel 136
Shock Theatre 176, 177
Showboat 74
The Shrine Auditorium 75
Shroyer, Fred 52
Shuster, Joe 34–35
Siegel, Jerry 34–35, 41
Silence of the Lambs 171
Simmons, Gene 191
Simon, Simone 143
Sinclair, Upton 106, 209
Sing-along Foo 74
The Skeleton Dance 7, 59
The Skylark of Space 106, 124
Slan 131
Slan Shack 131
Slate, Altheda 147
Slater, Kenneth F. 173
Smith, Clark Ashton 42
Smith, E.E. "Doc" 20, 37, 101, 106, 124, 158, 159

Smith, Skip 192
Snafu 140
Socialism 54
Society for Spaceship Travel (aka Verein für Raumschiffahrt) 70
The Solar Sales Service 34, 90
Something Wicked This Way Comes (book) 7, 11, 195
Son of Frankenstein 81, 177
Son of Kong 72
Sousa, John Philip 162
Soviet Union 89
Spacemen 179, 192
Spaceways 117
Spaghetti House 197
Special Services Division 140
Speer, Jack 51, 123, 150
Spielberg, Steven 9, 177, 184, 191, 194
Spies Like Us 193
Spock 183
Stagecoach 81
Stalin, Joseph 139
Star Trek 183
Starship Troopers 106
Startling Stories 36, 100, 158
Stay Tuned for Terror 158
Steeger, Harry 96
Steele, Barbara 184
Steinbeck, John 5, 12, 101, 205
Stevenson, Robert Louis 108
Stirring Science Stories 104
Stoker, Bram 182, 201
stop motion animation 56–60
Stovepipe Radio 15
Stranger in a Strange Land 106
Street & Smith 96, 157
Sullivan, Walter 27
Summoning the Spirits 57
Sun(t)rails 43
Super Science Stories 104, 107, 128
Superman 35, 41, 90
Superman's Pal Jimmy Olsen 188
Surround Yourself with Your Loves and Live Forever 144
Suspense 167
Sweet Idiocy 44, 146, 150, 153, 154
Sweetness and Light 112
Swisher, R.D. 206
Switzerland 134
Sykora, William S.: and the Futurians 92–93; and rockets 68–69; and the World Science Fiction Convention 84, 92, 99, 100
Syracuse, New York 69

Talmadge, Constance 74
Tanner, Charles R. 32
Tarzan 32, 53
Tarzan (comic strip) 8, 159
Tarzan (movie) 53
Tarzan at the Earth's Core 53
Tarzan of the Apes (book) 53
Tarzana 53
Taurasi, James 92, 93, 100
Taylor, William Desmond 162
technocracy 78–80
television: Gernsback writing of 15; LA's early broadcasts 7; and the World's Fair 89
Television and the Telephot 15
Television News 15
Temple, Shirley 10, 75
Temple, William 131, 134
Tendril Towers 146
Test, Roy 21, 24, 36, 63, 132; and World War II 139
Test, Wanda 24
Thanksgiving with LASFS 216
theatres (movie): in Los Angeles 29; tear gas bombings in 8; in Waukegan 7
Theron, Charlize 193
The Thief of Bagdad 29
The Thing 183
Things to Come 44, 72, 77, 81, 88, 176
Third Eastern Science Fiction Convention 54
Thornton, Billy Bob 191
Three Thousand Years 92
The 3 Worlds of Gulliver 186
Thrilling Wonder Stories 21, 23, 24, 32, 36, 37, 40, 45, 46, 69, 93, 100, 108, 133, 158; and artwork 97; and Heinlein, Robert 107
Tigrina (Eyde, Edythe) 154–156; and nudes 217; at World Science Fiction Convention (4th; PacifiCon) 158–159
Time Magazine 103, 123
The Time Traveller 34, 40, 90
Tippett, Phil 193
Torcon *see* World Science Fiction Convention (5th)
Toronto 159
Toronto, Richard 118
Torrance, Lew 133
Towry, Mike 187
Trans Atlantic Tunnel 72
A Tribute to Ray Bradbury: Thirty-Three Years of Inspiration at the Santa Barbara Writers Conference 195
A Trip to the Moon (Le Voyage dans la Lune) 56, 57
Triple Fan Fair 187
Triton 206

Index

Tucker, Arthur Wilson (aka "Bob") 79, 116, 121, 125, 159
Tucson, AZ 5, 8
Tulips Shall Grow 129
Tuomi, Dorothy 143
20 Million Miles to Earth 171, 182
Twilight at the World of Tomorrow 8

UFOs 118
Under the Moon of Mars 53
Unger, Julius 138
The United Artists (movie theatre) 75
The U.S. Treasury Department 131
University of California at San Diego 187
University of Southern California 62
The Uptown Theatre, 9, 74
Uranus (planet) 115
USSR 33

Valentino, Rudy 9, 12
Valier, Max 70
The Valley of Gwangi 186
Vampirella 220
Van Hise, James 179, 200
van Vogt, A.E. 131, 138, 152, 185; at the first Comic-Con San Diego 189; at World Science Fiction Convention (4th; PacifiCon) 157–158
vaudeville 74
the Vendome 10
Venice, CA 109, 145, 165, 168
Venus (zine) 147
Verne, Jules 20, 44, 95, 132, 157
Verrill, A. Hyatt 30, 95
Vice Versa 155–156
Vitaphone 208
Voice of the Imagination (aka *Vom*) 77–78, 112, 133, 134, 142, 155, 172

Wahrman, Mathilde *see* Ackerman, Wendy
Walking Dead 72
Wandrei, Donald 164
War of the Worlds 114, 183
War Over Lemuria 118
Ward, H.J. 97
Warner, Harry, Jr. 21, 41, 43, 69, 100, 139, 151, 206
Warner Brothers 73
The Warner Theatre 75
Warren, James 184; artwork 178; and the origins of *Famous Monsters of Filmland* 174–179; quitting Famous Monsters 199; soil from Dracula's castle 218
Waukegan, IL 7, 11, 101, 108, 187
Waukegan News-Sun 1, 50
Waukegan's Central School 7
The Way the Future Was 208
Wayne, John 71, 75, 140
Weinbaum, Stanley 98, 119–120, 183; stories by ("A Martian Odyssey" 119, 120; "Parasite Planet" 119; "Valley of Dreams" 119)
Weird Tales 20, 33, 50, 100, 101, 119, 132, 133, 147, 155; and Bradbury, Ray 128, 163; and Brundage, M. 123; and Lovecraft, H.P. 163–164
Weisinger, Mort 22, 34, 37, 40, 46, 89, **85**, 90; at the World Science Fiction Convention (WorldCon) 100, 119
Weller, Sam 7, 67, 195, 202
Wellman, Manly Wade **85**
Wells, H.G. 10, 20, 88, 120, 135, 140, 157
Werewolf of London, 72, 175
Wesso, H.W. 97, 147, 159
West, Benjamin 73
Westercon 159–160
Westinghouse 89
Who Goes There 139
Who Knocks 162, 164
The Whole Town's Sleeping 11
Why We Fight 140
Widner, Art 99, 138, 139
Wiggins, Olon F. 121, 136, 138
WingNut Films 171
William, Warren 143
Williams, Tennessee 12, 209
Williams, "Two-Gun" Montana 11
Williamson, Jack 108, 138, 159
Wilson, Dick 134
The Wireless Course 15
Wireless Telephone 15
Wizard of Oz 56, 183
The Wolfman (film) 72, 175
Wollheim, Donald 44, 104, 130, 135, 154, 213; and FAPA 41; and Michelism 54; and rockets 69; and World Science Fiction Convention (1st; WorldCon) 84, 91–94, 100, 111; at World Science Fiction Convention (2nd; ChiCon) 121; and World War II 139
The Woman in the Window 144
Woman on the Moon (Fraumi m Mond) 70
women: as science fiction fans 34, 44–45; as science fiction writers 109
Wonder Stories 22, 23, 24, 31, 33, 36, 37, 39, 47, 69, 83, 109; and Weinbaum, Stanley 119
Wonder Woman 90
Wonderama 175, 176
Wood, Ed 174, 177
Wood, Natalie 185, 203
Woodard, Wayne *see* Bok, Hannes
Woodman, Russell Harold 206
World Famous Creatures 179
World Science Fiction Convention (aka WorldCon) 65, 84–94, 99–100; aftermath 103; and cosplay 87; and the Exclusion Act 87, 93–94; and pulp art 97–99, 100, 103
World Science Fiction (2nd; aka ChiCon) 115, 116, 121–127; and auction 121, 125; and cosplay 126
World Science Fiction (3rd; aka Denvention) 104, 107, 112, 136–138, 155
World Science Fiction (4th; aka Pacificon) 157–159
World Science Fiction (5th; aka Torcon) 159
World Science Fiction Convention (15th; Loncon) 175
World War II 16, 70, 129, 136; and Ackerman, Forry J 141–144, 172; and fandom 134, 138, 139; and Harryhausen, Ray 129; and the LASFS Clubhouse 131, 139, 147
World's Fair, Chicago 64, 65
World's Fair, New York 8, 69, 89–91
Wray, Fay 55, 63, 170, 197
Wright, Farnsworth 100
Wright, Frank Lloyd 164, 180
Wright, Marjorie 100, 147
Wright, Weaver *see* Ackerman, Forry
Wyman, Belle 28, 29
Wyman, Carroll Cridland 28, 179
Wyman, George 28, 29, 82, 183

X Minus One 8

Yank Magazine 140
Yerke, T. B. (Theodore Bruce) "Tubby" 13, 22, 24, 25, 38, 43, 77, 111, 197; and Ackerman's collection 113; description of young Bradbury 27; and *Imagination!*

45, 48–49; and LASFS, quitting 150, 151; and LASFS Thanksgiving 216; and league librarian 132; and *Mikros* 51; and Michelism 53, 54; recordings of 112; and Technocracy 79; and the third World Science Fiction Convention 136, 137
YMCA 90, 100, 121, 124
Ymir 170
Yorkshire, England 133, 138
Young Communist League 54
The Young Diana 29

Zamenhof, Ludwik 36
Zekley, Zeke 143
Ziff-Davis 118
zines *see* fanzine
Le Zombie 111, 120, 125
Zukor, Adolph 210

www.ingramcontent.com/pod-product-compliance
Lightning Source LLC
Chambersburg PA
CBHW060340010526
44117CB00017B/2908